SO-CCK-787

3 1336 00057 2579

cop.a

B   Strode, H
      The eleventh house:
memoirs
                              1095

•   SAN DIEGO PUBLIC LIBRARY

STORAGE

ALWAYS BRING YOUR
CARD WITH YOU.

BRO
DART   PRINTED IN U.S.A.   23-528-002

The Eleventh House

Books by Hudson Strode

South by Thunderbird

Timeless Mexico

Now in Mexico

Sweden: Model for a World

Finland Forever

Denmark Is a Lovely Land

The Pageant of Cuba

The Story of Bermuda

Immortal Lyrics: An Anthology
of English Lyric Poetry

Spring Harvest: A Collection
of Stories from Alabama

Jefferson Davis: American Patriot

Jefferson Davis: Confederate President

Jefferson Davis: Tragic Hero

Jefferson Davis: Private Letters, 1823–1889

Ultimates in the Far East

The Eleventh House

HUDSON STRODE

The Eleventh House

MEMOIRS

cop. a

New York and London

HARCOURT BRACE JOVANOVICH

Copyright © 1975 by Hudson Strode

All rights reserved. No part of this publication may be reproduced or transmitted in any form or by any means, electronic or mechanical, including photocopy, recording, or any information storage and retrieval system, without permission in writing from the publisher.

Printed in the United States of America

Library of Congress Cataloging in Publication Data
Strode, Hudson, 1892–
The eleventh house.
1. Strode, Hudson, 1892–   I. Title.
D15.S89A33   973.9′092′4 [B]   74–34266
ISBN 0–15–128230–7

First edition
B C D E

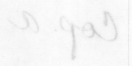

For Thérèse again
in loving appreciation

Beginnings

ELECTRIC lights appeared on Broadway for the first time (December 20, 1880) just a dozen years before my birth. Verdi's *Otello* had its debut at La Scala in 1887. Eugene O'Neill, America's foremost playright, and T. S. Eliot, our top modern poet, were both born in 1888. Jefferson Davis, the Confederate President, died in New Orleans in December, 1889. Grover Cleveland was on the verge of being elected President of the United States for his second term. Before I was one year old, Edwin Booth, America's greatest actor, died.

On October 31, 1892, Halloween, the school bells were ringing at eight o'clock in Cairo, Illinois, when my young mother was struggling desperately to bring me into this mortal world. The sound of bells was the last she remembers as the doctor administered chloroform. When I sniffed my first breath of earthly air it was nine o'clock and the constellation of Sagittarius was poised on the eastern horizon. According to the world's astrologers, the archer, half man, half horse, is an optimistic sign, ruled by Jupiter, the most benevolent of the planets, and indicates two concurrent interests or professions.

Cairo was not the place I would have chosen for my birthing, because all my antecedents were from Southern states. In latitude, however, Cairo was farther south than Richmond or Lynchburg, Virginia, where John Strode, my ancestor from Plympton St. Mary, Devonshire, settled in the 1640's. My father was born in Huntsville, Alabama, in the home of his maternal grandfather, Thomas Fuller Martin, who had removed from Hanover County, Virginia, in 1816 and built the first stone dwelling on Monte Sano. My grandfather, the Reverend Eugene Strode, and his wife had both died fairly young during Reconstruction, leaving five children to be parceled out among relatives. My father was taken by a Strode uncle, who had moved from Gainesville, Alabama, to the then prosperous Cairo. My mother's father, a colonel in the Confederate Army, was born in Macon, Georgia; her mother, near Lexington, Kentucky. Though Cairo had been established by Southern people and its sympathies were decidedly Southern, I never felt much connection with the town from which I was taken to the Deep South when I was four.

A whopping big infant, weighing eleven pounds, I had proved a terrible ordeal for my delicately boned mother, who was only twenty. Though I looked a prime specimen of infant health, it was discovered that some misplaced bit of skin or membrane obstructed normal urination. Three days later I underwent an emergency circumcision.

I was a friendly, smiling baby, they say, responding to strangers of every category, age, and color. When I was old enough to sit by myself and could say a few words, my mother would dress me in my best bib and tucker and put me on a hassock in a front window that went to the floor. Here I entertained myself by watching people pass on the sidewalk. When anyone stopped to speak to me I was delighted. I would bow and point to myself by way of introduction and say, "I'm Huddy Toad," the best I could manage out of Hudson Strode.

My first remembrance is of an event that might have taken my life. We had moved from the little cottage on Cairo's main street to a better place not far from the Episcopal church. When I was a toddler, hardly two and a half, I must have had already stirring within me the seeds of travel. In those days of open streetcars with two long steps on both sides, I tried to board one as it slowly rounded a corner. The conductor fortunately was quite near and scooped me up. The motorman stopped the car instantly when frightened passengers cried out to him. As amazed as he was agitated, the conductor asked, "Where do you want to go, little man?" Panting from the exertion of trying to board a moving vehicle, I said, "Take me to Auntie's." Auntie was Mrs. Charles Cunningham, who lived about a mile away on Washington Street. But I did not know her name. And she was not my aunt at all, but a dear family friend, who had taken my mother in when my Grandmother Hudson had virtually banished her because she refused to give up the idea of marrying my father instead of entering Wellesley. My grandmother had set her heart and jaw on her first-born daughter's becoming a lady professor.

My father appeared from a nearby tobacconist's shop, where I had given him the slip, and received me into his own arms from the relieved conductor.

My next memory is of the snows of Denver, Colorado, where we had gone the following year, because my father had developed what was then called "galloping consumption." Doctors said that the dry mountain climate was his only hope. His eldest sister, Mrs. Charles Pennebaker, my real Aunt Sallie, invited us to stay with her. Mr. Pennebaker had some executive position with my Great-uncle John Charles, one of the pioneers of Denver, who had prospered handsomely in real estate and erected the Charles Building.

My first accident I vividly recall, because I lost four front teeth at one crack. Being one who liked to make himself useful, even if a nuisance, I insisted, at three years of age, that I was big enough to carry a small bowl of raw oysters upstairs to my father's bed. When I begged, indulgent Aunt Sallie said, "Let him do it." So, walking with slow measured steps, as if I were bearing some ceremonial cup, I traversed the hallway from the kitchen to the front and started to climb the stairs, slowly but triumphantly. On the third step I stumbled and fell forward. Still clutching the bowl of oysters high in both hands, I could not save myself. My mouth came crashing down on a sharp stair tread. My teeth cracked. Four were broken off. Two I spat out with some blood. In my gasp of dismay, sense of failure, and pain, I swallowed two, which with no great ado eventually passed through my body. The other two teeth were found among the oysters on the stairs. I was to remain snaggle-toothed until the new teeth came in, strong and white and well-shaped.

My last remembrance of Denver is linked to the actual dying of my father. Until the twentieth century tuberculosis was not considered contagious. In all innocence my mother and I slept in the same large front bedroom with the patient. During the middle of my father's last night on earth I awoke in my crib because of the bright gaslight and the sound of my mother's uncontrollable sobbing. She was wearing a fuzzy ruby red dressing gown, redder than the blood my father had been spitting up. I stared over at the bed. Kneeling by his side, my mother was pleading without reason, "Oh, Tom, don't go! Don't leave me alone with this little boy to care for." In a faint voice my father kept insisting that he was not afraid to die, as much as he grieved to leave us. His assurance about not fearing death and whatever the next world might hold must have made an impression on my subconscious. Never in my life have I believed in any punishment after death, despite my boyish predilection for exciting tent-show "revivals" that graphically depicted the flaming horrors of hell.

When Aunt Sallie came in, I shut my eyes tight, feigning sleep. I knew that mysteries were going on which I could not understand. I was awed but still curious. As my father had his last hemorrhage I opened my eyes and sat up in the crib. My aunt took me up and carried me into another room, just as the doctor appeared in the upstairs hall. When my father took his last breath, he was only twenty-eight.

All through grammar and high school, long after I had lost my baby robustness and become excessively thin, I thought I might die of hereditary tuberculosis before I was thirty. I merely accepted a false verdict from the visible evidence I had in that early morning death-hour on March 27, 1896, in Denver, Colorado.

My father's casket was put on the same train with us at Denver for St. Louis, where we were to be met by Uncle Charlie Cunningham and change trains for Cairo. In the sleeping car, as we prepared to undress in a lower berth, I was fascinated by watching a pleasant-looking young man with a black mustache climb up a ladder to reach the upper berth opposite us. When my mother tried to draw our curtains, I held them open. Then I cried in my piping voice, very loud because of my snaggle teeth, "Oh, Mama, let's go upstairs there with that nice man!"

5

My mother blushed. The stranger, amused, replied politely, "I'm afraid, sonny boy, you'd find it a bit stuffy up here."

When we were about fifty miles out of St. Louis my mother led me into the ladies' toilet to let me relieve myself. She took occasion to do some primping in adjusting her long flowing widow's veil with the fetching white ruching at her forehead. As she raised the window to let in some fresh air a wanton gust seized the veil and carried it off. Mother let out a faint cry of desperation and thrust out a frail arm to draw it back. But the veil sailed over the bleak Missouri cornfield like a huge bird with gossamer wings. I can still see the voluminous black material—so essential to mourning in that *fin de siècle*—blithely soaring away over the tops of the winter-withered cornstalks. I thought it a jolly sight, but my mother was in despair. No widow appeared in public without her mourning veil, particularly only a few days after bereavement. And in those days no lady went out of doors in the daytime without some head covering. In a quandary, my mother pinned a black-bordered handkerchief on her top hair. But it looked so silly that I laughed, and she took it off. Finally, as the train was pulling into the St. Louis station, Mother seized my jaunty black-and-white-checked cap and pinned it on her head. If I had known the word "rakish," I would have said she looked more rakish than a freshly bereft widow.

When Uncle Charlie met us at the station's grilled barrier, he stared open-mouthed in astonishment at the unconventional head covering. Mother assumed what dignity she could command, as bemused passengers nudged each other and grinned. She flushed crimson and half stammered to Uncle Charlie, "My veil blew out the toilet window." Then she threw herself into his arms and burst into tears.

I was not taken to the funeral in Columbus, Kentucky, where my father was laid away in the Pennebaker plot overlooking the Mississippi. I remained in Cairo with Auntie and her two sweet-natured shepherd dogs to companion me.

After the funeral party returned, the question in my mother's mind was what was she to do now. She was a widow of twenty-three with a child to support and a pittance of life insurance to tide her over. One small fund she would not touch—a savings account in my name, earmarked for my education. My father had started it the day that I was born. He brought home from the barbershop his personal shaving mug with Thomas Fuller Strode painted in gilt. A shave at a barbershop then cost fifteen cents. So every time he shaved himself he dropped a nickel and a dime in a large clay piggy bank. When it was full, he would deposit the money in my name, and start to fill up another. To my mother this little fund was a sacred trust. She applied for a teaching position in her alma mater, Clinton College, Kentucky, where less than five years earlier she had been graduated valedictorian.

Shortly after my father's burial I had a scary accident which came near

6

being fatal. Cairo, lying at the confluence of the Mississippi and the Ohio rivers, was subject in flood seasons to what was called "seep water." The Cunningham residence on Washington Street, the town's longest and most prominent thoroughfare, was bordered on the south by a sunken side road that rose steeply at each end. Used as a shortcut in dry weather, in a wet spell, when the swollen rivers rose, the ten-foot-deep roadway filled with water. Because I was a rather responsible little boy I was allowed to sit on the bank above the seep water and pretend I was fishing.

I could easily amuse myself for an hour or so. Not understanding the technique of fishing, I used an empty shoe box to float as a hook, with a long string tied to it as the pole. I would pull the box by the twine along the surface of the water this way and that and imagine huge catches.

My mother, feeling a vague uneasiness, would from time to time come to the large window in the library to see if I was all right. Once, to be pleasant and to remind me that she had not forgotten me and loved me, she tapped on the glass to call herself to my attention. I squirmed around to face her and waved gaily. I half rose and shouted that I had already caught ten big fish. The next thing I knew I was head down in the water with my upended heels kicking wildly. Astonished, I struggled frantically to right myself. It was still chilly in April and my double-breasted blue reefer was heavy. Finally, however, my head emerged above the water. Spluttering, I clutched a thick clump of weeds, but I could not climb out. My terrified mother, followed by the cook and Auntie Cunningham and the barking dogs, arrived breathless at the spot of my humiliation and danger. Just as I was losing my grip on the slimy weeds and was about to slip under the water, somehow they pulled me out, dazed and badly scared. My mother trembled uncontrollably even after I was got into the house and changed into dry clothes.

The trauma of near drowning left me with a neurotic fright of water over my head. I could not learn to swim except in water that came only chest-high. Yet strangely I have ever had a strong affinity with salt seas and gulfs and bays when I am in a sturdy big boat. My spirits lift as soon as I am aboard an ocean liner. I am always a bit regretful when it docks. One of my favorite lines from Joseph Conrad, an idol of my late teens, runs, "A man can find his own soul only a thousand miles from land."

My mother's application to teach was accepted, to begin in September. In the meantime the Cunninghams insisted that we continue to stay with them. It was still hard for my mother and her mother to forgive each other. My Kentucky-born grandmother chose to forget that she herself at the age of seventeen had slid down a rope of bed sheets from her dormitory window at Monticello College in Illinois and eloped with a man named Sage. He had died within eighteen months, and she had been forced to teach for her living. The Widow Sage caught for her second husband the ex-Confederate Colonel I. B. Hudson, from Georgia. He had moved to Cairo to operate a commission business and be reasonably near his two newly acquired cotton plantations across the Mississippi in Arkansas.

Though my mother was a very good teacher, she did not relish the atmosphere of a girls' school, nor did she fancy the idea of an attractive young woman earning her own living. To her feminine mind men were born to support and cherish women. In the spring, after the conventional year of full mourning for a widow, my mother shed the black weeds and went into what was then called "second mourning," which was lavender or white. When the college term was done, we set off on a series of visits to various relatives in Mississippi and Alabama, and I think undoubtedly that my mother expected to pick up a husband somewhere along the way.

Wherever we went "company" came to see us. Soon Mother was having as many gentlemen callers as Amanda boasted of in *The Glass Menagerie*. When we made a prolonged visit to cousins, the Charles Gibsons, in West Point, Mississippi, on Sunday afternoons there might be as many as ten bachelors and widowers in the Gibsons' parlor. My mother was not only pretty, with delicate features, but she also had great charm and an inexhaustible store of small talk. She had little difficulty in entertaining several men at once. Proposals of marriage did come. The best offer was from an upper-crust plantation owner in Kentucky, but my mother had no notion of saddling herself with the duties of a plantation mistress.

An upsetting dramatic incident hastened my mother's decision to take a new husband. One evening at the Gibsons' supper table Cousin Ann (Mrs. Gibson) said sweetly, "Hope, why don't you go ahead and get married? It's been almost two years since Tom died." Casually, to pay a compliment to our host, my mother unthinkingly said, "Cousin Ann, I'm waiting to find a man as nice as your husband." The fork dropped from Mrs. Gibson's hand to her plate with a clatter that startled us all. Turning pale, with baleful black eyes focused on Mother, she muttered in a strained voice, "If you're so eager for my husband, Hope, you can *have* him!" She rose quickly, knocking over her chair, and fled from the dining room. A pained silence gripped the table. Mother looked as if she had been slapped in the face. The three young Gibsons, who were devoted to my mother, were appalled and cast sympathetic, affectionate glances at her. A bedroom door upstairs slammed with a bang. Cousin Charlie sat rigid, looking down at his plate. Finally he said, "Forgive her, Hope. She hasn't been well lately. It's that time of life."

About an hour later the twenty-year-old daughter went up to look in on Cousin Ann. In a frightened voice she called from the top of the stairs. "Papa, come quick. I think Mama is dead." All six of us rushed up the stairs, I tailing the procession. In bed, with her head resting on two pillows, our hostess lay white as whey and still as death. Cousin Charlie reached for her pulse and said hoarsely to the older son, "Call Dr. Ivy. It's an emergency—tell him to come at once. She has taken something. She's had spells of depression before."

As Mother, in a kind of daze, began to lead me away, the Gibson daughter rushed to kiss her impulsively.

In our room my mother tried to explain the incident to me by saying, "Cousin Ann has melancholia."

Dr. Ivy came and administered some antidote for an overdose of laudanum. Mother did not leave our room again that night, but she listened at the door and heard the physician say, "Mrs. Gibson will be all right. Just keep her quietly in bed tomorrow."

The word "melancholia" echoed pleasantly in my ears as I got into my little nightshirt. I liked new beautiful words. In the double bed my shaken mother held me close. She had not recovered from her dismay. She began gently to twist the lobe of my ear between her finger and thumb. Whenever she missed my father acutely she twisted my ear lobe. I found it an affectionate gesture and a strangely pleasant sensation. It made me drowsy now. Just as I was about to drop off to sleep, my mother murmured, "We shall have to find a new place to board."

Two mornings later Cousin Ann begged my mother's pardon, declared her affection, and pressed her to stay on.

We did stay, but my mother made a decision: she would marry another man who had proposed to her. He was a good man of pleasant personality, and nice-looking, with sandy hair and a healthy fresh complexion. Scotch-blooded on both sides of his ancestry, he was a Presbyterian. But he had no inherited means. He had dropped out of school to go to work in those reduced times following Reconstruction. He was now a traveling salesman for Simmons Hardware Company in St. Louis. Moreover, he was one of their top twenty, who earned bonuses and luxury trips. We could, my mother told me, "be comfortable." The prospective bridegroom promised to build her an attractive home in West Point. I liked the man; he liked me. His name was McMillen, spelt with an "e." His first name was Rane, pronounced like a "rainy" day. He said that it was the Scotch form of René. The wedding took place "quietly" in the Gibson parlor in December. Mother wore a white organdy dress she had made herself. The voluminous skirt had twenty or thirty ruffles, each bound with narrow white silk ribbon. I know because she had her picture taken in it in Atlanta. The couple left for a honeymoon in the East.

I recall no pang of jealousy or feeling of loneliness. The four McClellan boys in the next block were there to play with, and I stayed with them most of the honeymoon days and nights. One single incident marred my visit with the McClellans.

A visiting older boy told me to close my eyes and open my mouth wide and I would get the best thing I ever tasted. I had never had a reason to be

9

mistrustful of anyone. So, happily expecting some delicious morsel, I shut my eyes very tight and opened my expectant mouth wide. The boy rammed half a sack of Bull Durham smoking tobacco into the orifice. As the particles stung my tongue and almost choked me, I began to sputter and spit. Feeling betrayed, I struck out at my tormentor with my five-year-old fists. The boy's triumphant cackle at the success of his dirty trick died quickly when I yelled in outrage. He did not want to bring grown folks on the scene. He tried to soothe my indignation and the stinging sensation in my mouth by telling me that someone had done the same thing to him and told me it was sweet potatoes. I refused to be placated, even when he brought me a glass of cold buttermilk to wash out my mouth. I accepted the buttermilk and made a great to-do of spitting and gagging. For the first time I had encountered trickery. I would be more wary in the future. And that night at the supper table, to the surprise of my hosts, I declined a baked sweet potato. I have never since relished sweet potatoes, which are considered a typical Southern dish, tasty and very nourishing.

When the bride and bridegroom returned from the honeymoon, they took the upstairs apartment with a family named Davis, who occupied the lower half of the house. For five days of the week my stepfather was traveling. I was told that the more goods he sold the more his commissions would be above his salary. On weekend nights my parents would often go to euchre parties at a young couples' club over a downtown store. Alternate Saturday evenings they attended a so-called "magazine club," where members subscribed to a series of periodicals and discussed the contents at the meetings. With the Davises in the house I did not need a "baby-sitter." I could amuse myself with toys and picture books and solitaire, which my mother had taught me. I would play solitaire until I got sleepy and then put myself to bed. I was not a problem child.

In September I entered school. I enjoyed it from the first day. I liked to learn my lessons. I think I must have kept my hand up in the air in my eagerness to answer questions. I liked the boys on the playground. And quite naturally, in the first grade I became aware of the special attractions of girls.

I have forgotten the family name of the girl I first became fond of, but her Christian name was Lilly. We were together in a school play in which all the characters were birds. I was cast with her as a turtledove. Miss Howarth, our teacher, told us that turtledoves were highly regarded in the Old Testament, and she quoted a line: "The voice of the turtle is heard in our land." She explained that it did not mean the guttural grunt of a water creature with a hard shell, but the soft cooing of a gentle dove. Lilly and I wore identical pure white costumes and we were instructed to keep in constant touch. I was never to move from her side. The coach thought of tying us together, but I stoutly affirmed that I would stick to Lilly whatever might come. From time to time we had to lean our heads together and moan softly, "Coo, coo." I remember only a bit of one line of the several I spoke to the boy star who played the owl. It was about never leaving my beloved and ended "Coo, coo, wise owl, would you?"

So, in the progression of rehearsals and the performance, with all the feminine proximity and the tender cooing, I felt a stirring in my heart. I wrote my first love letter in the first grade and received my first love message from Lilly in return. One of her notes on a single sheet of tablet paper dropped out of my primer one spring day when I was entertaining an out-of-town business friend of my stepfather's before my parents returned home. He picked it up for me and asked me what it was. "It's a love letter," I confessed frankly. "From a girl." "Do you write them, too?" he asked, amused. "Naturally," I said. "How do you begin your love letters?" I said that I generally began: "I know you love me."

The man's eyes widened and he laughed out loud. Then he shook his head soberly and said, "Oh, no, that's not the way. It leaves nothing for her to say. Begin the next one with, 'I'm afraid you don't love me at all.' You'll get more reaction." I thanked him for his good lesson and determined to reform my style. He asked me how old I was. When I told him six, he shook his head again and murmured with an odd grin, "At nine Casanova just learned to talk." "Casanova—?" My query was interrupted by my parents' return. I hid the letter in my shirt and ran out to shoot marbles with some neighbor boys. "Casanova" was a big fine word to remember—like "melancholia."

One of the inducements to marriage with Mr. McMillen had been his promise to build my mother a house she could be proud of. For months talk went on about the kind of dwelling desired. The final plans called for a capacious one-story white cottage high off the ground. Mother wanted round columns with Ionic capitals on a veranda to extend the entire length of the front. For some reason she also fancied a large oval "reception hall." Father was amiable and went along with her in everything, but the oval shape of the hall gave the architect and the contractor some pause, and the lathe workers and plasterers did not find their jobs easy. However, the ovalness, with both ends like the large end of an egg, turned out to be a success, and Mother's reception hall became something of a small-town conversation piece.

The house was set on a corner lot and the lot next to it was bought as a green pasture for our horse's pleasure and for me to romp in with my friends. When the white picket fence was set up, the place looked very attractive and quite distinctive.

My parents paid off piled-up social obligations by giving euchre parties, followed by a light supper. If some guest declined at the last moment, I was available to take a hand. I felt no self-consciousness around grownups and was considered quite mannerly. I had a knack for cards and greatly enjoyed winning.

Though instructed in cards at my mother's knee, I never had a word of sex instruction from either parent. In the schools sex advice would have been thought indecent. Since most of the teachers were unmarried ladies, they were not supposed to know anything about sex. But children did know something about sex. I cannot say how, but esoteric knowledge seeped in. Little boys and girls sometimes played "papa and mama" in empty goods boxes or among cotton hulls in a barn. When I was in the second grade an open scandal occurred behind a pile of telegraph poles lying just beyond the edge of the school grounds. A handsome, rangy classmate of mine, an adopted son, was caught red-handed atop a little girl named Eunice by a group of us who wandered off at recess. By chance the principal also turned up. Three of us were questioned in his office as to just what we had seen. I have no idea how we explained the curious phenomenon. The highlight was the boy's bare bottom in motion. The principal gave the seducer a switching on his guilty rump. Eunice's mother was sent for and took the girl home to punish. A flurry of titillating excitement ensued for a few days, and then the affair blew over.

I did not mention the incident to my parents, and, though the whole town heard the story, they did not speak of it to me. It would have been embarrassing to us both. I never once thought of questioning either parent about the mystique of sex.

Looking back I discern no harm from avoidance of sex discussions between the generations. I recall little or no dirty talk at school or scrawlings on privy walls. Kids spoke of sex as "it," though they meant more than Elinor Glyn did when she created a mild sensation by declaring that Clara Bow had "it."

Some little girls of seven besides Eunice were not as ignorant of sex as their parents imagined. I was erotically attracted to one of my little sweethearts, who had beautiful long brown curls and who was named Lizzie, and I enjoyed fondling her on a couch in her family's back parlor when no one else was at home. Among some children no special sense of guilt attached to prepuberty sex. It was only after puberty, with the danger of "getting a girl in trouble," that sin came into the picture of boy-girl relations. Before puberty it was a matter of occasionally expressing affection and enjoying a tickling pleasure without removing all one's clothes.

From the second to the fifth grade in West Point I had three sweethearts—the same three—to whom I was almost equally attached. Besides Lizzie, there was the ladylike Laura Wildie, who lived on a many-acred estate. And there was Helen, who, after a fever, wore her hair cropped close, long before Mia Farrow. She kept the style because it set off her enormous brown eyes and her delicate features. Helen was something like a sprite. Her father, though wellborn, was, beyond his small business, a successful professional gambler. Her handsome mother had one blue eye and one brown eye. Her cute little brother, whom I recall as a mischievous pest, became in the twenties and thirties a noted female impersonator who got top billing in European music halls and was entertained at Windsor Castle by Edward, Prince of Wales.

There seemed to be a code among the four boys who were my closest friends not to speak of intimate relationships with girls. They did not kiss and tell. Casting my mind back to the early years of this century and recalling the cabalistic attitude of children toward sex, perhaps it should seem shocking. But I cannot think I personally incurred any psychological damage, nor can I feel I did any harm to anyone else. Today's sex education for school children with diagrams and pictures seems abhorrent.

In the fall of 1900 random talk of the race for President between William McKinley and William Jennings Bryan left little impression on me until the night when the returns began coming in by wire and my parents and I came near to being burned alive. The three of us had gone to the "theater" above a store, to listen to the early returns. The Methodist Church Guild sold tickets and were serving fried oysters. Oilstoves had been set up in the hall at the opposite end from the stage, on the street side and between the two stairwells. Some white-goateed dignitary up on the stage announced reports from the Eastern states. My mother expected McKinley to win big in the North and East, for she believed that there were no really "nice" Democrats above the Mason-Dixon line, just as she was not acquainted in the South with a single "nice" Republican.

While plates of fried oysters were being passed down the aisles by whispering church ladies, suddenly the old codger on the stage stopped dead still, broke off in midsentence, stepped forward and bulged his eyes wide in horrified amazement at something behind us. I twisted about in my seat to see what he stared at. Flames were leaping up to the ceiling at the back of the hall where the cooking was being done. Kerosene from the improvised stoves had caught fire. Someone yelled "Fire!"

Church ladies began rushing back up the aisles, not waiting to collect money. Half the audience was on its feet. Mother looked behind her and rose in terror. She cried out to my father, "Save my baby!" As he urged my mother out into the now crowded aisle, in her nervous agitation she left her black seal furpiece lying on the back of her seat. When my father bent to lift me in his arms I reached down and clutched it up. The stairs on the left side were too close to the flames to risk rushing by, so we made it to the jammed right-hand stairs. Everybody except Father looked wild-eyed in the violent shoving. Excitement on the street was heightened by the arrival of some fire-fighting equipment on wheels and two teen-aged girls indulging in hysterics.

On the sidewalk my mother breathed a "thank God" for our safety.

13

Then she confessed, "Rane, I left my fur collar. But let it go, let it burn!" As Father set my feet on the pavement I held the fur high and dangled it before her amazed eyes. "I saved it, Mother," I yelled triumphantly above the hubbub. "And I'm not a baby. I was eight years old last week."

My parents both smiled at my indignation. Mother stooped and kissed me and put the fur about her shoulders. It was a kind of wide collar that rose some nine inches high in the back like pictures of Elizabethan ladies. I remember how prettily it framed her face against the flames now billowing out of the front windows. We found our hitched horse and surrey and left the scene with moderate speed for home.

Though some persons were bruised, no one was trampled upon or actually burned. But the fire and water damage to the interior was so severe that the hall was never put into operation as a theater again.

McKinley won the election by a large majority, as the Memphis *Commercial Appeal* announced the next day. By chance I was to see this President in Buffalo with my own eight-year-old eyes the following September and to hear the revolver shot that killed him.

The year 1901 came and the century turned. The general mood was good, my father declared. His sales had waxed through 1900. The South was still poor and the price of cotton low, yet Americans in general felt that it was "a splendid time in a wonderful country." Food was abundant and foodstuffs cheap. A dozen eggs cost twelve cents; sirloin steak sold for twenty-four cents a pound. Each day in summer the iceman delivered a five-cent block to our "icebox" in the pantry. If unexpected company turned up and we were having calf's liver for lunch, the cook would send the stable-boy on his bicycle to the butcher shop to fetch another five cents' worth.

Despite the deplorable condition of poverty in some city slums, newspapers spoke of the "Age of Optimism." In the 1900 census three American cities had passed the million mark: New York, Chicago, and Philadelphia.

Industry was booming throughout the North. The average American blue-collar workingman received a wage of twenty-two cents an hour and worked fifty-nine hours a week. Immigrants were pouring in from Europe and finding jobs in factories, on railroads, and in what were called "sweat-shops" in New York: Italians, Hungarians, Poles, Irishmen, and Jews from Germany and Russia. Some held it healthful to get new blood and vitality and workers' arms into the expanding United States. But a few statesmen questioned bringing into the country "the scum and riffraff of Europe," including anarchists. Some said this flow of immigration was chiefly to benefit the very rich capitalists, who would exploit the unfortunates. The admired Senator Albert Beveridge of Indiana saw it differently and proclaimed in a much quoted patriotic pronouncement: "God has marked the American people as His chosen nation to finally lead in the regeneration of the world. This is the divine mission of America, and it holds for us all the profit, all the glory, all the happiness possible to man."

One cold afternoon, January 22, 1901, I went "to town" with a neighbor playmate to buy two spinning tops with some leftover Christmas money and unexpectedly ran into history with a capital H. In front of the shop window was clustered a knot of citizens staring at a small standing blackboard. Since the town boasted only a weekly newspaper and the Memphis *Commercial Appeal* did not arrive until midmorning, it was customary to announce a particularly outstanding event on a blackboard. Ever curious, I wormed my way up to the window to see what caused such respectful soberness in the crowd. QUEEN VICTORIA IS DEAD! In smaller printing the announcement stated that she had reigned for sixty-four years, the longest reign in English history. The new sovereign, King Edward VII, was already in his sixtieth year.

When I got home with my blue-and-silver top, having given one to my friend, I felt I was the bearer of great tidings. Mother was entertaining some friends in the parlor. I stood in the doorway and solemnly announced: "The Queen is dead!" The ladies turned to stare at me bemused. "Yes," I said emphatically, "Queen Victoria is dead. The news will be in tomorrow's paper."

When the company was gone Mother told me that Victoria was barely eighteen when she took the throne and that her long reign was called the Victorian Age. Now she supposed that her gay-hearted, sportful, aging son would change the tone of British society. I listened intently, because though only eight, I had a lively interest in English history, for my Strode aunts had told me that I was descended from Elizabeth, the youngest daughter of King Edward I. I found tales of kings and castles and manors far more to my taste than chronicles of pioneers in covered wagons chasing Indians off their own lands. I knew the slogan: "The sun never sets on the British Empire." Still, I could not help but wonder why the English were so bent on gobbling up other countries. My sympathies were with the Boers in the South African war that had been going on for more than a year.

Having such sporadic interests in world events gave me a slight reputation of being precocious, which I was not, though I did rank at the top or next to the top of my class. No one ever nagged me to do my homework, but my parents gave me help if I requested it.

One hears that only an unhappy childhood is interesting to read about. I have happy remembrances of my boyhood. I was fond of my stepfather and occasionally would go with him on a selling jaunt. While not robust, I was healthy and escaped most children's diseases. I had one physical disadvantage: I, who had weighed eleven pounds at birth, was now excessively skinny. As a friendly neighbor across the street said, "Hudson, you have legs like a kildee," that stem-legged field plover with the plaintive cry.

In one respect I differed sharply from the children I played with. I never had a regular nurse. Every other child I played with had had a Negro nurse. Mother herself had had a German governess in Cairo until Grandfather Hudson lost $75,000 in one week of speculation in wheat futures on the Chicago Exchange. He had wanted to retire from managing his two Arkansas plantations and his commission business in Cairo. He took plunges, lost heavily, and died of disappointment, though the doctor pronounced his malady a congestive chill superimposed on malaria contracted in Arkansas swamps. For economy's sake I was brought up entirely by my young mother, who could still sing "Holy Night" in German. Mother's closeness may have had a deleterious effect on my psyche, though I am not altogether sure. However, I missed that "amazing grace" that often came from the raising by a Negro mammy endowed with native common sense of "what is fittin' " and with an ineffable flow of sympathetic affection.

For his supersalesmanship Mr. McMillen won a bonus trip for two to the 1901 Pan-American Exposition in Buffalo, with an extra week at a swank resort hotel in Put-in-Bay Island, Lake Erie. I was taken along. On September 6 we were in the Hall of Music at the Exposition, where President McKinley stood on a dais shaking hands with a passing multitude. Father wanted to get in line so that his son might shake hands with a President of the United States. But my mother vetoed the idea. The throng was too dense, she said, and her nature revolted at standing in line for anybody. Moreover, she regarded Republicans as enemies of the South. So my father set me high on his shoulder that I might have a good long stare at the handsome, dignified man. As he put me down a shot rang out. Someone yelled that the President had been killed. Mother insisted on rushing away from the confusion and danger as quickly as possible. We saw no more exhibits that day.

At dinner that evening at the private home where we were paying guests—all hotels were jammed—there was much excited talk about the "assassination." However, the President was not dead yet, a newspaper extra announced. The culprit was an anarchist named Leon Czolgosz. He had approached McKinley with a revolver concealed in a scarf-wrapped hand. One of the guests, a Japanese diplomat—the first Japanese I had ever seen—declared that it was well known that world anarchists had been plotting to assassinate all the top rulers, beginning with Austria, Italy, Russia, England, and then the United States. They had already been successful in Italy, for King Humbert had been killed the year before. Back in our bedroom Mother said she thought there should be stricter immigration laws and that the U.S.A. should not admit aliens with such criminal-looking names as "Czolgosz."

The President died eight days after the shooting, when we were luxuriating in the resort hotel at Lake Erie. Vice-President Theodore Roosevelt,

16

called "'Teddy," was now President. In his newspaper photos he seemed to me to be mostly eyeglasses and enormous grinning teeth, like the wolf in *Red Riding Hood*.

Beyond the assassination I carried away few strong impressions of the Exposition except the luxuriant beauty of black-eyed Maxine Elliott, who had been selected as the most beautiful brunette in the Western Hemisphere. Her blown-up photographs were everywhere. Born the daughter of a Maine sea captain, she was an actress. Her goddesslike image was stamped or hand-painted on hundreds of Pan-American souvenirs. Someone at the Buffalo house had given my mother a plaque with Maxine Elliott's face in colors impressed upon it. I never expected to see her in the flesh, but some years later I did see her starring in a Broadway play. I never met her, yet by odd fortune within twelve years of the Exposition I was to know her sister, Gertrude, wife of the famous English actor Johnston Forbes-Robertson. In fact, I was to see her night after night behind the scenes at the brand-new Shubert Theater in New York in 1913–14, when I had a "walking-on" job as the fourth strolling player in *Hamlet*.

"For better, for worse," as the Episcopal marriage lines have it, I early exhibited traits of curiosity and impatience, which, combined, brought me to grief one bright Sunday morning when I was on my way to Sunday school. My stepfather was driving me in the surrey, because I was dressed all in white down to my shoes and socks and I carried an enormous letter W cut out of glazed lavender cardboard. I was to be the tail end of the rainbow in some tableau in which seven boys were to hold across their white chests letters of the alphabet to spell "rainbow." We left home extra early, because a business friend from out of town turned up and wanted to see Mr. McMillen at the hotel. After receiving compliments in the upstairs hotel lobby about the gleaming whiteness of my attire, I was left to amuse myself while the two men talked on a settee.

With the impending "show" at the church I was too restless to sit. I wandered about and gazed on the various boxes of brand cigars in a glass showcase. On the counter I noticed a curious nickel-plated contraption about seven inches square with a round depression the size of a pencil in its concave center. "What's this, Daddy?" I called out. I asked a second time. The men were so absorbed in their business talk that I got no reply. I decided to investigate on my own and jammed the forefinger of my left hand into the depression. Steel discs parted and then closed instantly. I let out a howl of dismay as the blades of the cigar cutter snipped off the end of my finger with half of the nail. Blood spurted over my immaculate whiteness as I held my finger close to my eyes to see what could have happened. The pain was so excruciating that I dropped my lavender W on the lobby floor to cover my bleeding left hand with my right. My shriek of pain and my bloody front threw the lobby into excited activity. Father wrapped his white handkerchief about my hand. "What on earth did you do that for?" he asked. "You wouldn't tell me what it was," I blubbered. "I thought it was a bell and I wanted to see if I could ring it."

"We'll have to take him straight home," Father said to the concerned room clerk. "Call Dr. Ivy at his house. Doctors' offices are closed on Sunday."

A kindly black porter picked me up in his arms to carry me down to the street where our horse was hitched. "Get me my letter!" I demanded. "Give me my W." The fellow stooped for the lavender W, now besmirched with gouts of blood and footprints. As we reached home my mother appeared on the veranda in her spring finery, preparing to leave for the Sunday school tableau. I had done my howling, and I determined to be brave as she stared aghast at her blood-besplattered offspring.

The doctor arrived quickly. He was dressing the wound when the doorbell rang. A messenger from the hotel had picked out the nipped-off end of the finger from among the cigar cuttings and presented it on a miniature tray—like an infinitesimal head of John the Baptist I had learned about in Sunday school. Dr. Ivy considered sewing the end back on after washing off the flecks of tobacco. Then he decided against it; it would be extremely painful. I was so young he felt that I might be able to grow a full-size nail again. (I never did; the left forefinger has remained forever a bit truncated.)

While my impatient curiosity had taught me a painful lesson, I had not lost all sense of responsibility or duty. "Run," I begged the hotel messenger, "please run and take my W to the Sunday school superintendent and tell him to get some other little boy to hold up the letter and say my words." Father gave the youth two bits and sent him posthaste to the church.

Curiosity remained a trait for the rest of my days, which perhaps was not bad for a writer. And I have had a devilish lifelong struggle trying to curb my native impatience.

Undoubtedly these traits caused many of my problems. But another brush with death came within a year after the theater conflagration, through no fault of mine. Although my father had given me a much loved yellow bicycle, I often liked to ride the family horse. The lot boy would saddle him for me, for I was too small to set a saddle on the horse's back and I could not reach high enough to bridle him. The horse was gentle enough and we were friends, but one day he came near to killing me. As we trotted home from an afternoon ride, a vagrant sheet of newspaper blew up out of a ditch under his nose and frightened him so badly that he ran away with me. Turning into the open gate of our pasture, he bolted straight for his stall in the stable. If I had not had the presence of mind to flatten myself backward with my face to the sky I would have been beheaded by the low lintel of his stall door. Had I leaned forward I would have had my brains knocked out. As it was, the horse came to a stop with such an impact against his feed trough that the saddle was jolted loose and I did a tumble that knocked the breath clean out of me. I found myself wildly gasping for air on the straw under the horse's belly. A second time in my life—after the near drowning in Cairo seep water—I brought an excited household to my rescue. The Negro boy got there first, then my mother, followed by the frantic cook, who was sure I was killed. The quivering horse was still panting furiously and snorting a little, but he stood rigidly still while I was pulled from under him, breathless and bruised, but not seriously hurt. For the next fortnight I would have nothing to do with the horse. Then, when my yellow bike was stolen, I made up with him and rode again—a bit mistrustfully.

During a week of street fair in the fall, I lapsed from grace. The carnival had set up its tents and booths in the heart of West Point in the open space between the M. and O. tracks and the two front blocks of the more prominent shops. Going alone in the late afternoon I saw my first motion picture: *The Great Train Robbery*. I was chilled with apprehension when the bandits lined up the unlucky passengers outside the coaches with their hands in the air and robbed them of their valuables. They turned men's pockets inside out and dumped the contents of ladies' handbags into croker sacks, while two of the brigands brandished menacing revolvers. It was all so exciting that I stayed through a second show. Then and there, I think, my passion for the theater was born.

Intoxicated with this new experience, although it was dusk and I knew that I should go home, I bought a ticket to the next-door attraction, where a gold-wigged lady in a spangled white dress was hypnotized and made to rise prone six feet in the air. She lay there unsupported like a floating angel. A bearded man produced an iron hoop and passed it through the air from her feet to her crown to prove the levitation without wires. The miracle so amazed me that I stayed through a second show to try to figure what kept the lady up in space. Dazzled by such legerdemain I finally left the tent to find the night pitch black.

With the barkers' cries ringing in my ears, as if to emphasize my guilt of tardiness, I ran all the six blocks home. A policeman was at our door trying to calm my near-hysterical mother, who was sure I had been kidnapped and was demanding that "the bells be rung." My mother had an odd idea that if a child was lost after dark the thing to do was to "have all the town's bells rung." As she stopped to gather her wayward boy in her arms, I did not say "I'm sorry to be so late," but declared with breathless enthusiasm that I had seen unbelievable wonders.

An advantage I had for eleven years was that I was an only child. People often shook their heads and said it was a pity, for an only child was prone to be self-centered, selfish, and spoilt. However, I was far more of an extravert than an introvert; I did not mind making advances to a stranger, child or grownup, if I was attracted. I was generous with my toys and cookies and even marbles, though not with my pennies. I had a stingy streak that made me reluctant to part with money; I would like to call it frugality. Spare change went into a succession of clay piggy banks—for deposit in my savings account.

Just before I was twelve I ceased to be an only child. My mother confided to me that God was "going to send me a little sister." I took the news philosophically and was delighted to go for a fortnight's visit with friends and relatives in Cairo.

Father put me on the northbound M. and O., in charge of the conductor, and I put myself to bed in a lower sleeping-car berth without any fuss. In a black October night at half past two in the morning, Uncle Charlie Cunningham was at the station to meet me, cheerfully. I had a wonderful time visiting here and there, at my grandmother's and with first cousins.

The most memorable and exhilarating event was my first ride in one of the new automobiles. It belonged to a rich young man who roomed with one of my relatives and had a new 1904 Packard. We drove eleven miles to the next town, called Mound City, and back. The speed seemed terrific compared with our horse and buggy and I automatically pushed my feet hard against the floorboards again and again to help brake the car.

News came that the baby sister had arrived and that I was to return home at once. When I got there I found the squalling, red-faced, homely infant extremely disappointing. She was to howl for three months with colic. Something in her mother's milk must have disagreed with the baby. In that first decade of the century "formulas" were hardly known. But there was one blessed panacea then that could be bought without prescription: "Mrs. Winslow's Soothing Syrup." Oh golden remedy! The thickish white-green liquid came in a narrow round bottle about seven inches high. A spoonful of Mrs. Winslow's slipped into the baby's mouth while it was wide-open yelling would stop its crying.

Of course, I did not know the magic ingredient was laudanum, but it would have made no difference to me if I was trying to do my homework while temporarily minding the baby in the crib. When little Hope—she had been named after my mother—annoyed me beyond endurance, I would reach for the soothing-syrup bottle.

Another change was more upsetting than that of a crying baby. My father announced that we were moving to Demopolis, Alabama, a town in the rich Black Belt that had been founded by French refugees. He had formed a partnership with one of the local citizens to establish a new hardware store. Mother had never felt content about being married to a "drummer," a condescending term used then for a traveling salesman. And she wanted a husband at home all week and not just weekends.

We left our home with its white columns and oval reception hall shortly before Christmas. Temporarily we boarded in the home of the new partner. It was pleasant enough, but on Christmas Day Mother wept for the loss of her beautiful house. I longed for my West Point playmates and moped. The baby continued to scream her protest against colic. Together the three of us made my poor stepfather's yuletide miserable.

However, when the new school term began in late January, we were established in a pale yellow cottage. It sat next door to the Episcopal church and only half a block from Bluff Hall, an elegant mansion built in 1832 on the Tombigbee River's white cliffs, which reminded me of pictures of Dover in my geography book.

Demopolis was about as pleasant a small town as possible for a boy to grow up in during that first decade of the twentieth century. It had tradition and a unique history. It was founded in 1817 by Napoleonic refugees who fled France after the Bourbon restoration. A vast acreage had been acquired —at two dollars an acre—to cultivate the vine and the olive. An allotment of 480 acres was assigned to General Count Charles Lefebvre Desnouettes, a favorite of the Emperor who had often shared his carriage on the disastrous retreat from Moscow. Desnouettes was the leader of the band of pioneers. The main body of French exiles sailed on a chartered ship from Philadelphia and arrived at a landing called "White Bluffs" on July 14, 1817. The town-to-be was given a Greek name meaning City of the People, and the county was called Marengo in honor of Napoleon's victory over the Austrians. Later the county seat, twenty miles south of Demopolis, was to be called Linden, after the village of Hohenlinden near Munich, site of another Napoleonic success. A settlement to the east of Demopolis was named Aigleville, in honor of Napoleon's ensign.

Though the French came with stout, hopeful hearts, life was tough in the canebrake, where they erected rude log cabins. Men who had known little but sophisticated Paris or battlefields had to be taught how to plow. Many of the ladies, daintily brought up, learned to scrub and to milk cows. But they attempted to be gay. In the evenings they brought out their musical instruments, put on their French finery, and danced minuets on cleared ground by moonlight. Some of them made the best of their arduous situation and their poverty by pretending it was all a masquerade. Colonel Nicholas Rauol, who had accompanied Napoleon in his first exile, to Elba, became a ferryman over French Creek. His vivacious Italian-born wife, the one-time Marchioness of Sinabaldi, a former maid-of-honor at the Neapolitan court of Queen Caroline, made ginger cakes to peddle to travelers at the creek crossing.

Among the more prominent settlers who soon joined the Bonapartists were several French plantation owners escaped from the Negro insurrections in Santo Domingo: the Ravisies, the Stollenwerckes, and the Chaprons. Jean Chapron had recovered some of his fortune in Philadelphia after his losses in Santo Domingo. He was rich enough to have portraits of himself and his wife painted by Rembrandt Peale before becoming a pioneer in the Alabama canebrake. They now hung on the drawing room wall of Mrs. Adelaide Garber, a direct Chapron descendant, who became our family friend. I greatly admired these elegant portraits of a distinguished-looking man and a beautiful woman in a red velvet evening dress, painted before 1820.

Count Lefebvre Desnouettes, too, had private wealth, partly through his wife, said to be a sister of Laffitte, the celebrated Paris banker. She purposed joining her husband later in Alabama. In the meantime she sent him luxuries and vintage wines.

It was the hopeful idea of the count and the leading exiles to prepare a future home for Napoleon at Demopolis, after effecting his escape from the island of St. Helena. He was to be brought across the Atlantic to Brazil and thence to Alabama. Desnouettes had a one-room cabin erected near his own log house as a shrine to the fallen Emperor, where he displayed battle trophies, captured flags, swords, and pistols. In the center of the room a bronze bust of Napoleon stood on a huge block of cedar. While no trace of the Desnouettes houses was left in 1907, Mr. Jesse Whitfield, engineer and surveyor and father of my classmate Tom, drove me to the site, and showed me a cedar peg with the letter D, which he had himself driven there years before.

When Napoleon died in 1821 at fifty-two, the motive force of the enterprise was gone. Desnouettes' wife had been seeking assiduously to secure him a pardon; with the exiled Emperor dead the French king had nothing to fear from his former supporters. Desnouettes gave a farewell dinner to his disheartened compatriots and left for Philadelphia, from whence he took ocean passage on the *Albion*. But he never reached France. His ship was wrecked off the rocky coast of Ireland. The leader of the faltering Vine and Olive Colony was drowned.

The experiment in cultivating olives and grapes had been doomed to failure from the first. The first vines brought over by ship had not been properly packed and had dried out. The Demopolis limestone soil was not suitable for olives and the occasional winter freezes were deadly to the tender young trees. Grapevines were damaged by severe frosts. The more prudent of the settlers like Chapron turned to cotton cultivation after 1824 and prospered. Most of the French refugees gradually dispersed to Mobile or New Orleans. Some eventually returned to France. Colonel Rauol turned soldier of fortune and sold his services to the Mexican government.

When I was a boy a few surviving olive trees stood in the Winns' back garden. Out of curiosity and respect, I tried eating some of the small bitter fruit. The experience was disappointing.

To me Demopolis possessed one very special distinction besides its fascinating history. It boasted a real theater, with parquet seats, a balcony, and boxes. The town's geographical position, halfway between Meridian, Mississippi, and Selma, Alabama, made a convenient stopover for theatrical troupes. The Braswell Theater on Strawberry Street occupied the upper floors of the Braswell Hardware Company, the rival business to my father's. It was only a few yards north of the railroad track that split the town down the middle in almost equal halves. The cottage on the south side of the track directly opposite belonged to a family named Newhouse. Here Julia Newhouse, the mother of Lillian Hellman, the future playwright, had lived, as Miss Hellman tells in the first sentence of her autobiography *The Unfinished Woman.*

The first stage play I saw was *Faust.* I found it the more exciting because I conversed with two of the "stars" the afternoon of the performance. They had wandered over from the Demopolis Inn to our hardware store and pretended to be interested in buying a saddle. "Marguerite," blond and slightly buxom, told me that she called Waco, Texas, home. I assured her that we could ship the saddle she admired by express to Waco. I was eager to make the sale because I got a ten per cent commission on all I sold when I "clerked" after school hours and on Saturdays. I noted the odd smile on the swarthy face of the Brooklyn man who played Mephistopheles and realized that they were just killing time. The pretty lady took my hand, thanked me for my courtesy, and said that she would think about having the saddle sent to Waco. I was not fooled. But I was delighted just the same to have talked with live actors, who were to me like creatures from another planet. I was never to miss another show during my school days.

I next saw Joe Jefferson's two sons in a performance of their famous father's *Rip Van Winkle.* And then I was enraptured with my first light opera: Reginald De Koven's *Robin Hood,* composed two years before I was born. I carried away a vivid memory of the future Mrs. Grant Wood, who, as Alan-a-Dale in beige tights, sang "O Promise Me" right down at the footlights. She was young and golden then and had an appealing contralto, but what I was to remember best were her fine legs. In 1938, in Iowa City, when I taught Shakespeare in the University of Iowa summer school, she was a handsome white-haired lady, considerably older than her renowned artist husband, who became our friend. My wife and I were invited to a dinner party at the Grant Woods' home, and during cocktails I spoke to her of my boyish infatuation. Mrs. Wood was puzzled. I told her that I had seen and heard her in *Robin Hood* when I was twelve, and added out of devilment, "I have never forgotten your surpassingly beautiful legs." The amazed old lady blushed with pleasure. "You hear that, Grant?" she called to her husband, with a note of triumph. She switched place cards on the dining room table and I found myself at the hostess's right.

In April of 1905, when I was going on thirteen, I decided that I was not getting enough interest on my savings account. So I called on the president of the Robertson Banking Company and said I would like to buy stock in his bank. Smiling indulgently he sent for my statement: I had accumulated some $265. The stock was priced at $125 a share and paid eight per cent. "I'll take two shares, please," I said. A certificate for two shares of bank stock was duly made out in my name. As I shook hands with this small, kindly, dark-eyed man named William Sylvester Prout, I did not dream that in little more than a dozen years he would become my second stepfather. I still possess the two original shares bought when I was twelve. But the stock has been divided again and again, until now there are forty-eight shares. Dividends and extra dividends have never ceased to be paid semi-annually.

When Mr. McMillen bought the vacant corner lot on Main Street opposite the west side of the Demopolis Inn as an investment, with his cooperation I erected a large billboard on which might be pasted advertisements of coming theatrical attractions. The cheap lumber and the labor cost me about five dollars. For renting out my billboard I received two complimentary choice seats to every theatrical show or circus that came to town.

I had found no difficulty in adjusting to the new school environment. I liked the teachers and I liked the pupils well enough. A boy named Simon Mayer and I almost instantaneously took to each other and we were to eat our lunches together at recess until graduation from high school. During Passover Simon would bring a double supply of matzo wafers in his lunch box to share with me. I liked the novel taste of unleavened bread. Simon's father, we were told, had come to the South from Germany with a peddler's pack on his back. Now he was senior partner of Mayer Brothers, the largest department store within a sixty-mile radius. He had married an aristocratic Jewess from Meridian, a tall, slender, low-voiced lady of great dignity, whereas he was roly-poly and heartily expansive. Mrs. Mayer rarely went out except for an afternoon drive in her carriage. She was completely absorbed in her home and her five adoring offspring, of which Simon was number four. In all my intimacy in the household during the next four years I never detected the faintest objectionable trait of the "Jewish mom," so flaunted in novels in the 1960's.

Simon and I played together, rambled along the riverbank among cotton bales, and watched the steamboats pass. We visited the attractions at the periodic street carnivals. Except for his lack of interest in books, we shared common pleasures and found each other thoroughly *simpatico*. I came to wonder years later if this empathy had been due to the planets' configurations at the time of our birth. We were born a day apart under that determined sign of Scorpio in its first decan. We never had a disagreement. Simon was amazed and delighted to discover one day as we relieved ourselves at the edge of the Tombigbee River that I had been circumcised, and five days earlier than his own eighth-day ritualistic operation. Our friendship was to last firmly until Simon died of diabetes at twenty-four, just one year before the discovery of insulin.

A family event early in 1906 was the birth of a second sister, on the seventeenth of January. In those days babies were born in the home—and at that time Demopolis had no hospital. I had been sent to spend the afternoon and night with John Bestor Meriwether, a boy a year younger than myself. His father had recently become president of the new City National Bank and Trust Company. His beautiful mother, with a golden voice as thrilling as Sarah Bernhardt's, according to people who had heard the French actress, had become my mother's best friend.

That mid-January day turned so unseasonably warm that peach trees in backyards burst into bloom. After school I shot marbles in my shirt sleeves. I had turned thirteen in October and this was about my last game of marbles. That same night I emerged "physically" from childhood to adolescence. My first reaction was one of repulsion and resentment at the problems that went with puberty.

At breakfast I was relieved to note that none of the Meriwethers seemed to regard me as different. As we started off to school, Mrs. Meriwether, with a twinkle in her lustrous brown eyes, said, "Now I shall tell, Hudson. You have a new little sister, born yesterday afternoon. Your father telephoned. I am to be her godmother. After school you are to go straight home to greet her."

When I saw Ruth, who was named for my mother's only sister, I marveled at the vagaries of nature. Hope had been a homely baby, but Ruth was pretty when one day old. Hope did not turn pretty until after her second birthday.

My concern about puberty dissipated quickly enough. Nothing serious troubled me except a matter of church doctrine. My Sunday-school teacher at Trinity Episcopal thought that I should consider confirmation and began to instruct some of us teen-agers. I balked at the doctrine of the Trinity: three Gods in one: God the Father, God the Son, and God the Holy Ghost. To me they were separate entities. If Jesus on the Cross was really God incarnate, I asked, why did he cry out so piteously to the Father up in Heaven? Could God the Almighty suffer? Where was God, I demanded, when Jesus was enduring torture on a cross? I accepted the divinity of Christ, but I insisted that he was a man, born to be an example to us, as well as a beloved Son of God. And if God and Jesus were one person, I persisted, how could Jesus sit on the right hand of God's throne? My teacher struggled in vain to straighten out my thinking. But I could not be persuaded to accept the doctrine of the Trinity. I learned by rote, however, what else was required to ready me for confirmation. When the bishop came he laid his blessing hands on me as on the other, more submissive, ones kneeling at the altar rail.

When an attractive, recently built two-story house on Strawberry Street came on the market my father bought it promptly. It had the distinction of being the only centrally heated residence in the town, with a coal-burning hot-air furnace in the large basement. A Northern gentleman had built the house for comfort as well as for appearance, and then he had had reasons for moving to California. What particularly attracted me was the library-den, with bookshelves, an open fireplace for coziness, and an outdoor entrance. Since Mother had her parlor, I came to assume the library as largely my own preserve for homework, desultory reading, and playing parchesi with friends. A "geographical" advantage was that the school was now only four blocks away. And just five blocks southeast stood ante-bellum "Gaineswood" in all its fading glory. This splendid Greek Revival mansion was one of the South's showplaces, noted especially for its ball-room with walls lined on three sides by floor-to-ceiling mirrors.

It had been eighteen years in the building—from 1842 to 1860. General Nathan Bryan Whitfield was his own architect after studying numerous plans of great houses of Europe. He had used mostly slave artisan labor, but he imported much of the ornamentation, the mantels, and the chande-liers. The artificial shallow lake on the front garden was dry when I first saw Gaineswood, but on one of the islands a circular pavilion with fluted narrow columns still stood. The house had not had any restoration work since 1900. During my school days it was untenanted except for care-takers.

Because I was friends with several young Whitfields I often played with them around the old slave quarters. Twice we were permitted to play inside the house. I was intrigued by the mirrored ballroom and pictured it glitter-ing with the reflections of a thousand candles when some gala occasion brought "beaus and belles" from various plantations. In the midst of the echoing emptiness, where we children all but tiptoed, I realized in myself a strong taste for elegance. I had no desire to live in such a place myself, but I would have relished being a welcomed guest.

Naturally I did not imagine that my mother would be offered Gaines-wood as a wedding present by my future second stepfather, the banker, who handled the estate for the absentee "landlords," two Whitfield female descendants living in New York City. They wanted to be shed of the place and the expense of gesturing to keep the house in repair. They urged Mr. Prout to take full ownership for $9,000 cash. My mother flatly declined the gift. She wanted no responsibility of any old house, however beautiful and historic. She argued cogently that the upkeep would be far too dear for a small-town bank president. And besides, she said, it was too far from the town's center. She would feel lonely surrounded by those spooky groves of cedars. When in the middle twenties a sudden-rich lumberman bought the place, restored and refurnished it, my mother had no envious pang but only renewed jubilation at having escaped a white elephant.

In January, 1972, I thought of that $9,000 asking price in comparison with the announced $200,000 appropriation to the Alabama Historical Society for restoration. This did not include the undisclosed purchase price of 1946 and the $40,000 for the new copper roof. If times had changed drastically in 1972 they had also changed sharply the first decade of the twentieth century. Instead of attending balls in a room of mirrors with crystal chandeliers, we danced in the Elks Club over a store.

While lacking former ante-bellum elegance, Demopolis, with its French memories and Southern traditions, still reveled in hospitality and party-going. Young folk seemed to have as many parties as the grownups. Some children's parties were at night and we walked our dates and were not afraid, for Demopolis streets were deemed so safe that parents did not worry. By a town ordinance that lasted until 1914 black citizens were under curfew to be off the streets by nine, except on Saturdays. The chief policeman, Mr. Monnier, descendant of an original French settler, would sound curfew by beating with the heavy key to the jailhouse on one of the hollow iron pillars that supported the roof of the Robertson Bank's portico.

Teen-agers who lived on plantations often gave quite lavish house parties. One I attended when I was fifteen at the Wooten-Whitfield place some ten miles in the country is the most memorable, because of the tubs of ripe figs, my favorite fruit. Whereas the girls stayed in the big house, eleven of us boys were domiciled in what was known in slavery times as the detached "office" where plantation business was transacted. Seven cots had been set up along with the two double beds always kept in readiness for unexpected guests. But what seemed to me the high spot in the hospitality was the quantity of figs and pure cream served every morning for breakfast. We consumed them by the thousands. It is tedious to peel a fig. Several spinster Whitfield cousins of our hostess would rise at mid-July sunup for the fig-peeling. Though servants were plentiful, they could not possibly do all that peeling by breakfast time.

The blessing of servants in that so-called "Age of Contentment" made family life the smoother. My mother maintained an all-day nurse for the little girls and a cook who prepared three meals a day, and carried all the leftovers home in brown paper bags.

Mother seemed allergic to a kitchen. A thorn in my boy's content was her dread of having to get breakfast. Before seven she would awake, wondering if the cook had come. A little after seven she would begin to call in a low monotone, so as not to wake the girls and her husband, "Hudson—Hudson. Look out your back window and see if there's smoke coming out the kitchen chimney." I would creep to the window with hope and trembling. What a difference smoke or no smoke made! Joy surged in my heart if I saw gray wisps arising; I would get back into bed and snuggle gratefully under the covers. But if no smoke, I was consternated. Mother hated above all to make biscuit, and Southerners seemed to think hot biscuit for breakfast essential.

As far as I know, Mother never possessed a cookbook. She was not the kind to enjoy swapping favorite recipes. She justified her attitude by saying with a gay little laugh, "A lady can't be in the kitchen and the parlor at the same time." And she belonged to the parlor, where she exhibited a sparkling charm. She made the shyest and most humble of her callers feel at ease and important. She sent them all off liking themselves better.

Besides my own party-going, reading, schoolwork, chores, and clerking at the hardware store on Saturdays, I really enjoyed my small vegetable garden. A black man did the initial plowing and the laying out of rows. Then I took over with the planting and the cultivating. I made the soil very rich by scattering the rotted manure from the stable lot. I got a kick out of chopping weeds with a sharpened hoe. I took pride in bringing in my own butter beans, tomatoes, and roasting ears. In hot July and August I watered my garden with a hose while most gardens "burnt up" in the Alabama heat. It was my pleasure to be alone with the soil for an hour or so in my daily routine. If I had boyish worries, they seemed to dissolve into the soil. Today, in 1974, my favorite recreation, besides reading and foreign travel, is still gardening, where the tensions of these disturbed times seem to disappear in working the good earth.

Two pomegranate trees, planted by the previous owner, graced our front lawn. Pomegranates were rare in Alabama. They seemed an anachronism, belonging to the Bible or to tropical Asia and Africa. I liked the distinctive taste of the grenade-shaped fruit, the size of an orange with a very tough skin and filled with scores of seeds in a crimson pulp of agreeable acid flavor. I paid off many a boyish obligation with gifts of exotic pomegranates.

I was nibbling at half a pomegranate one rainy summer afternoon while reading alone in the library when a strange thing occurred. I was "aroused" by the most unexpected "pornography." As I perused for the first time Shakespeare's *Rape of Lucrece* I felt a stirring in my groin. In the brief introduction I had learned that the poem had been printed three centuries before, in 1600, and that it had been an immediate popular success in London and gone into many editions. *Lucrece* tells of the sad fate of a beautiful and virtuous woman ravished at sword's point by her husband's perfidious friend and her houseguest. I had never heard the word "voyeur." As I turned the suspenseful pages I became an involuntary voyeur. Shakespeare is extremely vivid as he has Sextus Tarquinius treacherously steal into his hostess's chamber, violently ravish her, and speed away at dawn.

I was somewhat shocked at what I read and shocked at the erotic effect the poem had on me. I felt defiled sitting alone in our library. I became acutely aware that I had a lot of growing up ahead of me.

I played in all the school plays that were put on each year at the Braswell Theater. But I never quite got over my humiliation at forgetting a piece of doggerel about ten little Elks in the entr'acte of an Elks' benefit performance put on by a professional lady director. Suddenly I forgot what happened to the seventh little Elk. I stood there before the curtain, almost touching the footlights, and turned numb. The directress finally appeared at one end of the proscenium and prompted me with what the sixth little Elk did. "I've already said that," I called to her, loud enough for the balcony to hear. "Well, start from there anyhow," she urged. So I began again with the sixth Elk and continued to the end: "And then there was none."

With the applause and laughter ringing in my ears, I flew from the stage without bowing and jumped into a wicker basket of costumes, feeling more embarrassed than I had ever felt in my life. This fear of forgetting lines dogged me through my amateur theatrical years at college. Even now, I never give a public "dramatic reading" of a Shakespearean tragedy without the reassurance of the text before me, however seldom I glance at it.

At school, there was one ubiquitous fly in the ointment of my content. A girl just six months older than I always led the class, while I trailed in second place term after term. Though she wore glasses, she was a pretty girl, named Bessie Rae Burnitt. Her father, the local photographer, had been born a cockney and was called "Dad Burnitt."

Frankly I did not think the extra amount of study necessary to beat her was worth the effort, even if I could have, which I strongly doubted. I read book after book for pleasure. I reveled in Mark Twain, Edgar Allan Poe and Rudyard Kipling, as well as Shakespeare. I ordered the better novels of Dickens and Walter Scott in cheap editions, and read and read.

Far from the fashion-conscious world of Edward VII, we in Demopolis yet knew from the newspapers and magazines much that was going on in London and New York. We were aware that Caruso was the top star of the Metropolitan Opera, that Sarah Bernhardt was making farewell tours and drawing enormous crowds in Texas, where under a circus tent she played *Camille,* though few Texans understood a word of French. My father bought records for our phonograph. I got a special lift out of the dramatic arias, and particularly Caruso's *"Ridi, Pagliacco."*

I read several magazines that contained stories of New York and London stage productions. To conceal the open fireplace in summer I made a large screen of heavy gray Beaverboard and pasted on photographs of stage stars clipped from periodicals. In the montage, I reserved the center spot for Maxine Elliott, and placed on either side of her pictures of Johnston Forbes-Robertson, the great British Hamlet, and E. H. Sothern, then the best of the American Hamlets. I was significantly aided in the creation of my dramatic screen by a windfall of three years' accumulation of copies of *Munsey's Magazine* with sections of pictures of stage stars.

The thirty-six issues were given me by a new friend of my mother's, whose husband, Julius Marx, was the great-uncle of Lillian Hellman.

So, besides my normal routine of everyday play and school, I had a secret life in the theater which I did not share with anyone, not even Simon Mayer. Altogether I was a happy teen-age boy in that small southern town.

In general, though I was considered a mannersome, satisfactory boy, in looking back I discern traits in my boyish nature that could not be called admirable. I was not too congenial with teamwork. I disliked anything called "a committee," with its arguing back and forth. If I was on a committee, I wanted to dominate it and settle the matter quickly. My mother tried to give me piano lessons, but I found practicing such a bore that after six months I gave up any attempt at learning to play. I enjoyed good music, but I would have hated marching in a school band.

Games in which I could not naturally do well I avoided. My hands, inherited from both sides of my ancestors, the Strodes and the Hudsons, were too small to make me a passably good ball player. I liked tennis and played occasionally, but the competitive excitement made my face turn so flaming red that, skinny as I was, I was told such violent exercise might be dangerous to my health. Only in one pseudosport did I shine: roller skating, then in vogue over the nation. A large roofed skating rink had been erected within three blocks of our place. From the first I was a whiz on roller skates and won prizes in competitions. I never had one pratfall. I was a good volunteer instructor and eager to help smaller boys and timid girls and pretty young married women. From thirteen to sixteen I had to content myself with calling roller skating my sport.

When religious revivals came to town they were held in our skating rink. I attended many sessions, more for the excitement and the gospel singing than the idea of being "saved." Episcopalians did not seem to like to be saved in public. But I enjoyed witnessing the salvation of other people as they came down the aisles to sit on the mourners' benches. I never missed the "men only" night, with its dramatic depiction of lurid sins. Evangelists would portray certain sexual doings in such colorful language that some of the town's "fast" young men would be impelled to repair to the local sporting house after the service.

One night the graying Reverend Mr. Culpepper, a noted evangelist from Texas, announced that he would speak on a very solemn theme. He fore-warned the all-male congregation that he had never broached this special subject without some fellow fainting. In a voice quavering with emotion, he waxed eloquent on the harmful effects of masturbation. He hammered his points home—with a glittering eye. When it seemed that he was failing to bring on a fainting spell, he stepped near the front edge of the platform, teetered there, and tearfully told of a fine young man turning into a maniac and being incarcerated in an insane asylum.

Suddenly I heard an ominous thud behind me as someone on the aisle two rows back hit the floor. A beam of triumph suffused the evangelist's features as he signaled quickly for music. Men turned openly or furtively to see who had fainted. It was a scion of one of the town's prominent old families, an amiable, shy young man who had finished high school two years previously. As friends carried him out, the revival pianist pounded out a triumphant march.

Sensational evangelism was still being practiced in the South at least until 1922, after which I lost track of it. But in 1922 in the Morgan Hall auditorium at the University of Alabama, when I was a young associate professor, I witnessed the same sort of melodrama as in the Demopolis skating rink. At a "men only" session, when the evangelist got on the subject of "self-abuse," one of the most admired students, a football player and a brilliant graduate student in physics, who had just won a Rhodes scholarship, keeled over in the middle of the sixteenth row.

Despite my own deficiency in sports I was an ardent baseball fan through the newspapers. My prime hero was Ty Cobb, the Georgia-born small-town player, who became a major leaguer with the Detroit Tigers in 1905 when he was only eighteen. A left-handed batter and a right-handed thrower, he scored more runs, totaled more hits, stole more bases than any other player. When the daily Montgomery *Advertiser* was delivered I would turn immediately to the sports page to see what Ty had done the preceding day. In 1911, I was to behold my lanky idol in person at a preseason game with the University of Alabama's nine. He cleverly tore a sizable three-cornered hole in the back of his left black stocking so that he could be easily identified by the crowd in the stands when he faced the pitcher. And to my utter astonishment I was to see him struck out by my college chum Charlie Greer, a sophomore pitcher from Marion, Alabama. I was to keep up with Cobb's brilliant record until another athlete across the Atlantic supplanted him as my hero. This man was Finland's track star, Paavo Nurmi. Between 1920 and 1932 Nurmi was to set twenty world running records. After he had won six Olympic championships, his meteoric career came to an abrupt end when he was disqualified as an alleged professional just before the 1932 Olympic Games in Los Angeles. Bitter, he returned to Finland and made a small fortune in the construction business as well as owning the most popular haberdashery in Helsinki. I was to meet the athlete who had so captured my imagination in Helsinki in early September, 1939, a few days after Britain had formally declared war on Germany.

After Ty Cobb and Nurmi I was never again to feel such enthusiasm for any single athlete, though I was to have close friendships with such admired Alabama football stars, decades apart, as Johnny Mack Brown, running back, and Scott Hunter, quarterback.

Dividends on my five-dollar billboard had continued to pay bounteously. With two tickets to every play and a pair for circuses I would take Simon Mayer or one of my girls or my mother with me. Once the Braswell management offered me a box with six chairs for an afternoon performance of Paul Gilmore, a matinee idol who looked like a Gibson man and who played on the road the society dramas that John Drew essayed on Broadway. So I gave a box party, followed by chocolate ice-cream sodas and Nabisco wafers at Simmons Drug Store, and felt very much the man of the world. My special date was Willey Gayle, who eventually was to marry a Maryland cousin of Wallis Simpson, Duchess of Windsor. Willey's family lived in Montgomery, but she spent the summer months with her idolizing grandmother, Mrs. Willey Winn, who was "the" *grand dame* of Demopolis, a figurine in Dresden china, not five feet tall, with forget-me-not blue eyes and white white hair.

When a young widow, she had made an arduous journey to Gettysburg to bring back the body of her twenty-four-year-old soldier husband. She had had him dug up out of Yankee earth and had sat with his coffin in a freight boxcar all the way from Pennsylvania to Demopolis. I marveled at the fiber, that vein of iron in those tiny, fragile Southern ladies. I admired the quiet elegance of the Winn drawing room with its gilded Venetian mirrors and the handsome dining room with its tall silver epergne. Besides outlying plantations, Mrs. Winn owned nearby Winns' Grove, where Napoleonic refugees had simulated gaiety in 1819 and where Fourth of July barbecues and horse races were currently held.

Willey Gayle, who was a year older than I and a grade ahead, was touched with inherent glamour at fourteen and I thought I was in love with her. But she outgrew me so rapidly that at fifteen she led the ball of the year in Tuscaloosa in a gown of gold lamé. The state papers were full of her photographs. I felt extremely callow. But we continued devoted friends after Willey had gone to New York to study for a stage career, which she did not follow. When I was twenty-one I took her to a matinee at the Hudson Theater in New York to see *The Dummy* with Ernest Truex. But the real star to me was an exquisite, golden-curled darling of eleven in a black velvet dress with a wide collar of white embroidery. On the program she was called Joyce Fair. Years later she would become internationally known as Clare Boothe Luce. Our friendship began in 1932 when Clare Brokaw wrote me inquiring about renting the cottage we were leaving in Bermuda on our imminent return to the States. In replying, I told her that I had loved her when she was eleven and called Joyce Fair.

Year after year I played in all of the school shows and was never to forget my lines again. But in my senior year I faced breaking my neck because of a mechanical malfunction. I was playing the lead in some silly dream play in which I wore silk pajamas throughout the show. At the end a six-year-old yellow-haired girl named Carol de Feu, wearing only a sash and carrying a Cupid's quiver of fake arrows, lured me into a wooden crescent moon covered with silver foil. We were to be cranked on wires up to the stage sky as the curtain slowly descended. Rehearsals at the Braswell Theater had all gone smoothly enough. But on the night of the performance the moon contraption stuck twenty feet above the stage floor. One wire finally went up while the other stayed stationary. We were perilously clinging to the lathes. Cupid turned deathly pale and tears of terror began to flow. But she did not scream. Thunderous clapping and laughter greeted our near disaster as the curtain dropped. A tall ladder was reared quickly against the flimsy, wavering moon. A thin stagehand brought Carol down in his arms, and then I descended gingerly. The curtain suddenly rose again as I hit the floor. I grasped the still terrified Cupid by the hand and muttered under my breath: "Smile, dammit, smile!" I dragged her to the footlights with aplomb, where we bowed and bowed and smiled and smiled.

After I turned sixteen and was shortly to be graduated, the question of my college education became urgent. One thing I knew full well: I had no intention of stepping into my father's hardware business. Although I seemed a natural-born salesman, I was determined to avoid what the English call "being in trade." My Aunt Franc, my father's second sister, who was married to a British consul and plantation owner in Guatemala, had told me once that no Strode was ever "in trade." But I had no imperative promptings as to what profession to pursue. I had a slight leaning toward architecture, and, because I liked travel, I considered a diplomat's career. In my subconscious I had a hankering to be an actor or a writer. Considering my lack of robustness, my stepfather suggested civil engineering: he thought that in the outdoor life my strength would increase. I took a romantic interest in his picturing of the possibility of building bridges in Peru. I had my heart set on going to Vanderbilt University and then on to Oxford.

A staggering blow struck us two months before graduation day. My mother had earmarked all the money she personally possessed for my higher education. She had put it in stock of the new National City Bank and Trust Company. One Monday the town was rocked with consternation when the bank doors did not open. I recall the lines of depositors formed around the block. Pounding on the doors and windows had no effect. Bank examiners were working inside. Then the shocking news broke. The president, John Meriwether, and his cashier had together taken out $90,000 of the $100,000 capital to speculate privately in cotton futures. Their gamble had lost. The bank failure was complete. Depositors got back only a small percentage. Holders of bank stock received not a red cent. All my higher education money was wiped out.

During the excitement Mother kept outwardly calm and spent hours attempting to console Mrs. Meriwether, who had to give up her big house and her jewels. The Meriwethers moved to a house not much better than a cabin on the railroad track about fifteen miles to the west. I went with Mother to say good-by to Mrs. Meriwether at the station. Her golden beauty was almost extinguished by a plain checked gingham dress. To complete the picture of the malevolent change in fortune, she, who had had three servants, boarded the train with a new broom in her hand. Yet she managed to wave bravely to us from the back coach platform, as a French aristocrat might have done from a tumbrel on her way to the guillotine.

Many persons expected Mr. Meriwether to land in the penitentiary. But, this being the South, it was finally argued that the president and the cashier had simply "borrowed" the $90,000, however illegally and ill-advisedly, and were unfortunate in the turn in the market. They were never officially indicted.

The big question in our family now was where my education money was to come from. My father did a good business, yet with his trusting, kindly nature he gave credit to anyone, and a proportion of customers did not pay their bills. Some accounts would run for over a year. One socially prominent old widow, who lived across Main Street from the Episcopal church, where she knelt in her own pew, ignored thirty-six months of hardware bills. Then she declared, with a kind of coquettish cackle, "The statute of limitations has taken care of my bill. It's been over three years now, and so I can't be sued." She never paid.

With so many hardware debts outstanding I was loath to accept money from my stepfather, who had always treated me with the indulgent affection of a father by blood. I felt that I must somehow make my own way.

Vanderbilt was now definitely out of the picture and Oxford too, unless I was fortunate enough eventually to win a Rhodes scholarship. I decided on the University of Alabama at Tuscaloosa where there was no state tuition and where board and room could be had for about twenty dollars a month.

Since I ranked second in the graduating class I had been designated "salutatorian." Bessie Rae Burnitt, who always stood number one, had her valedictory, "The South in Song and Story," already written. In the midst of the spring round of parties I became seriously anxious, for I could not think of an original subject that appealed to me.

Mother sensed the depth of my concern. One afternoon, noting my gloom, she had an inspiration. She quietly went upstairs and got down on her hands and knees before an old trunk in the hall. When I rushed up for something, for a moment I thought she was praying. Then from the very bottom of the trunk she unearthed a sheaf of thirty pages of very thick

34

narrow, cream-colored paper. As I helped her rise she put the manuscript into my free hand. I recognized her extremely legible large handwriting. "My valedictory address at Clinton," she explained.

I went down into the library and shut the door. The title page read "We Die: We Live" by Hope Hudson. At first glance I thought that she had got the phrases reversed. On page three my eye paused at the lines: "The seed sown in life springs in harvests of blessings or harvests of sorrow. The grave buried the dead dust, but the character walks the world and distributes itself a benediction or a curse among the families of mankind."

Certain words were underscored for emphasis. In one margin a prompting in pencil read "Soft and pathetic." I noted references to what Cato and Sir Isaac Newton had left behind them. "When Edison dies," one sentence ran, "will he not live a *thousand* lives in all lands where the electric light sheds its beams?" The address ended with a rousing summation: "So *our* lives glide on; the river ends, we know not where; and there is no jumping ashore. We live and we die, but the good that we do lives after us, and is *not* buried with our bones."

"This is it!" I cried aloud. "This is what I need." I gave a whoop of relief and rushed to embrace my mother.

On Commencement night to a packed audience at the Braswell Theater I gave "We Die: We Live." I had learned to throw my voice to the back row. After a funny case of goslings my voice had emerged as a pleasant deep baritone. I felt an impostor when I received congratulations on my original and thoughtful address. But we never divulged the secret.

It occurred to me to wonder why my mother, who had been valedictorian at Clinton College, had little interest in "doing anything" with her mind. She had no ambition to achieve. She was content to be admired as a charming woman in a small-town atmosphere. She opposed women voting or any mixing whatever in men's affairs. Mother was no ardent clubwoman. She belonged to only one small literary club, and she worked on her "papers," which were said to be unusually good. In later years she did found and organize the Demopolis Music Study Club and when she died in her eighty-ninth year she was still its honorary president.

In one special respect my mother and I differed sharply. She was instinctively orderly and neat. I was not. Her house was ever spick-and-span. Even at night she wanted everything straightened up—no stray magazines or papers left lying about in the living room, no jacket flung on a chair. She would say, "You never know when there might be sickness in the dead of night and the neighbors come in." "What the neighbors might think" held some special importance in her thinking. Even as a teen-ager I disliked such an attitude. I did not care too much what the neighbors thought.

The only open clash I recall during adolescence, when I completely lost my temper with my mother, occurred in my last school year. I had left the house on my way to work one Saturday when she called from an upstairs window for me to come back. Thinking she might be in trouble, I bounded up the stairs. She was standing in my room in no trouble whatever. She merely glanced meaningfully toward my chiffonier. "You left that drawer wide open," she said. In cold fury, I gave her a withering look, scorned the open drawer, turned on my heel, ran down the stairs, and slammed the front door with such violence that it cracked the glass. At that moment I wrenched myself free from any maternal domination. Oedipus lay in the dust, wounded beyond recovery, if not completely dead.

In the summer vacation, to make up somewhat for the loss of my education money, I accepted an offer to solicit subscriptions for two Hearst magazines: *Cosmopolitan* and *Good Housekeeping*. The publishers were making a real bargain rate for the two and gave me a high percentage of the take. In 1909, I was one of the first youths to indulge in such self-employment. At the beginning my pride suffered sharply when I hesitantly rang the first doorbells. I did not like to ask favors. But I so stressed the bargain subscribers would be getting that I eventually made myself feel that it was I who was doing the favor. The job turned out to be so easy and profitable that I began to ring strange doorbells in nearby towns. In Uniontown one day I cleared $14.35 between the morning and the evening trains. I was to continue the magazine subscription solicitation in Tuscaloosa during my first two years at the university until the Hearst people withdrew their bargain rates. I had gained a surging feeling of independence to be able to buy my clothes and pay for incidental expenses. Later I was to think of the bank failure as a blessing instead of a catastrophe.

Few Alabama high school graduates went on to college in 1909. During my freshman year at the university the campus enrollment stood just above 400, as against 14,000 plus in 1970. I was the only student from my hometown. Family friends prophesied that I would be homesick. I doubted it. I was seeking new green pastures and I was eager for learning. Though I had agreed with my stepfather that civil engineering might be good for my health, I began to think less of the idea as September approached. What I enjoyed most was good prose and good poetry.

On the train to York, Alabama, where I had to change to the A.G.S. for Tuscaloosa, I began to waver. We had a three-hour layover at York, which meant a bursting fried chicken dinner at the hotel with half a dozen vegetables in little side dishes like those in canary cages. A wizened Negro part-time preacher acted as porter and carried my suitcase across the street to the station. Just as the northbound train from New Orleans rushed in, I asked "Preacher" to tell me his favorite text in his sermons. Looking at me with wise little eyes, he said: "Pray, and don't think." With a smile I asked why he did not want his congregation to think. Narrowing his eyes, he said with conviction, "Because, brother, thinkin' is weaknin'." I was never to forget the text, though I was to stray far from it again and again and again.

36

Twice later in my life I was to receive illuminating advice from black strangers.

As I settled back into the green velour of a Pullman seat—despite my inherent frugality, I indulged myself by riding in the Pullman when I traveled—I tried to shut thinking out of my mind. When I got very still, instinct murmured: "Major in English literature."

At Tuscaloosa I was met by a personable young civil engineer, Jim B. Abbott, whom I had met in Demopolis, and who wanted me to pledge Phi Gamma Delta. With Abbott were three of his fraternity brothers in a hired carriage. They bore me off to a large private home, where Fred Maxwell, a college junior, was my host. I knew little about social fraternities (I was laughed at for speaking of Sigma Nu as Sigma Numa), but I chafed at being held in something like luxurious incarceration for two days.

Entertainment for rushees in 1909 would be incredible to today's college boys. Instead of kegs of beer, hard liquor, and "groovy" girls, we were treated to lemonades and buggy rides. Clement Wood took me for a drive in a smart horse-and-buggy outfit. A Tuscaloosa native, Wood was to become a well-known poet and an early advocate of nude bathing and sexual freedom. Now still more or less conservative, he was helping with fraternity rushing before leaving for his last year in the Yale Law School. I was impressed by his sophistication and the tilt of his straw boater as he sought to persuade me to pledge his fraternity. But I was suddenly moved to say, "Stop the horse a minute!" Surprised, he amiably drew up under one of the famous Tuscaloosa oaks that bordered a wide avenue. "I want to ask you one thing. Which fraternity here has the best *national* rating? You have lived in the East and you *know*." He looked at me oddly, started to evade, then answered without equivocation, "Delta Kappa Epsilon," and added, "It was founded at Yale."

"Thank you," I said. "The Dekes want to reach me, but Abbott won't let me communicate with them."

A senior Deke, who came from a plantation at Faunsdale, near Demopolis, found me the next day, and took me to lunch at his fraternity house. It was an old brick mansion of many rooms built by Dr. Lafayette Guild, chief medical officer on General Robert E. Lee's staff. In 1909 it was the only fraternity house in Tuscaloosa. I had dreaded living in Wood's Hall dormitory, where hazing with bed slats was said to be an everyday practice on the "rats." So the idea of a home away from the campus appealed to me greatly, although it meant almost a mile's walk to classes.

The clincher came after lunch as a group of us were chatting on the columned veranda. A brisk young man in a flat-brimmed straw hat set at a cocky angle got out of a horse cab and came up the brick walk beaming. He held a longish rolled-up magazine in his hand like a scepter. (A recently graduated law student from Mobile, Greer Maréchal was to become a noted patent attorney in Akron, Ohio, and to marry the daughter of a member of Woodrow Wilson's cabinet.) The latest issue of the *Saturday Evening Post* was unfurled and opened to a certain page. Maréchal declared triumphantly: "Here is the kind of man a Deke is: Robert Edwin Peary! The Deke flag now flies at the North Pole." Peary had joined Delta Kappa Epsilon, Maréchal added, at Bowdoin College in the 1870's.

I knew that Peary had "discovered" the Pole in April, when, with four Eskimos and his Negro bodyservant he had made a final dash for it. Now I read the account in the *Post* of how he had stuck in the ice the United States flag, the Navy flag, and then the Deke flag. Because I was an admirer of achievement, my adolescent heart swelled with pride to think that this arctic explorer had actually reached his goal.

"You can't do better than Deke," an inner voice prompted. When I went to get my jacket I held up the buttonhole in the lapel to the senior from Faunsdale for the triangular pledge button. I moved to the Deke House late that afternoon. Room and board in the fraternity house cost twenty dollars a month.

At registration, when I faced the stern, aristocratic academic dean, Charles Heyward Barnwell, a Harvard Ph.D. from South Carolina, I did some persuasive talking. Though I came from a ten-grade school, I pled with him not to make me take Freshman English. I told him that I had a wide appreciation of first class literature. I reeled off dozens of works I had read and admired. At last, he said thoughtfully, "I shall put you in my own class in Sophomore Literature, which is a survey of English poetry, beginning with Chaucer. If you do well on the six weeks' examination, I'll let you stay. If not, you go back into Freshman English." I studied hard, and on the first six weeks' test I made an A minus.

Tuscaloosa was a pleasant university town with many ante-bellum homes. Its chief glory was its great oak trees, hence its epithet "Druid City." On Broad Street, from the old Governor's Mansion to the old State Capitol, oaks marched down the center of the wide boulevard as well as along both sides. The university buildings at the city's eastern edge were set in groves of oaks and hickories, adorned here and there with dark green magnolias. The original buildings, patterned after those of the University of Virginia at Charlottesville, had been burned by Federal troops a few days before Lee's surrender at Appomattox. The commanding officer had refused to spare even the handsome domed library with its thousands of valuable volumes; but for some whimsical reason he allowed a copy of the Koran to be saved. When the President's Mansion, perhaps the most beautiful Greek Revival house in the South, had been set on fire in the reception hall against the curving staircase, the president's wife, Mrs. Garland, had persuaded the young officer in charge to put it out, appealing to him as a gentleman to leave standing the home of her and her daughters. The other building not burned was the students' mess hall, which was later to house the family of General Josiah Gorgas, the Confederacy's Chief of Ordnance and the father of Dr. William Crawford Gorgas, whose work in eradicating yellow fever made the construction of the Panama Canal possible.

A social practice of college life in 1909–10 that would bring whoops of derision from today's young men was the custom of calling in clusters on the attractive local girls. Upperclassmen went voluntarily, but Deke freshmen were made to spruce up and go. We walked miles on Sunday afternoons in varied directions. The young ladies were sometimes hard put to entertain a gang of ten to twelve boys at once, followed by another group, and another and another. One of the most popular girls, Mary Nuzum, who had a sweet singing voice, sang "The Land of the Sky Blue Water" six or seven times every Sunday during the nine college months.

The word "relevance," which came into prominence in the late sixties, would have seemed absurd to us in 1910. An insistent student with "demands" would have been sent packing as a troublemaker. We expected the Administration to administer. We had respect for the judgment of older and more experienced professors, whose good breeding created a kind of supplementary school for living.

No student in 1909 would have thought of going into a classroom without a tie and standing collar. I was not at all happy about my own stiff collar because my skinny neck took a measly size 13. I recall that one rainy fall afternoon in my freshman year, while reading an adventure novel by Jack London, I felt a sharp pang of envy because the lusty hero had a 17-inch neck. In subsequent years I never gave up wishing for a larger neck measurement. Then when I reached fifty and steadied at 16 inches, I longed to return to 15 or even 15½. One has to be careful what he wishes for, because he might well get it and be sorry.

Each fraternity member was urged "to go out for something." Since I had not the physique for athletics, I tried out for the dramatic club, called "Blackfriars" after the London theater where some of Shakespeare's plays were produced in his own time. For days I practiced that rich old chestnut, Mark Antony's oration over the murdered Caesar. I had developed a deep baritone voice in my frail body, and I could call up emotion with ease. I made it. Professor Frederick D. Losey, who taught Shakespeare, had founded the dramatic club. He had studied under Harvard's George Lyman Kittredge, America's foremost Shakespearean scholar, and he had also studied acting for a year in England. Losey was a magnificent physical specimen, six feet one in height. He wore a neat black beard trimmed like that of the classroom plaster bust of Shakespeare that stood on a bracket directly above his head. He was the most inspiring professor I was ever to know and he had a direct influence on my career.

My first role at one of the club meetings was that of Mephistopheles in Marlowe's *Dr. Faustus*. I was told quite frankly by the casting committee that I was chosen for the simple reason that with my long nose I looked more like the devil than any other club member. With my kildee legs in red tights and a swirling black cape about my shoulders, I must have resembled something to scare pilfering crows. Everything went well enough until the last moment, when I was to re-enter, clutch poor Faust, and lead him to hell. In the excitement of my performance I had forgotten about that last entrance, smeared cold cream over my make-up, and was stripping off my red tights when a cue echoed ominously. Horrified, I rushed to the exit and watched helplessly as Faust mouthed his last lines three times over center stage, waiting for Mephistopheles to conduct him to hell. Frantically I gestured to my smeared face, my down-hanging tights. The actor rose to the occasion by grimacing in despair and staggering toward me in the wings as if the devil unseen was drawing him like a magnet. Twice I had made a mess of a public appearance, once when I forgot what the seventh little Elk did, and now at the university before the Loseys and an audience of my peers. Only four years hence I was to witness two slip-ups on the New York stage in the great Forbes-Robertson's *Hamlet* that came nearer to being disastrous.

In disgust for my blooper—though only two or three of the audience realized that something had been amiss—I doubted if I should ever be given another part in a Blackfriars performance. But when spring came and Dr. Losey began rehearsals for a road trip of *Twelfth Night,* in which he played Sir Toby Belch, I was assigned the part of Sebastian, Viola's twin brother.

The senior girl who played Viola and I practiced making up before a mirror side by side to look as much like twins as possible. Both of us had brown eyes, moderately large. Identical russet pageboy wigs helped much. The costumes had been rented from New York. Viola and I wore high gold kid boots slashed in front and laced with thongs. But Losey and the entire cast were concerned about my calves. They had to be padded nightly with face towels.

We played *Twelfth Night* not only at the Elks Theater in Tuscaloosa, but at the leading theaters in Birmingham, Montgomery, Mobile, and Selma. On the road trip an unprecedented phenomenon in weather occurred. When we entrained for Mobile on April 20 the men wore Palm Beach suits and straw hats; the girls were in summery muslins. When we got to Selma, on Shakespeare's birthday, April 23, we alighted in a snowstorm. Our hosts and hostesses—the Blackfriars were always lodged with alumni or friends of the university—met us in furs and winter coats. At the station the entire cast was in a compulsive shiver, as if we had caught some tropical shaking disease on Mobile Bay. Carriages rushed us to our respective hospitality homes. I was the guest of Sam Hobbs, an Alabama Deke who was now a promising lawyer and a future U.S. Congressman.

Sam was big: six feet three and weighing 230 pounds. That night I must have been a sinister sight in Sam's long black overcoat as I tramped through the snow to the Dallas Theater four blocks away. I had to clutch the front of the coat and hold it up to keep from tripping, while the back trailed the snowy sidewalk like a prelate's train. And because Sam's felt hat came down to my lips, I wore my own straw boater with its light burden of snow. The sudden cold wave, however, gave us a potent shot of energy. Dr. Losey said he had never seen a more spirited performance than we gave that night in Selma. It was a Shakespeare's birthday to remember.

College days passed agreeably without benefit of radio, television, motion pictures, motor cars, or marijuana. Cocktails, so far we knew, had not been invented. Because Tuscaloosa was a university town no saloons were permitted. However, there were none of the disillusioned, defiant, and lost faces that one sees on campuses in the early seventies.

The nearest Alabama students came to a marching "demonstration" were nightshirt parades after some football victory. Word would fly that we were to don nightshirts. (Only the local Chinese laundryman wore pajamas.) We would join the crowd from the university barracks at the corner of Queen City and Broad by the old Governor's Mansion, and with flaming torches march to the end of Broad Street and the old State Capitol.

The Capitol, dating from 1820, had been converted into a Baptist Girls' Seminary. We would march up the stairs and around the inner balcony railings under the rotunda, shouting victory slogans and singing college songs. We did not attempt to snatch panties. But the girls would shiver and pretend to hide their faces at the scandalous sight of boys in nightshirts, though they knew perfectly well that we wore clothes underneath and not just bare skin. The towering, stout old president in a sputtering rage would raise his heavy gnarled walking stick and threaten us; but he never actually struck anyone. Having tramped through the upper halls and received the tribute of girlish screeches and the blazing indignation of the lady teachers, we would depart satisfied.

No movie houses existed in Tuscaloosa in 1909–10. (Griffith's *Birth of a Nation* was five years in the future.) But the town boasted an Elks Opera House, which drew good attractions, with well-known Broadway stars like May Irwin, Virginia Harned, Margaret Anglin, and William Faversham. Birmingham with its Jefferson Theater was only sixty miles away by train, and during my college days I was to see there such luminaries as Pavlova, Nijinsky, Sarah Bernhardt, E. H. Sothern, Julia Marlowe, and Minnie Maddern Fiske.

Mrs. Fiske was the first great actress I saw perform—in January, 1910. To me her Becky Sharpe in a dramatization of *Vanity Fair* was sheer genius. She could suggest emotion with remarkable restraint. I was tremendously impressed by her unintelligible chattering when her husband returns unexpectedly and finds a would-be lover in her boudoir. That January evening in 1910, when I was seventeen, turned out to be doubly significant as a milestone.

I had gone up on the afternoon train for the Fiske show with a Deke brother named Alonzo Hill, two years graduated and now working in a local bank. His tall, lithe figure enabled him to wear tails with casual elegance and to lead balls with grace. His hair was fair to tow, his complexion all over pink, and his ears stuck straight out. Strangely, the spread ears gave him added attraction. Alonzo, versed in worldly ways at twenty-three, did not lead me astray. I asked to be led down the primrose path.

After Mrs. Fiske's performance, over a chocolate ice-cream soda at Hyler's, the fashionable downtown gathering place for Birmingham society, I expressed a desire to visit a "house." So Alonzo took me by cab to a place he knew on Avenue A. It was definitely not a home, but the red light did not glare blatantly. Of the six brick houses attached like New York brownstones, Genie Gilbert's was Alonzo's favorite. We were admitted to a small private parlor. Genie assured Alonzo that his favorite girl, Beatrice, was free. Middle-aged, middle-sized, plump, executive, Genie was dressed in plain blue cotton chambray. Alonzo explained that he did not want Beatrice for himself this night, but for me. The madam turned to me with speculative eyes, but remained impassive. "I'll send beer," she said, and left the room.

"She seems like a pleasant, respectable woman," I remarked, to Alonzo's quiet amusement. She was so different from pictures I had seen of voluptuous women in crinolines and extreme décolletage in New Orleans houses with crystal chandeliers. My thought was interrupted as a tall, inoffensively pretty woman of about twenty-eight entered. She had gray eyes and indifferent blondish hair and was wearing a long black skirt, a white shirtwaist, and no make-up. She and Alonzo greeted each other like friends. As I was being introduced, a black maid brought in a tray with six small glasses already filled with beer and surrounding the empty bottle. Alonzo paid for the beer with a dollar bill, when I knew a bottle elsewhere cost a dime. We each took a glass. Beatrice belched, blushed with embarrassment, covered her mouth with the back of her hand, and said, very ladylike, "Do pardon me. I'm so sorry. I have been drinking so much beer tonight."

While Beatrice sipped her one tiny glass, I had two and Alonzo drank the other three. I was not at all certain how beer would set on a whopping chocolate ice-cream soda. We chatted about Minnie Madden Fiske, whom Beatrice had once seen at a matinee in Cincinnati. "Why," I thought to myself, "except for the beer, this is like a Sunday-afternoon call on one of the older girls in Tuscaloosa." At last I made the bold move. "Well, shall we try it?" I asked with civility, rose, and held out my hand to Beatrice. As we ascended the stairs, the walls of which were painted an intense red, I ventured to put an arm around her. "Why are your walls so red?" I asked, something like Little Red Riding Hood. And Beatrice replied like the Big Bad Wolf, but sweetly, "To make you the more passionate." I squeezed her slightly and we passed into her bedroom. "You get undressed," she said, "while I excuse myself for a minute." I supposed that she had gone to the bathroom.

I was dazzled by the brilliance of her large dressing table. It gleamed with dozens of pieces of cut glass, reflected again in the dresser mirror and the double-doored mirrors of her wardrobe. Two of the bowls were like small punch bowls. Carafes and candy dishes jostled pin trays and candlesticks. These objects were not cheap, I knew, for I had sold cut glass in our hardware store. Was she a collector? Were these tokens of affection from grateful clients? I tapped various glittering pieces, lost in amazement. In the great old New Orleans houses the shining glass was in the chandeliers. Here they reposed on a courtesan's dressing table. I did not like the word "whore"; it sounded degrading. I had taken off my coat and tie and begun to fumble with my shirt buttons when Beatrice returned in a flowered pink dressing gown. "You aren't undressed!" she exclaimed. "I was admiring your cut glass," I said. "I know cut glass, and you have a valuable collection." "It is my one obsessive vice," she said with a slight smile. "Do other . . . girls . . . like you," I partially stammered, "go in for cut glass, too?" "Quite a number. My sister does."

"Is this your sister?" I asked, picking up a small unframed snapshot of a fully clothed woman in a floppy summer hat. "Her name is Louise," Beatrice said, almost tenderly. "Does she—too?" I asked, pulling off my shirt and unbuttoning my trousers. "Yes, she's in a house in Cincinnati." Then, sensing my thought of "how-could-a-nice-girl-like-you?" she said, "We were orphans." I was slightly moved to pity as I dropped my pants. "Do you like this life?" I asked, as she threw aside her robe and stood naked beside me. Her figure was excellent. I had never actually seen a flesh-and-blood grown woman completely naked before. She replied with candor, "I don't like living in a sporting house, but I do like to screw." I caught my breath. It was the first time I had ever heard a female use that titillating word. I got off the rest of my clothes quickly, all except my socks. Beatrice's next move took me by surprise. She grabbed a pillow from the head of the bed and placed it at the foot where it was about four feet from the mirrors of the wardrobe. "Let's lie this way," she said, "and watch ourselves."

This was a wrinkle I had never heard about. I was really being initiated into bacchanalian mysteries. I did not exactly desire to look, but I did steal a couple of glimpses.

When it was over and we were on our feet, I politely said, "Thank you." I gave her a quick hug and slipped three one-dollar bills onto the dressing table among the cut glass. I knew the price. Every boy knew that; whether the girl was in a house or brought by a bellboy to your hotel room, the fee was three dollars, and it remained the same at least into the twenties.

Beatrice put on some underclothes and her shoes and stockings and then again donned her robe. She wanted to say good night to Alonzo—perhaps she wondered if he had changed his mind, and was now in the mood. He was waiting where we had left him, chatting with Genie Gilbert as he might with an aunt. But he said he only wanted one dance with Beatrice. So we went into the small ballroom where he dropped a quarter in the music machine, and he and Beatrice waltzed. Genie came over to me and held out her arms in invitation. The plump woman was remarkably light on her feet as I whirled her about. When the music stopped we made our adieus.

It was now about one in the morning. Snowflakes were swirling briskly. Not a cab was in sight. So we began walking the ten blocks back to the Hillman Hotel, where we had a room for the night.

"Well, how about it?" Alonzo finally asked.

"No problem at all," I replied, man-of-the-world fashion. "I just did what came naturally and she co-operated. I must say I was a bit dazzled by all her marvelous cut glass."

I was ever inclined to play with my superiors when they would accept me as a friend. I had much to learn in this growing-up process from men and women older than myself. My closest friend among fraternity brothers was a senior four years older than myself. Wilkes Banks came from a well-to-do plantation family in next-door Greene County. He had such a good mind that throughout his four university years he never made a grade below an A. We had similar tastes in literature and theatrical performances and even girls. One girl in particular, the prettiest in college and the most sought after, was a senior from Birmingham, whom I had the nerve to date. Though she was known as the uncrowned queen among the coeds at the time, she was a straight-laced, strict Presbyterian. She would never go buggy riding on Sundays. She was so careful of her maidenly attributes that in dancing no male body could get closer to her than the breadth of her extended hand, palm down, which she held up and dangled to keep her partners at a four-inch distance while giving them the most beguiling smile. Of course, I had other dates with less puritanical Tuscaloosa girls and I still corresponded with three girls in Demopolis.

My interest in the theater stood me in good stead with Wilkes's father and stepmother, who were ardent playgoers. They would take me along with Wilkes on train trips to Birmingham to see some star perform. I was often invited for weekends down to Eutaw, thirty-five miles southwest, to their white-columned town mansion under ancient magnolias. I enjoyed driving to various plantations. I liked bridge and happily made a fourth hand. I admired the second Mrs. Banks's prize conservatory of rare flowers and the outdoor camellia bushes that soared to the second-story balcony. I liked Mr. Banks's custom of saying grace with everybody standing and particularly the brevity of that blessing: "We thank thee, good Lord!" I felt quite grown-up when each night I found a carafe of imported sherry and a wine glass on a silver tray on my night table.

44

Distinguished-looking, with a neat white mustache above his protruding upper teeth, Jamie Banks had been born with several silver spoons in his mouth. He was the first autocrat I had encountered. Until his only daughter ran away and married at seventeen, his will had never been crossed by his offspring, his sweet-natured second wife (the first wife had died with the birth of the sixth child), or the blacks who tenanted his plantations. But he took a kind of liking to me because I dared to express views contrary to his. He tolerated no independence in his own family, yet he found it intriguing that a whippersnapper like myself would be so bold as to disagree with him.

In those days, long before air conditioning, no male from eight to eighty ever sat down at Jamie Banks's dining table without a jacket, even if the temperature soared beyond ninety degrees. Somehow, in spite of a slight internal rebellion, I admired his sticking to Southern tradition. Once when I was staying with Wilkes at the Banks's summer home in Chautauqua-oriented Monteagle in the Tennessee mountains, I almost disgraced myself by rushing to the midday dinner in my shirt sleeves. I had just come in full of excitement from interviewing the great Ernestine Schumann-Heink, who was giving a concert that night in the auditorium and who was a paying guest in the house across the street. This hefty Austrian opera star had been so warm and friendly and so motherly concerned about my thinness that she had called me "dear" three times on the veranda as we chatted. I was thinking about the interview I was to write for the Birmingham *News* and unthinkingly dropped my jacket on a hall chair.

After saying grace, Mr. Banks remained standing and eyed me balefully. Everybody began casting anxious glances at me, including the youngest boys. Suddenly I realized my gaucherie. I excused myself to get my jacket and then we sat down. Mrs. Banks began questioning me about Schumann-Heink.

Wilkes and I were to remain devoted friends until his death at sixty-five. To me he had one flaw: like so many Southerners, he had not a shred of ambition. He was content to live in the little town of 1,500. I had urged him to go to some ivy-league Eastern university for graduate work or take a couple of years at Oxford, but he was not interested. He did make one grand tour of Europe and occasionally he would spend a fortnight in New York seeing shows. Wilkes read the best of the current literature, kept up with world events, invested in blue-chip stocks, dispensed gracious hospitality, shot quail and deer in season, and took pride in his rose garden. His personal ambition, however, extended no further than the senior wardenship of the local Episcopal church. Perhaps if I had been born to inherit plantations, I, too, would have felt differently, but I do not think so.

In my sophomore year I was accepted in Dr. Losey's course in Shakespeare for upperclassmen. We spent an entire semester in intensive study of two tragedies and read three comedies collaterally. Losey would read each scene dramatically, taking all the parts, and then give us scholarly notes line by line. I hung on his every intonation and gesture. The bare wooden platform of the classroom became the stage of the Globe Theater. In a flashing second Losey could change from Othello to Iago, to Desdemona or Emilia. He became the jocular, rustic gravedigger as readily as the brooding young Prince Hamlet. His reading of Falstaff was the best I have heard on any stage. I have never seen any actress approach the depth and variety of his presentation of Cleopatra. I am eternally grateful to Professor Losey for bringing Shakespeare to life for me.

While recognized as a brilliant teacher, Dr. Losey had a facility for making enemies among faculty members, students, and townsfolk. One early spring he decided by example to teach Tuscaloosans how they should treat blacks. He hired a fifteen-year-old boy, midnight-black, for his driver and houseboy. Shortly, he announced casually at parties that he and his wife had adopted the boy, not legally, but just with an understanding. After a few weeks of ostentatious pampering, one morning while the boy was milking the much loved Jersey cow, Losey was appalled to see him brutally kick the cow in her bag. Furious, Losey took the buggy whip to the boy and gave him a lashing. The next morning the professor did not meet his classes. He and Mrs. Losey had been taken violently ill. In fact, they almost died. The "adopted" son had put rat poison in their breakfast coffee. He fled and was never heard of again. The town did some snickering. Losey now drove his own horse and never again openly challenged Southerners for their handling of race relations.

My junior year in college was different in that I stayed out the first semester. I was trying to put some flesh on my frame. So I spent the fall and December visiting relatives on a farm at South Columbus in western Kentucky. My Aunt Sallie Pennebaker and her husband, who had just retired, were temporarily domiciled in one of their tenant's cottages while their permanent retirement home was being built in the woods. Only a few miles to the west lay the Mississippi River and the town of Columbus, where my father lay buried.

When I saw my father's grave I found the cemetery green and serene, high above the Mississippi bluffs. It lay directly opposite the historic Missouri hamlet called Belmont, where the Union almost lost the Civil War, because General Grant barely escaped capture or killing on February 23, 1862. That day General Bishop Leonidas Polk routed the forces of Grant, who fled to his gunboats anchored in the river, leaving his caissons and supplies behind and many bewildered soldiers to be taken prisoners. The Federal hero of the battle was Grant's sure-footed horse, which slid down a high cliff and negotiated the narrow gangplank of the last retreating boat that was about to steam back upriver to Cairo. Thus the prime Union commander was spared to defeat the Confederates in Virginia in the spring of 1865. Without Grant, old-timers in Columbus told me, the North could never have won the war.

I thoroughly enjoyed the activities of farm life and the association with tenants and hired men. I relished the copious cream, the fresh eggs, the chickens, the sausage, the battercakes and molasses. I liked, too, the physical exercise of farm work of my own choosing, and the small tasks I could perform at hog-killing time. I helped shingle the roof of my aunt's new one-story house until I took a headlong tumble and broke my hand when I hit the ground.

Though I got much reading done I had a complete academic rest and proudly weighed 119 pounds when I returned to the university in January to buckle down to nineteen hours of classwork. The theater continued to be my absorbing extracurricular interest.

A minor distinction came to me at the beginning of my senior year, when I was made the first "student assistant" the university had ever employed. I graded the test papers of septuagenarian Colonel Thomas McCorvey, one-time Commandant and now Professor of History. His course in English history was required of every freshman. Of all the remarkable answers on the papers I corrected only one has stuck in my mind. A rich playboy from Birmingham wrote that the significant event of Richard Coeur de Lion's funeral in 1199 was that "hordes of American tourists crossed the Atlantic to witness the royal obsequies."

Commencement Day at the university came at the flowery end of May when magnolia blossoms scented the campus's unpolluted air, even though Tuscaloosa now boasted almost thirty automobiles. My mother came for the graduation, went to the dances, and looked so remarkably young that many persons at first glance thought that she was my date. My happy undergraduate days were over. I had acquired a sheepskin and some academic honors and I had formed friendships that were to last until the friends shed their mortality. But now what to do was the question.

Back in Demopolis for the vacation, I was facing a blank wall. I had no skill to bring in cash. No compass needle pointed to a definite profession. So, for the nonce, I turned *régisseur,* fancy name for stage director. When one of the ladies spoke to me of the debt owed by the United Daughters of the Confederacy for the local Confederate monument, I suggested that I be hired to put on a benefit theatrical performance. It would be a variety show giving talented townsfolk a chance to dance or act. Many citizens had only seen magazine pictures of the new dances like the tango, the turkey trot, and the grapevine, all of which I had learned in Tuscaloosa. I enlisted the services of six prominent "society" girls, six of the town's attractive beaus, and a young matron who ran a dancing school. The dances would be interspersed with dramatic sketches and specialties.

We worked fast and furiously and rehearsed for hours on end. The

Demopolis *Times* of June 12, 1913, announced: "Vaudeville for U.D.C. Benefit Monument Fund, directed by Hudson Strode, at Braswell Theater, Friday evening, June 20."

For the main act I dramatized two scenes from a recent popular novel called *A Fool There Was,* and cast the beautiful young wife of the new druggist, Hobson, as the vampire and myself as the victim in her toils. I became a bit anxious at the dress rehearsal when, after a torrid scene, someone called out to me from the back of the theater, "That's where Mr. Hobson is going to put a bullet through your heart." (This was two years before Theda Bara became an overnight sensation in the motion picture *A Fool There Was* and the number one "vamp" of her day.) Some say the ending was "sensational" when I died with an empty liquor bottle in my lifeless hand and with my head hanging off the couch—taking care to face the audience—while Mrs. Hobson, wearing a low-cut black lace evening gown, leaned over me, plucked red rose petals from her bouquet and scattered them over my degenerate body as the curtain slowly fell.

The show was a huge success in that the theater was sold out. There were curtain calls. The U.D.C. had cash to finish paying for the Confederate monument. I had money to bank for my next move.

I went to bed exhausted but triumphant. And then, to my mother's shame, all hell broke loose on Sunday when three ministers of the gospel denounced the show and me from the Baptist, Methodist, and even the Presbyterian pulpits. The Baptist reverend, who had not seen the performance, preached a hellfire-and-damnation sermon and urged the city council to close the doors of the theater and the dance halls on the grounds that "they were immoral and a disgrace to common decency." Letters pro and con flooded the newspaper office.

After the talk subsided I decided that I might teach English in the Demopolis high school for a year, though I had never taken a course in so-called "education," which I regarded as boring and unnecessary. I consulted with two members of the local school board. During the interview I split an infinitive. One of the men, a stout lawyer, handicapped by a St. Vitus dance that jerked his head about on his massive shoulders, smilingly called my attention to the split infinitive. From my blank reaction he divined correctly that I did not know one when I heard or saw it. A fortnight later I got official word that the Demopolis school board would not have a place for me for the term beginning in September. My specific lack of grammar proved a blessing. Had I been more knowledgeable I might have wasted a year or maybe two teaching in a small town. Perhaps the recent "scandal" of being preached against added a factor to my turndown, but I attributed it chiefly to my not recognizing a split infinitive. A divinity was shaping my end.

The day after the negative reply, while reading of some forthcoming Broadway production, suddenly the word "Columbia" flashed in my consciousness. I announced to my parents that I would take a Master of Arts degree in English at Columbia University while I considered my future. I chose Columbia rather than Harvard or Yale because I desired to see plays. As soon as I was officially accepted, I booked a room at Livingston Hall, the graduate dormitory. Then I engaged passage on a steamship from Savannah to New York. The price of the combined rail-and-boat ticket was exactly the same as a direct one-way fare on a Pullman. The two days and three nights at sea would mark my first of many ocean voyages.

New York Interlude

ON my first evening in New York I was taken to hear *Aïda* sung in English at the vast and splendid new Century Theater. I found grand opera thrilling. It seemed a bright omen for my Columbia interlude.

The room at Livingston Hall, the graduate dormitory, turned out to be a suite with a study and a bedroom. I shared it with an older law student from Birmingham who had recently been private secretary to the president of De Pauw University. We discovered a decent restaurant close by, where we could get breakfast for twenty cents, lunch for twenty cents, and dinner for thirty cents.

Looking through the thirty-one letters of introduction with which I had left home fortified, I was guided to telephone Virginia-born Irving Brock, an editor of the New York *Post*. I hoped that he might suggest some part-time job that would provide me with spending money. Brock invited me to dinner the next night at a Swedish restaurant called Henri's. He said his wife was visiting her parents in Virginia and he was batching it. "What show would you like to see?" Without a moment's hesitation I said, "Marlowe and Sothern. They're at the Manhattan in *Much Ado About Nothing*. I saw them in *Hamlet* in Birmingham." "Fine," Brock said. "Their publicity manager, Paul Wilstach, happens to be a good friend of mine. He'll get us good seats."

The restaurant was gourmet. I don't recall what I ate except the marvelous Swedish pancakes as dessert. At first I was stunned by the cold akvavit, that innocent-looking Scandinavian appetizer. The first swallow bulged my eyeballs with astonishment and burned my gullet with icy fire. I was not much accustomed to hard liquor. I had been really drunk only once before, at the national Deke convention in Memphis. But Brock, taking for granted that I, coming from the South, was a seasoned drinker at twenty, kept ordering imported beer until I was floating on two planes. At the end of the meal I could hardly rise from my chair. We had sat there sipping brandy and chatting until long after curtain time. Then we strolled —I doubtless lurched—to the Manhattan Theater.

Paul Wilstach, who happened to be in the lobby, escorted us to our aisle seats in the intermission after Act I. I had only a kaleidoscopic impression of flashing silks and velvets on the stage, but I was conscious of the rich, beautiful diction of Julia Marlowe and E. H. Sothern, her husband star. In Birmingham I had seen them play *Hamlet* when I was cold sober. I told Mr. Brock of Marlowe's innovation in Ophelia's mad scene. She carried a basket full of white roses, which in her distraction she named columbine and fennel and rue, as she presented blossoms to the king and the queen.

Although I was too much affected by the alcoholic libations to follow alertly the progress of Shakespeare's comedy, an idea for a job was born in the midst of the fourth act. When Brock and I went into the lobby during the last intermission to thank Mr. Wilstach for the choice seats, I boldly inquired about the possibility of a job as supernumerary for the rest of their New York run. I said I needed the money and that I had no night classes at Columbia. Wilstach looked me over and took me straight to the office of his brother Claxton, the manager, a handsome, white-maned man with an actor's strong features. I briefly related my amateur experiences. He wrote a note to George White, his agent on Broadway, and asked him to give me an extra's job beginning the next week. "But it only pays a dollar a performance," he said. "That will feed me for a day," I replied gratefully. I walked back down the aisle for the last act in a state of euphoria.

The next morning I presented Claxton Wilstach's note to Mr. White, a black-mustached Jewish gentleman. "Wilstach says you are a friend of Irving Brock of the New York *Post*. Of course, I could hire you as an extra with Sothern and Marlowe, but I doubt if you would be happy. They are not easy to work with. Their fellow players don't altogether like them." He paused and took up a paper on his desk. "I have something better in mind. Next week the English actor Johnston Forbes-Robertson arrives to begin his farewell tour in repertory. He opens the brand-new Shubert Theater with *Hamlet* on October 2. He's the world's greatest Hamlet since Edwin Booth. Ever hear of him?"

My heart leaped. "He's my idol," I said. "When I was a kid I cut his pictures from magazines and pasted them on a fire screen."

Surprised and amused, White gave me instructions as to the appointed hour at the Shubert for rehearsals. I floated down Broadway, more intoxicated than I had been on the various liquors at Henri's. Another idea was born: I would write my master's thesis on the stage history of *Hamlet* from Burbage to Forbes-Robertson. I would be getting original material—I hoped—from the world's foremost living Hamlet and watching him from the wings night after night.

Dazed by my good fortune, I walked into two male figures that seemed mistily familiar. I had met them at the Deke convention in Memphis the previous December when I was the delegate from Alabama. Phil Stone, the Mississippi delegate, had come to see his friend, who had won a Rhodes scholarship, off on the steamer for England. Phil recognized me instantly and deliberately walked in front of me so that I bumped into him with a jolt. "Where the hell do you think you're going, Strode?" he demanded with a grin.

"I'm about to go on the stage, I think." Then I told of my evening with Irving Brock and my forthcoming "engagement" at the Shubert. The boys from Mississippi would not hear of my leaving them the rest of the day or that night. So we slept three in a bed in the old Herald Square Hotel. Phil Stone, who was to become a judge in Oxford, Mississippi, and William Faulkner's mentor, encourager, punctuator, and most severe critic, was to keep in touch with me for years, until after Faulkner left for Stockholm to accept the Nobel Prize, with Phil running along by the moving train repeatedly instructing Bill to "Do right" in Sweden.

At the hour designated I was at the stage door on Shubert Alley between Forty-third and Forty-fourth Streets. I handed my engagement slip to Mr. Rutherford, the stage manager, and joined a group of miscellaneous Americans hired to "walk on," as the English call it. I was standing in the front row as Rutherford looked us over to assign parts. Someone reminded him that a fourth strolling player was needed; it had not been worthwhile to bring the silent fourth one from England. As Rutherford's dark eyes ran along the group, I raised my head, put on an expectant expression, and stepped slightly forward. "You," he said. "You know the play, I'm sure. You are to enter with the players. Hamlet will give his advice to the players, and you will respond accordingly. Silently, of course. Down in the wardrobe room someone will give you your costume. The boots will be too large for you, but you will have to make do."

There was a slight stir and everyone turned as Sir Johnston and Lady Forbes-Robertson came onto the stage. (He had been knighted earlier that year.) Tall and extremely slender, he wore a formal gray suit and a gray top hat. With his superb aquiline profile he looked the epitome of distinction. How, I wondered for a moment, could this actor who had turned sixty the previous January become the young Hamlet, as full of agility and fire as melancholy. Radiant beside Sir Johnston, in a smart black coat suit and a frilly white blouse, stood the world's second most beautiful woman, Gertrude Elliott, younger sister of Maxine, but more delicately feminine and more appealing.

Here I was, I reflected, less than a fortnight in this reputedly heartless New York, standing on the same floorboards with the celebrity I so admired. Fortune was indeed smiling on me.

When the Shubert was dedicated on Thursday, October 2, 1913, I was lifted into higher realms by Forbes-Robertson's acting—for he *was* the young Hamlet of my imagination. He illuminated the poetry, the philosophy, the wit, and the moving tragedy of the role. In my rough brown wool costume I stood entranced in the wings, drinking in every word he uttered, noting each piece of business. When Hamlet died sitting on the throne I

55

was wet-eyed, like most of the rapt audience. Richard Le Gallienne was to write in *Century* the next February that Forbes-Robertson's dying as Hamlet was the most moving aesthetic experience of his entire life. He wanted every friend he loved to have the experience of seeing so transcending a work of art.

Night after night as I stood with the other three "players" listening to Hamlet's advice on acting, I felt I was being instructed by some highly literate demigod whose beautiful smile might have dissolved a revolution. Since 1913 I have seen all the important British and American Hamlets and to me none of them has ever approached the performance of Forbes-Robertson.

Of course, I still went to my classes at Columbia; two in dramatic history under Brander Matthews, one in eighteenth century literature, one in literary criticism, and one in playwriting. I enjoyed them all, but my heart's interest lay on the Shubert stage. I was navigating in a totally new world, and incredibly content there, however lowly my status.

Gradually I got to know various members of the cast. Some were much nicer to me than others. Several of the younger men contemptuously ignored me. The fellow who played the despicable Rosencrantz with a lisp invited me several times to his apartment for supper, in which the main dish was invariably salmon mayonnaise, which I came to think was the only menu Englishmen living temporarily apart from their wives knew how to prepare. Gertrude Elliott was kind to me and once granted me a half-hour interview, which I published in the Sunday Birmingham *News*. Her favorite role surprised me: Cleopatra in *Caesar and Cleopatra,* which Bernard Shaw had written for her husband.

Often I stood in the wings beside her, holding her huge basket of artificial garden flowers until she was cued for her entrance, when I would place the basket in Ophelia's hand and she would turn mad.

Even Sir Johnston came to acknowledge my greeting backstage, and one night he, too, received me in his dressing room during the fourth act, in which in his own version of *Hamlet* he does not appear. (He laid the entire Act IV in the castle orchard with fruit trees in full bloom; most of the act is given over to Ophelia's madness and Laertes' exciting return.) The star answered numerous questions about the character of Hamlet. He said that the prince came near to the very edge of madness but that he "never quite went over." Later he gave me a handsomely printed copy of his playbook of *Hamlet,* as he had cut and arranged the text. It is an oversize book with illustrations, printed at the end of 1897, after his first performance of *Hamlet* at London's Lyceum Theatre on September 11, 1897, with the young Mrs. Patrick Campbell as his Ophelia.

One night at the Shubert a catastrophe was barely averted during a performance of *Hamlet*. It reminded me sharply of my own freshman blooper in *Dr. Faustus*. The "leading man" of the company, named Cookson, the most beloved member of the company, with premature white hair covered by a wig, played a near-perfect Horatio. During the third act he was brewing tea two flights aloft in his dressing room, which he shared with Sir Alexander Scott-Gatty, the Cassio of *Othello*. Hamlet had dismissed the players, after giving us advice, and, full of excitement about the coming play in which he would test the conscience of the King, he called for Horatio. I heard Forbes-Robertson give the familiar "What ho, Horatio!" Horatio is supposed to enter immediately, answering "Here, sweet lord, at your service." I heard the call repeated, and then a third time, louder, with a slight hint of desperation. Horatio always entered from the right, on the far side away from the door that led to the tiers of dressing rooms. Standing in the doorway, I saw the baffled Hamlet leave the stage and start around the backdrop to see what the hell had become of Horatio. Poor Cookson, all but falling down two flights of narrow iron stairs and adjusting his wig and costume, asked me, as he flew past, "Has it been very long?" He rushed out onto the empty stage, almost out of breath, shouting "Here, sweet lord, at your service." But there was no Hamlet. By now Forbes-Robertson had made his way entirely around the backdrop and had to re-enter behind Horatio and speak those tender words of one admiring friend to another:

> "and bless'd are those
> Whose blood and judgment are so well co-mingled
> That they are not a pipe for fortune's finger
> To sound what stop she please."

When the scene was over, poor Cookson stood speechless in an agony of contrition and apology. Forbes-Robertson merely pressed his arm forgivingly and silently passed into his dressing room.

Some jinx was on that particular night's performance. Just before the final curtain begins to fall slowly, "four tall captains" (stout supernumeraries in armor) bear the body of the dead prince on locked war shields and start up the five steps to the back corridor with the head foremost so that the last tableau centers on the slanted stretched-out hero. I, in the first-row group, "kneeling in awe and grief," looked up to take a last glance at the dead prince. The two supernumeraries on the right, thinking the curtain was full down, lowered their side of the shields and Forbes-Robertson hung precariously at a listing angle. I stopped breathing. I thought that he would surely roll off. I saw him turn paler under his pale make-up. When the curtain reached the floor several members of the company rushed to catch the star as he did roll onto the shoulders of the two maladroit extras. Forbes-Robertson had really been frightened and trembled visibly. His eyes blazed at the stage manager, whose eyes in turn blazed at the guilty men, who were summarily fired then and there. Even in top professional companies things sometimes go dangerously amiss, as well as in amateur performances.

On the stage-level floor at the Shubert there were only three dressing rooms: one for Sir Johnston, one for Gertrude Elliott, and the middle one for Adeline Bourne, who played Queen Gertrude and who was a magnificent Emilia in *Othello*. Miss Bourne had created Salome in Oscar Wilde's censored play at the private Court Theatre in London and also Monna Vanna in Maeterlinck's censored play. She had been born in India, where her father was a British army officer, and her complexion was as dusky as Shakespeare's dark lady of the sonnets. I wondered if her mother had been a Hindu. She had a regal dignity, but in the scene when the ghost of Hamlet's father appears in her boudoir, her scream could jolt spectators almost out of their seats. I stood in awe of her because she was like a "tragedy queen" and I never got up the nerve to address her backstage. Then, by strange chance, in late November I became what might be called her gigolo.

At Thanksgiving Miss Bourne gave a Sunday-afternoon dance and supper at the British Imperial Club in the East Thirties, where she resided along with ten other Britishers of distinction. I was surprised and delighted to be invited. I knew the new dances, so I got along well, but I noticed that few of the young British actors could dance. I danced first with the hostess and then twice again. She was surprisingly light and graceful. She seemed pleased with me, and was anything but formidable.

I happened to be waltzing with Gertrude Elliott when supper was announced, served in the club dining room half below street level. I asked her if I might have the honor of escorting her down to supper. I shall never forget the open-mouthed surprise of several of the young Englishmen who had snooted me backstage when they saw me walk down the stairs with Lady Forbes-Robertson on my skinny arm. Later, at the theater, they began falling over themselves making up to me, and two of them begged me to teach them the one-step. But I turned British cool and had little interest in their belated friendship.

I do not think that I ever heard the word "gigolo" until I first went to Paris. But, in a "quite high-minded sense," that is what I might have been called during the ensuing months. I was Adeline Bourne's unpaid escort on days she did not play in *The Merchant of Venice* and *The Light That Failed*. We went dancing in that era of smart *thé dansants* at the Astor and the Waldorf. Miss Bourne would slip a greenback into my hand just as we reached the hotel. At first I felt unchivalrous, even though I always gave her back the change. Often I would dine with her at the British Imperial Club and escort her to some current theatrical performance for which Belasco or another manager had sent her special seats.

Though Adeline Bourne was a strict vegetarian, doubtless from her rearing in India, she would order prime steaks or chops for me. After she had dined me several evenings at her club I felt that I should take her to luncheon on my own. She was anything but costly, for she never touched alcohol in any form. She insisted that she only wanted a salad. When I asked "Lobster, shrimp?" she said brightly in her inflected English accent: "I do like a potato salad." It was the cheapest item on the menu. I could not talk her out of it. "No, I really enjoy a potato salad," she insisted. And she looked at the bemused waiter with such a queenly smile that he thought surely there must be some wonder in a potato salad that he had never imagined.

It was an enriching experience to companion this intelligent British woman, sixteen years my senior. Some evenings after dinner she would show me her scrapbooks and scores of professional photographs of herself in various roles. She talked not only theater and the British Empire, but Eastern metaphysics and some movement coming into America called "New Thought." Though she never bragged, she had a sense of her own worth. For a party to which she took me one night she wore a dazzling evening gown of white taffeta created just for her. As we started down the inner staircase of the club, she paused before a gilded pier mirror on the landing and regarded herself. Then she exclaimed admiringly, "See! I look like Rachél!" She did look like pictures of that nineteenth century French tragedienne, but she had a beauty Rachél never possessed.

Because she did not play on Christmas Eve, Miss Bourne asked me to dine with her. Then with raised umbrellas we went shopping in the rain to get last-minute gifts for some of her compatriots living at the club. We jumped sidewalk puddles and laughed and were silly and banished homesick feelings.

After the Forbes-Robertson company moved on to another city in the spring, we corresponded. Later I saw her twice in London. For a wedding present in 1924 she sent us a handsome outsize book of *Hamlet* with the John Austen drawings. In my studio today hangs an inscribed photograph of Adeline Bourne as herself beside one of Forbes-Robertson as Dick Helder in *The Light That Failed*. Sitting in a high-back chair semiprofile and wearing an elegant dinner dress, she has the eyes of an Eastern mystic.

I made use of only one other letter of introduction—to Mary Kilpatrick, play broker and actor's agent, born in Montgomery, Alabama. It, too, brought me a part-time job as a play reader. But the week before I presented the letter I had met her at Adeline Bourne's dance. She knew who I was and many of my Alabama friends. She said in surprise, "But what are you doing *here?* How did you *get* here?" When I explained, she said, "That's fast going, to have just arrived from Demopolis." I would take batches of one-act plays from her Broadway office back to Columbia, read them, and write a paragraph of appraisal. Then on certain afternoons by appointment I would discuss their virtues and their flaws with her less important clients. Fortunately, after a few weeks the job petered out, for I needed to finish my thesis.

From the beginning my favorite professor had been gray-bearded Brander Matthews, the drama specialist. He would not permit any female to take his course in Molière, even if she were born speaking French. He told the wife of Charles Darnton, dramatic critic of the New York *World,* that her presence might embarrass the ten young men in the class, for naturally he would speak of risqué matters. He admitted to me that he was breaking university rules to exclude women. The truth was that the old gentleman had a rich repertoire of French off-color stories which he enjoyed telling, to our huge delight. An ardent Francophile, he declared that he loathed German jokes, which generally dwelt on the digestive tract. He said he could not understand why Germans seemed to get more fun out of the bowels than the genitals. As he dilated on the Molière dramatic art or regaled us with stories, a lighted cigarette dangled from the right corner of his mouth. His copious beard and mustache were brown with nicotine stain. At his home, to which he would invite a few favorites in the evening, he had a collection of hundreds of ashtrays, and he could tell what noted person had given him each one. Among his favorites were those from Mark Twain and Theodore Roosevelt.

New Orleans-born Brander Matthews had been a gay blade in his youth in Paris. Later he had stunned his family and shocked his friends by taking for his lawful wedded wife an English chorus girl from the notorious "Black Crook" company, a musical extravaganza in which women appeared in tights for the first time on the New York stage. It had proved a most happy marriage, and now the aging couple—Mrs. Matthews was short and dumpy—looked the very image of Victorian probity.

I had not let study at Columbia consume too much of my time. I had indulged myself in playgoing and the Metropolitan Opera. After all, I had chosen Columbia because of the New York theater. One of the top thrills of my life had come in December when I froze my ears and my toes standing in line outside the Metropolitan in seven-degree temperature to buy standing-room space to hear Caruso sing *Pagliacci* at a matinee. He was in superb form. Two critics declared that on this particular afternoon he gave perhaps the greatest performance of his career. He had fainted in his dressing room after Act I. The curtain was held down for forty-five minutes. I have not heard such magnificent singing in the half-century since in Europe or America. No later operatic singer has equaled Caruso.

I heard both Caruso and Scotti sing twice, and Pasquale and Amato, Frances Alda, Louise Homer, Ernestine Schumann-Heink. I heard Geraldine Farrar in *Butterfly.* I saw every leading theatrical star who performed that 1913–1914 season: among them, Maude Adams, John Drew, Ethel Barrymore, Margaret Anglin, Cyril Maude, Bertha Kalish.

That second decade of the twentieth century was a climactic time of artists. Sarah Bernhardt and Eleonora Duse, who died about a year apart in 1923 and 1925, were incomparable in their divergent techniques. No later ballet dancers have displayed the utter genius of Anna Pavlova and Vaslaw Nijinsky. In time I came to believe in good part Oswald Spengler's views on the decline of Western civilization.

My year in New York, during which I turned twenty-one, had a radiant glow for me. I relished whatever good things New York had to offer; the bad are not incised in my remembrance. In the entire nine months I had had only one sharp disappointment, caused by my one gesture of self-sacrifice.

Sir Alexander Scott-Gatty invited me, as Adeline Bourne's escort, to a dinner for twelve at some exclusive club with dancing afterward. Gertrude Elliott, who enjoyed dancing, was the guest of honor. Then I got a telegram from Lister Hill, my fraternity brother, and a future United States senator. He was coming to spend that one night with me on his way to Cambridge to consider entering Harvard Law School in the fall. (He eventually took his law degree at Columbia.) With painful regret I canceled my acceptance of Scott-Gatty's invitation, which would have been the top social event of the season for me. I met Lister at the station, took him to a balcony seat to see Bertha Kalish, the Polish actress, in some melodrama, and nobly forbore to tell him of my sacrifice.

In early May I had a surprising and delightful experience that almost made up for my disappointment about missing the Scott-Gatty dinner. I was a houseguest in the Garden City home of Walter Hines Page, ambassador to the Court of St. James's. There I ran into one of the most unorthodox vices in which a man may indulge. It was no appetite of Mr. Page, who was in London, but of a man who had leased his beautiful estate. The lessee was a Mexican, or, rather, a highborn Spaniard reared in Mexico, named Dick Mestres. Out of friendly interest my Aunt Franc had taught him English when she and her British husband were living in Mexico. She had known him first as a poor, proud lad with a widowed mother and four sisters to support. He absolutely refused to allow his womenfolk to demean themselves with a job—ladies in Spain then took no salaried positions. Eventually he had struck it rich in mining properties in Mexico. Now he was a partner of the noted mining engineer John Hayes Hammond. In 1914 they had world-wide business interests, so that they needed the whole twenty-fourth floor of the new skyscraper, the Woolworth Building.

Aunt Franc, on her way to England to visit her dead husband's relatives, had wired me to meet her train at the station at eleven. Standing on the platform near where her Pullman was expected to stop I noted a smartly dressed young woman with a fetching nose veil. She was slim and willowy, and strikingly beautiful. She wore a corsage of Parma violets. In her hand she held a nosegay of violets. As we were the only two persons on that part of the platform, we exchanged glances. I moved discreetly nearer. Her eyes seemed to be the color of the violets. When the train came to a stop I was there at the vestibule to embrace my aunt. Then, to my surprise, she turned from my arms into those of the girl. I was introduced to Dick Mestres' youngest sister.

Suddenly both women were saying that I was to come to Long Island and spend a couple of nights. I protested that I had no pajamas, no toothbrush. The girl waved my objections aside. "You will find a supply of both." My Columbia classes were dismissed as airy trifles. Within minutes we were speeding in a chauffeured limousine to Garden City.

While a fuss of love and affection was being made over my aunt by the mother and wife of Mestres in the drawing room, I was taken by the young lady up to my vast bedroom, which was really that of the absent host. "Most of the furniture belongs to the Pages," she said, "but these Chinese chests are my brother's." I remarked the antique lacquered chests of drawers with exquisite enameled designs in gold. The young lady—I have forgotten her name, but it was something like Gilda and she was twenty-one—began opening drawer after drawer. Altogether there were seven chests, containing nothing but silk pajamas—from Japan, China, Paris, London, St. Petersburg. "You have more than a hundred pairs to choose from," she said. "One pair for tonight and a different pair for tomorrow. My brother never sleeps in the same pajamas two consecutive nights, except when he is on some distant travel. Now you know my brother's secret vice—a passion for silk pajamas. He does not drink or smoke, and we believe him to be a faithful husband. But he is obsessed with a neuroticism of early poverty, so he is addicted to the luxury of elegant pajamas."

In my bathroom I found a new toothbrush and an unopened tube of toothpaste. On bookshelves in my room were Ambassador Page's books to browse through. The next morning, after breakfast in my room brought up by two Mexican servants, I wandered into the back garden. There under a blossoming apple tree I found the girl stretched out on the green turf. As I came near she let her gorgeous lashes close. I hesitated only for a minute, then on impulse I knelt and gently kissed her forehead. She stirred lazily. I lay down close beside her on my back and looked up through the haze of scented apple blossoms to a blue sky. I reached for her hand. She turned toward me and opened her beautiful eyes. I sought her lips. It was a sweet hour to remember.

That night I indulged myself in the vice of wearing a second pair of my absent host's monogrammed pajamas—from Doucé's in Paris. The next afternoon several of us saw my aunt off on a Cunarder, and I returned to my studies at Columbia. I became deeply involved in preparing for final examinations. I never saw that lovely girl again.

A temporary setback had come when I failed to pass the three-hour comprehensive examination in English literature. I had not studied enough, partly because I knew that there would be a second chance a month later if I failed. On the second go I came through all right.

I vividly recall one smarting blow to my ego when Professor John Erskine, who questioned me on my thesis, "The Stage History of Hamlet," asked what I planned for my lifework. Though I did not mean to be cocky, I confessed that I had no intention of being a teacher. "I want to be a playwright!" I declared, expecting to be complimented on such an interesting ambition. Erskine snorted with contempt, "Who wouldn't?"

I felt like the fool I was and I began to take stock of my abilities. The very next week, when the head of the English Department of Syracuse University came to Columbia scouting for an instructor, I changed my tune. Now I declared that I desired to teach. I gave as a reference the name of Frederick D. Losey, who had taught at Syracuse before coming to Alabama. Dr. Losey's letter of recommendation was so enthusiastic that it got me the instructorship over ten other applicants, all of whom were my superiors in age and training. The letter of Brander Matthews, who sent me a carbon copy, helped too.

A few days later Professor Matthews showed me a letter from Syracuse, thanking him for his recommendation and saying that they were offering me an instructorship. "We shall keep him for two or three years, and then send him back to you for his doctorate." The last words sort of chilled me. Matthews regarded me shrewdly. With quiet but decisive emphasis, he said, "If you can *write,* don't take a Ph.D. If you cannot, and stay in the teaching profession, you will *have* to. But getting a doctor's degree may be a blighting experience for one with creative talent. I avoided that unholy grind myself. Kittredge of Harvard, reckoned as America's top Shakespearean scholar, has only an A.B. But this Germanic obsession with Ph.D.'s will undoubtedly expand. A doctorate never made a natural-born good teacher a better teacher. Sometimes it ruins him. Of course, I've always been unorthodox—and much in the minority." His words penetrated to the heart of my being. By lucky chance, though Fate decreed me a teaching career, I would never have to take the higher degree. I never doubted that I was the better teacher for that minus.

I wrote my mother that because of my youth I had decided to teach for a year, instead of going to London to study at Beerbohm Tree's dramatic school, and that I had accepted a position at Syracuse University. She was beside herself with joy. Her wire was so out of all proportion to the fact of my very simple employment that I was embarrassed. She used only six of the allotted ten words: "Thank God for such a son!"

The telegram arrived on Columbia's Commencement Day early in June. I had earned my M.A. in nine months, but I had no desire to rent a gown and march to the "exercises." Instead I went to a matinee at The Palace, where the star vaudeville "turn" was Ethel Barrymore in Barrie's *Twelve Pound Look.* Then, after taking a farewell present to Mary, the genial Irish waitress at the restaurant where I had been sustained for seventy cents a day, I boarded a southbound sleeper for the vacation in Alabama.

The following two years in Syracuse turned out to be agreeably pleasant despite the gray cold days of upstate New York winters. I found both English faculty members and the townspeople not only cordial but also abundantly hospitable. As I taught six class hours a week—three classes of two hours each in English composition—I had time to do book reviews for the Syracuse *Post-Standard,* and later to be a second-string dramatic critic, when two plays opened the same night at the city's two theaters. Syracuse was one of the favorite places for "trying out on the dog" new productions before they opened on Broadway. The short-lived National Drama League was then in its heyday. Soon I was talking on the modern theater at various clubs and giving occasional Shakespearean readings in James Street drawing rooms. So I got to know the leading "hostesses." Being a bachelor of twenty-two, I often made the needed extra man at supper parties. People were generous not only with their dinner tables, but also with theater seats. When I was not myself covering a show, I was often invited to accompany a family with a young daughter to star attractions. I particularly remember the American première of Mrs. Patrick Campbell as Liza in Bernard Shaw's *Pygmalion,* which he had written for her and which was eventually to be turned into the bright musical comedy called *My Fair Lady.* Mrs. Campbell was fifty and a bit plump, but she was such a superb actress that she gave the illusion of being a seventeen-year-old cockney flower girl.

When Forbes-Robertson in the second year of his farewell world tour came to Syracuse in *The Passing of the Third Floor Back,* my new friends Mr. and Mrs. John Hazzard of James Street offered to give an after-theater supper party for eight chosen members of the cast. The star himself never went out to evening parties, even in New York. But he sent me a nice note from Albany explaining. His brother Ian, the Polonius of *Hamlet,* was pleased to come, as well as the lovely Laura Cowie, who now took all the Gertrude Elliott roles. When I called on the star in his dressing room Sir Johnston told me that his wife was at home in England about to bear their fourth child. (The baby turned out to be another daughter, Diana, who was to marry Vincent Sheehan, the American writer.) I already knew that my special friend Adeline Bourne had plunged into patriotic war work in London, for we corresponded.

We ate at small tables set in the two Hazzard drawing rooms. The hostess placed Ian Forbes-Robertson and me at a table with herself and the scintillating Kentucky-born wife of New York Supreme Court Judge William Andrews. She wrote stories under her own name of Mary Raymond Shipman Andrews. Her agent, Paul Reynolds, Sr., never had trouble selling them. Her chief achievement was a slim book called *The Perfect Tribute*, about Lincoln's brief address at Gettysburg, which was then required reading in New York schools. Mrs. Andrews and I hit it off famously and she seemed delighted when I told her that she was "the most Southern thing" I had seen in Syracuse.

The Andrewses lived on an estate called "Wolf Hollow" some miles from the city. I was to spend many luxurious weekends there. Their only child, Paul, a promising young lawyer of twenty-five, would pick me up in his little Ford roadster and take me out.

Mrs. Andrews, knowing my interest in story writing, would read me her new manuscript. I did not hesitate to criticize and make suggestions. If snow lay heavy on the woods and fields, she and I would go snowshoeing. I had never walked on snowshoes before and I found it an exhilarating experience. When we returned to the house after a long tramp on snowshoes, if the judge was home and not in Albany, he would prepare superlative mint juleps, which his wife had taught him to make in the Southern way. Frosty juleps seemed more civilized than bourbon highballs or the new cocktails just coming into vogue. They were as cheering indoors in a New York winter as on an Alabama veranda in midsummer.

Paul and his mother told me a funny thing that had happened to Judge Andrews. Because a court case involved hashish, that North African hallucinatory drug, to be absolutely fair Judge Andrews had decided to try some himself in the privacy of his home. Mother and son laughed to recall the totally unexpected effect it had had. They swore me to secrecy, but after half a century I think I can tell. The judge got down on all fours and thought he was a puppy. He scampered about and barked and whined. They were first aghast, and then convulsively amused. When he came out of what today might be called "a trip" he had no recollection of his antics and insisted that his wife and son had made up the ridiculous story. But he never tried a second experiment.

I relished those stimulating weekends with the Andrewses, both in snow-covering weather and in late May, when a thousand giant peonies bordered the broad stone stairs that led down in three terraces to the rose garden. I enjoyed having breakfast brought to my room on a tray. I was learning fiction techniques from a popular writer, who sold every story she wrote in a range between quality *Scribner's* and slick *Saturday Evening Post*. I was myself working on what I thought was a good story, but I could not get an effective first line. Mrs. Andrews said, "Catch the reader's attention with movement in the first sentence." She dictated: "The hot August breeze of a

New York summer blew the curtain in with a puff against his face." I did use the line later in the story, but began my story thus: "Dr. Villier stepped out and noiselessly closed the door of the prison cell behind him."

This story eventually appeared in *McClure's* under the title "Number 29." On hunch, I sold it without benefit of agent to Charles Hanson Towne, the first editor I offered it to. His letter of acceptance gave me one of the thrills of my life. In his congratulatory remarks he said, "I predict a great future for you." For a few weeks I walked on air, thinking that I was independent, that I could throw over teaching and make my living by writing in any part of the world. Though my second story, "The Imperial Battle," appeared in *Forum* before the *McClure's* story came out, I had a rude awakening in the following years and sold little fiction.

Among the extra-curricular activities in Syracuse besides book reviewing, I found time to direct a few one-act plays at the university. The first was Shaw's *The Dark Lady of the Sonnets*. I persuaded the Dean of Women, Jean Marie Richards, niece of President Day, to do Queen Elizabeth. She was a tiny, acidulous, gray-haired spinster who taught a course in modern drama. She had superior diction and plenty of spirit. A senior girl made a voluptuous Dark Lady. I was a skinny Shakespeare. But it was done in modern dress, so I suffered no embarrassment over tights.

Along with my good times and outside activities in Syracuse I found teaching a most pleasant profession. My classes in English Composition went well. I varied textbook stuff with readings of English poetry. The students were responsive. I got good work out of them. They treated me with respect, though I was only a year or two older than some of the freshmen. I enjoyed the personal contacts of the individual conferences on their themes. I let them talk about themselves, their problems, their aspirations. It was really a boon to me to teach English, for I had talked the dean at Alabama out of my taking composition, and, though I held a master's degree from Columbia, I had gaps in my knowledge of rules of grammar.

In my second year, to vary the monotony of Freshman Composition, I volunteered to add to my schedule an upper-class course in the development of the drama, beginning with Greek tragedy. I more or less "played back" what I had learned from Brander Matthews' lectures to the thirty upper-classmen and graduates who registered for the course.

The faculty member with whom I was most closely associated had a distinguished family background. We roomed in the same private house and took our meals together across the street. His name was Eugene Bradford. He was a ninth generation direct descendant of that historical William Bradford who at a comparatively early age became the first governor of Plymouth Colony and was re-elected governor thirty times. This Bradford, a graduate of Maine's Bowdoin College, had also been a Deke. He had earned his Ph.D. at Harvard and now taught Anglo-Saxon and Old English. He was a handsome, serious-minded, shy fellow, with a somewhat grave

Roman face and an impressive dignity. After three centuries, some of the original Puritanical strain still ran in his blood. Though of strong masculine physique he was still a virgin at twenty-nine, which seemed rather incredible to a Southerner. But Bradford was perfectly normal. He just had not found the right girl to marry, and he could not bring himself to dally with prostitutes. He said his gorge rose at the idea of a bawdy house and he feared "the pox."

His down-East restraint made it difficult for him to relax in company. So about once a fortnight he would slip away to one of the more obscure Syracuse beer parlors. He did not invite me to accompany him in his mild debauches, but he got in the habit of bringing me back an ordinary building brick. He would lay it outside my door to let me know that he had been working off tensions. I never knew where he found loose bricks at midnight, and he would not explain how or why.

For all his dignity, secrecy, and introversion, he was a most interesting companion. To his astonishment and dismay the upstate New Yorkers at Mrs. Worthy's boardinghouse thought that we talked exactly alike because we did not roll our R's.

In my second winter Bradford found the right girl—on a moonlight skiing party on the gentle snowy hills of a friend's estate. She took the six of us back to her family home in town for a midnight supper. He married her the next year. Later he became academic dean of two of America's foremost universities.

I, too, thought that I had found "the right girl" in Syracuse about the time Bradford did. And I felt more sure on a week's visit at her family's vacation home on an island among the Thousand Islands. Her name was Eleanor Pass. Her deceased English-born father had owned the Onondaga Pottery Company, which made fine china. Her younger brother, Richard, just my age, invited me out to their country estate for weekends. Again, as at the Andrews', I was lapped in the luxury of trained white servants. Eleanor was extremely pretty, with delicate features and large brown eyes. She was a year and a half older than I. She was so obviously a lady. And I always preferred girls to be instinctive ladies. Bold, boisterous tomboys bored me. She liked to read and we talked hours on end. I spent the first week of my second summer vacation with the Passes at their place, "Swift River Point," in the Thousand Islands. Two young men were employed to tend the motor boat and sail boat. We sailed the blue St. Lawrence almost daily, picnicking on various green isles near the Canadian shore. In the course of the week I felt I was in love. Six months after my return to Alabama I received what was later to be called a "Dear John" letter. Eleanor was engaged to a handsome young man whose father was a millionaire manufacturer of boys' clothes. I liked him very much the one time I met him. But the news crushed me for a couple of days, making me feel very young and very callow. Then I soon began to realize how much I enjoyed being free. Eleanor and I have kept in touch through the years. In April, 1972, on sudden impulse I telephoned her in Boston and asked her birthday, month and year. Our stars were not congenial.

Twice serendipity blessed me in the spring of 1916. At the Syracuse *Post-Standard* I was permitted to choose whatever books I wanted to review. I went off one day with a book on Browning by the well-known William Lyon Phelps of Yale. I was delighted with the clarity of his interpretation of the poems, and thought the book ideal for teaching Browning to college students. I gave it a long, detailed, and enthusiastic review, which appeared two weeks before the one in the New York *Times*. Then Dr. Phelps came to Syracuse to deliver the Phi Beta Kappa address. I was invited to a champagne dinner for ten given in his honor in a private home. Before I arrived he asked about the Syracuse reviewer of his Browning and said the review had much gratified him. On being introduced we became friends. After dinner he asked my plans for next year and the future. He wondered if I would care to teach Freshman English at Yale. I said I would indeed be flattered.

Then in one week in late April three significant things happened. My salary at Syracuse was raised. I was offered an instructorship at Yale. And at the end of the week I received an offer of an associate professorship to teach Shakespeare at the University of Alabama.

Not long before, I had received a batch of clippings from Alabama newspapers from my friend Lister Hill, now studying law at Columbia. He had written in ink at the top of one cutting: "Ill blows the wind! I trust you realize what this may mean to you!" I did not. But Hill, the future United States senator, with an inborn political acumen, had foresight.

A dramatic row had occurred in Tuscaloosa between Dr. Losey, my brilliant Shakespeare teacher, and the university's powerful president, George H. Denny. Dr. Denny was accused of tampering with an F grade on the report card of Asa Rountree, son of a prominent citizen. Denny was so passionately interested in keeping up the enrollment that he would make flattering notations to parents on report cards, like: "Splendid young man—Should go straight on to graduation and law school!" Asa had innocently taken his report to Professor Losey to inquire what his grade really was. Losey saw instantly how the president had obliterated the F by writing with his heavy hand "Excellent student." The professor's F had become the E of the president's "Excellent." Losey publicly declared that Denny was morally corrupt and demanded that the Board of Trustees fire him immediately. The trustees met. Losey was said to have put on a magnificent performance in his recriminations in the closed-session trial. When it was all over, President Denny announced to the press that Losey had proved himself "temperamentally unfit to teach." The trustees dismissed the professor.

Within the month I was offered Losey's position. Partly because my stepfather had died that year and I felt that my mother and two little sisters might need me close by, I chose the Alabama offer. It was a difficult decision—to turn down an offer to teach at Yale! I wrote Dr. Phelps that I had decided to return South. He replied that he thought I had chosen wisely. To get to teach Shakespeare and English Literature instead of Freshman Composition, he said, was a rare thing so early in one's career.

I recalled Dr. Losey's emphasis on Hamlet's line: "There's a divinity that shapes our ends, rough-hew them how we may." My future destiny was shaped by the heavy stub pen of President Denny, who had turned an F into "Excellent" on a student's report card.

Return
to
the
South

BACK at the University of Alabama I boarded with family friends named Quarles in the same house on Queen City Avenue in which Professor Losey had lived. I had the small downstairs bedroom, which I imagined the Loseys had given the black boy whom they "adopted" before he put rat poison in their coffee. It was a pleasant enough room looking out on trees.

Shakespeare was my special delight to teach. But I had the burden of fifteen hours of classroom work. Besides teaching poetry and Modern Drama, I was the entire staff of the public-speaking department. In my first year John Sparkman, who became a United States senator and Adlai Stevenson's running mate for Vice President, took the course under me, and we have kept in touch ever since. Senator Claude Pepper was in another section of the public-speaking class.

For the Blackfriars Dramatic Club I staged and directed two major productions a year. We went on tour for a week in the spring, playing in Birmingham and other cities. I put on Wilde's *The Importance of Being Earnest,* in which my future brother-in-law, Chappell Cory, Jr., played Algernon. Because I was dubious about the diction of the law student who played Ernest—he would sometimes unpredictably lapse into Alabama vernacular—when we played the Jefferson Theater in Birmingham I took the part of Ernest myself. It was easy enough as I had directed the comedy and played the lead in the outdoor theater of Syracuse University only a year before.

As if I did not already have enough to do, I began giving occasional dramatic readings of modern plays at club meetings—for pay to supplement my low salary. I continued to write stories when I had spare moments. At an Easter service in Christ Episcopal Church, a story suddenly came to my mind full blown. I promptly wrote "The Imperial Battle" and sold it to *The Forum,* which was then an influential literary magazine.

Tuscaloosa had a most pleasant social life. Several young married couples were about as attractive as must have existed anywhere. The parties were many. The husbands liked me, because I was always the first to leave, which generally broke up the party. I had a need for sleep with my heavy schedule the next day. I was invited to most of the fraternity dances.

I was not much older than many of my students, but they always treated me with respect. I could be on most friendly terms with them out of class, but when I entered the classroom the picture was quite different: I was "the professor."

A senior student of mine was Chappell Cory, Jr.; he was only four months younger than myself. He had lost some years because he was threatened with tuberculosis. He invited me to his home in Roebuck Springs, Birmingham, for a weekend. He prepared me for the informality of the house by saying, "Don't be surprised if you find a garden rake in the parlor. It's a very relaxed household. My mother isn't much of a housekeeper. She is a clubwoman, preserving the Montgomery home of Jefferson Davis for posterity, among other things." The house was old and rambling, sitting in the middle of sixteen acres across from the swank Roebuck Country Club. It was reached by streetcar from Birmingham, and there was a shortcut through the meadows, across a footbridge, and over a stile. From the first I loved the relaxed atmosphere of the place. Chappell's mother possessed great charm. She had been a beauty in her day and was decidedly feminine. But she kept a German woman as housekeeper and cook, for she was often absent, going to United Daughters of the Confederacy conventions and lobbying at the state legislature for the passing of some welfare bill or other. His father had been editor of the Birmingham *Age-Herald,* but the position did not pay enough to enable him to educate three children, so he was now in the building and loan business. In his younger days he had been private secretary to Governor Forney Johnston, and when a daughter was born she had been named for the governor's wife.

Thérèse was now sixteen and in high school. She was shy, elusive, tiny, and very pretty. She was also proud, sweet-tempered, and "different." I felt like an older brother to her and did not dream that eight years later she would become my wife. Nor did she, for to her I was a university professor and, as she said, might have been from another planet.

One of my Shakespeare students, Charlie Johnson, from Montgomery, whom I cast for my leading man the second year, would sometimes drop by to see me in the afternoons. One day he brought along a packet of letters from his girl. He wanted to read them to me, for he thought they were exceptional. The girl was Zelda Sayre, daughter of a Supreme Court judge. In four years she was to become the wife of F. Scott Fitzgerald. Now she was just sixteen, while Johnson was twenty-one. I have always been able to spot talent. The girl had talent to an extraordinary degree. Her letters were original. They had a keenness and a sharpness; they were pungent, slightly racy, and humorous. "Zelda has such a distinctive style," Charlie said. "I can't come up to these; I don't try to. I send her about three lines in return. Is she in love with me, do you think?" I thought that there was no doubt about her being in love with this handsome, blond chap, who was inclined to treat her somewhat cavalierly.

"Yes, at least for now. It may be just puppy love. When you get out of Harvard Medical School I don't know how she will feel."

"Well, she kind of fascinates me, but she's a madcap. I can't bring myself to actually say I love her."

I first saw Zelda atop a loaded baggage truck at the M. and O. Station in Montgomery. I had stopped by on my way to Savannah and an ocean voyage to New York to spend a couple of days with Charlie Johnson's family. Without his knowledge Zelda had come to meet me. Even at sixteen she was touched with glamour. I never thought her beautiful, but with her gold hair, green eyes, and fine complexion she had something about her that was arresting and even exciting. I thought then that she faintly resembled a handsome hawk, as Ernest Hemingway, who hated her, later saw her as a predatory hawk. She swung down lightly from the topmost trunk on the moving truck and dropped in front of us in a crouching position. "Hi, Zelda! Mr. Strode, this is Zelda," Charlie said with small welcome in his voice. We had plans for the evening that did not include her. Zelda had been told that I was arriving on the afternoon train and she had ridden her bike to the station to see what I looked like, and then climbed on the baggage truck to make an original entrance. I don't know what she thought of me, but we liked each other guardedly. She shrewdly saw that I was not taken in by her unconventional antics, atop a moving loaded truck. I am inclined to think she perhaps liked me better for it.

When she came to the university dances, she pinned a sprig of mistletoe to the tail of her green wool suit, flaunting right and left the invitation to kiss her ass. I walked over to her, broke in on her dancing partner, and said, "You take that off." She looked defiant for a moment, then she said, "But I can't reach the pin." So I turned her around and did the unpinning myself in the middle of the dance floor. "Thank you," she said, and the dance resumed.

My first two busy years at the university passed pleasantly on the whole. I felt that I had to prove myself worthy to be an associate professor. I was twenty-three when I began. But I loved teaching and I was overworked without realizing the fact. Nervous energy kept me going. At the end of my second year I was turned down in the army draft as 4F. In weight I had dropped from 119 pounds to 109.

I decided that I might help somewhat with "the war effort" by becoming an educational secretary of the Y.M.C.A. It ended in my producing plays and vaudeville for the troops and arranging dances and entertainment for their pleasure.

I was stationed at the Naval Air Base in Pensacola. So much talent was in evidence on the base, from Ringling Brothers tightrope walkers to top night club singers from Manhattan, that I arranged a seven-act vaudeville. It was quite a society event, with the admiral and all his staff in attendance. In a hilarious but silly one-act play called *1999,* when the price of eggs is supposed to have reached astronomical proportions, I played the husband to a well-known female impersonator who was four inches taller than I. I was the only amateur in the line-up.

The biggest excitement of my stay in Pensacola was the burning of the base blimp in midair. Men and officers watched horror-stricken, wondering who were the victims. Because the blimp's chief pilot was a friend of Commander Leslie Walker, who was my good friend from Alabama, he had been persuaded to give me a ride that afternoon at four. We sailed over the green land and out over the blue sea. I found it thrilling. That very same night about ten o'clock the blimp burned in the sky. It was an agonizing sight. Some women in Pensacola fainted. Many a serviceman had tears in his eyes. I trembled to think of what a close shave I had had. Leslie Walker was appalled to realize that the fire could have occurred six hours before and I would not have survived the flames.

The next morning we learned that the three men in the blimp had jumped to safety when the airship caught fire at takeoff. One sustained two broken ankles, but the other two were merely bruised and badly shaken.

From Pensacola I was transferred to the naval base at Gulfport. A lieutenant commander there turned out to be an excellent actor. After I had put on a series of one-acts with men and noncommissioned officers, he persuaded me to put on Arthur Schnitzler's *Anatol,* a sophisticated Viennese comedy. Of course, it belonged on a small stage, but the huge auditorium was jammed. I played Anatol and the officer played my friend.

Then I came down with flu in that killing epidemic of 1918. I was literally the last man among thousands to get it. I had a bad case of it. My new stepfather, Mr. Prout, the banker, whom my mother had recently married, was as worried about me as my mother. Then in the dark of early morning one cold January night, when the Gulf Shore temperature was below freezing, the wooden section of the hospital in which I was a patient caught fire from the kitchen and burned rapidly. Some twenty-five or thirty bedridden men were still in the ward. I quickly packed my suitcase, put on my overcoat over my pajamas, and walked to the front door. Expeditiously we were all moved by ambulances to an empty barracks where cots and bedding were provided. And expeditiously we got breakfast served from another kitchen. Not one patient suffered a relapse.

When I was dismissed after six weeks' recuperation, men were being let out of the service. The war was over. I had made friends with the director of vocal music, who ate at the Officers' Club with me. He was from Connecticut. He had a splendid bass baritone and could stimulate the men to sing lustily. I can't recall his name, though I visited him and his wife in Connecticut during the Harvard-Yale boat races several years later. But he did me a blessed service. I had about six months before I was to return to my university. I wanted some delightful but simple and inexpensive place in which to write. He said, "Go to Carmel-by-the-Sea in California. It has everything you want." I went by Demopolis to say good-by to my mother and little sisters and my second stepfather and left for California.

Carmel had been given its special cachet by Jack London, who had settled there a few years before his suicide in 1916. But he had had a difficult time getting established as a writer and people told me that he had collected a four-foot stack of rejection slips. I had enjoyed London's lusty stories of his highly adventurous life, and particularly his novel about a dog, *The Call of the Wild*. In his heyday he had been one of the most popular and highly paid writers in America. He managed to produce fifty-odd books in seventeen years. A compelling alcoholism and an accompanying dark depression had been the cause of his self-destruction at forty. Though a confessed socialist, he was much admired even in Czarist Russia. London had loved Carmel, but excessive booze finally got him.

I managed to rent a small furnished house, which was mostly a large living room with a fireplace. Behind it were two rooms, a kitchen, and a bedroom with an exposed bathtub and a stationary bowl. The toilet was outside the house between two more tiny bedrooms. The place was owned by a lady artist, who now lived in a mansion next door. Formerly it served as a dame school, whereby the artist had supplemented her income. The location was quite central with the post office just around the corner. I paid twenty dollars a month rent. Beauty lay only three blocks away at the sea with its sculptured rocks and twisted pines. Golden poppies by the billions climbed the summer-bronzed hills in the background. Fragrant mariposa lilies and white roses bloomed in the flower gardens. Refreshing fogs rolled over the landscape periodically. Interesting people were always coming and going. I was happier than I had ever been.

I engaged an untalkative Chinese to clean my house on Thursdays. He was so thorough that he moved every stick of furniture out onto the brief lawn, and then put everything back again in the proper place. Although I had never cooked in my life, now I tried my hand at cooking on a two-burner oilstove. I had very simple meals. Artichokes were then three for a dime (artichoke farms belonging to Italians surrounded the village) and they were no trouble to boil. So I existed largely on rare steak and artichokes and milk.

Fewer than two thousand people lived in Carmel in 1919. Tourists were not encouraged. The inn could accommodate only a few. The city streets were kept unpaved by design; some roads were blessed with cracks like crevasses. Everything was done to make the town safe for the writers, of whom Robinson Jeffers and Van Wyck Brooks, both in their early thirties, were currently the best known. By preference Jeffers lived on an isolated stretch of rocky coast some miles south of the little town in a stone house he built with his own hands. Only rarely he would come into Carmel for his mail. He did not care to mix. Nor did he bother to answer letters unless they were about some special business. His long-suffering wife said it was a kind of insanity with him not to answer letters. He brooded over life's tragedies and man's alienation from nature. His poetry is decidedly masculine and rich in elemental power. But he did not become really famous until *Roan Stallion* was published in 1925. I met him only once, in the post office. He reminded me of an intense eagle, anxious about many things.

The most important event of the year, a performance at the famous out-of-door Forest Theater, took place about a fortnight after my arrival. People came from Monterey, Palo Alto, and San Francisco to see these annual shows. A London director who was "at liberty" had been brought in to put on Alfred Noyes' poetic drama *Sherwood,* laid in the days of Robin Hood. Most of the talent was local or came from nearby towns. The part of an old man whose son is killed in the action was the only part that had not been cast. I tried out for it. It was a small part, but it called for a depth of emotion. I got the role.

A handsome British woman with real stage presence played Queen Elinor. Some weeks later at my house she confidentially told a bit of her story. As a girl she had been sent out from England to South Africa with a contingent of ladies-of-the-evening to add spice to the monotonous life of the Dutchmen. She was now a widow with a small competence. Why she had crossed the continent to reside in Carmel I do not know. But she was a compelling actress, and had been in three of the Forest Theater productions.

The Queen of the Fairies was played by Mrs. Phil Gordon, wife of a vice-president of the Southern Pacific Railroad. She was small and beautiful. Before her marriage she had played the girl in a year's run of *Maryland, My Maryland,* produced by Belasco and starring Mrs. Leslie Carter. Marie Gordon was Charleston-born, but she had excellent diction. I had noticed her in the post office and the grocery store in smart riding togs. She looked somewhat imperious despite her small stature, and I hesitated to speak to her. In shimmering white, she was perfect for the Fairy Queen. Backstage I got up the courage to speak to her. She was charming and Southern. She invited me to dinner to meet her husband. They owned a house in Carmel. Thus began a lifelong friendship.

The out-of-doors performance with the natural forest behind us was lighted artistically. Seats were arranged in tiers before us. The theater was sold out. Van Wyck Brooks and his wife were in the audience. He seemed so impressed by my performance of what might be called a "cameo" role today that he waited after the show to congratulate me. He was a shy little man with a large mustache. The Brookses invited me to tea at their cottage. They were not having too easy a time. He was writing *The Ordeal of Mark Twain* and translating French novels for a living. His wife, too, was translating novels from the French. They had two small boys to support and educate.

78

I began dining out with people who had servants. When there was no servant and they did the cooking themselves, I asked to watch them, to learn for myself. But I never tried anything the least bit complicated and I doubt if I really learned much.

I met the wife of a naval commander named Maxwell, who was lonely while he was at sea. I often dined with her in her gem of a house set at the far end of the town and furnished with rare Chinese pieces. Mrs. Maxwell was an artist, who did atmospheric seascapes. One evening in her patio she told me a true story about a mysterious painter whom she called "the Ibsen lady." Her little boy had died before he was five and she painted a full-size portrait of her dead son on each successive anniversary of his birth until he was nineteen. She was an English gentlewoman, daughter of a baronet, and had made a bad marriage to a French diplomat in Russia.

I asked if I might use the material in a short story. She gladly gave me permission. I let it incubate for about a year. When the story was done I called it "The Painter of Ghosts." I sent it to my new agent, O. K. Liveright, brother of Horace Liveright, the publisher. He telegraphed me he had sold it as Blue Ribbon fiction to the Chicago *Tribune Magazine* for a big price. Later I took it along with other stories to the Curtis Brown agency in London. I changed the title to "The Phantom Model." Curtis Brown first sold it to the *London Magazine*. Then it was published in Danish and Hungarian translations.

I sent Mrs. Maxwell a copy of the Chicago *Tribune* story, romantically illustrated in colors. Though she had known the Ibsen lady in San Francisco I had laid the story in Carmel—in the Seaside Inn and in her own house. She was pleased with my dramatic ramifications.

At some weekend convention I became a landlord and a profiteer. I rented out the two tiny detached bedrooms in my backyard for enough to pay for a full month's rent. Then I rented one room to a youngish Hungarian artist, who had come to the States to do a portrait of Woodrow Wilson.

Work hours for writers and artists in Carmel were sacred. No one intruded. Social events occurred at night. Ladies who had said good-by to Puritanism would discreetly tap at my door. Sex life was no problem.

Carmel was so beguiling that I did not want to return to professorial harness. I considered getting a job with Standard Oil in China. It would be romantic, and it would give me a store of fresh material. But the fact that one had to sign up for a stay of three years was something that gave me pause.

Although I was an associate professor at my university, my salary was absurdly low, even for those moderate times. Because I was so young Dr. Denny had got me cheap. I decided to take a gamble. I wrote the president that I could not return to the university unless I was promised a raise of $800. After the letter was dispatched, I trembled inwardly at my boldness.

I knew how hard-pressed the president was for funds. No such thing as government subsidies existed then. The state was really poor. And no Alabama student was asked to pay tuition.

I began to realize how greatly I enjoyed teaching Shakespeare, among my four other courses, and would miss it as a vital part of my life. In my profession I could always have at least three and a half months of vacation in which to write. Van Wyck Brooks was on the verge of a nervous breakdown. Because of absolute necessity he was forced to translate French novels for bread and butter. He was soon to suffer a collapse.

Some afternoons Brooks would drop by my place and I would make tea. One day when he was having tea with me, I inadvertently offended him. I knew that his literary criterion was high, that he believed only in top-quality writing, and that he had no interest whatever in popular commercial stuff. I recall slapping a nearby manuscript for emphasis, and saying with a kind of defiance, "I'm writing to *sell!*" Van Wyck actually paled. I saw the disappointment and hurt in his eyes. Though he said nothing, in that moment he gave me up. He had no further interest in me. He never asked me back to his home. And once when I passed him walking with his houseguest Edward Sheldon, whose play *Romance* was a tremendous success in two hemispheres, he smiled wanly, but he did not bother to introduce me to the playwright.

Years later I wrote Van Wyck to tell him what he had done for me: made me doubt the value of fiction in slick magazines. I gave up entirely when Henry Backman Sells, editor of the *Delineator,* softened the blow of a rejection by telling me I would never be a successful writer of popular fiction. He flattered me by declaring that I had a first-rate mind, and should perhaps turn to nonfiction. He said that my fiction would always sound a bit phoney, because I did not believe in it myself. After 1923 I never attempted another short story. The last one, called "The Canceled Line," laid in Provincetown, appeared in the prestigious *English Review* when Ford Madox Ford was editor. So both Brooks and Sells had an influence on my career.

Years later I heard from Brooks, who was enthusiastic about my Jefferson Davis biography. He said that it was not only absolutely first-rate, but it had so much "go." I met him at the Harvard Club at lunch one day, after his mustache had turned white. I recalled to him his giving me up at Carmel. He remembered me well, but he had no recollection of the incident.

In Carmel Brooks had shocked me into taking stock of my abilities. I had once had an idea that I might make a decent living out of fiction, but now a mistrust was about to overwhelm me. Happily, the answer from the president at Alabama came back positive. Along with many commendations for my work, I was assured of the raise. Again I felt that a divinity had a hand in shaping my ends in sending me back to the security of Alabama.

I decided to go to Provincetown for the summer vacation of 1921 because I hoped to meet some writers. On a stopover in New York I had the good fortune to meet Lucy Huffaker of the Theater Guild, who gave me a letter of introduction to Eugene O'Neill. He had just won the Pulitzer Prize for *Beyond the Horizon,* his first full-length play. O'Neill was the person I desired to see above anyone else. But I was not sure that even this letter from his close friend would get me to him. I was told in Provincetown that the playwright was peculiar and reclusive and did not care to meet strangers. I also learned that he did not live in Provincetown, but about two miles away across the sand dunes in a cottage on the Atlantic shore.

Hopefully, I mailed Miss Huffaker's letter and gave the address of a Portuguese fisherman's house where I had found a nice large room with a private entrance. An answer surprised me with its promptness. O'Neill's wife, Agnes Boulton, invited me to tea and gave some directions about finding the lonely place.

Next day O'Neill himself wrote me.

Better postpone the long-trail walk until Sunday p.m. The latter part of the week—what with our slavey taking her weekly vacation, etc.—is always a hectic time for us. And just now, to make matters more complicated, our pump has gone bust and we are having no end of household worries. By Sunday, praise God, the sky will have cleared somewhat and we will be less disagreeable.

See you then. I hope. This in haste.

Sincerely,
Eugene O'Neill

So, on Sunday, wearing my best summer sports jacket, I set off across the white sands in joyous anticipation. The midsummer June sun beat down relentlessly. I soon felt as if I were traversing the Sahara desert. I took off my jacket, then my necktie, then my shirt. I plodded on and on, wondering if a sunstroke might stretch me out to expire on the dazzling sands. When I felt almost burnt to a crisp, I saw the silhouette of a cottage and heard the roar of the sea. As I approached the house with a surge of relief, I put on my shirt and tie and jacket.

Within the house I saw that I had had small need to re-dress myself. For there in the very center of the living room on a pillow lay the future Mrs. Charles Chaplin naked as the day she was born. Oona was then just one year old. Four-year-old Shane came forward to greet me solemnly in his cherubic nudity. Then the playwright strolled in from an ocean swim dripping a watery trail. Wearing the briefest of black trunks, he sat on a sofa, glistening wet and burnished a dark bronze from weeks of sunning on the sands. He sat mournfullike, half bent over. His ribs were all but visible beneath the wet swarthy skin.

Agnes Boulton was fully clothed in a summer dress with a skirt of the length then fashionable. She was a woman of instant charm and made me feel very welcome. I learned that her father was an English artist. And I also learned that O'Neill had an older son, Eugene, Jr., by his first wife. This first-born was to become a university instructor of some erudition and a coeditor of two thick volumes of Greek dramas before he eventually committed suicide.

Teatime passed pleasantly, with little Shane, who was to know such an unhappy, checkered career, diligently passing the cupcakes. He reminded me of an unsmiling cherub in an Italian Renaissance painting. His mother told me that he had been named after that sixteenth century Irish chieftain, Shane O'Neill, who had defied both Henry VIII and Queen Elizabeth.

Eugene was anything but talkative, but he freely answered questions that occurred to me. Born in New York, he had been partially brought up in musty stage dressing rooms and cheap hotels, when his matinee idol father, James O'Neill, played the romantic Count of Monte Cristo for sixteen consecutive years. After a series of boarding schools, in 1906 Gene had gone to Princeton for a year. But he had not taken to university life, he said, and flunked out in the spring. He had gone to sea on voyages to South America and South Africa and become saturated in the salty talk of sailors, stevedores, and outcasts. In 1912 he was forced to spend months in a sanatorium because of tuberculosis. There he began creating one-act plays, drawn from his sea-going associations. In 1914–15 he studied playwriting under George Pierce Baker at Harvard. Then he became associated with the Provincetown Players, where his short plays were first produced.

O'Neill told me that his father, who was pathologically stingy, had generously paid for the private publication of his two volumes of one-act dramas. I knew, of course, that with the production of his *Beyond the Horizon* his reputation as an important American dramatist had been established—when he was thirty-two. *The Emperor Jones* had followed shortly, and recently he had finished *Anna Christie,* which he showed me in manuscript. His handwriting was so tiny that one almost needed a magnifying glass to read it. The next year he was to win a second Pulitzer Prize with this play, which was later to be Greta Garbo's first vehicle in talking pictures.

As the afternoon progressed O'Neill became more mellow. After tea he took me on the small veranda facing the ocean and pointed out a rotting derelict ship that had been washed up on the beach, a hundred yards east of the O'Neill cottage. He had used it as a model and inspiration in writing *Anna Christie,* he said. We strolled down the sands to the east to get a closer view. Robert Edmund Jones, the New York scene designer, just returned from an errand in Provincetown, joined us. He was the O'Neills' houseguest and he had been commissioned to do the sets for the play. The night before, Jones told me, they had clambered over the wreckage and hung ships' lanterns here and there to note the best effects.

When we turned back, some distance away I noticed a second house on the beach. To my astonishment, a man was hanging on a cross. His head was sunk to his breast; he looked dead. The hair and beard were bright auburn. Instead of a loincloth the figure was wearing kelly green swimming trunks. Dumbfounded, I stopped and stared. O'Neill and Jones were amused at my perplexity. Jones said, "An artist lives over there. He's doing a crucifixion on canvas. The man modeling Jesus is Ernest Boyd, the Irish critic, now living in New York. You can't see the artist or the easel because they are just around the corner of the house."

Back in the cottage, where I made my adieus to Agnes O'Neill, Oona still lay on her pillow, cooing sweetly and kicking her baby legs in unbreached freedom. A writer must need to be free of restraining conventions, I thought to myself, as the naked Shane handed me my straw hat. It was all so different from the way of Tuscaloosa. Maybe one did have to be strange and different to be a great writer.

To my surprise and delight O'Neill followed me out the door and said, "I'll walk you partway." As we headed across the dunes toward the town, he became sympathetically amiable. I told him that I had strong doubts that I had enough talent ever to be a writer, though I had had several stories published: in quality magazines, in slicks, and in pulps. Had he had doubts about himself? He smiled slowly. "Of course," he said, "we all do. Remember? My father paid to have my first plays published, so that I could see my name in print. You have already published on your own. Keep at it. Don't let teaching consume all your time. Writing is a rather lonely business. Be careful it doesn't enslave you. Now I think you can find your way." He stopped on the rise of a dune and held out his hand rather shyly. But I felt as if he were blessing me. I said to myself, this man is full of kindness, though it is hard for him to show it. When I looked back and waved he was standing on the ridge of a dune. I can still see that bronzed skeletal form clearly outlined against the sunset's afterglow.

I saw Agnes O'Neill many times later: twice she lunched with me in Provincetown. And I met her in New York and in Bermuda. One evening after a party in Greenwich Village, when I was Agnes's escort, we sat past midnight on a park bench in Washington Square talking about her famous husband. She told me something of her early married life with Gene. His heavily tinctured melancholy and his excessive shyness were painfully real. She said that on their honeymoon and through the early years of marriage when he went up to a hotel desk to sign the register he would "get the shakes." He could write his own name all right, but his hand trembled so violently when he tried to add the customary "and wife" he simply could not do it. He would blush furiously, and she would have to take the pen and finish the line herself, while the room clerk looked on, embarrassed or suspicious. Agnes said that Eugene O'Neill never could understand why he was fearful of mere living and she herself never really knew. She pointed up his perplexity by quoting from one of his similarly tortured characters in a play: "Why am I afraid to dance, I who love music and rhythm and grace and laughter? Why am I afraid to live, I who love life and the beauty of flesh and the living colors of earth and sky? Why am I afraid of love, when I love love. Why was I born without a skin, O God? Why the devil was I born at all?"

"Those are the questions he asked himself," Agnes said, "but he never knew the answers."

Gene found comfort as well as inspiration in the Greek tragedies, she told me. He was fond of quoting that last line in *Oedipus Rex:* "Therefore, while our eyes wait to see the destined final day, we must call no one happy who is of mortal race, until he hath crossed life's border, free from pain."

O'Neill's withdrawal, I think, made him the more dedicated writer. During the three years my wife and I lived in Bermuda I got to know Joe Powell, the old blue-eyed Negro boatman who instructed the playwright about the channels and the rocks in the bays. When O'Neill bought the beautiful century-old house called "Spithead" on a point of land jutting into the Great Sound, Joe found O'Neill very different from Mark Twain, "a magnificent gentleman in a white doeskin suit," whom he had often taken sailing before 1910. At first he was awed by the dramatist, who wrote *Strange Interlude* and *Mourning Becomes Electra* at Spithead. "A very *conservative* man was Mr. O'Neill," he said. "When he was in his study writing he looked more like a lunatic than anything else—and you better hadn't go near him. But when he came out to the water to swim or sail he was completely changed, the nicest man you ever saw—a *solid* man he was."

When O'Neill succumbed in 1953 to a longtime muscular disorder that caused him to shake so uncontrollably that he could not hold a pen, he left the manuscripts of three finished plays. One, *Long Day's Journey Into Night,* produced in New York in 1957, was autobiographical: about himself as a brooding, poetic young man, his older drunkard, hell-rake brother, his pathetic, dope-addicted mother, and his tight-fisted father with an aura of jaded glamour. Seeing this play unfold gave me more insight into the tragedy of O'Neill's psychology. "Genius," I said to my publisher, who companioned me, "isn't worth the price of such suffering."

In Bermuda in 1931 when Agnes O'Neill was staying at Spithead I had not thought it fitting to ask her why she and Gene had parted. With her sweet disposition and keen perception she had seemed the perfect wife for his complicated nature. From Stark Young, the dramatic critic of *The New Republic,* who knew them all well, I got some hint of his attraction to the glamorous Carlotta Monterey. I never met the third Mrs. O'Neill, but I had

84

seen her on the stage in *The Hairy Ape*. She was considered beautiful, but to me there was a hard streak under her high polish that I found not *simpatico*. I wondered why she had sought to catch this timid, sensitive man with his air of brooding mystery. Young said that at heart O'Neill was really a romantic and that after he was famous and had plenty of money he wanted a dash of elegance in his somewhat monkish life. When Carlotta took him shopping with her once in expensive boutiques he had been astounded by her imperious manner with shop assistants, who kowtowed to her in a way he had never witnessed before in his life. And when she had him feel the exquisite texture of imported dainty underwear, the like of which he had never dreamed, he was carried away. Young said that he had been "quite content if Agnes wore a slip made of sailcloth." But these fine silks and organzas went to his head and he desired a new environment with all the sophisticated appurtenances that Carlotta was so equipped to supply and grace. She wanted a famous man for a spouse as background to lure into her circle celebrities of high distinction. The O'Neills moved across the continent to California and lived in style with chauffeur, chef, servants, highbred dogs, and gardens. Carlotta entertained with discreet elegance and saw to it that her husband's sacred working hours were never violated. When America entered World War II the O'Neills' satisfying way of life began to break up as servants were drafted or entered some kind of war work. They had to leave their suburban estate because they could not get another chauffeur and neither one could drive a car, I was told. Gene was so undone by the war (he always felt the woes of the world keenly, Agnes had said) that he could no longer write. Then the strange shaking disease seized him and he was further incapacitated. Carlotta Monterey had the care of his invalidism during his last years. After his death in 1953 she arranged for the posthumous production of his three manuscript plays, first in Stockholm and then in New York. So, doubtless, despite early prognostications of O'Neill's friends, she had proved as good a wife in her way as Agnes had in hers.

The last letter from O'Neill which I can find in my files is dated April 3rd, 1938, from Tao House, Danville, Contra Costa County, California. I had written him about an anthology of English lyric poetry I was preparing, and said I was asking twelve persons of note in two hemispheres to name their three favorite poems. O'Neill replied promptly.

No, I am not enough of a critic of lyric poetry to venture my special definition. And my admirations will have to be from admiring memory. It is a long time since I have read them. First, far above all others, Keats' "Ode to a Nightingale." Second, Swinburne's "A Forsaken Garden." Third, Francis Thompson's "The Hound of Heaven."

I remember you well at Provincetown.

Greetings—and all good wishes to the book and you.

O'Neill's emphatic first choice "far above all others" was gratifying, for along with "Ode to a Grecian Urn" it ranked with my own top favorites. The other two choices somewhat surprised me. But, taken together, his taste bore out what both Agnes Boulton and Stark Young had said: that basically he was an incorrigible romantic.

He sent my publishers a generous letter of commendation on *Immortal Lyrics* for use in publicity and he particularly praised my "fine" introduction on the history of English lyric poetry. Basically, Eugene O'Neill was a generous-hearted man, as well as the greatest dramatist America has produced.

Meeting the O'Neills was the high spot in my Cape Cod summer. I also met prominent artists, including Gilbert Miller, the beautiful violinist Thelma Given, and America's highest paid illustrator, Dean Cornwell, who became a real friend. Then there were the radicals Max Eastman, Harry Kemp, and Mary Heaton Vorse, and several personages well known in Greenwich Village.

I learned something more about the domestic life of authors when I spent a weekend with Susan Glaspell and George Cram Cook at Truro, a few miles away by bus. This husband and wife were cofounders of the much talked of Provincetown Players, that experimental theatrical group organized in 1915. The first year they had put on O'Neill's *Bound East for Cardiff,* which helped to launch him on his illustrious career. They were a prime motive force in the renaissance of the American theater of the 1920's. Their first wharf theater was built out over the bay less than two blocks from my lodging.

"Jiggs" Cook, as he was called, met me barefoot at the Truro bus stop in the late afternoon. As a young man he had sought freedom and culture in Greece and was still throwing off the inhibitions of a small town in Iowa. He was a large, handsome man with a magnificent white-haired head. From the bus he took me straight to the kitchen to meet the middle-aged cook, a character well known in Bohemian circles in the Village. She could not shake hands with me because both hands were busy: one frying onions for our supper, and the other holding high an open book she was reading, as if she did not want her left hand to know what her right hand was doing. Curious, I asked what she was perusing with such absorption. It was Strindberg's *Dance of Death,* one of the Swede's most difficult and esoteric dramas.

In the small living room Miss Glaspell greeted me, standing quiet and serene in the middle of the checkerboard floor painted in glossy blue and white segments of a square foot each.

After supper Jiggs stretched out prone in the very center of the checkerboard, his unconstrained belly rising prominent between white head and bare feet like a treeless hillock. He discoursed on this and that, Greece and

O'Neill and the future of the American theater. He seemed utterly contented with his lot in life, and found it sweet to do nothing in the summer.

His wife, who wrote every day, was outwardly a placid woman, happy to ply her needle in the evenings far from the stirring tumult of Greenwich Village. I asked her questions about the technique of fiction writing. I confessed that I was concerned about acquiring a first-rate style, and that I would not find Robert Louis Stevenson's apprenticeship in duplicating various kinds of styles to my liking.

Miss Glaspell put by her needlework and said quietly, "Don't worry about style. If you are a first-rate person, you will find that your style is eventually first-rate."

That is all that I specifically recall of our weekend of conversation at Truro, except for the fact that she told me that neither she nor her husband had been psychoanalyzed, simply because they felt no need. I had been hearing much about this new psychoanalysis and Freud for the first time in Provincetown. I had heard the terms "mother-fixation" and "father-fixation" and "libido" and "id." I was told the Freudian idea that dreams, however disguised, had sexual significance. This was all new to me. There was no analyst in Alabama in 1921 so far as I knew, and, to my shame, I had only barely read of Sigmund Freud.

Many a day I lunched at the same table with Grace Potter, a well-known New York analyst who had studied in Vienna. One day Dean Cornwell was lunching with us and he told the white, bobbed-haired Miss Potter that he had been having a recurrent dream about his teeth loosening and falling out. Could it have a meaning? "Indeed," she said. "You have a subconscious fear of impotence. Many men past thirty often dream of teeth falling out." Dean and I were astounded. "Well," I said, "I've never dreamt of loosing my teeth. I'm not yet thirty. But I had an odd dream two nights ago. I was in some small railway station waiting for a train. A burly, bearded stranger standing near me was holding a stack of silver dollars about eight inches long horizontally between his two palms, as if about to juggle them. As the train rushed in the stack of dollars in the man's hand began to buckle upward and finally disintegrated and spilled to the floor. I woke before boarding the train. Can you make anything out of that?"

Miss Potter smiled. "You, too, have a subconscious fear of impotence," she said. "A train and a railway station have sexual connotations in dreams. The eight-inch-long stack of silver dollars represents the penis. Its breaking up suggests a hidden fear of impotence, just as Mr. Cornwell's loss of teeth. In the subconscious dreams take on bizarre disguises."

I was as flabbergasted as Dean had been. On leaving, after thanking Miss Potter for our initiation into the interpretation of dreams, Dean mentioned a pseudoscience that he followed: astrology. He said that he went at regular intervals to Evangeline Adams about business matters, favorable days for signing contracts, and even marital problems. He ran off a list of noted persons who consulted her, including the banker J. Pierpont Morgan. In my abysmal ignorance I said I thought the whole thing was crazy. But he maintained that it had been most helpful.

I continued to scoff at astrology until in Bermuda I was given a book by Evangeline Adams called *Astrology, Your Place in the Sun,* published in 1928. I read it with absorbing interest. I was a Scorpio. And I learned after five years of marriage with a Pisces that I had made the best possible marriage. My wife's stars and mine melded in a most remarkable way. My moon sign was in Pisces, her sun sign, an excellent thing for marriage. After reading the grave faults of a Scorpio man, I used astrology as a kind of therapy.

That revealing summer at Provincetown was one of the tops of my life. Besides the good times and enlightening growing up, I had managed to get some writing done. I had received checks for short stories that paid for my seaside vacation. When I returned to Tuscaloosa, I had high tales to tell of new things abroad in the world. I also had a healthy deep tan, a small mustache, and discreet sideburns. I thought I looked Spanish. I hoped I resembled a writer.

Settling back in the university routine in the fall of 1919 was, in fact, comforting. I took to lecturing on Shakespeare with enthusiasm after a year's absence. I continued to go for weekends to stay with the Corys at Roebuck Springs. Chappell was now out of the service as an infantry lieutenant and had begun the practice of law. I gave Thérèse, who was now having beaus, brotherly advice about which of her suitors to consider seriously for marriage. She said that for her family's sake she thought she should marry a man with money.

Thérèse had gone to Montevallo College for two years, where she had taken courses in what was then called "domestic science," cooking and sewing, among other subjects. Then she had entered Goucher in Baltimore, and the pressure of beaus increased. She spent about as much time going to dances at Annapolis as she did on her studies. She attracted the affectionate interest of the Naval Academy senior who stood at the top of his class. He was a splendid young man from Chicago named H. M. Pino, called "Piney" by his admiring fellow midshipmen. He was president of his class and captain of the football and baseball teams. Besides being an athlete, he played the violin. This Piney asked Thérèse to lead the senior ball of the year with him. I was tremendously proud of her.

Her friends in Baltimore and Annapolis smiled, wondering how Thérèse would get on with Piney's Midwestern parents. The Pinos were concerned when they heard that their only child fancied a girl from the South. Naturally, they were expecting him to give them many strong-boned grandchildren. They came to his graduation, and when they met this girl, who weighed no more than ninety-five pounds, their fears were confirmed. Mrs. Pino, who wore sensible low-heeled shoes and walked with the strong stride of her husband, did not conceal her shock, even belligerence. The first question she put to Thérèse was: "Can you make hot cakes?"

"Well, I have never actually made any," Thérèse replied politely, "but I've seen our cook make them."

"Well, Piney *has* to have his hot cakes for breakfast!"

Thérèse was astonished to realize that they took it for granted that she was going to marry Piney. Leading the ball with him was one thing, but marriage she had never contemplated. The Pinos were quite well-to-do and it did not occur to them that any girl who had the chance would not marry their son. But Piney understood; he was as sensitive as he was strong and stable. He would gladly have forgone his hot cakes to have attracted this delicate girl with something more than the fondness everyone felt for him.

When she left Baltimore for Birmingham, Piney settled her in the Pullman solicitously. They said farewell with no more than affectionate friendliness. Two years hence she received a letter in which he said he wanted to resume their relationship. Before she could write him that she was soon to be married, a Baltimore friend sent her a newspaper cutting about his death. Pino's submarine had sunk to the ocean's bottom through some mechanical malfunction. Deep-sea divers found his body with his violin at his shoulder.

When Thérèse next came to the University of Alabama dances she stayed with some of my friends. I recall that I was standing in the drawing room when she walked down the stairs as my date for the evening. Seeing her looking so adorable and so desirable in a simple low-cut black evening dress, I fell in love—for the first time in my mature life. She was even prettier than I remembered her, with more distinction to her delicate features.

But I was not ready to settle down—yet. I had planned a year of writing in Italy. Thérèse encouraged me to go. In truth, she did not want to consider marriage—yet.

It was in January, 1920, that Thérèse first met Zelda Sayre. Fresh and unsophisticated despite Annapolis, by chance she drew Zelda as a roommate at the S.A.E. house party at the midterm dances. She found Zelda, who seemed to have been born worldly-wise, dazzling. Zelda was given to impulsive and unorthodox gestures. When she was not getting the attention she desired, she might go to the French doors and kick out the bottom glass. Then she would complain of cold, and at the raised inglenook of the S.A.E. house, with bookshelves on either side of the fireplace, she indiscriminately threw volumes into the fire to keep the flames going. This was at three or four in the morning, when girls had "late" after-the-dance dates.

89

I had noticed myself that in the grand marches when Zelda was not leading the ball she would invariably take the end and keep a little behind the line so that the chaperones and all the sitting guests could readily identify her.

One night, Thérèse remembers, when Zelda was putting on heavy mascara, a third roommate from her hometown asked solicitously, "Zelda, what are you going to do?" In a tone of quiet desperation, she replied, "I honestly don't know. I just honestly don't know." In her voice was a fear that her decision might presage some future tragedy. Of course, Thérèse had no idea who or what they were referring to. It was to her marriage with Scott Fitzgerald. Zelda had had another of several special delivery letters from Scott pressing her to marry him. Scott had been stationed in Montgomery as a lieutenant with his regiment and had fallen in love with her.

Born in St. Paul, educated at Princeton, Scott had as much glamour for a man as Zelda did for a girl, and more beauty. In his family line was Francis Scott Key, who wrote the words of "The Star-Spangled Banner"— and who was his namesake. He had never met anyone like Zelda, with her aristocratic Southern lineage and her hoydenish ways. (She had been named for a gypsy in some romance that her mother had read.) She continually shocked Montgomery, but most people were rather fond of her. Any outlandish thing she did was more or less excused as "Oh, well, that's Zelda." She had started young in her exhibitionism when she secretly telephoned the fire department that a little girl was trapped on a roof and should be rescued. Then she climbed a ladder to the roof and kicked the ladder away.

Her wild antics fascinated the handsome young lieutenant. He saw her as the glittering heroine of a dozen short stories and novels. She was wonderful copy. He was to claim that she was the first "flapper," and that he had virtually invented her. But now she hesitated to say yes to his marriage proposal. She did not want to chance a man who, for all his parlor graces, had no way of supporting her.

Then on March 26, 1920, Scribner published *This Side of Paradise*. The advance notices presaged a hit. In February the movie rights to a *Saturday Evening Post* story of Scott's called "Head and Shoulders" had been sold. His career was launched. Zelda's engagement to Francis Scott Key Fitzgerald was announced in the Montgomery *Advertiser* of March 28. Zelda's mother, Miss Minnie, who had misgivings about the match, warned the Catholic Scott in a letter: "It will take more than the Pope to make Zelda good. You will have to call on God Almighty direct."

Largely for reasons of economy, the marriage took place in the rectory of St. Patrick's Cathedral, New York, on April 3. A priest relation of Scott's performed the ceremony. There was no music, and no flowers. Judge and Mrs. Sayre did not attend the ceremony. The honeymoon at the Biltmore Hotel was so wild that the management asked the couple to leave.

Less than three years after her marriage Zelda told her sister Rosaline that she never had wanted to marry Scott.

By the time that the Fitzgeralds were back in Montgomery visiting Zelda's family, Scott was getting top prices for his stories. I was invited to an informal small party for them at Eleanor Browder's. I had never met him before. Scott was not drinking that week. He looked as fresh as he was handsome. Both he and Zelda had gold hair and gray-green eyes and beautiful smooth complexions. At first glance they looked like brother and sister. But his eyes were larger than Zelda's and more widely spaced. And his mouth was more generous. He was wearing plus fours and jacket of a muted mixed green color. Zelda wore a coat suit made from the same cloth. Leaving the others inside to make merry in their fashion, Scott and I sat on a swing on the porch and talked for two hours. I found his conversation fascinating. And then he shocked me with his aims. His ideal, he said, was to live the life of a hedonist. He argued that pleasure is the sole or chief good in life and that moral duty is fulfilled in the gratification of pleasure-seeking instincts. "We shall get all the joy out of life we can," he said. "And then when I reach thirty-five I shall do away with myself. There is no sense in growing old. What do you think?"

I was appalled. He might have been spoofing, but I took him to be at least somewhat serious. I told him I thought his philosophy was rotten. He did not resent my frankness. He only gave me a strange smile, a bit sad.

At first Scott encouraged Zelda in her exhibitionism and drinking. Then Zelda gave him no peace. The more she disturbed him, the heavier was his own drinking. She was now hellbent to gain fame for herself. Her talents were really opulent, but she never could quite bring them into order. She tried both writing and painting. In her late twenties she strove to become a ballerina, practicing ballet in Paris under an expensive Russian woman teacher with almost lunatic dedication.

Though Scott was providing the cash for her extravagant taste in fur coats and other luxuries, she seemed to resent his successes. A young couple who had known the Fitzgeralds on the Riviera told me in Bermuda in 1931 that Zelda would preside over impromptu wild parties that swirled around Scott as he sat trying to write at a small marble-topped table in the living room.

Ernest Hemingway, who was in Paris in the twenties with the Fitzgeralds, was to write to Arthur Mizener, a biographer of Scott, "I never had any respect for him ever except for his lovely, golden, wasted talent. I think Scott in his strange mixed-up Irish Catholic monogamy wrote for Zelda and when he lost all hope in her and she destroyed his confidence in himself he was through. He never slept with another girl except Zelda until Zelda went officially crazy. She was crazy all the time I knew them, but she was not yet net-able."

Zelda first entered a sanatorium for mentally disturbed persons on April

23, 1930, when she was twenty-nine. She was in and out of hospitals the rest of her life, in France, in Switzerland, in Maryland, and in North Carolina. She was a frightful drain on Scott's pocketbook as well as on his uncertain nervous system. And he had to be both father and mother to their daughter, Scottie, who had been born on October 26, 1921.

When Scott, who gradually became a wreck, went to Hollywood to work on pictures, Sheilah Graham, a beautiful English columnist, took loving care of him. Though sometimes he treated her abominably, she nursed him tenderly, and even moved for his sake to a house in the San Fernando Valley, where he could have peace and quiet, which he had never known with Zelda. He and Sheilah lived openly together. She loved him in spite of his faults and his drinking, and struggled to lessen his alcoholic intake. In early November, 1940, at a drugstore, he blacked out. Thoroughly frightened, he stayed in bed and even stopped drinking Coca-Colas. Writing on a lapboard in bed, he desperately tried to finish *The Last Tycoon* in his absorbing need for another novel and for money for Zelda.

On November 20, he felt able to go to a movie, but at the end he said he felt awful and could hardly walk. The next afternoon he was up sitting by the fireplace, nibbling on a chocolate bar and reading the *Princeton Alumni Weekly*. Suddenly he rose, made a gasping sound, and fell dead. What he had told me he planned to accomplish by his own hand, nature finally accomplished for him. In the meantime, he had renounced his Catholic faith. But there had been no time to send for a priest to give him extreme unction. Scott had wanted to be buried beside his parents in the Catholic cemetery of Rockville, Maryland. But holy ground was forbidden him by the bishop. So he was laid away in the little Protestant cemetery nearby. Among the twenty-five mourners was his lovely nineteen-year-old daughter, Scottie, a student at Vassar.

I ran into Zelda on a Montgomery sidewalk near her home on Sayre Street in one of her more lucid periods. It was in November, 1947. I hardly recognized her. But we were very glad to see each other. She was extremely pale and wore no make-up whatever. Her hair was graying and straggled, but her facial bone structure was still excellent. Her rusty black skirt hung to her ankles. She wore a large floppy hat. In her hand she carried a small Bible. I had heard that she went by streetcar among black people to give them Bible lessons. She asked me to come in and said she would make me a cup of tea. But, unfortunately, I was on my way to another engagement. We stood on the sidewalk and talked of Edmund Wilson, who had been Scott's Princeton friend and admiring critic. Zelda said that though "Bunny" Wilson claimed not to believe in God, he lived more or less by the Sermon on the Mount. He had proved it again and again. She said she had written him to that effect. Then she added, "Religion is my only strength." Zelda was so wistful and appealing that I regretted I could not have tea with her then, and I was leaving Montgomery the next day. I would have liked to reminisce with her. I promised to call her the very next time I was in Montgomery and fully intended to. I found a new sweetness and a humility in her that I had never seen before. But she was so obviously the embodiment of the last act of the tragedy that I walked away saddened.

Shortly she was returned to the mental hospital in North Carolina. On the night of March 10, 1948, a fire broke out in the kitchen and spread rapidly. Nine women, Zelda among them, were trapped on the top floor. Their bodies were so badly charred that the authorities were not really sure which was hers. But some remains, believed to be those of Zelda, were sent to Rockville, Maryland, and were buried beside Scott. Scottie, who was now married, was at the graveside.

Scott and Zelda have become golden legends of the flowering twenties. They were the most glamorous couple of the Jazz Age. Cyril Connolly, the British critic, said of Scott that he was "firmly established as a myth, an American version of the Dying God, an Adonis of letters."

Zelda and Scott had managed to destroy each other. It is my opinion that Zelda, in her childish selfishness, her abnormal egotism, and her compulsive exhibitionism, would have spoiled the life of any man she married. But Scott refused to divorce her after she went insane. He continued to visit her and he paid enormous bills to keep her in the best private institutions. He could have committed her to Bryce's Hospital for the Insane in Tuscaloosa, where the cost was nothing or minimal. He behaved generously to Zelda partly, perhaps, for their daughter's sake. And he may have hoped the numerous psychiatrists would restore her to sanity. He continued to pay for her care on borrowed money until his death and after that out of his estate.

One facet of Scott's nature that I have not touched on was his generosity and helpfulness to young aspiring writers. He would read their amateurish manuscripts and even try to get agents for them. He secured his own publisher, Scribner, for Ernest Hemingway, after singing his praises to Maxwell Perkins. Zelda resented the money Scott lent Hemingway in Paris. She and Ernest had loathed each other from the first. Each saw the other more clearly than Scott saw them. Hemingway was to prove ungrateful for the favors Scott did him. He chose to blot them from his mind. He wanted to think that he had done everything for himself. Scott had an essentially obliging and indulgent nature, unless he had had too much to drink. Then he could be rather horrible.

When Scottie Smith, the Fitzgerald daughter, came to tea at our home in 1970, I asked her which parent she had loved better. She gave me no clear-cut answer. "Well, you see, my mother was almost always sick. And my father was almost always drinking." Scottie, who was then forty-nine, had turned out to be a pretty, charming, well-integrated woman with apparently none of her parents' faults. She had what they lacked: stability.

Europe
in
the
Twenties

THE New York editor, Irving Brock, who had been indirectly responsible for my treasured experiences with the Forbes-Robertsons and Adeline Bourne in 1913–14, now in 1921 more directly used his magic "open sesame" at a special door. I had called on him about the possibility of getting a couple of my one-act plays produced. Colonel Brock took me to the office of a homely, lanky young man, who, at the time, was assistant dramatic critic of the New York *Times*. His name, which was just beginning to be known, was George S. Kaufman. His first comedy, *Dulcy,* starring Lynne Fontanne, was a current hit on Broadway.

Although nothing was to come of my plays then, the meeting was fraught with rich personal dividends. George invited me to his apartment for dinner to meet his stunning wife, Beatrice. Through the Kaufmans I was later to know Edna Ferber and other of George's collaborators. More significant to me, they would be responsible for my meeting the two American critics who in the twenties, thirties, and forties ranked above all others in my esteem: H. L. Mencken and Stark Young. I was to be twice the Kaufmans' houseguest in different apartments as they rose in affluence.

In the meantime I took off for a year abroad—a leave of absence without pay. I chose Sorrento on the Bay of Naples because the name attracted me, and because F. Marion Crawford, the successful novelist, who had ventured far, said it was the most beautiful and harmonious place in the world. There he had built a great stone house high above the sea.

I stayed at the Cocumella Hotel. The boatman who rowed out to meet the ship had a most musical voice as he sang out, "Coc*umel*-la, Coc*umel*-la." The hotel was everything I could desire. It possessed four acres of lovely garden with orange trees and scores of different flowering plants. A decorative iron railing marked the sea boundary more than a hundred feet above the water. Through a cavern the way wound down some two hundred stone steps to the curl of white sand which was our private beach.

The Cocumella had been founded as a monastery in 1557 and became a hotel in 1777. It had its own domed and frescoed church attached at right angles to the western façade. Shelley, Goethe, Murat, and Wellington were among the guests who had enjoyed the inn's hospitality. The Garguilo brothers ran it. The youngest, a tall and distinguished-looking man, was the manager. The elite gave it custom, and it was quite inexpensive in 1922.

I had a small room at the back of the hotel with a superb view of quiescent Vesuvius, which would have its crown of snow in December. My room had floor-to-ceiling French doors opening onto a small iron-railed balcony. The deep blue Bay of Naples lay stretched out before me and the patterned flower beds and orange orchard lay beneath. I was situated in eternal beauty.

Sorrento has been both a summer and a winter resort since Roman times. The district produces oranges, lemons, and nuts. The renaissance poet Tasso was born here in 1544. His statue graces the town square. But Sorrento has stayed a small commune with a population of about twelve thousand. Although it is the seat of a bishopric, there is little memorable about its cathedral. Shops that sell fine linens to tourists abound, but even the trading has a relaxed rhythm.

I was aware that first day that I had found the ideal spot for my psychic needs. I had left all sense of responsibility behind me, and I was feeling the hungry futurity of youth.

With me had come a talented young man from Meridian, Mississippi, named Russell Wright. He was to study musical composition in Naples. Several retired British army officers were guests for the winter season with their wives and daughters. The noted Swedish sculptor Lundberg was here with his writer wife and his son Bengt, a madcap cutup of twenty-one. Many Scandinavians came to avoid their dark winters. Alfred Bishop Mason, a retired mining engineer, accompanied by his wife, the composer, were guests. Count Dante Serego-Alighieri, a charming, shy young man and Dante's direct descendant, was recovering from an operation. He had a six-hundred-year-old name and the nose of his great ancestor. I was glad to let him practice his English on me when we bathed in the sea or had tea together.

Then Miss Margaret Booth, mistress of a fashionable school in Montgomery, Alabama, whom I knew well, turned up with sixteen young society girls. When she became ill, I was summoned. She gave me money and asked me to take her charges onto the Capri steamer, show them the sights, buy their lunch, and take them into the Blue Grotto. Because of the low-hanging rock at the entrance of the eerie Grotto, I had to lie down with one of the girls in a small boat. This girl, then in her late teens, was Sara Mayfield, the daughter of an Alabama Supreme Court judge. In her sixties she was to write an excellent life of Henry Mencken, whom she knew in Baltimore, and also to write intimately of Scott and Zelda Fitzgerald in a fascinating book called *Exiles from Paradise*.

In October, desiring a break from writing, I took Russell to Germany where he and I could hear grand opera. (La Scala in Milan did not open until Christmas.) In 1919 I had already visited France, Switzerland, and England. In England I had reveled in Shakespeare country and stayed as a houseguest in a seven-gabled Elizabethan manor adjoining the forest of

Arden, where Shakespeare's mother had been born. But I had never seen Germany and among other objectives I wanted to see the Passion Play at Oberammergau. So we headed straight there.

The village in the spectacularly beautiful Bavarian Alps, lying some forty miles from Munich, was a storybook place, with scenic paintings on the outside of the rococo onion-towered church and on some façades of shops and dwellings. Athletic young men with shoulder-length blond hair, which they had grown for the performance, acted as porters at the train station and carried our bags to an inn where we had reservations for two days and nights. The wood-carving industry of Oberammergau is famous and many of the long-haired youths walking the streets were engaged in the family tradition. The village population amounted to only about four thousand, and in the season of the Passion Play the daily tourists surpassed that number.

The audience is seated in a roofed auditorium which provides for 5,200 spectators. The origin of the Passion Play goes back to 1633 when the village was stricken by the plague. For its deliverance a vow was given to enact on the stage the Passion of Christ every ten years. In the aftermath of World War I and Germany's defeat, the 1920 performance was postponed until 1922, when Russell and I saw the tragedy. The playing time takes almost eight hours. The whole performance was more moving than I could have believed.

Munich is famous for its grand opera, where perfection is the goal. The handsomely laid out city with spacious parks and green belts was fortunate to have three art-loving nineteenth century kings in succession who strove to create a "modern Athens" as a cultural and artistic center for Bavaria and for Germany. In 1922 Russell and I saw a performance of *Siegfried* that was as near perfection as possible. Then we went to Dresden for a full week of opera.

Dresden was overcrowded with tourists in 1922. We were lucky to be housed comfortably in a private home. We got three choice opera tickets, including one for our landlady's daughter. It was a treat for her and she was our guide, though she spoke little English. Two productions were particularly outstanding. One was a magnificent *Otello;* only one man in Germany was capable of singing the title role, a guest star from Berlin. The golden-haired Desdemona was young, an excellent actress, and the most beautiful woman we had seen in Germany. We heard a stunning dramatic actress, lithe and lean, with a rich mezzo-soprano, named Irma Travani, sing an exciting Carmen. Everything was extremely cheap, even grand opera. The exchange for German money was so advantageous that we could get a good meal for twenty-five cents.

I found both Munich and Dresden cities of singular beauty; particularly Dresden, which in its downtown area was all baroque white. The savagery of the punitive allied attack just before the end of World War II, when the

99

central area was devastated and more than 150,000 persons were killed by phosphorus and high explosive bombs, seemed to me one of the most horrible and unwarranted incidents in the entire conflict.

When we got back to Italy from Germany we visited the Serego-Alighieris at Gargagnago, near Verona, on an estate bought by Dante's son Piero in 1353. It has been in the family ever since. Not only were there leased farms, but on the property were the San Ambrogio red marble quarries, also leased. It was much like staying in a country estate in England. There is something of an international common denominator among European landed aristocrats. I was later to find this true among the Danish and Swedish nobility.

In the pleasure of passing one friend on to another in a different country, I was reminded of the American South, too. When I mentioned that I was going to Algeria in the early spring, the Countess Papafavo of Bologna, a sister of the Countess Serego-Alighieri, who happened also to be visiting her, gave me a letter to the Countess de Brazza, a great-granddaughter of Lafayette, living in Algiers. Her late husband, the African explorer and empire builder, had opened up the Congo for France.

Dante's mother encouraged the friendship between Dante and me. She said I gave him more confidence in himself. He may have been troubled about his responsibility in bearing his great ancestor's name and, when his father died, on becoming head of a large family with many estates. Dante remained my friend through the years and we kept in touch through occasional letters. In 1971, on our way from Milan to Venice to embark on a Black Sea cruise, Dante met us in Verona and took us to lunch. We had not seen each other in forty-nine years, but there was instant recognition and affection.

Russell and I came to Rome in late October, 1922, with its Colosseum and the Arch of Constantine and all the effulgent glories of antiquity. A natural phenomenon, which I had not believed possible, appeared as an extra dividend: an apple-green sunset over St. Peter's. We saw it from the height of the Pincio Gardens. The whole sky was a green of an ethereal radiance. For more than half an hour the phenomenon lasted. It was extraordinary in that we had seen in Dresden a green sunset done by theatrical lighting in the performance of *Otello* some days previous, and we had declared there could be no such thing in nature. But in August, 1935, I was to see at Montevideo another apple-green sunset.

In Rome we each have our favorite spots. Mine is the Scala di Spagna, that noble staircase so named for no better reason than that the Spanish Embassy was on it. The young John Keats, my favorite lyric poet, died in the building to the right side of the stairs, and Axel Munthe, the Swedish physician and author, lived there a century later. Lord Byron resided elegantly on the piazza, facing Bernini's fountain made in the shape of a boat.

At the wide base of the staircase are the canopied stalls of the flower sellers. I bought a dozen pink roses to put on the marble mantel in the small narrow room where Keats died and where two windows look down on the Spanish Steps.

On the morning of October 28, 1922, we were in the capital when Mussolini made his historic "march on Rome." But we missed the event by an hour, for our train to Naples had departed. The new Fascism was to have its brief period in the Italian chronicles. When we returned to the Cocumella, some of our young Italian friends were in a state of high elation, repeatedly toasting Il Duce, the leader.

A fascist convention at Naples on October 29 provided a pretext for the concentration of armed squads. But on October 28 virtually no opposition was to be met from either the civilian or military authorities in Rome. Mussolini was saying for all Italy to hear, "So far, Communism, and no farther."

Russians of the upper classes were still fleeing the Bolsheviks. An exquisitely lovely Russian girl named Katia, with her mother and nineteen-year-old brother, had gradually made her way to the Cocumella. Here her little family stayed for three weeks while awaiting a ship bound for Brazil and a new life. The mother—her husband had been killed by the Bolsheviks—stayed in her room most of the time. She could not reconcile herself to the loss of her estates or quite understand what had happened to her. But Katia put a brave face on everything. Of necessity, the family had to travel second class to Brazil. A dozen of us saw the little group off on the steamer that ran from Sorrento to Naples, where they would board an ocean liner. Katia waved gaily until the boat receded in the distance. Going second class was to her something like Marie Antoinette's playing at being a dairymaid.

In late November I had received a letter from George Kaufman.

It was pleasant to hear from you, although we are somewhat surprised to have you turn up in Italy. However, even over there, you won't be forgotten. On this side of the water things go along about the same, the heartaches alternating with the spasms, if I may grow poetic. Beatrice joins me in sending regards, and let us hear from you in less sketchy fashion.

It was brief and to the point. One significant line pleased me: "Even over there, you won't be forgotten." But what did he mean by "the heartaches alternating with the spasms"?

For two weeks at Christmas an elaborate crèche was set up in the church attached to the hotel. Large figurines made of plaster and wood in the eighteenth century were used. Joseph and Mary and the Christ child, with the ox and the ass and the wise men, were all in place. People were rushing down hillsides to get a view of the baby or winding along twisting paths among palm trees. The scene was illuminated at night and the church doors stayed open. I paid a tribute of looking in on the crèche each day, for it was much like a work of art. The figures would be carefully packed and ticketed and stored until the next celebration.

The Count and Countess Serego-Alighieri came to the Cocumella with their five children to spend the Christmas fortnight and give the servants a holiday. There was a gala Christmas party. I had written a song called "An Orange Garden in Sorrento," which Mrs. Mason had set to music. It was first sung on Christmas night by Ruth Thompson, an American soprano, who had to sing it twice over.

Dante's mother, tall and elegant, was lady-in-waiting to the queen whenever she came to Venice, where the family had an inherited *palazzo* on the Grand Canal and in which my young friend Dante was born. A remark by Mrs. Mason, a beautiful old lady herself, stuck in my mind. "How is it that the Countess Serego-Alighieri in a simple black velvet gown and a string of pearls can make every other woman in this room look cheap?"

But the Countess complained that all of her children but one were "camels," with no style at all. Kiki, the eight-year-old, was the exception. He wore black velvet suits with elaborately embroidered collars. His hair fell in black ringlets with a natural curl. His black eyes were large and sparkling. He had a graceful, assured walk. He was the handsomest of the children and made an impression on entering a room. The second daughter, Moochi, aged fifteen, was a passionate admirer of Mussolini. Her ideal woman was the heroine of the opera *The Girl of the Golden West,* who packed a revolver. In time, she became a leader of *Fascistas,* marching at the head of her women's "army."

Life at the Cocumella was like an international kaleidoscopic house party, the figures always changing. Some came for two days and some for an entire season.

Marion Olcott Dix, the widow of a New England writer, had settled permanently in the hotel. She had been my friend from the first week. Eventually she would read my stories in progress. I was a slow writer, and I worked only in the mornings. The central heating was not turned on in the hotel until eleven o'clock, but my best hours for work were the morning hours, and so, because Mrs. Dix had persuasive influence with Mr. Garguilo, an oilstove was put in my room at no expense to me. In the afternoons, I would often have tea with her, and after Russell Wright left I generally dined with her.

One afternoon Mrs. Dix asked me to accompany her to call on the Princess Sumonti, who lived in a villa several miles away. I was immediately struck by the pink camellias that grew up to the second story. We found the princess in winter tweeds. She was an attractive woman of much practical sense and good humor. She was the very last baby to be born in the Borghese Palace in Rome. After tea in the drawing room, the princess showed us her Italian garden. She maintained this winter villa in the south, she said, where she could avoid "society" on a "take-it-or-leave-it" basis. If there was something really important she would make an effort to go. She seemed very fond of Mrs. Dix and was loath to say good-by. When we finally did leave, she had her gardeners heap quantities of pink camellias into our carriage until we were knee-deep in blossoms. Protesting did little good. All the hotel's dinner tables were festive for several nights with camellias.

The young Marquis Benzoni, called Giorgio, came down from Rome for a brief holiday in a little car of his own. Automobiles were still scarce in those days. The Benzonis were friends of the Serego-Alighieris. Giorgio took me on an all-day excursion to see the temples of Paestum on the Gulf of Salerno. The road lay along the curves of the famous Amalfi Drive, almost always in sight of the blue sea. Then down to Salerno and twenty-two miles below that.

The Greek city of Paestum had been founded by colonists from Sybaris about 600 B.C. Under Augustus and Tiberius the area was highly cultivated and celebrated for "the twice-blooming roses of Paestum," which are mentioned by several Latin poets. But deposits of silt at the mouth of the Sele River had long since made the neighborhood unhealthy. Malaria and typhoid were rampant. Giorgio had ordered box lunches packed for us with a Thermos of drinking water and a bottle of wine. Only the foolhardy would take chances in such a fever-ridden region. This day we were the only sightseers.

I was unprepared for such splendor and beauty in a flat area. I had seen nothing so impressive in all Italy. It seemed odd that the Greeks would erect three superb temples in a field instead of on an eminence. Yet here they were, strung out at intervals about two short city blocks distant from each other. Once a thriving seaport, the ocean had now receded from Paestum about a quarter of a mile. The three Doric temples are in a remarkable state of preservation. Each massive column is standing. The southernmost temple honors the god Poseidon. There are six great columns at each end and fourteen at the sides with two inner rows of seven columns, each supporting a second smaller column. It is the best preserved of the three and dates from about 460 B.C. A different quality of marble was utilized here; it is pale yellow in color, something like a dusty chantarelle mushroom.

Giorgio told me that all the exterior columns and the architraves were standing after some 2,400 years. They are without parallel in Doric architecture. The circuit of town walls, well built by squared blocks of travertine limestone, was fifteen feet thick, he said. He pointed out the remains of a Greek agora. "All three of these temples," he said, "are older than the Parthenon set on the Acropolis in Athens."

We spread out lunch amid the ruins on the porch of one of the temples. We leaned back against a column and looked out to the deep blue sea. The town of Paestum had been extremely vulnerable to passing ships, and was consequently sacked many times. Then fevers came and made people desert the spot.

I would not have seen the temples if Giorgio had not had his little car. And, though he knew their history well himself, he had never seen the temples before. This Paestum excursion was perhaps the high point in my Sorrento sojourn, and I am eternally grateful to the young marquis for taking me.

In 1969, almost five decades later, I took Thérèse to see the temples. She was as deeply impressed as I had been in 1922. But now the malarial swamps had been drained. New streets had been laid out in the village. A museum to house the priceless artifacts had been erected. An inn to accommodate overnight guests had been built. Here an excellent lunch was served. The "twice-blooming roses of Paestum" flourished again profusely, planted in orderly beds, and in the open fields wild flowers covered the ground.

In January, 1923, a surprise letter awaited me at the Cocumella from Beatrice Kaufman. She was coming to Italy very soon and bringing with her a Vassar graduate, "as lovely as the new crescent moon," she wrote. They would come on a ship direct to Naples and stay at my hotel for a week. The girl's name was Margaret Leech. She was hoping to be a writer. In time she would win two Pulitzer Prizes for nonfiction.

The Shelton Martins, who were later to play an extraordinary role in my life when I had desperate need of them, came to the Cocumella in mid-January. They were a highly cultivated couple from Peapack, New Jersey, a fox-hunting region. They lived at Valley Brook Farm, kept four hunters, and rode to hounds. Shelton had won numerous silver cups for his skill in jumping. One day they took me for a return visit to Pompeii, which had suffered a violent eruption in 79 A.D. and buried citizens in the ashes. We had not chosen the day wisely, for it began to rain as we stepped from the carriage. But I got the impact of a civilization of luxurious living and voluptuous vices almost 1900 years in the past. The rain became steady until it was a downpour. I had not thought to bring a raincoat. Charlotte's umbrella gave her some protection.

Two days later I came down with influenza. Though I had fever I felt no real need of a doctor. But Mrs. Dix asked me if I would let a woman physician who called on her about twice a year look in on me. She was downstairs now. Mrs. Dix prepared me for the woman's masculinity. She said that she carried her own cigar case and she would always light up with the men. The woman came up and was tenderly solicitous. She was huge and an American of good family. She made out a prescription. I never saw her again. That spell of influenza was my only illness in the year abroad.

Later I learned more about the doctor. She was the reputed lover of a Russian princess who lived on the estate next door. The villa was set close to the sea, so I never saw the house itself; it was hidden from the gateway by masses of flowering vines. I was told that the princess had been in Sorrento at the time of the revolution and that her husband had been executed. I did see the princess's daughter and the young woman she was living with, for they had a strange sort of little Russian buggy in which they rode about. The villa came to take on a sinister mystery. For the first time in my remembrance I had run into the phenomenon of lesbianism, but I do not believe that even then I had ever seen the word in print.

An old friend of the Masons came to the Cocumella: a Mrs. Florence Bissell, pronounced Bizéll. She lived mostly in Europe and spoke perfect French, but her daughter was married to Robert Bigelow, a prominent Wall Street broker, who had a large house on Martha's Vineyard. Mrs. Bissell wore a high-style golden-brown wig, which slipped a half inch one evening and revealed her white hair. Her conversation interested me. She would say, "I was sitting on the davenport with Oscar Wilde when Henry James came up with one of his long involved sentences." Her son-in-law in Vineyard Haven, whom I visited in 1931, said, "She's a nice old lady, but her head is too full of dukes and duchesses." She did in fact know many of the European nobility. She would always preface the mention of the Duc de Richelieu as the *premier duc,* emphasizing the *premier.* She was a kind of walking *Almanach de Gotha,* but she had known also writers of achievement and men in high positions of state. I think that she was enjoying her widowhood greatly. I recall her remark, "A widow with a checkbook can do much." I was to see her again in Paris in May and afterward in London, where she took me to a ball given by the Marchioness of Carisbrooke.

Mrs. Bissell, like the Shelton Martins, was to remain a friend after my marriage. I began to wonder if Mrs. Dix had been right when she told me that I had a gift for friendship. In 1922 I knew nothing of astrology, but now I know that the Sun, Uranus, and Saturn were in the eleventh house of friends at the hour of my birth, and I have come to attribute some especially benign influence to their position in that part of the heavens.

Beatrice Kaufman and Margaret Leech arrived in late January. They were enchanted with wandering about the little winding streets of Sorrento and with the shopping. Beatrice and Peggy were excellent foils for each other, the one with her rich, black-eyed Eastern appearance (John Weaver called her the Queen of Sheba) and the other a pale golden beauty. But the fragile one could be very stern if an overloaded burro was beaten on the Sorrento roads. Though she did not speak Italian, she could make her meaning most effective. I did not go to Capri with them or on the Amalfi Drive. But I was there when they returned in the evenings for dinner. It was Beatrice who held my affectionate interest. After a week Beatrice and Peggy went north to look at cathedrals and museums. I was about to go south: to Sicily and North Africa.

Enriching was hardly a strong enough word for my nine months experience in Sorrento, with that week of opera in Dresden, the Passion Play in Oberammergau, the temples of Paestum, and that visit with the Serego-Alighieris in Gargagnago.

I had known for months that I was going to the Sahara Desert's edge in Biskra, and looked forward to the venture. Yet I could hardly bear to take myself away from the Cocumella. But the time had come to make my farewells. When I came to settle my bill, Mr. Garguilo began scratching off item after item so that I had to pay very little for extras. My bill for board and room was only two dollars a day. Everyone had been exceedingly kind to me. The servants knew my means were extremely limited and never expected large tips. Yet they had been most attentive. I came to love Italians above all other peoples for their kindness.

I said good-by to Mrs. Dix in her hotel room. All along the way down the winding steps of the cavern friends were sitting on ledges to say *a rivederci* to me, including the hotel's head waiter. My wardrobe trunk, a gift from my university students, was to be sent by American Express to Paris, to be held for me there while I traveled in Africa. It was already in the rowboat. My heart was full. My last *abbraccio* was for Fortunato, a young Sorrentino destined to rise in Mussolini's *Fascisti*. I have never had such a going away in my life. When the little steamer arrived and I boarded it, I waved once and then I went within quickly.

Taormina rises on Sicily's east coast almost perpendicularly from the sea. With Mount Etna to the south, its setting is spectacular. Only Rio de Janeiro rivals it. The volcano was currently in mild eruption and spouting flames. The little town itself is a flower garden at all seasons.

I was surprised to find a letter from Margaret Leech forwarded to me from the Cocumella.

Palace Hotel, Perugia
February 20, 1923

Perhaps it's the breath of the sirocco from the pages of *South Wind*—or maybe all the miracles I've been hearing about—or even a sensational spring this first bright day. But anyway I'm seized by a sudden unescapable longing to fracture every appointment, smash my fist through every plan—in a word, go South.

At noon, I was incredulous, at tea-time diffident. Tonight I believe that Taormina will see me some two weeks from now.

I want to rest in the sun at Taormina and decide critically if it's the most beautiful place in the world. And visit the bazaars of Tunis.

If this does reach you, answer it, Am Exp Co. Florence. I'll be there for, anyway, I expect two weeks.

Hudson, do send along some good tidings. I can't bear more than two weeks of puss-faced Madonnas.

Yours for the pagan South,
Peggy Leech

I had no time to answer, and I did not know if she would come. I thought she might be a nuisance.

Sauntering out onto the streets I ran into Sir Johnston Forbes-Robertson. There was no mistaking that handsome profile. Much surprised, I introduced myself to him, recalled my "walking-on" job in New York, told him how much he had helped me with my master's thesis on "The Stage History of Hamlet." I said that I was now teaching Shakespeare at the University of Alabama. He was on his way to the Greek theater and he would be glad to have me accompany him, if I had nothing special to do. His daughter Maxine, called "Blossom," was buying a pair of snub-nosed scissors in a shop "back there." She was hoping to cut asphodels among the ruins. I said I did not think that asphodels were real, but flowers of some mythological paradise. "Well, here she comes, and we shall see," Sir Johnston said.

Accompanied by a handsome young cavalier, a count from Palermo, she joined us. She was the most beautiful of the four sisters and the eldest. But none of the girls was as beautiful as their mother, Gertrude Elliott. If Blossom turned one way her eyes were deep blue, and if she turned the other way her eyes were brown.

There *were* asphodels, both white and yellow, of the lily family, with narrow leaves and particularly delicate blossoms. "Do they grow only on sacred soil?" I wanted to know. "Well, they seem to be in some profusion here," Sir Johnston said. "You know this famous Greek theater was rebuilt in Roman times, and so is really a Roman theater. It stands on a spur of Mount Lauro, which affords a splendid view of Etna from base to summit on one side."

We looked back. It was breath-takingly beautiful. The crown was like molten diamonds. Almond orchards climbed the mountain as far as they dared. They were now in full pinkish bloom and the volcano was flaming. "What a superb backdrop!" I exclaimed.

We sat down in an advantageous spot facing Etna. I asked Sir Johnston how he was enjoying his retirement. I had not seen him since 1915 in his Syracuse dressing room eight years before. He had passed his sixty-ninth birthday in January, but he was looking extremely fit. "I have returned to my first love: painting," he said.

It was peaceful and exciting to be sitting here in the ancient theater with the foremost actor of my time, while his lovely daughter cut asphodels below us. No one stood higher in my esteem than this Englishman. Richard

Le Gallienne had written that the most moving aesthetic experience of his life was seeing Forbes-Robertson as Hamlet die on the throne. Having witnessed his death night after night I could agree with him. I did not think there was any other actor, living or dead, who had such sensitivity.

When Blossom and her cavalier came up to us, she held out a bouquet of asphodels for us to admire. "See," she exclaimed, "they *are* real!" The swain was carrying the snub-nosed scissors. We got up and began to descend. The young lady was so elated with her flowers that she rushed down the tiers of seats followed by her count. Sir Johnston and I took it more slowly. We stopped for another long look at Etna, with its fire and dazzling snow and almond blossoms.

He told me that he was leaving the next day for Palermo. As we were saying good-by on the street I felt that it was the last time I would see my one-time idol. Then Peggy Leech suddenly appeared. I was really surprised to see her, and I was glad to be able to introduce a great man to her.

Peggy and I stayed in different hotels. Hers was more expensive than mine, but mine was comfortable and had a lovelier garden. After three more days of beholding Mount Etna at various times of day and night on walking trips, we took the train to Syracuse, a port on the Ionian Sea. Founded by Greeks from Corinth in 735 B.C., according to Thucydides, it became the leading city of ancient Sicily.

The modern districts of Syracuse project in long straight lines among orchards and flower gardens and stone quarries. The ruins of the vast theater are most impressive. It is by far the largest in Italy. In its heyday it could accommodate almost all of the city's forty thousand population. We noted the ruins of scores of different civilizations, and then drove to a place where rowboats with rowers were for hire on the narrow tributary, the Cyane. It is famous for its papyrus.

A channel had been made between the thick rows of papyrus, a variety of tall water plant of the sedge family, which grows three to twelve feet high. The writing material of the ancient Egyptians, Greeks, and Romans was made from this plant, which branches out at the top into a wide feathery crown. At certain places we could reach out and touch the stems, as the papyrus stirred gracefully with the little breezes. That anything so fragile-looking could have so many utilitarian uses! The ancient Egyptians, who got their supply along the Nile, used the roots as fuel, the pith as food, and the stems for cloth, twine, and sheets of writing material. Papyrus was also adaptable in the fabrication of boats. (In 1970, a sailboat constructed of papyrus triumphantly crossed the Atlantic.)

I had hardly realized that papyrus still existed. It was, to me, somewhat in the category of asphodels. And here we were gliding between walls of the pale green plants that rose canyonlike above our heads. What ingenuity first discovered the trick of fashioning writing material from these reeds?

"Think of all these unwritten books," I said to Peggy. "It's like a silent voyage through a wavering library. 'Heard melodies are sweet, but those unheard are sweeter.' " I trailed my hand through the lacquer-dark water. We hardly spoke for the two hours. Our boatman only smiled from time to time.

When Peggy left for Girgenti, I took a small ship to Malta. We were to meet again in Tunis.

I proved my immunity to seasickness on a tempest-tossed voyage to Malta. Even the grizzled captain of the ship was forced to his bunk. I ate a hearty meal. I have never felt the slightest queasiness on any sea and I have been a passenger in some really severe storms.

When our ship docked at the deep-sea harbor of Valletta, the capital of Malta, after choosing my hotel I called on the gray-haired American consul. He received me most cordially, invited me to dinner that evening with his wife and to go to the Italian opera for a performance of *La Traviata*. Then he assigned an amiable and knowledgeable young Maltese on his staff to show me about that day. The dark-eyed, swarthy fellow drove me to the spot where Saint Paul was shipwrecked in 60 A.D. The bay bears his name today. "The island of Malta," he said, "in early times belonged successively to the Phoenicians, the Greeks, the Carthaginians, the Romans, and the Saracens. We are an odd mixture of races here. Perhaps our chief claim to fame is the fact that the Knights of Saint John of Jerusalem and their hospitals were located here from 1530 to 1798."

"They really date from the Crusades," he went on to explain, "when there were no hospitals to care for the wounded. When the Turks drove them out of their stronghold on the Island of Rhodes, Charles V of Spain offered them sanctuary in Malta. The Knights paid one falcon as annual tribute in acknowledgment of allegiance to Spain. The men were a military-religious order of uncommon dedication. The rule of the order was entirely beneficial, yet admission became more restricted as a test of nobility of birth. From estates all over Europe the Knights drew their resources, but most of the wealth came from Spain and France. The symbol of the order of Saint John was a white cross on a black robe. So, in time, they came to be called Knights of the White Cross. They were valiant fighters as well as compassionate nurses."

"What became of the Knights?" I asked.

"The order received its death blow when Napoleon on his Egyptian campaign took Malta in 1798. He stayed six days on the island and compelled the Knights to leave—to go back to their own estates. Soon afterward the British took over."

One day the consul and his wife took me on a picnic among some picturesque ruins near the catacombs. They were both concerned about my sailing as a deck passenger on a Russian cattleboat for Sousse in Tunisia. I had ascertained that the ship was going to Africa to *get* the cattle. I protested that it was only for one night aboard. Sousse was directly west of Malta and surely nothing could happen to me in one night.

Because Mrs. Dix had been enchanted with ancient Kairouan in Tunisia I had decided that I must see it. It was once one of the holy cities of Islam, ranking after Mecca and Medina, which were prohibited to men of other faiths. But when the French got control of Tunisia in 1881 they demanded that the mosque be open to all men, for here rebellions might be incubated. Tunisia was to remain a protectorate of France until 1955.

Despite the consul's warning, in a misguided spirit of adventure and a sudden compelling sense of economy, I bought a ticket as a deck passenger on the cattleboat. I had not expected the veritable swarm of Arabs who embarked with me. A delegation of Dutch businessmen were traveling first class. I was the sole American aboard.

I tried to make friends with the Arabs. I even squatted down and joined one of their card games. It was a game new to me, but I had beginner's luck. The stakes were small enough. But after about a quarter-hour I noted that the best dressed among the Arabs was getting restive and would prefer me out of the game. So I played my cards foolishly until I had lost all that I had gained. Then I smiled, bowed politely, moved away, and sat on my luggage on the deck.

I had a sudden foreboding that I might be robbed in the night. I had taken the precaution of wearing about my neck under my shirt a necklace of hundreds of seed pearls, with a pendent cross of seed pearls. I had bought it at a highly recommended antique shop in Syracuse. It had belonged to a Spanish baroness and was two hundred years old. It was really a lovely thing. I was taking it back to Alabama to the girl I hoped would marry me.

When dusk fell I began to feel lonely and did not set a high value on my status as a deck passenger. I got out my boxed lunch and prepared to eat it, but without appetite. Then I was conscious of a man standing before me with a quizzical expression on his face. He was the first class steward, a White Russian from Kief. He had blue eyes and blond hair, and he spoke English. He did not look unlike an Englishman of the upper class. He made polite inquiries. "This won't do," he murmured. He was obviously ruminating as he walked away. After some minutes he returned. He picked up my suitcases and told me to follow. I docilely obeyed. We went down some stairs. "This is my cabin. You are to sleep here."

"But you?"

"I shall occupy an unbooked first class cabin."

He left me alone again. I realized that he thought it unsafe for me to sleep on the deck.

After a few minutes the man tapped gently on the door and re-entered, bringing me fruit and four hard-boiled eggs with salt and pepper. I learned that his name was Constantine. We spoke of the Bolshevik revolution. He said that after his escape from Russia this job was the best he could get and that he really liked the sea. "Better days will come," he said cheerfully. Then he left me to go and turn down first class beds. I did not see him again until morning when he brought coffee and toast and jam. Our little conspiracy had not been discovered. When the proper time came he took my luggage up to the deck. He did not want to accept money from me, but I pressed some on him. I shall never forget my gratitude to this Constantine. He may have saved me from a traumatic experience.

Kairouan lies thirty-eight miles inland by rail from the port of Sousse in a semidesert alluvial plane. On reaching the French-operated hotel a little before midnight nightingales were singing in the feathery pepper trees that almost touched my second-story windows. It was full moonlight. I had never heard the plaintive song of nightingales before and I was lost in enchantment. When I turned around three Arabs in white burnooses were standing in my room. They were respectfully waiting until I came out of my reverie. I had not locked my door. Puzzled, and a bit uneasy, I asked what they wanted. Each wanted to be my guide the next day. I chose the sturdy one with the mustache who spoke some English.

I had a sudden inspiration. "Will you take me out now?" I asked.

"Now? It's midnight!"

"I'd like to walk about this town by moonlight."

He hesitated and then agreed. Kairouan was all gleaming white, enhanced by the brilliance of the moon. We saw mostly walls and doorways, for the Arabs have their life behind walls. We walked to the *medina* forming the old town, which occupies the northeastern part of the city and is surrounded by a high crenelated wall. In the northeast of this section is the great mosque, gleaming like white enamel in the moonlight. Naturally, we did not attempt to enter. It was mysterious and something like a dream walking with this husky Arab in the dead of night in a city that seemed empty. We passed only three persons lurking in doorways. One white-clothed loiterer came forth to accost us, to question what we were up to. My guide assured him that all was well.

When I returned, outside my window the nightingales were still singing as if their hearts would burst. I felt that I was committing sacrilege in closing the shutters, but I desired sleep.

The next morning my guide was waiting in the lobby at nine. We saw the interior of the mosque by daylight and the prayer chamber, the roof of which is supported by some two hundred columns. The floor was covered with handsome oriental rugs. Rugmaking is the handicraft of the area.

My guide told me that educated Muslims make pilgrimages to Kairouan when they cannot get to Mecca in Saudi Arabia. And they pray at the tomb of Sidi Sahab, a companion of Mohammed who died after the leader did. He is buried with three hairs plucked from the prophet's beard in a leather pouch on his breast.

I left by train for Tunis the next afternoon, taking with me a profound impression of a once holy Muslim city. But I could rejoice that France had left an imprint of its civilization in the hotel refinements. This time I bought a first class train ticket. The locomotive, however, broke down on desert sands. We had expected to arrive in Tunis in time for dinner. But here we were stuck for hours with no food. And I was hungry.

At a distance I recognized voices speaking English. I hesitated and then began strolling toward them. "Do I hear American voices?" I called. "English voices," a woman replied promptly but not unkindly. Six persons were sitting on the sands about a spread-out picnic. They were all about the same age, three men and three women. "Are you, too, on this train bound for Tunis? I did not see you on it." They said that they were and asked me if I would like to share their supper. I accepted with pleasure. I was somewhat chagrined when the train was ready to go and I saw them all enter a third class carriage. The English seemed to know how to travel inexpensively. But they would never have been deck passengers on a Russian cattleboat.

I called Peggy Leech at her hotel to announce my arrival. She had been concerned about me and had tried vainly to locate me through the American consul. She feared I might have contracted a fatal fever on one of our rambles to a village north of Taormina, when she had strongly suspected the town well of being contaminated and had asked me not to drink. We had noticed posted on every door a black-bordered card commemorating the death of one relative or many. Not a single house was without the death card. But I was so thirsty I took a chance. Now here I was in Tunis, feeling fine and still under the spell of Kairouan and the nightingales.

Tunis, like ancient Carthage, which is really a suburb of the modern city, stands on the threshold of a western bay of the Mediterranean. Peggy and I took a victoria and drove to pay our respects to one of the most famous ruins of antiquity. The site of the city was admirable in every respect, with safe deep-water anchorage and easily defensible low hills and a promontory. It knew centuries of prosperity, but declined after Hannibal's defeat in Italy, and was totally destroyed by the Romans in 146 B.C. Virtually nothing remains but a few Punic cemeteries, shrines, and some ruins of fortifications. There are Roman remains, too, including baths and amphitheaters. But the place is depressing and it is not hard to believe the legend that the Romans plowed salt into the soil so that nothing could ever grow. A wind was howling about us to make the place more desolate. Peggy had such an aversion to strong winds that it amounted to a phobia. She became infuriated with me because I did not want to leave Carthage at once. I was asking our driver if he knew the exact place where Saint Augustine had preached.

I tried to pacify her by a drive through a beautiful Tunisian park in its first spring rapture. But she was not interested and took from her handbag something on a newspaper sheet she called a crossword puzzle. I had never heard of such a thing. It was a new invention. She began by asking me to give her a seven-letter word beginning with Z. Wanting to enjoy the exotic flowers and trees, I was annoyed and took an intense antipathy to crossword puzzles. It proved a bit embarrassing when Dick Simon, a friend of the Kaufmans, took me to lunch in New York and proudly displayed a copy of the very first book his new firm, Simon & Schuster, was publishing—crossword puzzles. "And see," he said, "it comes with a pencil that slips in here." I have yet to undertake my first crossword puzzle.

Peggy had already been visiting the *souks,* the little Arab bazaars that are so endlessly fascinating. They open onto narrow tortuous streets covered by arches or roofs of planks, where only pedestrians go. She had made many friends among the dusky-hued proprietors. Her blond beauty was a novelty among the mass of dark complexions.

We bought souvenirs in the different *souks.* But the proprietors did not seem to care whether we made purchases or not. They welcomed us with small cups of sweet strong coffee almost everywhere we stopped to look at this or that.

Peggy had also made friends with a Swiss lady, whose husband was an importer. While her spouse was absent evenings amusing himself seeing live "adult" shows in harlotries, she was at loose ends. A hotel waiter, whom she had known on previous trips, said that he could get us in at an Arab wedding in the better part of town. In a spirit of adventure we accompanied him. He was a friend of the gatekeeper, but the gates were barred to women. A generous bribe could not persuade him.

Now here we were on an Arab street with apparently nothing to do. But the ladies were to get more of an adventure than they had bargained for. The hotel waiter and the Swiss woman discussed the matter. We took a carriage and arrived at the threshold of a house that was not a home. The waiter explained that desert girls of the Ouled Näil tribe came to the city to earn a dowry, and that when they had a sufficiency they loyally returned to marry the nomad they loved. Surprised as she was by the sight of the foreign women, the madam had the presence of mind to serve us tea. She was a motherly type who had not gone back to the desert, because her fiancé had been killed. The first girl came in with demure modesty. She wore a French evening gown of lavender silk with many ruffles. But because there was a chill in the April night she had on her long-sleeved fleecy underwear which came up to her neck and covered her arms. She found no incongruity in this style. She was pretty, with enormous doelike eyes, but she was so shy she kept her head tucked. She answered our questions sweetly in monosyllables, not looking up. A second girl was bolder. She had greenish eyes and wiry reddish hair. Her arms and shoulders were bare. She looked more experienced and ready for any wickedness.

We were ushered into a bedroom where the large bed was the most conspicuous piece of furniture. There the second girl and the waiter entertained us with an elaborate dance in which four handkerchiefs were fluttered and licentious glances exchanged.

While they were dancing, suddenly I recalled Judge Andrews in Syracuse and his experience with hashish. I knew it was commonly procured in Tunis and could be chewed or smoked. I thought to chew some while I had Peggy and the Swiss woman to look after me. I had never actually seen the stuff and was curious. "Could I order some hashish?" I asked the waiter when the dancers paused. Peggy strongly put her foot down on any such diversion. She had a very determined "No!" So I gave up the idea completely and I never was tempted again.

In the meantime, patrons were arriving and glancing in at us, for the madam had purposely left the door open. They were polite and tried to hide their amazement at the sight of white women. They were also patient about being kept waiting. I shook hands with each of the Arabs as we departed, after the Swiss lady had settled up. I have long carried the vivid memory of the girl with the doe eyes and her union suit protruding out of the lavender silk. I wondered if she would take the dress back to the desert with her along with her accumulated dowry, and if she would tell the bridegroom about her experiences. I also wondered if Margaret Leech would tell Ralph Pulitzer, whom she was to marry, about our "bizarre" evening in Tunis.

I had made friends with an Arab who held a university degree. He told me that there was to be a gala engagement party in a fine house and he would be glad to take me to it. There was no trouble getting in here. We were warmly welcomed. The bridegroom was seventeen. His father was quite rich. The three-story dwelling was built around a fountained courtyard, where some two hundred guests, all male, were circulating. At the end of the court opposite the entrance a stage had been set up for the musicians and the entertainers. Refreshments were spread in profusion on long tables for the performers. The singing star was a handsome woman, a bit plump, and famous throughout Tunisia. She, too, wore a French evening dress of lavender-colored silk, very décolleté, and her arms were bare. The oddity here was that when she finished each song, she would step to the refreshment table, pick up a peeled hard-boiled egg and eat it.

The other custom I found strange was the enforced absence of the bride. She and her mother and the other women had been relegated to observe the festivities from behind a screen of pierced marble on the third-floor gallery. In the land of the Muslims in 1923 it was still very much of a man's world.

Our last afternoon Peggy and I went to make our farewells to special friends in the *souks*. Everywhere they served us sweet thick coffee "strong enough to bear up an egg." We appreciated their hospitality and I felt I had to drink the coffee, but after the eleventh cup I could take no more. It made me drunk, and a more unpleasant drunkenness I have never experienced.

Peggy took a ship for Marseilles the next morning, and a few hours later I left by train for Algiers. I had determined to see the Sahara Desert that began at Biskra and I hoped to sleep one night out under the stars.

In Algiers when I telephoned the Countess de Brazza she invited me for luncheon. Her villa was in a fashionable suburb. Her father, a great-grandson of Lafayette, had been French ambassador to the United States during the Rutherford Hayes administration and when a tiny girl she had learned English from black nurses and cooks, which had given her an extraordinary accent. She had married an Italian-born count with the long name of Pierre Paul François de Brazza. Her husband became a French citizen after he had made explorations of the West Coast of Africa for France. On orders of the French government he returned to Africa in an attempt to forestall Stanley's efforts to annex the whole Congo basin for Belgium's Leopold II. Although he partially failed in this project he added almost 200,000 square miles in central Africa to the French empire. He died in Dakar, West Africa. Brazzaville, capital of the Congo, was named for him. His handsome portrait hung in the drawing room of the villa.

De Brazza was one of the great explorers of modern times. But in one thing he was unlucky. His two sons, aged about twenty and twenty-one, were gentle idiots. They looked much like identical twins and they smiled and smiled amiably at me. They had lunch with us and their table manners were good. The countess and her lovely eighteen-year-old daughter, Marthe, who spoke British English, pretended not to notice anything amiss with the boys. I, of course, showed no sign. When I addressed some simple remarks to them they nodded their heads and smiled in agreement.

While Marthe and I strolled about the garden, the Countess de Brazza wrote a note to her brother's wife, Clara de Chambrun. She was the sister of Nicholas Longworth, and was "mad about Shakespeare." As I made my adieus, the young men waved me off with grinning countenances.

As a sad footnote to this visit, I received a letter from the Countess de Chambrun dated March 29, 1950.

Speaking of friendships: You probably know that my husband's dear sister Thérèse died two years ago at a ripe old age. There would have been little real sadness in that had it not taken place at the same time as her only daughter, Marthe, married to a colonial inspector at Fort Lamy—the place where Adelbert was wounded fifty years ago—and where poor Marthe took some deadly infection, was transferred to her mother's care in Algiers, and died there where both were too ill to see each other.

My husband was able to take a plane and be with them at a few hours' notice. His presence was a great comfort.

We shall go again shortly, this time to present Dar-el-Snagha, where Thérèse and Brazza gave their home to the State to be made into a colonial museum—souvenirs of his explorations in Africa and also a memorial to their family life: paintings, furniture, and especially books, for a part of his library was early fifteenth century.

On the train to Biskra we came to the city of Constantine, which had been founded by Carthaginians, rebuilt by the Emperor Constantine, and finally ruled by the French, who made it into a modern city. Constantine is a city of storks, which breed there. It is considered lucky if storks choose your chimney for a nest. In April the sky was dotted with the white birds. They were taking their young on trial flights, preparing for an imminent migration to Denmark. And flamingos in droves near the marshes were likewise giving lessons to their fledglings. They would rise up in sudden glorious pink clouds. I did not know their particular summer destination, but I was enchanted by the delicate pinkness of their wings and bodies. Flamingos seem tribal by choice. Storks are more individualistic, like family men.

Constantine, like Kairouan, was a whitewashed city. But here it was the quaint custom to paint the doors of the harlotries a heavenly blue.

The name Biskra, like Sorrento, had long stirred my imagination. The town lies at the threshold of the Sahara Desert. The ancient Romans, who managed to get everywhere, made it a military base. Later it became an important Muslim town. In 1844 it was garrisoned by the French. Many contingents of the Foreign Legion passed this way into the burning sands. Villagers cultivated the surrounding five square miles of oasis, planted with some 150,000 date palms and fruit trees that bore apricots, pomegranates, and olives. The mild winters, where the temperature never goes below fifty degrees in January, has made Biskra a popular and pleasant winter resort. The town has about twenty thousand permanent residents.

I was immediately discouraged by the hotel manager from fulfilling my romantic desire to sleep a night on the desert. It would be costly. It also might be dangerous because of robbers. Besides, the time of the full moon had passed.

When I first emerged on the street lined with palm trees and flowering shrubs I was accosted by a horde of Arab bootblacks. I insisted that I did not want a shine. But one likely light-skinned lad, far more refined-looking than the dirty-faced crowd about him and wearing a clean white smock and a new red fez, simply dropped to his knees, took my right foot and lifted it up on his little box and proceeded to shine my shoes. He was about thirteen, and his name was Salah. By the time he had finished, I had decided to let him be my guide. Like the puppy in the petshop, he had chosen me.

Salah took me here and there, even where the camels were tethered at the edge of the town. The shacks of the poor were made of sun-baked bricks. Salah told me that his father had been a railroad worker and was killed in an accident the year before. He had a sister of fourteen, whom he said was quite beautiful. She had had a baby only two days before. The baby's father was a hotel waiter. "Since I am the head of the house, I can invite you to see where I live," he said. I hesitated; my intrusion might be unwelcome. But he wanted to show me his two-day-old nephew. The place was not more than three blocks from my hotel.

I confess that I was curious to see how ordinary folk lived. I had been only in a rich man's home at the engagement party in Tunis. Salah's apartment was on the second floor. We entered a large room, almost bare of furniture. The boy's mother was squatting over a brazier cooking couscous. She was surprised to see the foreigner he brought up. But she rose to greet me politely, if shyly. The baby was asleep in a wooden box suspended from the ceiling by ropes. It made an excellent cradle. I was pretending to admire the nephew, when another door opened and a girl appeared. I caught my breath. She was beautiful, as Salah had said, the most beautiful girl that I had seen since leaving Italy. Her features were delicate. Her gray eyes were large and lustrous. She wore her wavy brown hair loose. Her dress was a faded soft yellow. She did not smile. She was still weak from the experience of childbearing, looking as if a terrible thing had been done to her. She walked to the crib and caught onto the ropes for support, but she did not glance at her boy child. I left a token gift of money on the baby's swinging crib. I made my adieus and did not tarry. But I would never forget the fragile beauty of Salah's sister.

As we went down the stairs, Salah was murmuring *"Toujours* couscous." It is a stew made of cracked wheat, meat, and tomatoes and other vegetables, seasoned sometimes with spices. We stopped at a French restaurant, and I bought Salah a continental meal. I was not in the least embarrassed by his table manners.

A sophisticated Arab of gracious mien, whom I met and found *simpatico,* had played in Maugham's *Garden of Allah* with Nazimova for a full year in London. He liked England very much, but he felt he should return to his native land and his properties. He was quite tall for an Arab and good-looking, with chiseled features and gray eyes. He was a direct descendant of Mohammed. We had interesting conversations over tea. He surprised me by saying that loose married women would often trip over the flat roofs to an illicit rendezvous when they had the chance.

I did not get to meet this highborn Arab's wife or see inside his house. His sophistication stopped short of asking a stranger to be a guest in his home.

Only Salah, whose father was dead, had been able to do that for me. Salah looked as if he might have been accepted into one of the best preparatory schools in Switzerland. Some special strain of blue blood must have been in his ancestry. He came to the Biskra station to see me off. His last words as the train moved were: *"Je ne suis pas content."* He was unhappy to see me depart. I hoped others would appreciate his dignity and character.

I had relished North Africa. Muslims were something new in my experience. In general, I had liked the Arabs I had met, from the *souk* owners in Tunis to Salah, the bootblack, and the highborn scion of Mohammed.

May in Paris is generally the perfect month, when all the leaves are unfolded and most of the flowers are in bloom. I sent the letter from the Countess de Brazza to 52 Rue de Vaugirard, which I had ascertained was neighbor to the Luxembourg gardens. The Countess de Chambrun invited me for tea. I was the only guest and we talked nothing but Shakespeare until her son René, called "Bunny," came in and then we talked American baseball, his passion. We shared an enthusiasm for Ty Cobb. The general, a great-grandson of Lafayette, was absent with his forces in Morocco.

One evening Madame de Chambrun took me to the Odéon to see *The Merchant of Venice* with the great Firmin Gémier in the role of Shylock. Gémier, a friend of hers, had sent her tickets, although she had quarreled with him in rehearsals about his light treatment of Portia.

After her marriage, this sister of Nicholas Longworth had earned her Ph.D. at the Sorbonne, because, she said, the French critics would not take the American dilettante seriously when she wrote of Shakespeare. Now they heeded her as an "authority." She had published three books on Shakespeare.

Madame de Chambrun was presently engaged in writing a life of Shakespeare in which the Dark Lady of the Sonnets is identified as Ann, wife of D'Avenant, the keeper of the inn where the dramatist was pleased to stop overnight on his journeys between London and Stratford. Sir William D'Avenant, the playwright, often boasted that he was Shakespeare's illegitimate son.

I had noticed that Madame de Chambrun invariably wore black. I asked Bunny if she was in mourning. He said, "Yes, for my sister." Her death had come about in a strange way. The young lady was in her bath when a telephone call came for her. Her maid brought the phone to the tub. The water acted as a conductor and she was electrocuted before she could say the French equivalent of hello. "My mother has not entirely recovered from the shock," Bunny said. "My beautiful sister was nineteen and the only girl. I have no brothers." René was eventually to marry the only daughter of Premier Pierre Laval, who was then extremely popular with the French people, but who was later accused of being a collaborator in World War II and suffered a grisly death.

In Paris, I again saw the Shelton Martins and Mrs. Bissell, whom I had known at the Cocumella. The Martins, who were childless, were expecting to adopt a boy baby in London. Mrs. Bissell asked me if I would care to accompany her to the theater to see a Cocteau play. Another day she thought that I might like to see the Cluny Museum with her as guide, for she knew where the choicest items were located. And a third time she wondered if I would go—as part of my education to gather material for writing—to a "showing" at one of the top couturiers in Paris. As many men as women came, she reassured me. So, for the hell of it, I went. Some of the models were strikingly beautiful, not like many of the half-starved skeletons of today. The clothes had grace and elegance.

When we came from the showing Mrs. Bissell said, "You are going home to be married. In Fanny Burney's phrase, I want to have a little 'chattery' with you." We had stopped at a sidewalk café under the trees for coffee. "Without your permission I have made out a check for you, which I beg you to accept for a wedding present. I travel about so much that if you should send me an invitation, it might never reach me. There is always something that your future wife might want that you don't find among the gifts. So I hope you will accept this token of friendship."

She took an envelope from her bag. "I am very grateful," I said. "In fact, quite overcome."

We sipped our coffee. I saw her to her hotel. Her conversation was still mostly about Whistler and Wilde and Henry James, all dead before 1916, and princes of various ranks and countries, many of whom I had never heard of. But she was invariably interesting.

When I got back to my hotel room I ventured to look at the check. It was on a New York bank for five hundred dollars. I first thought of returning it, for it was much too much. Then I reasoned with myself and decided that she had wanted us to have the money. It would certainly cause her no sacrifice. I sent her a warm note of appreciation. In reply, she said she was leaving for London and gave Claridge's as her hotel.

When I got to London I called on the literary agent Curtis Brown and offered stories that I had written in Sorrento. I left them with a Miss Pearn to read. She asked me to return in two days, if convenient. In the meantime I telephoned Mrs. Bissell. "The Lord has delivered you into my hands," were her first words. "I am invited to a ball and supper given by the Marchioness of Carisbrooke at her home. Her husband is a first cousin of George V. I need an escort. Will you accompany me? You must, of course, wear tails." "But mine are too seedy," I protested. She countered, "Proper outfits are always for rent in London." I couldn't quite picture myself going in rented evening clothes. But I said I would see what I could do.

When I returned to Curtis Brown I found that Miss Pearn had already sold one of my stories, the poorest of the lot, in my estimation. Maxwell Aley, fiction editor of *Woman's Home Companion,* came in while I was discussing with Miss Pearn how to go about renting an outfit for the next evening. Aley and I had never met before, but we liked each other. I told him my problem. "Look here," he said, "I have just had tailored very elegant evening togs. You and I are the same size. Why don't you come to my hotel and try them on? I initiated them over a weekend at the home of W. L. George, and I am next to dine formally with Rebecca West. I am not using the outfit for two days." I did not even protest. I accepted with gratitude. The Englishwoman held her mouth open in amazement at such a quick camaraderie.

As a footman called out our names, the Marchioness of Carisbrooke received us with that utterly charming graciousness the English can turn on so readily when they want to. In one of the drawing rooms I recognized from his photographs the man who was crown prince of Sweden. After the death of his first wife, Princess Margaret of Connaught, Mrs. Bissell told me, he was now courting Lady Louise Mountbatten, whom he would marry within that year of 1923. I did not meet the crown prince on this night or fancy that I ever would. But in 1939 he received me at the palace in Stockholm. On the death of his aged father in 1950, he was crowned Gustaf VI Adolf. On November 11, 1961, his birthday, I was knighted by His Majesty and decorated with the Royal Order of the North Star.

I do not recall many other guests, but there was a Germanic-looking oldish granddaughter of Queen Victoria, and Clara Butt, the concert singer, a huge woman with a powerful contralto and a long train, which a gentleman stepped on and stopped her in her tracks.

After dancing with Mrs. Bissell, I suddenly found myself facing the golden young Duchess of Hamilton. We had stayed at a small hotel in Perugia together, and, not knowing her identity, I had asked her to dance. She had been writing a letter at a corner desk in the room where a three-man orchestra was playing. Politely she had declined. The next morning at breakfast her lady-in-waiting companion had told me who she was. We left for Florence on the same train. She distinctly recalled having seen me somewhere before. And now in London she waltzed with me.

A supper with champagne was served on a lower floor at midnight at tables for ten. There were no place cards. I sat at Mrs. Bissell's right. The food was marvelous, beyond anything I had had in my year abroad: caviar, fresh salmon, birds in aspic, and chocolate mousse. My educational year was almost ended.

The Shelton Martins had a surprise for me: an infant boy whom they had legally adopted in London. They had named him Richard for their friend Dick Sheppard, the popular rector of St. Martin's-in-the-Fields. I attended the christening, and I dined with them in their suite afterward. This couple from Peapack New Jersey, were to prove invaluable friends within a very few years when I had urgent need of them.

I visited Earl McGowin, a former student of mine, now a Rhodes scholar at Oxford at the time of the bump boat races, and there I met Lady Astor at a university club party, where she spoke with wit and charm. She was already in Parliament. Later we became firm friends and met in

London and Delray Beach, Florida. I have saved some thirty letters from her. She and Lord Astor will appear in a later chapter.

I had had such a heady year abroad that I can hardly recall anything about the return sea voyage.

When I was about to return to the States, the Kaufmans invited me to stay with them in New York. They rightly surmised that I would be broke after a year's leave of absence without pay.

Beatrice took me to luncheon at the Algonquin's famed Round Table. Just after the first arrivals were seated Heywood Broun, the dramatic critic of the *Tribune*, brought in a stranger who had obviously never been there before. I was impressed by his distinguished large nose. After he had been introduced around, the newcomer took the chair at my right. I had not caught his name. So I turned to Beatrice and asked *sotto voce* who was the man with the big nose on my other side.

"Stark Young," she replied. "He has just become the dramatic critic of the New York *Times*."

I said with enthusiastic delight, "Are you really Stark Young? You are the person in New York I most wanted to meet. Just before I left Sorrento Lincoln Steffens gave me two old copies of *The New Republic*. I read your piece about John Barrymore in *Hamlet*. I thought it brilliant. I greatly admired your distinctive style. And in another issue was an amusing piece about an old black woman in Mississippi who had such advanced ideas on feminine behavior. How do you up here in New York understand the Southern Negro so well?"

"I was born in Como, Mississippi," he said with a grin. He told me then that he had his first dramatic assignment for the *Times* that very evening. He was covering Eugene O'Neill's *All God's Chillun Got Wings*. Paul Robeson, the Negro actor, was starring with Mary Blair, the wife of Edmund Wilson, who was Stark's literary colleague on *The New Republic*.

"By the way," he said casually, "Doris Keane is supposed to go with me. But this morning she wasn't well. If she isn't all right by five this afternoon, would you care to meet me in the lobby?"

"Would I!" I said with an exclamation mark. I could hardly believe my possible good fortune. Young promised that he would phone me in any case. I doubtless hoped that Miss Keane's indisposition would not clear up until the morrow.

That afternoon I hovered near the telephone at the Kaufmans' apartment. They were both out. Exactly at five the phone rang. It was Stark Young. Doris Keane still felt unwell. Could I make it?

A little after eight I was waiting in the theater lobby. When Young joined me he was carrying his portable typewriter, which he said he was used to.

A play about miscegenation was a daring theme for 1923. Paul Robeson played the sympathetic role of a law student, whose neurotic wife (Mary Blair) drove him almost to desperation.

In his criticism in the morning *Times,* Young, while complimenting Robeson's dignified bearing and rich speaking voice, pointed out certain deficiencies in his technique. Few Negroes had ever then played on Broadway and none, so far as I knew, in a leading role. It was customary for critics to overpraise black actors. The Algonquin crowd, who prided themselves on their so-called liberal views, were not enthusiastic about Young's review. But George Kaufman had nothing to say against it. Robeson was a better singer than actor. He was great in concerts. Later, in Edna Ferber's musical, *Showboat,* he absolutely thrilled his audience with his performance of the black roustabout who sang "Ole Man River."

Young's contract with the New York *Times* ran for a year. Then he resigned and returned to his former post at the weekly *New Republic.* He had never felt congenial with dashing off reviews between 11:00 P.M. and 2:00 A.M. He liked time for reflection.

With a classical Mississippi background, Young had not stopped cultivating himself. He read Italian poetry in the original and he translated Chekhov's plays from the Russian. He was a delightful raconteur. As a conversationalist I rank him along with H. L. Mencken and Aldous Huxley.

I was soon writing reviews for *The New Republic* of books by James Branch Cabell, Wyndham Lewis, François Mauriac, and others. I was happy to know that my reviews pleased Edmund Wilson, who even in the mid twenties I regarded as the most perceptive literary critic in America. Wilson wrote me that he found my review of Mauriac's *Thérèse* "absolutely first-rate."

Despite his sophistication after years in the East, Stark Young remained appreciative of what cultivated values of the Old South were left. He and my wife, Thérèse, an unreconstructed rebel, became devoted friends after they met in 1928. They corresponded occasionally through the years. Stark would entertain us as we passed through New York on our way to Bermuda or Europe, and send Thérèse inscribed copies of his books. I have a letter from him on *New Republic* gray stationery dated August 2, 1928, after his first meeting with Thérèse, when I was at the MacDowell Colony. He described her with keen perception.

I have been meaning to write you for a week ever since Thérèse was here. But I've been trying to get a first draft of my novel [*So Red the Rose*] done before I go abroad next week. I must not wait any longer to tell you how much I enjoyed seeing Thérèse.

She is very fine and aristocratic, as well as charming looking, and she wears her clothes beautifully. You get, too, a sense of character, as well as distinction, and I'm not modern enough to despise either. She is the kind of person that makes you want to defend her and fills your heart with wishes for her happiness.

Since I considered that Young wrote with a sixth sense even in his critical reviews and essays, I saved this particular letter. In cleaning out an old trunk on August 10, 1972, I came across it, where it had lain forgotten for forty-four years. Stark's description fits Thérèse perfectly today.

The second night after I arrived in New York in 1923 I was taken by the Kaufmans to dinner at Robert Sherwood's. He was then a budding playwright. I recall, oddly, that on that occasion I had my first corn on the cob in a year. After dinner I learned of a raging pastime of the young literati. The game was parchesi, which I had first enjoyed at the age of six. A man named Herman Mankiewicz, of some importance in the theatrical world, was the only extra guest, besides the Kaufmans and me. Such high stakes were set that I was glad to stay out of the game. I watched for a while, and then I wandered off, found a convenient bed, lay down without ceremony, and went to sleep. I was awakened by Mary Sherwood's screaming at Beatrice, because she would not break her blockade. "I hate you! I hate you!" she cried. "I'll never speak to you again!" I arose to question the fury. Mary Sherwood was a tiny little thing, hardly five feet, little more than half the height of her rangy and now embarrassed husband. When I appeared, she quieted down, but still bristled with suppressed frustration and rage. When we were kids, I thought, we never reacted to a game of parchesi so intensely. Mary Sherwood bade us good night, without apologizing for her violent outburst. Beatrice went off with the major loot.

The second time I was the houseguest of the Kaufmans they were in a very handsome apartment. Because George was called unexpectedly out of the city one night, I got his ticket to a dinner for authors and publishers at the Brevoort Hotel celebrating the defeat of a censorship bill in the New York Supreme Court. Horace Liveright, the publisher, was the principal speaker. Beatrice was now working for Liveright, so we got a good table. Seated at my left was Charles Hanson Towne, the editor of *McClure's,* who had bought my first story in 1916. He recalled it and the letter he had written me about it. Later, when he became editor of *Harper's Bazaar,* he published poems, articles, and a one-act play of mine.

The chief excitement of the evening for me was meeting H. L. Mencken. He was also placed at our table for twelve. Mencken surprised me by his spontaneous geniality. I admired him above other critics of contemporary life for his pungent, original comments. He ridiculed "organized" religion and jeered at business and the middle classes. He had called the South "the Sahara of the Bozart," declaring there were no first class writers below Richmond and not one symphony orchestra or a decent art gallery in the region. No one used words that so got under the skin. He enraged people. In Mississippi, after his Sahara piece was published, he was burned in effigy. He was the bane of pompous politicians. In literature he fought against the phoney success of such popular authors as Harold Bell Wright.

At the Brevoort dinner he was so amiable and jolly that by the time the dessert was served I felt I could challenge him on anything. I said across the table, "You don't seem to like Southerners a bit. In fact, you don't seem to like anything or anybody. Please just tell me if there are any people you do like." He bestowed on me what I might have interpreted as a benevolent grin. "I like Turks," he replied. "Turks!" I reiterated in astonishment. "Yes, Turks. Did you ever know a Turk who wasn't an absolute gentleman?" "I have never known any Turks." He reeled off a string of reasons for admiring Turks. It was that element of surprise that made him such a stimulating conversationalist. I delighted in his unorthodoxy.

After dinner I said, "I would like to talk to you some more."

"Good as done," he said. "Here's a bona-fide invitation. Come to Baltimore to see me next Saturday week. We have a little amateur orchestra and we make music at my house at 1524 Hollins Street every other Saturday. We drink Würzburger beer and have a high old time. Burton Rascoe is coming down. You know him. Come with him. We'll find time to talk."

Rascoe, the literary critic of the *World-Telegram,* said he would be delighted for me to accompany him. It was one of those invitations that rarely loom in an aspiring young man's life. But I was compelled to return to Alabama before that second Saturday rolled around.

A few August nights later, because I was the Kaufmans' houseguest, Edna Ferber invited me to her birthday dinner for ten. Just as we were going into the dining room a man delivered a standing ashtray made in the form of a messenger. Miss Ferber casually tore off the wrappings and held up a birthday card from Nelson Doubleday, her publisher. "It was sweet of Nelson to remember my birthday," she said. A white slip of paper drifted to the floor. One of the guests picked it up. It was a royalty check of over $30,000 for *So Big.* Maxwell Aley, who had lent me the tails in London, told me that a few weeks before he had paid $30,000 for the first serial rights. I had just read that the motion picture rights had been sold for a huge sum. It forcibly hit me that popular writers could make big money.

Immediately after dinner George slipped off to the dress rehearsal of *Old Man Minick.* He and Miss Ferber had collaborated on the play made from one of her magazine stories. I was asked to bring the hostess down to the theater later. In the meantime four of us had a game of lotto, another favorite pastime of the literati. I had not played lotto since my early teens. The players were Franklin P. Adams, the columnist, Harold Ross, the editor of *The New Yorker,* Peggy Leech, and myself. There were no stakes. It was all for fun. I won with the word "bewigged." Peggy vehemently declared that there was no such word. But F.P.A. insisted there was, and proved it by the dictionary.

Miss Ferber and I went by taxi to the dress rehearsal. And on that ride I learned how extremely kind and generous successful writers can be. I had been having considerable difficulty with my eyes, but I had to go back to my teaching job. Miss Ferber was concerned. Her father had gone blind.

She offered me a thousand dollars to give the eyes a complete rest for several months. "I have lots of money now," she said. "A thousand doesn't mean much to me. Some day if you are flush and insist, you may pay me back. But take the thousand as a gift."

I could not accept. But it was a sweet gesture to remember.

During the rehearsal I noted some stage business I believed could be improved. At Childs at 2:00 A.M. George and Edna and I ate pancakes. I told them what could be easily remedied, before the play opened in Greenwich, a few days hence. About a fourth of the audience on the right side of the theater could not see Phyllis Povah, the star, in a crucial scene at the back of the stage in an oblique breakfast nook. "Have her leave the table," I suggested, "with her cup of coffee in hand, saying she didn't want breakfast, only coffee, and come out into the open living room for her big speech." The collaborators agreed with me, as in the other two cases. George said, "When you are putting on a play you are grateful for all the help the good God can send you."

I went up on the train to Greenwich for the opening with Beatrice Kaufman and Edna Ferber. George was already there. That night I saw that all my suggestions for revised stage business were enacted.

And that night I got my first inkling that all was not well in the marital relations of Beatrice and George. George was the soul of discretion, but there was a girl named Myra Hampton who had come up to Greenwich to see the play. Her objective was to get the role of one of the minor characters, which she did. The actress playing the part of an aggressive club-woman had her two weeks notice of dismissal the next day.

The house was sold out. George had not thought to provide a seat for Myra. She was piqued. I heard her tell George in the lobby that she had come to see the play and would very much like to do so. He seemed nonplused. I think a chair was provided for her. He himself was always too nervous on first nights to sit anywhere.

Myra was not to be seen in the hotel dining room at the supper party following the opening. "Who is Myra Hampton?" I asked Beatrice. Her reply surprised me. "She's the kind of a girl who will meet George at any appointed New York lamppost. He likes to be able to treat his girls casually. He doesn't want one who is a nuisance." I said no more. I felt it was touchy ground.

Beatrice made an odd remark after our return to New York. "George makes a good man to be married to. I wouldn't want to be married to anyone else. But he is not much of a husband."

Later I learned that the couple was sexually incompatible almost from the first and that Beatrice and George were both virgins when they married. George was a virgin until twenty-eight. In the first year of their marriage Beatrice became pregnant. But things did not go well. A baby boy had to be taken from her, stillborn and deformed. Thereafter Beatrice had a kind

125

of loathing for the birthing of an infant. She told me that she found child-bearing appalling and rather disgusting. She did not tell me that George found it physically impossible to have sexual relations with her after the malfunctioning. I learned this later from a close family friend. And George's analyst failed to enable him to make love to his wife. With Beatrice he remained permanently impotent.

Apparently George's libido had got a sudden stimulating jolt. He had an arrangement with Polly Adler to have her girls meet him on street corners, whence he would take them to a private apartment. He did not want to be seen at her "house," where he had a charge account.

George was far more complicated than Beatrice, who was a normal attractive woman with obvious sex appeal. He was very dependent on Beatrice, who ran his home efficiently and harmoniously. He followed her advice above that of all others. I never heard a cross word between them. And they seemed to have a definite fondness for each other. I came to believe that they were living as brother and sister. Years later, when Mary Astor's husband procured her secret diary and began to publish it in lurid installments because she was suing him for a divorce, Beatrice was in Europe. She came straight home. George met her at the ship. They did not kiss. But she stood by him and said to the reporters that many married men, in the way of their profession, enjoyed flirtations with actresses. Was there anything so strange in that? Then she bought a place in Bucks County, Pennsylvania, called "Barley Sheaf Farm" as a refuge for George, to get him away from reporters and the tactless questions of their acquaintances.

I did not see much of the Kaufmans after the Mary Astor scandal made front-page headlines. But one evening I was invited to Edna Ferber's, when she was living in the elegant Park Avenue penthouse that had formerly been owned by Kruger, the Swedish match king. The Kaufmans were up from Bucks County. George was still looking somewhat hangdog. Out on the terrace, while I was admiring the tomatoes and green beans that flourished there, Edna told me how crucified George had been by the salacious publicity and the crude jokes about the affair. He had wanted above all else to keep his private life secret. He resented being dubbed "America's male sex symbol." "You know how abnormally sensitive he is," Edna said. "He will step only ankle deep into the ocean—literally."

Beatrice was to die of a cerebral hemorrhage early in 1945. In his crushing grief at losing her, George actually beat his head against the wall. Two years after her death I had a late breakfast at George's apartment alone with him. I recall that we had loganberries with rich cream. When Moss Hart, his favorite collaborator, arrived, he had had breakfast, but he too was served loganberries.

About the collaborations Beatrice had told me that it seemed to take the sting and burden out of a single-handed job. George said: "It is marriage without sex and subject to vexations. But two people working together often fly far above their talents."

Before I left I went to see the guest room in which I had once spent a week. I wanted to know if the framed photograph of Lynn Fontanne was still hanging above the bed. It was. She had written: "You made me what I am today, I hope you're satisfied—Love—Lynn." She had taken the words from a current song. After *Dulcy,* Fontanne had gone to the top. George had also certainly gone high, with a string of twenty-seven hits, including two Pulitzer Prizes. Neither scandal nor the death of Beatrice had put the brakes on his compulsive playwriting. He had collaborated on forty plays altogether, and represented so-called "commercial" Broadway at its best.

The Kaufmans had been extraordinarily kind to a young man from Alabama with no claim whatever to fame and absolutely no personal claim on them. For a wedding present they sent us a chocolate set from Austria with stylized floral design. On some chilly nights we still drink hot chocolate from the Kaufman cups. In 1974, none of the six cups and saucers have been broken. On our drawing room hearth stands an antique bellows of beautifully carved wood, which Beatrice sent me from Italy. It works perfectly and stirs flames in our log fire, as well as a rush of gratitude for the two Kaufmans, George and Beatrice.

I admired so much a piece H. L. Mencken had done on Joseph Conrad that I wrote him. On April 15, 1924, he replied.

You missed a high-toned affair by not coming to Baltimore that Saturday night. The club drank two kegs of beer. But now there is another party every Saturday. The next time you come North by all means stop off.

Thank you for what you say about the Conrad essay. Conrad said he liked it too.

In May, I submitted a short story for *The American Mercury,* which drew a gentle rejection.

This is an excellent story, but it so happens that we are unable to buy any fiction at the moment. I am very sorry. We are using but one story a month and we already have twelve or fifteen in type.

Have you something else? That is, something in the way of an article—not fiction.

I wrote Mencken that I might come by to see him the first week in August on my way to New York. He answered promptly.

I'll probably be back in Baltimore Monday or Tuesday. How long I'll remain I don't know. But the chances are at least ten to one that I'll be there on Wednesday. I suggest that we have lunch together on that day. Please let me hear from you at 1524 Hollins Street.

On Wednesday Mr. Mencken came to fetch me at my Baltimore hotel to take me to lunch at a restaurant noted for its gourmet food. It was a very hot day and I was unprepared for his being so smartly turned out. He was even carrying a cane; few gentlemen were still carrying sticks in the middle of the twenties.

He wore his hair parted in the middle and plastered down. Just under medium height, his figure looked squat despite the excellent tailoring. He had no neck to speak of and wore the highest detachable starched collar he could manage between his shoulders and jaw. When he stepped out on the Baltimore sidewalk to hail a taxi he was as jaunty as if he were strolling down the Boulevard des Italiens.

We lingered over our meal. Mencken saw he had captivated me. And I realized that he had to have an audience. When we rose to go he invited me to his house on Hollins Street that evening. "Come at ten," he said. "I shall have finished my day's work then, and my mother will have gone upstairs. I'm sorry I can't give you music."

Mencken and his bachelor brother August still lived with their mother in a narrow brick three-story house in an old-fashioned neighborhood of Baltimore. I raised the polished brass knocker at precisely ten o'clock. It was a sweltering evening. When I left the hotel the outside thermometer stood close to a hundred degrees. Mencken came to the door in his shirt sleeves. He had loosened the neckband of his collar. The customary gold-filled collar button still stuck in its button hole. He looked quite different from his soigné appearance at midday. He ushered me through the two parlors to his study. "Would a Tom Collins be acceptable? It's the best drink I know for beating the heat." He proceeded to mix the gin, lime juice, carbonated water, and ice in tall glasses. "Take off your jacket and loosen your tie. This is about the hottest week I can recall in Baltimore."

We were in a library at the back of the house. Outside the open door and open window was a small patterned flower garden, surrounded by an ivy-covered high brick wall. With a frosty Tom Collins in my hand and the electric floor fan blowing full upon us I soon forgot the heat and was conscious only of Mencken's talk. He reminded me of a wise, pudgy Zen priest I had once seen in a Japanese motion picture. He talked wittily. Yet after almost a half-century, I cannot recall the specific words.

What surprised me most was Mencken's profound interest in heritage and breeding. His principles were aristocratic rather than democratic, and he amusingly excoriated the "boobocracy." In the line of his German ancestors there was a plenitude of Ph.D.'s. He was extremely eclectic, with strong admirations and prejudices. Unlike Carl Sandburg, who told me at my home that he thought "exclusive" was the dirtiest word in the English language, Mencken gloried in it. He was really sympathetic to the Southern way of life, its emphasis on family and ancestors. On a visit to Richmond, when Joseph Hergesheimer and he were houseguests, the novelist had been dubious about the critic's behavior. But Mencken had been immediately accepted as "belonging," and Hergesheimer had been regarded as not.

128

I refrained from bringing up Bobby Burns, for I believed there was a special quality about the Scots that lifted them above the average. And Mencken might have countered that perhaps half the blood in the plowboy's veins could have been blue for a special reason. Nor did I cite Sandburg, who was obviously of peasant stock, and had no idea from what province in Sweden his unlettered father came.

On one thing we had a difference of opinion. He despised the music of Ravel, the French composer. I enjoyed it. Mencken's passionate enthusiasm was for the German composers. The amateur orchestra that gathered in the Mencken double parlors on alternate Saturdays made German music almost exclusively: Wagner, Bach, Beethoven, and the Strausses.

We talked and talked, or, rather, he talked and I listened. And every now and then we had a fresh Tom Collins. When our bladders needed emptying, we utilized the pebbled paths of the flower garden.

I was in accord with his opinion of virtually all books brought into the conversation. I happened to like the writers he did. But I told him that I found Dreiser hard to take. Though Mencken himself found Dreiser's style massively clumsy and his diction often trite, he said that his "realism" was something new and important when Doubleday published his first novel, *Sister Carrie,* in 1900. When his publisher printed only a thousand copies of his book and made no effort to promote it, Mencken told me, Dreiser went into a nervous breakdown and contemplated suicide. I confessed that I might have been unfairly prejudiced.

As the old-fashioned clock struck two I rose unsteadily. My host called a cab for me.

My long evening with Mencken at his home made me understand why his friends had such affection for him, for he gave so generously of himself. As a slight token of gratitude for his hospitality I sent Mencken an original etching that I had got in Nuremberg. He replied promptly and characteristically on October 3.

My best thanks for that charming etching. I am delighted to have it. I am not far from the Einganstor of the Kloster myself. I must begin to prepare myself for Heaven.

I take it you are back in Alabama. Don't forget that you are to compose a treatise on life there for *The American Mercury.* Don't denounce the State unless you want to! Let us hear what is charming in it.

He sent me a signed photograph of himself, dated 1924, which now hangs in my studio.

After my return from Sorrento in the summer of 1923 and a stopover with the George Kaufmans in New York, I came straight to Roebuck Springs to the Cory household to see the girl my heart was set on marrying. She had plenty of beaus and danced often at the Birmingham Country Club, although she had never made her formal debut. She was hard to persuade that I was the right husband for her. But she had already learned to type after a fashion and now she took typing lessons to perfect her skill and asked me for lists of books she might read.

Finally the wedding was set for December 20, 1924, when I would have my Christmas vacation. We had planned the honeymoon to be spent in Havana. And then one of Thérèse's relations offered to give us for a wedding present a week at a pleasant hotel he owned in Winter Haven, Florida. I canceled reservations on the ship from New Orleans to Havana and added a week in St. Augustine.

Three weeks before the marriage Thérèse's home, which had been rebuilt and much extended only two years before, burned to the ground at dawn. In the servants' quarters the Negro butler had made too roaring a fire, which caught the roof and then jumped to the roof of the big house. Thérèse managed to save most of her trousseau and about half the wedding invitations, which were already addressed. Some of the family portraits were rescued and a few pieces of downstairs furniture, including a library table in which was found a first edition of *Babbitt* that belonged to me. Thérèse had jokingly said that she suspected I might be marrying her for her father's fine collection of first editions. All the books on the shelves were burned to ashes.

I came at once at Thérèse's telephone call and did what I could to console the Corys for the loss of their house. The family moved into a fashionable downtown furnished apartment.

We were married as scheduled on December 20 in a church wedding at the charming Wilson Chapel in Roebuck Springs and left for Florida on the midnight train.

When we returned to Tuscaloosa, the parties my friends gave for us were a bit of a strain on Thérèse, who never cared greatly for them at best and only played bridge when she could not gracefully get out of it. But I was happy to see that she really liked the tree-shaded town and especially my friends.

My eyes had been giving me serious trouble ever since I foolishly, heedlessly, typed for four hours on the back veranda of our Demopolis house in the blazing August sun with the red half of the typewriter ribbon because the black half had paled. I was writing a story of the Cocumella, about an old one-eyed room boy who drank by mistake a bottle of embalming fluid and was discovered dead in a position of prayer before the church altar. He was eventually declared a local saint. As I finished the typing my vision was blurred. When I got up, I staggered, and could hardly get downstairs for lunch. "Something terrible has happened to me!" I announced. I do not know how much the brilliant sunlight and red ribbon combination was responsible. But I felt stricken, like Saul of Tarsus.

For several days I was half-blind. For the next two years reading was painful for me. I could not bear to look at the fine print of the stock market report, even though my few shares were holding up well. I recall having to dictate a book review for *The New Republic* to my patient bride, who read the volume of poetry aloud to me, and then made four typed drafts before we were both satisfied with the review. My classes suffered. I would read Shakespeare's tragedies aloud and go home with a splitting headache. Nonetheless, occulists could find nothing wrong with my vision, and I did not need prescription glasses. But I found a magnifying glass helpful.

My good friend Dr. William Partlow advised a complete change and rest for my eyes. So it was that in the summer of 1926 I took Thérèse to France. Tourist class had just been introduced on the Cunard Line and was heavily advertised. It was all we thought we could afford. We had a fairly large stateroom, but the food was dreadful, British cooking at its worst. Happily for us, there was aboard, with a party of young ladies traveling first class, Mrs. Saffold, wife of the Professor of Latin at the university. She would invite us to tea on the first class deck and to dinner—when some of her girls were seasick. The University of Georgia Glee Club was aboard, going on a singing tour of European capitals. Thérèse never lacked attractive dancing partners.

The first night in Paris at a good restaurant I ordered for myself *champignons Provençal*. I was very fond of fresh mushrooms, but I did not know that *Provençal* meant they were cooked in heavy garlic. The dish made me ill, and I have never been able to abide the taste of garlic since. I still think it strange that Provence, that region of flowers and perfumes, should have garlic associated with its name in the otherwise superb French cuisine.

In Paris one evening we engaged expensive orchestra seats for a *Samson and Delilah* performance at the Opéra. I did not know that it was then mandatory for men in the orchestra to wear dinner jackets. I had not brought dinner clothes, but I was wearing a dark blue suit. The ticket taker in black tie regarded me with surprise and exclaimed, *"Pas de smoking!"* He seemed genuinely distressed, and procured us seats in a box on the first tier. In those days of the mid twenties strict etiquette was, logically, strict, as it is not now in these oddly permissive times. We went often to the Opéra-Comique, where black tie was not required.

I took Thérèse to call on Madame de Chambrun. It was unseasonably chilly for a July afternoon. A welcome grate fire burned cheerily in her study at 52 Rue de Vaugirard. The lady received us in a padded black satin robe embroidered in gold thread. It had lost its center button and was pinned together with an enormous safety pin. But her conversation was as stimulating as ever, ranging the globe, while we drank tea. Madame de Chambrun told Thérèse of Lafayette's utmost efforts to save Marie Antoinette by trying repeatedly to awaken her to the reality of the revolutionary fervor. Then in the tenderest way she described the love of the queen and the Swedish Count Fersen.

When the countess invited us to dinner, the general had returned from Morocco. This great-grandson of Lafayette was very distinguished-looking and a charming man with pink cheeks and luxuriant white hair. He told us he would never march his native troops in the light of the full moon, not even to spare them the burning desert heat of midday. Something got into their blood and he had disciplinary troubles. Being moonstruck, he said, was not just a fanciful idea.

On the delectable menu there was corn on the cob. That was thought to please the American guests. Madame de Chambrun said that the French considered it good only for horses. This corn had been allowed to stay too long on the stalk before gathering and was indeed fit only for horses. Madame de Chambrun and I were the only ones who took a third bite. We both had strong teeth.

After dinner Madame de Chambrun described their home in Morocco. It sounded alluring, with a runnel of fresh mountain water coursing through their dining room to cool it. She and the general hoped that we would some-day visit them when she was in residence there. But it never worked out. On the Chambruns' last trip to America in celebration of their golden wedding anniversary, they sent us their photograph, taken on board ship, and Madame de Chambrun wrote that after a visit to her hometown, Cincinnati, they were coming to Tuscaloosa to see us. But my mother-in-law was then ill and occupying our guest room, so with profoundest regret I had to cancel our invitation. It was one of the hardest letters I ever had to write. She replied understandingly, "Another time." But there was no other time, for they both died shortly afterward.

Montclair friends, whom we knew through our very good friend Leonard Beecher, the great-nephew of the odious-to-us Harriet Beecher Stowe, entertained us to pressed duck at the Tour d'Argent. Later they drove us to a château in a stately park, not far from Chartres, where recommended paying guests were accepted. Reservations had already been made for us for a three-day stay.

We were both feeling somewhat ill when we arrived and went straight to our luxurious room. The widowed chatelaine blamed our indisposition on the drinking water of Paris. We could hear the villainous words *"l'eau de Paris"* echoing down the corridors to the various maids and eventually to the sweet old mother-in-law of the countess. Solicitously the old lady came in to see us. Her English, she explained, was a "little constrained—is that the right word?" Nowadays she had so little practice, she said. I recall her gently insistent advice: "All that is in must go out," for which she provided a laxative. We went to bed and skipped dinner that night.

The next day we were fine. Wandering about the grounds, I began happily to pick and eat a few luscious strawberries that grew temptingly in the garden, until the head gardener like an avenging angel swooped down upon us to say, "It is forbidden." If you eat strawberries now, he declared, you won't enjoy them at dinner. I was virtually chased out of this sweet-smelling Garden of Eden.

From the château we took a train for Brittany, passing the imposing Mont-Saint-Michel on the way. Our prime objective was Pont Aven, a quiet little fishing village to which the artist Paul Gauguin in 1889 had retreated for two years before going native in Tahiti. Here we found the perfect resting place in an attractive small hotel run by an Englishwoman and her French husband. We had a relaxing week at the Mimosa Hotel, with its clipped lime trees. It sat by a stream of clear water bubbling over gray rocks. In the village the Breton natives still wore their starched white coifs with the black flowing skirts. The chief event of our days was having tea with delicious jam made from fresh strawberries in a small shaded garden on a narrow peninsula that thrust itself between two tiny rivers that were hardly more than brooks. A lulling music was made by the water where the crystalline stream played over and under and around the rocks. In all the world this spot holds the chief place in our memory as the most delightful for enjoying tea.

It happened to be owned by a successful sculptor from Paris who spent his summers here. He was a splendid figure of a man, with a handsome face and curly black beard. His workshop lay at the entrance to the tea garden. He noticed our presence after repeated visits and one day he came and joined us at our table. He had been commissioned by New York's Metropolitan Museum to search out and buy Breton objects in ancient carved wood. He showed us his collection. Thérèse and I immediately fell in love with a church chest from the sixteenth century. It had three separate front panels of graceful madonnas holding the child. I had ever had a penchant for beautiful wood, and this chest of rich dark oak really thrilled me.

Each late afternoon the sculptor would take a breather and have his tea at our table. He knew well the Chambruns in Paris. Finally, our last afternoon, since I saw that he had become rather fond of the gentle Thérèse and incidentally liked me, I was emboldened to beg him to let us have the chest instead of sending it to the Metropolitan. I told him that he could surely find other good chests in old churches that had gone into disrepair. He already had three large elaborately carved ones that it was obvious the museum would like. Finally he said that because we were so enamored of the chest he would let us have it.

He would personally see to the crating after we had left Pont Aven and send the chest by American Express on the next ship. It arrived in perfect condition. We have never ceased to bless this accommodating and more than kind man. When one rails against the mercenary character of the French I recall this sophisticated Parisian sculptor, who asked me only sixty dollars for the priceless piece.

133

Following the relaxing week in Pont Aven we went to Biarritz on the Bay of Biscay near the Spanish border and found a pleasant hotel where we dined in a shaded garden strewn with small white pebbles. This town had been made fashionable as a favorite resort residence of Napoleon III and his Empress Eugénie. The sea beaches were very fine and extended far. Colored pavilions of the well-to-do dotted the sands. The surf was so high that the "life-savers" were almost constantly blowing warning whistles at the more adventurous swimmers.

Biarritz was an advantageous place from which bus tours radiated. One took us to St. Jean-de-Luz, the beach resort, where Louis XIV married his cousin, Marie Thérèse of Austria, in 1660. Then we drove on to the stark, barren Loyola, where Saint Ignatius founded the Roman Catholic order of the Jesuits in 1540.

Another day we went to Pau, a tourist center at the foot of the Pyrenees renowned for its scenery. It became the residence of the kings of Navarre and here in the château the great Henry IV was born. Another notable person born in Pau was Jean Baptiste Jules Bernadotte, Napoleon's general, whom he made marshal of the empire and whom Sweden later chose for her king.

In 1946, on the library wall of Prince Wilhelm, only brother of King Gustaf VI Adolf, I was to see a large painting of the city of Pau done in the early nineteenth century. I think that the prince took some pride in the common origin of this Bernadotte, who had risen from the ranks, and served brilliantly under Bonaparte.

I was still having a miserable time with my eyes, and glasses were no remedy. When we returned to Paris, through the American Hospital I was recommended to a French physician, who gave me a thorough examination. His explanation of why I needed an operation on my brain did not satisfy me. I did not believe him. But I confess that he gave me a dreadful fright.

In the meantime we crossed France by bus to look into the University of Grenoble in case I should ever want to take a Ph.D. abroad, as two of my colleagues had done.

The city of Grenoble in southeast France is beautifully situated on the Isère river at the foot of the Alps. But I did not find the university attractive at all. The buildings looked grimy and musty. There was no campus. It all looked rather seedy after the beautiful campus at the University of Alabama. I gave up any lingering idea of ever taking a Ph.D.

But we enjoyed our stay in Grenoble. From our hotel balcony we could look up beyond the hills to Mont Blanc covered with dazzling snow. Through binoculars we could plainly see black streaks of people skiing down the thrilling slopes.

As a last treat, just before sailing home, we took a bus tour to the "highest carriage road in the world." Above the tree line on the barren slopes lavender grew in profuse clumps. The bus stopped to give the drivers a break and we were invited to gather sprays of lavender to our heart's content. In the shadows of the towering peaks we garnered quantities of this sweet, pungent European mint with its spikes of small lilac-blue flowers. On our balcony rail Thérèse spread the lavender out to dry in the hot sun. We said farewell to France with four sweet-smelling suitcases, which caused even the Havre porters to sniff the air appreciatively.

Crackup

ON shipboard we came to a decision. I would stop in Baltimore and consult a noted brain surgeon, Dr. Dandy. Thérèse would return to Alabama to pay family visits.

In Baltimore Dr. Dandy declared there was nothing wrong in my brain. He sternly warned me: "Stay away from those fellows who want to operate, or that will be the end of you." He also said, "You have been building up pressure for years from overwork and nervous tension. It will take you just about as long to unwind."

That afternoon I reached a crisis. Looking at some wild animals in the Baltimore zoo—I had gone because someone had told me that watching animals was soothing to the nerves—suddenly I was consumed by a terrible weakness. I quietly, undramatically went to pieces. I could hardly breathe. I could not think clearly. My feeling of inadequacy appalled me. I knew just enough to take the right streetcar into the city.

Back at the Knights of Columbus Association, where I was staying—it was the most reasonable place in town for a room and meals—I became frantic within. After a completely sleepless night, the next morning I went to the office of Dr. Baker, one of America's foremost physicians. I saw his second in command, who was sympathetic in his examination and diagnosis. I was told verbally and in writing that I was cyclothymic, meaning in psychophysical terms that my temperament was characterized by alternations of lively and depressed moods. I must acquire a more even temperament. He sent me to two psychiatrists for two sessions each and to a doctor of nervous disorders. The latter recommended a complete rest in bed for at least one month in some sanatorium for nervous diseases. I felt I could not afford it.

I telephoned Thérèse, who was visiting my mother in Demopolis, and gave her the verdict, to which I myself had no answer. My mother came to the phone and urged me to come to her big house for my rest. It was the last thing in the world I wanted. She demanded constant attention and entertainment. Together she and Thérèse went to Tuscaloosa to explain my situation to President Denny. He could not have been more understanding. He asked them to assure me that my interests would be protected absolutely. He told them that I was "invaluable to the institution" and that it would take three men to fill my place.

On passing the Fidelity Bank Building after leaving Dr. Baker, who prescribed a glass of milk after each meal, I was arrested by a sign announcing a health club on the top floor. I had never been in such a place, but I was clutching at straws. In a tremble I took the elevator. The manager was a big blond German named Roland Forelifer. The interview ended with his offering me free for a fortnight the facilities of his club, with exercises, steam baths and all.

While I was taking tests and talking with psychiatrists, I accepted his surprisingly kind offer and diligently took advantage of the services. Forelifer was my guest at lunch at the gourmet restaurant where Henry Mencken had entertained me. In my unsettled state of mind I did not want to see Mencken. Forelifer, incidentally, told me that he himself had once had a smashing nervous breakdown. Regarding his gigantic muscular size I could hardly believe it. He also told me a nephew of his had committed suicide after three sessions with my young Jewish psychiatrist. I should be on my guard, he said. Forelifer was a good psychologist himself. He advised me to eat no sugar and no meat, but this advice I disregarded after the fourth day.

Since I could not afford a sanatorium, in my quiet desperation I suddenly thought of the Shelton Martins in Peapack, New Jersey. They had a large spreading house with many bedrooms and a staff of three or four servants, besides a head gardener and a groom for their four hunters. I had spent a weekend with them after my return from Europe in 1923. I telephoned them and invited myself for a visit—"to rest my eyes." I dared not mention a nervous breakdown. They seemed delighted to have me.

Shelton met me at the nearest railway station to Peapack. I steadied myself not to reveal the state of my nerves. I was warmly welcomed at Valley Brook Farm by Charlotte. To my surprise I found that the Martins "dressed for dinner" every evening, as did the English nurse, Miss Trewin, whom they had brought from London for their adopted son, Richard. I telephoned Thérèse for my tux and all that went with the outfit. When the box came, I felt more comfortable.

Charlotte Martin had suffered from her eyes and had an elaborate set of glass prisms supposed to strengthen the eye muscles. She turned them over to me. She would often read aloud to me after dinner. One of the books she read was Stefan Zweig's *Marie Antoinette*. After the first few days I wanted outdoor work to do. So Shelton let me clean underbrush from a ravine. Then I took on the duty of feeding the turkeys and ducks, which I enjoyed. I discovered that ducks were far more intelligent than turkeys.

Some evenings I excused myself early and joined Nurse Trewin in her sitting room to listen to her radio and to talk privately of my problems and my nerves. We listened to the Tunney-Dempsey fight together. I enjoyed little Richard, who was then a charming, well-mannered boy of three. The Martins said I was a help to them entertaining their guests at dinner, since I had traveled extensively and knew many interesting people. They took me out occasionally to dine with them. At one home in nearby Gladstone I was amazed to find two Rembrandts hanging on the walls.

On the days of foxhunts I liked watching the jumps over the hedges and fences. I learned that I must never say "the dogs barked," but "the hounds gave tongue." One day I "rescued" a lady who had been thrown from her horse, brought her back through the meadows to the Martin house, gave her sherry, and telephoned her home to let her husband know that she was perfectly all right.

Day by day my nerves became steadier and my eyes gradually became more normal. I stayed with the Martins in luxurious comfort for two months.

On returning South, I tried out the efficacy of my recovery by stopping for some days at "Lang Syne," the plantation home of Julia Peterkin and her husband near Columbia, South Carolina. I had met her at the Maxwell Aleys in Connecticut on a weekend visit. She had done a book of Negro sketches called *Green Thursday,* which had received a fine critical press. Now she was correcting galleys of a novel about a plantation black man who once stood six feet four, but who contracted some strange disease that caused his toes to drop off one by one and who then suffered the amputation of both legs, and finally died. His Christian name was April, and Julia was calling her novel *Black April.* As death approached he begged her to bury him "in a man-sized box," for he had been "six feet fo', six feet fo'," he kept repeating. So she got the longest coffin she could find for him.

Julia asked me to read the last half of her galleys and make suggestions. I thought the publisher's editing had been far from perfect. In the very last chapter much new extraneous matter was introduced that took away from the impact of April's dying, which was very moving. I shook my head and said, "Oh, no!" Then with a pencil I began to delete sentences and paragraphs. At first Julia regarded my depredations on her galley sheets with some alarm and questioned my high-handed doings. But when I was done and she read it over, she exclaimed, "The Lord sent you to me!"

Wandering about the plantation I met many of the blacks who worked the land. Sister Mary, called "Si' Mai," was a splended specimen of a strapping middle-aged woman, who was not above sinning by her own code. I found her chopping wood, but she stopped to chat with me. She was to be the heroine of Mrs. Peterkin's next novel. Two years later, walking through the forest of the MacDowell Colony with Julia one afternoon, I found that she was concerned about a title. "Why not call it *Scarlet Sister Mary?*" I suggested. "You have a black and a green in your other titles." She agreed, and that was what she called the book, which won the Pulitzer Prize. Ethel Barrymore played the part in blackface, but she knew nothing about Southern Negroes, and she did not please Mrs. Peterkin. When Julia went to Columbus, Ohio, for the final rehearsals she wanted to have the production stopped. Miss Barrymore called her a bitch and pulled the heads off the two dozen pink roses Julia sent her on opening night.

Sister Mary had a daughter, born on the plantation, who had married the proprietor of a well-known Harlem night club, also raised on Lang Syne. One evening he sent his car and white chauffeur for Mrs. Peterkin at her hotel. A table for one had been prepared for her on a dais as if for a queen. The best menu and champagne were set before her. Si' Mai's daughter came to tell her how terribly her mother had behaved when she was in New York for a visit. When she first got on a subway she "screamed and hollered" the whole time until she got off. She liked nothing about Harlem or its foreign ways. "One day," the daughter said, "there was thunder and lightning, and Mama jumped up and down shouting, 'Thank God, that's somethin' Ah know.' "

One afternoon Julia took me to call on an old Negro woman called Aunt Hester. It was chilly in mid-December, but not cold. Julia thought we would be more comfortable with a fire in the old stone fireplace. So I gathered sticks and wood from the yard and Aunt Hester furnished an old newspaper. It was soon warm and cozy in the one-room cabin. We sat on three cane-bottomed chairs. After chatting about this and that, Julia said, "Aunt Hester, Mr. Strode is troubled in his mind." The old woman looked at me and said sympathetically, "Is you, honey?" Then she studied me shrewdly with her small black eyes. For a minute I thought she had gone into a trance. Then she made a pronouncement. "I see what's botherin' you. You is tryin' to move too fast." She held up the fingers of her black hand. She touched the first one and then the third with a fingertip of her other hand. "Don't try to jump from here to here by yo'self. Wait for the Lord to move you. He'll know when you is ready to go from here—to here."

Aunt Hester had said something that went beyond the skill of the two Baltimore psychiatrists. I cast my mind back to the favorite text of the wizened black preacher who carried my suitcase at York, Alabama, when I was about to enter the university: "Pray, and don't think. Because thinkin' is weakenin'."

When I left Lang Syne I felt that I had really proved my cure. I had read galley proof and my eyes had not caused me any pain. My nerves were steadier. I was returning to my patient, understanding wife with high optimism. I was ready to take on the full teaching load at the university after Christmas.

For two consecutive summers I was invited to the MacDowell Colony at Peterborough, New Hampshire, which Mrs. MacDowell had created in 1911 as a memorial to her composer husband, Edward MacDowell. No one from Alabama had been invited before. Thérèse urged me to accept because the heat in an apartment before the advent of air conditioning was not the best place for creative work. She would go to her family's summer place at Shadow Lake in the cooler atmosphere of the hills of Jefferson County.

I found arrangements for work at the Colony ideal. We were each given a one-room commodious studio located somewhere in an enchanting forest. Each cottage possessed a stone fireplace and a pile of stacked wood lay convenient to the front door. My cottage had five windows and a comfortable couch for resting. Different patrons had given the money for the construction of the varied studios, which were in most cases named after the donors. Mine was called "The Wood Cottage," though I never knew the identity of a Mr. or a Mrs. Wood. It was the farthest away from headquarters except one, which was used by Marc Blitzstein, the composer, who was creating a grand opera.

We men slept in bedrooms of a male dormitory about a quarter-mile from the MacDowell dwelling place, where we took breakfast and dinner. Hot lunches were brought out by pick-up truck and left in baskets on our doorstep.

I reveled in my first morning's walk to my studio through the woods, over paths of pine needles spongy with moss. I was fascinated by the Indian pipes, those ethereal waxy flowers that resembled something ectoplasmic. They are leafless, almost translucent blossoms, pencil thin, that grow to a height of six or seven inches out of decaying organic matter. They reminded me of congregations of miniature ghosts. The air was fresh and cool, and scented with pine. I soon had a log fire blazing. In my studio I was supremely content.

The chief luminary at the Colony was Edwin Arlington Robinson, then considered, in 1927, America's foremost poet. At dinner that first evening I took the chair at his right, left vacant for a good reason. He was deaf in his right ear. But because I had a strong voice he could hear me.

Maine-born Mr. Robinson was a large man, quiet and gentle, with bright black eyes behind his spectacles. He had already published *Merlin* and *Lancelot,* narrative poems in blank verse, and had been awarded the Pulitzer Prize in 1921 for his *Collected Poems.* He was now finishing his long poem *Tristram,* which would be a Book-of-the-Month Club selection and which would win him another Pulitzer Prize. As a young man Robinson had had a struggle with obscurity and poverty. After two years at Harvard, because President Theodore Roosevelt admired his early peoms, happily he secured for the poet a sinecure in the New York customs house. Although he went only occasionally to work, he found the job irksome. After four years he resigned the post to devote all his energies to poetry. In 1911 he spent his first summer in the congenial, creative atmosphere of the MacDowell Colony. He always stayed the full four months. He continued to return until the year of his death in 1935. Mr. Robinson was the only "cre-a-tor," as Mary, the cook, called the colonists, permitted to have his domicile in the big house, where he was allotted the master bedroom upstairs.

Among other writers who were in residence with me were Padraic Colum, the gnomelike Irish-born poet, and his red-haired Irish wife, Mary, the literary critic. My friend Julia Peterkin, mistress of the South Carolina plantation, was here, and Frances Newman, the Atlanta spinster librarian, who had just published *The Hard-Boiled Virgin,* highly praised by Mencken and James Branch Cabell. Du Bose Heyward, who had written a story of waterfront Negroes in Charleston called *Porgy,* was here with his wife, Dorothy, as collaborator in dramatizing the story for the stage. It would make a tremendous hit on Broadway, and in 1935 be made into a folk opera called *Porgy and Bess* with music by George Gershwin. Lewis Browne, the ex-rabbi, who had written two best sellers, *This Believing World* and *That Man Heine,* was a twinkly eyed wit, who would often preface a remark by quoting his immigrant English grandfather: "As my old grandfather never tired of saying, 'Vonce an Englishman, alvays an Englishman.' "

Among the composers who rose to eminence in various musical media was Aaron Copland. He had studied free composition and orchestration with Nadia Boulanger for three years in Paris, and had been soloist in his piano concerto with the Boston Symphony Orchestra under Serge Koussevitzky earlier in the year of 1927. He was to rise higher and higher in musical fame and would eventually travel widely as conductor in Europe, Russia, and the Far East.

Marc Blitzstein, who was as handsome as Copland was homely, also composed in a variety of styles and was shortly to have a grand opera produced at the Metropolitan. But his career was cut short when he was brutally murdered by unknown assailants in Martinique.

Altogether we were twenty-two residents, then the capacity for the Colony. On the whole the colonists, of widely diverse backgrounds, from Brooklyn-born Aaron Copland to South Carolinian Julia Peterkin, got along together very well indeed. There were no personality clashes. Everybody was busy with his own interests. Apparently no one left his studio until around four-thirty. Blitzstein, who worked in my part of the woods, would sometimes send word by the deliverer of lunches that he would give me tea if I would come to his studio, where he would play for me.

The only other studio I ever visited in the late afternoon was Mr. Robinson's, which was also in my neck of the woods, but closer to headquarters. The cleared ground surrounding his place was studded with chanterelle mushrooms, those pale yellow edible fungi that are trumpet-shaped and delicious. The poet had never thought to gather them. But I did delightedly with his permission. Mary, the sweet-tempered, accommodating cook, broiled them for us as side dishes. I never revealed the secret of my source of supply. But occasionally there would be enough to serve the six who happened to sit at Mr. Robinson's table.

The poet had some congenital foot trouble and he was forced to wear iron in his shoe soles. I discovered this infirmity one stormy night when I had stayed too long talking with him at the big house. Mr. Robinson insisted that I take a spare bedroom on the upper floor and not risk the half-mile walk to the dormitory in the pelting rain without a flashlight. He walked into my room in his stocking feet to see if I had made myself comfortable, and I could not help but notice his deformity. His toes bent backward and inward. He had to walk more or less on his heels. My thought went immediately to Lord Byron's club foot.

One night when Mary Colum and I had been taking a walk around ten o'clock, talking of the Irish theater, we returned to the cottage where the two married couples were accommodated to find tears streaming down Padraic's cheeks. "What on earth?" we exclaimed together. He looked up from reading Hervey Allen's *Israfel: The Life of Edgar Allan Poe.* "Poor Poe was hungry," he half sobbed. "He actually suffered from hunger." "Come with me," Mary said to me. Outside, she whispered, "Padraic is hungry himself." We walked over to the empty kitchen of the big house and made him a quick roast beef sandwich and rushed it to him. As he began to munch, his grief was assuaged, and he laid by the biography.

Thornton Wilder, who was somewhat shy, with an amiable toothy smile, came to the Colony for a brief visit. He had lived and written there the year before. His first novel, *The Cabala,* attracted some favorable attention in 1926. He had now brought along with him two sets of galleys of *The Bridge of San Luis Rey.* I was flattered that he asked me to read one set. "Please note any misspelling or dubious punctuation," he said. I found only trivial printer's errors. The book fascinated me and was beautifully constructed. I predicted a huge success. I had not yet been to Peru. But neither had Thornton. I recalled that when I was about to enter college my stepfather had suggested civil engineering and the possible romance of building bridges in Peru.

Thornton had been born in Wisconsin and received his early education in China, where his father was in the consular service. He returned to the United States at seventeen and was graduated from Yale at twenty. Then he taught French at Lawrenceville for seven years. He insisted to me that the routine of class hours was good for his creative work. He claimed that when he was not teaching he was "all at loose ends" and got little accomplished. I wondered. But his words helped reconcile me to my professor's job, which took more than a major part of my time and energy. Thornton was now an instructor at the University of Illinois. In the future he was to write a series of highly original plays, beginning with *Our Town*. He became absorbed in the theater and, incidentally, very rich. We corresponded off and on until 1970 when Thornton had serious trouble with his eyes.

Lewis Browne, the one-time rabbi, was generally considered the life of the party, though his humor was not always appreciated by the other Jewish colonists. He loved an audience, and sometimes would be carried away by his own anecdotes. One night after dinner when he was playing a casual game of billiards with Mr. Robinson, he paused to relate a story of low life in London. Two middle-aged virgins from Georgia and one from New York State were idly watching the game. Marc Blitzstein and I were standing on the other side of the table. As Browne rose to his climax he shouted, "No bloody f———g bastard is going to make a fool out of me." Robinson's mouth fell open and he dropped his cue with a clatter. Suddenly, when Browne did not get the laugh he expected, he realized the words he had used and flushed crimson. He began to stutter in the direction of the ladies, "I was sure that you wouldn't understand that Cockney slang." I picked up Robinson's cue for him, which he accepted vaguely. But the game was over. The ladies beat a decorous retreat. Browne was overcome at his gaffe and left for the men's dormitory. Blitzstein murmured something in my ear about "that jewel of a word."

At breakfast I generally sat by Frances Newman, who had a dripping sweet Southern voice that was almost a lisp. I found her comments on life and letters amusing. She had had the misfortune to be born an ugly duckling into an upper-class family of beautiful sisters and handsome brothers, leaders in Atlanta society. Frances had made a name for herself as an acidulous reviewer of books. She was an ardent admirer of H. L. Mencken. She explained the current Southern literary renaissance by saying, "We Southerners did not dream that anyone expected *us* to write, but as soon as Mr. Mencken let us know, everybody started writing from the Atlantic Seaboard to the plains of Texas."

I found Frances rather unresponsive to great poetry. She dismissed Shakespeare with a categorical: "He talks too much." And one of my favorite novelists, Joseph Conrad, she put down with "He talks too much, too."

Willa Cather, who had been with Miss Newman at the Colony the previous year, came in for strictures. In speaking of her novel *The Lost Lady,* she sniffed, "Miss Cather from Nebraska doesn't know the first thing about a lady."

Frances was eccentric in the chosen color of her clothes and the bindings of her books. They must be in two tones of fuchsia, deep pink and purple. When she went to Paris she had Patou design her frocks in those shades. I think that her distinctive clothes were to distract attention from her plain face and her mouse-colored hair. While highly controversial in her opinions, Frances's lengthy book reviews and articles always had a special cachet.

One evening at dinner my helping of carrots was somewhat skimpy. "I think," I said, "I would like some more carrots." "God knows, nobody would begrudge you a few carrots," Frances observed quickly. She took my plate out to the kitchen and brought it back replenished.

Later she would write me amusing letters and never failed to send "salutations" to my wife. She sent us a copy of her translation of *Six Moral Tales* by Jules Lafargue, that nineteenth century French symbolist poet, who was one of the first to use blank verse and who influenced Pound and Eliot. One day a satirical piece of mockery about her appeared in *Vanity Fair,* in which Miss Newman was pictured as committing suicide when she realized she was not appreciated. It was meant in fun, with only a tinge of malice. Frances was in her suite at the Algonquin when she read the article. She promptly and deliberately took an overdose of Veronal, lay down fully clothed in one of her fuchsia creations, dropped the offending copy of *Vanity Fair* on the floor, lost consciousness, and died. Sylvia Chatfield Bates, a novelist friend who had been with us at Peterborough, wrote me that she looked "as if she had just done something smart" and was almost pretty in her casket of mauve velvet.

Sometimes Mrs. MacDowell would ask some of us to her small house in the town for a buffet supper. She was an indomitable little woman with piercing black eyes and a frank smile. At an advanced age she still gave concepts to support the work of the Colony. She managed the place with sustaining skill, engaged the house servants and the gardeners, saw to it that everything reasonable was done for our comfort. She never questioned what we were writing or composing or asked what progress we were making. But she kept a wary eye on everything. She had only one rule: no studio was to be used at night for work or rendezvous. Her excuse was danger of fire; no hanky-panky was the real reason. The only cottage wired for electricity was the one with the grand piano nearest headquarters, where any of the four pianists could play for his friends.

Mrs. MacDowell gave up her life to help the "creators." For our meals and rooms we paid a nominal fee of two dollars a day. And unless both spouses were writers or composers, Mrs. MacDowell discouraged visits from the noncreative partner, even though they stayed at the local inn.

Each one was allowed to follow his inclination and predilection. One New England lady preferred not to enter the dining room for breakfast; she did not like to speak to people before she began her day's writing. So Mary would hand her a raw egg in the kitchen to swallow when she got to her studio.

In 1927–28 we were so close to the Soviet Revolution that Communism naturally came up in discussion. Marc Blitzstein seemed to favor it. But

Eva Goldbeck, the plain daughter of the beautiful Viennese creator of the title role of Franz Lehar's *Merry Widow,* stoutly declared that her principles were aristocratic. Later Eva, who was doing a stream-of-consciousness novel, and Marc, the composer, were married.

I enjoyed every hour at Peterborough. I did not accomplish as much as I would have liked. But I wrote a one-act play that was published in *Harper's Bazaar,* put into booklet form by Samuel French, and found its way into an anthology of twenty plays. I did several book reviews for Edmund Wilson at *The New Republic.* I wrote some poems that were printed in *Bookman,* the New York *Herald Tribune Books,* and *Harper's Bazaar.*

It was by strangest chance that we went to Bermuda. After Christmas of 1928 I had been sent by physicians to the mild climate of Miami Beach to recover from a virulent case of influenza that had left me collapsed. I was also having something like a nervous breakdown from overwork: teaching fifteen hours a week, directing the university's dramatics, lecturing here and there, and writing articles and book reviews for magazines. Doctors in Tuscaloosa and Birmingham had suspected tuberculosis might be imminent and urged upon me a year's stay in Arizona. But we were told that a servant was hard to come by in the Far West; Thérèse, who weighed less than a hundred pounds, would have to wash our own sheets. That was a nightmarish thought to me. Still, we reckoned on going to Arizona until I took up with a semiprofessional hobo in Miami Beach. Actually, he picked me up one balmy January night as we sat reading under the brightly lighted marquee of the Spanish Inn. He was small, with curly blond hair, and dressed smartly in expensive clothes. He appeared to be just under thirty.

We both held thick books. I had noticed him eying me several times to see the title of the volume I was reading. When at length he made out that it was a novel of Dostoevsky, he decided I was worth addressing. "I see," he volunteered, "that we share a taste for Russian literature." He held the back of his jacketed book toward me. It was Tolstoy's *Resurrection.* As he rose to come over and introduce himself, the latest copy of *The Nation* dropped to the pavement. "Do you read that?" I asked. "Occasionally," he said. I mentioned that I sometimes did book reviews for *The New Republic.* His round blue eyes widened. He had found someone worthy of his conversation.

From that evening on I saw him almost every day. We went to the beach together, to dinner at various inexpensive restaurants, and we talked hours on end. His last name was Condon. I have forgotten the first. He claimed Indiana as home, but he confessed that after high school he had made a career of hoboing. He said it was in his Irish blood. Though his father now owned a ten-room house, where he was always welcome, the old man had been a hobo in his youth. Condon had even "ridden the rails" a few times when there was nothing better and sometimes he had accepted the hospitality of hobo jungles. But, he said, he was the hitchhiking type of tramp. "I specialized in middle-aged persons who looked well-heeled. I would tell a touching story about going to Frisco to see my dear old mother. Husband or wife would often slip me a twenty-dollar bill surreptitiously and admonish me not to tell the other spouse. The woman would beam with delight and exclaim again and again, 'Won't your mother be surprised to see you!' And I would say, 'Yassum,' like a twelve-year-old."

"You see," he philosophized one evening, "life to me is a kind of joke. I cannot take being born into this ridiculous world too seriously."

Remarking his good-looking, stylish clothes, I asked, "What do you do for a living now?"

Condon grinned. "You might be embarrassed if I tell you. I am being kept by a wealthy Chicago woman. Well kept, in fact. She'll be coming down later. She's married, but her husband is near impotent. She likes my mind, she says—and my technique—and other things." He laughed, then added, "When God was giving out cock, I was really there!" It was the only "coarse" remark I ever heard Condon make.

"I do have a profession," he admitted. "I can make money whenever I need it. I am a musician. I'm good on the trumpet. I'm signed up to play with an orchestra at a debutante dance next week. I do it for kicks mostly. It amuses me to watch the gilded youth at play, with their designing mammas in the background. I have good manners, and I can stop playing and dance with some sweet young thing if she attracts me."

One day on the beach I mentioned that there was only one woman in a mile of sand that I would like to know. "Which?" Condon asked. "The one who looks like a lady." Condon glanced in four directions and spotted her quickly not far from where we were sitting on his fine terry cloth blanket. "Yes," he said; "of course." She was blond and Nordic-looking and she wore an expensive cream-colored bathing suit. She sat under a pale blue umbrella, playing idly with her little girl. I had never seen her speak with anyone on the beach. "I don't quite know how to go about meeting her," I said.

"That's easy." Condon nonchalantly got up and strolled near her. Very politely, he said that his friend had lost a quarter just about where she was sitting. The lady looked surprised, but she moved and began helping him in the search. Then I was standing there. And within half an hour serendipity had worked its odd magic directly through a hobo.

The lady had been born in Scotland, as had her husband, whose surname was Smiles. He was a grandson of Samuel Smiles, a best-selling Victorian author of inspirational books like *Self-Help, Character,* and *Thrift,* which had been widely translated. For some years her husband had been a New York jute importer.

Since I was obsessed with the dismal prospect of a year in Arizona, where my little wife would have to wash our bed sheets, Mrs. Smiles was all sympathy. "But why must you go to Arizona?" she said. "There is Bermuda, two nights by ship from New York." She and her little girl had spent the winter months there the year before. She assured me that I could get a furnished cottage by the year for about sixty dollars a month and a servant for a pound a week. The moment the words were out of her mouth, I knew that Bermuda was the answer. I wrote Thérèse that night about the high probability of Bermuda, where frost was never known, where flowers bloomed all year, where the seashore was only a short walk away from any spot on the islands. I felt I had glimpsed paradise. I wrote to the Fred Heyles, native Bermudians, whom I had known as a lad in Demopolis, when Mr. Heyle was in the lumber business. I asked about a house. Mrs. Heyle replied promptly and sent snapshots of a cottage and garden with birdbath that would be available from April to October at fifty-five dollars a month, off season. I grew stronger week by week, envisioning Bermuda.

When we gave up our apartment and stored our furniture, we sailed from New York to Bermuda. The owner of the house, a spinster, met us at the dock in a red linen dress for identification. She was the daughter of a deceased English colonel and a professional florist—without greenhouse. A steak was in the refrigerator and a full tea caddy on a shelf. The lady was staying with a friend until she left for England three days after our arrival. Masses of Dutch iris were blooming in the side garden, where, with the help of a gardener, she cultivated flowers for sale. We settled in comfortably, in peace and blessed quiet. No motorcars ran about the coral roads: they were banned by law. The sound of the sea came faintly. We had found the ideal haven. We planned a stay of months. We remained in Bermuda for three years.

The second day after our arrival Fred Heyle came in his buggy to call with his wife. They brought a sack of new potatoes, a variety of green vegetables, fresh butter, a jar of milk, and a layer cake. It was like the Old South.

In September, when our landlady returned from England, we rented "Knollwood," a pleasant cottage furnished with antiques. Taking it by the year it was priced at only sixty dollars a month. The widower owner, descended from an early eighteenth century governor, had decided to reside in England for several years. I raised our vegetables in the back garden where papaya trees flourished. My six white Leghorn hens supplied all the eggs we needed. We had a maid named Rhona from St. Kitt's who came by bicycle. Her asking wage was a pound a week, when the pound was still worth about five dollars. We had no water bill, for our water came from heaven as rain that ran over the whitewashed roof and was stored in a huge cistern beneath the house. On chilly nights we burned fragrant split cedar logs in our fireplace.

Knollwood happened to be next door to "Inwood," once the home of the beautiful Mrs. Peck of Springfield, Massachusetts, who entertained Woodrow Wilson there and earned him the dubious nickname of "Peck's Bad Boy." Inwood in our day was owned by Mrs. Peck's stepdaughter, Harriet Smither, who had furnished it handsomely. The property had originally been bought by Francis Jones in 1700. The house, constructed later, was perhaps the finest example of Bermudian eighteenth century to be found on the islands. Built of the native coral limestone, it was covered with plaster and painted pale oleander pink with black trimmings.

Our geographical situation could not have been more fortunate. Behind us on another knoll was "Woodhaven," which sloped down to our place and was divided by a stone wall two feet thick and two and a half feet high. The garden and the mansion were owned by the Misses Wood, white-haired spinsters whose father had been a Chief Justice of Burma. After receiving a formal call from the ladies, we were privileged to show the garden to friends. It was without doubt the most beautiful on the islands. Most of the formal designs were originally created by Miss Tottie, the masculine sister. Here and there a detail was copied from some European spot. The inspiration of one of the flower beds came from a similar form on the Piazza Michelangelo in Florence. A pergola in the quarry garden was suggested by one in Mentone. A balustrade with flower troughs was copied from the veranda of a Pyrenees village hotel. Many of the coral stone steps and pillars were suggested by Italian memories. The garden was constructed more or less on eight levels, descending from the dwelling on the ridge, with its superb view of the harbor, downward to the back lawn tennis court. It was full of surprises and delights, with a deep ferny grotto and a pergola which supported climbing roses and mauve passion flowers in season.

The stock market crash came in the October after our arrival and the Depression in the States was soon in full swing. Though the value of my few stocks sank to a low level none of them quite expired and I held on for recovery. In the meantime, however, dividends dropped to almost zero.

Thérèse secured a position as secretary to a lawyer and member of the Bermuda Parliament, her first and only paying job. Her hours were ten to four with about a two-hour lunch period. She walked to work or crossed the bay in a rowboat for twelve cents. Her small salary took care of our grocery bill. She would buy T-bone steaks and filet mignon at the farmer's market, where all cuts of beef were the same price. We would wrap our roasts, or "joints," as the English call them, in large papaya leaves, which contained pepsin that tendered them.

Thérèse also got at a bakery delicious fresh orange cake which we would serve guests for tea. The climax would come when we led our visitors over the wall and let them feel the enchantment of Miss Tottie's garden. Oddly assorted persons, from John Walters, part owner of the London *Times,* and the Reverend Endicott Peabody, headmaster of Groton, to Agnes Boulton

O'Neill and Lady Plunkett-Ernle-Erle-Drax, Lord Dunsany's charming sister-in-law, had tea or dinner with us.

Bermuda was an extremely sociable place. But because carriage hire was expensive and Thérèse could never learn to ride a bicycle, we rarely went to evening parties out of walking distance, unless our host kindly sent his carriage for us. I had to conserve my strength and Thérèse never cared greatly for parties. The Bermudians could not well understand my depleted health, but they could understand the stock market crash, to which they attributed my breakdown.

On one of those ineffably beautiful late April mornings that illuminate the islands, I biked from our place in Paget around the east end of the bay to Hamilton, where the ships docked. Pleasant excitement pervaded the throng that had gathered all along the quay and sidewalks to witness the "official" arrival of the new vice-admiral who was to take command of the British fleet in the Atlantic. He bore a renowned family name: Haggard. He was a nephew of that best-selling author of exotic tales of Africa, Sir H. Rider Haggard, who as a staff officer had hoisted the flag of annexation of the Transvaal in 1877. And now at eleven o'clock the admiral was scheduled to step ashore officially at the Yacht Club dock with a proper bit of British pomp, including brief speeches of welcome by the mayor of Hamilton and one or two members of Parliament.

Eager for a good stare, since I was going to write a book on Bermuda, I managed to worm my way to the front row of spectators. I found myself brushing shoulders with a tweedy, middle-size man with heavy eyebrows and spectacles. He was meticulously smoking a cigarette in a short holder. He seemed to be alone. I took him for a tourist. As I cast oblique glances at his physiognomy, I knew that I had never seen him before, yet he looked distinctly familiar. Just as the admiral's boat hove into sight, I addressed the stranger. "Do you know," I ventured, "you resemble Rudyard Kipling." The man turned and eyed me sharply, though not unpleasantly. With an amused smile he said, "I *am* Rudyard Kipling." Dumbfounded, I asked, "But what are you doing here, sir?"

He explained that he and his wife were on a cruise ship, that his wife had become ill, and when the ship called at Bermuda two days ago the doctor had put her in the hospital. "She is there now, getting good attention," Kipling said. "While she was napping, I slipped away to see this little show. I knew Rider Haggard well."

I was so excited at finding myself talking with Kipling that only in a kind of shadow play did I notice the man I had come to see step from his motorboat onto the landing to be officially greeted by the local dignitaries. Then I got a full, long look as he passed quite close to us. He was tall, about six feet two, lean and blond, with blue blue eyes. Immaculate in his stiffly starched white uniform with the discreet gold braid, he looked cool and "clean." He walked with natural, easy grace. He was not just handsome in a British manner—he was noble-looking.

Kipling murmured, "He seems perfectly cast for his role, doesn't he?" But to me the man in uniform was more than that. I felt an inexplicable attraction to him. When I got home to Knollwood, even before I told Thérèse about meeting Rudyard Kipling, I announced that I had seen a man I greatly desired to know—the new admiral of the British fleet. Thérèse smiled at my presumption. Neither of us dreamed that Sir Vernon Haggard and his lady were to become our most cherished friends in Bermuda, and that I would tour eastern England with him the first summer of his retirement and visit Lady Haggard, the widow of Rider, in Norfolk.

The brief ceremonies over at the water's edge, Mr. Kipling turned and asked me to recommend a good tobacconist. Happily, I offered to escort him to a shop I knew. I then introduced myself as a university professor on leave and told him that I lectured on Shakespeare and taught him—Kipling—in a course in the modern novel. I said that my students were amazed to learn that he had lived in Vermont for four years in the 1890's on a place inherited by his American wife. I did not mention that the rugged New Englanders were not in the least impressed by his fame, and resented his regarding Americans in general as men of a "lesser breed." I did tell him that my students found it hard to believe that he had written the first *Jungle Book* and *Kim* in Vermont.

As we made our way through the dispersing crowd, not one person recognized him. I was struck by his comparatively youthful appearance. Since he had been a "classic" for three decades and had won the Nobel Prize in 1907 (the first Britisher to be so honored), he seemed to me a phenomenon of agelessness. Though sixty-five, he looked like his newspaper photos of two decades earlier. His hair was mostly dark and his thick eyebrows showed only a scattering of white hairs. His speech was energetic, vivid, concise. His manner was surprisingly informal and cordial for a man once reputed to dislike Americans. Kipling bought a cigarette holder of imitation amber and threw his old one, heavily stained with nicotine, into a waste basket. He said he would like a carriage to return to his wife.

I found a passing Portuguese driver I knew. When Kipling asked if he could give me a lift, I told him that I lived in Paget and that the hospital was in Paget. Without a moment's hesitation I left my bike where it was parked and got into the victoria beside him. For twelve cents I would take a rowboat back from our place across the bay to Hamilton and pick up the bicycle later.

I confess I felt a thrill to be driving between flowering oleander hedges with a man who was Mark Twain's chief literary enthusiasm. In his autobiography Twain declares: "There is a man whose name and words stir me more than do any other living man's. That man is Rudyard Kipling. I know his words better than I know anyone else's books. They never grow pale to me. They keep their color; they are always fresh." He declared that he read *Kim* every year and that in this way "he could go back to India without fatigue." As a young man of twenty-four and a correspondent for an India newspaper, Kipling had crossed the United States gathering material for articles. He stopped in Elmira, New York, to interview Mark Twain, who was thirty years his senior. Kipling was then unknown except in India.

I spoke of Twain's soaring admiration and the fact that the author had made winter retreats to Bermuda when he was a widower. I told him I knew the Allen family with whom he had stayed and the little girl, Helen, who held first place in his affections. She was now in Bermuda with her English lieutenant commander husband. She had shown me the table at which she had played hearts with Mark Twain night after night. He could never sleep without his game of hearts with Helen. He virtually commanded her to sit beside him on his afternoon carriage drives. Though people had thought her the luckiest little girl in the world, she said that frankly she had found Mark Twain a "consuming, colossal old bore."

Kipling smiled with surprise, and told me that he had "stopped off" in Bermuda in 1898. He found the place "delightfully simple." He claimed that he had discovered the identical setting Shakespeare had in mind for *The Tempest*. He had written a provocative article about it in *The Spectator*. I told him that my friend Christopher Morley, who had recently spent a fortnight in Bermuda, wrote whimsically in the *Saturday Review* that he had used a copy of *The Tempest* as a guidebook.

No, Kipling said, he was not writing anything at all now. He declared that he had been "more or less loafing for nineteen years" and enjoying his house and beautiful garden in Burwash, Sussex, which he had bought in 1902. I was aware that Kipling's best work had been done before 1910. Yet he seemed so vigorous I felt that he might surely have another book in him. "Aren't you going to write one more novel?" I asked, with a persuasive intonation.

"Good heavens, no!" he exclaimed. "A novel is too much work. You have to have a beginning, a middle, and an end."

Kipling said that he was staying at "Inglewood," a private guest house in Paget East. I knew it well and passed it every time I biked into Hamilton or picked up my mail at the Paget East post office, which was set in a field of Easter lilies cultivated for export. The mansion had been built by the Triminghams, one of the foremost old families. It had once been leased to Princess Louise, Marchioness of Lorne. In 1930 it was an expensive and exclusive inn, accommodating fewer than twenty guests.

On the ride we spoke of the caliber of American Rhodes scholars. When I told him that our current scholar from Alabama had become the new golf champion at Oxford, Kipling was delighted. Apropos of something, he expressed enthusiasm for Edna Ferber's *Cimarron*. As a young man he had

154

traveled through that raw Oklahoma Territory, he said, and he thought she had captured its spirit "superlatively." And he added, "I think some of her short stories are unbeatable."

Kipling offered to drop me at my place, but I insisted on riding to the hospital with him, and then letting the driver take me home. "When I am not with my wife," he said, as he stepped out of the carriage and paid the driver, "I tell stories to the little ones in the children's ward. One red-headed boy won my heart immediately by putting me on my mettle. I offered to help him pass the time by telling him some stories. He regarded me dubiously, and challenged, 'Are you sure you know any good ones?' "

Kipling said that I might come to see him some late afternoon at Inglewood. But because of his wife's condition he could not accept any social engagements. Noting his agility when he sprang up the hospital steps, it seemed incredible that this man was already famous in 1892, the year of my birth. His first book, *Plain Tales from the Hills*, written when he was scarcely twenty, had been an instant success and gone into numerous editions. He seemed equally gifted in verse. When *Barrack Room Ballads* appeared in London in 1892, some enthusiastic reviewers accorded him the place in current British letters left vacant by the death of Tennyson that same year.

England was thrilled with Kipling's tales and light verse, not just because of his vivid depictions of soldier life in Victoria's far-flung colonies, but because of his ardent imperialism. "All for Empire" became a patriotic slogan. Kipling devoutly believed in Britain's civilizing mission to those underdeveloped nations she so handily conquered, annexed, and ruled. Americans got their most vivid impressions of India from his stories.

Returning to Knollwood I had the elated feeling that I had "seen Shelley plain." It was one of those unexpected and fortuitous happenings that seem to come by chance, for which Horace Walpole coined the word "serendipity."

I was to learn other things about this particular "immortal." I called on him one late afternoon the following week. I took him a small basket of the fine papayas which grew on a flourishing tree in our back garden. He would take half to his wife, he said gratefully. He was still anxious about her health, though he assured me she had passed the critical stage. I was surprised to find Mr. Kipling such an uxorious husband. Most of the day-light hours he spent with her—and some in the children's ward telling stories. The little red-headed boy had decided that he did know some good ones. Kipling's interest jumped to my South. He inquired about the blacks, their proportionate number. He asked how they "managed." I told him that the races got along very well together. He had not long since been in Spain, he said, where unrest was rampant, though King Alfonso XIII was personally popular. He told me a story of Primo de Rivera, whom the King, dissatisfied with the functioning of the parliamentary government, had supported in establishing a military dictatorship. The new dictator, digging into graft and corruption, discovered that one greedy official was actually drawing monthly pay as "Wet Nurse to the Orphanage."

While intensely British, Kipling was bitter against certain practices in English schools. As was the abominable custom of colonial parents, he said, he was sent from India to England at the tender age of six and "boarded out" while he attended an inferior school. Then at about twelve he was entered in a new, raw, public school in the unattractive part of Devon. A sensitive boy, he loathed the bullying and caning in vogue for centuries. He never entered a university; he returned to India at sixteen and became a journalist.

I wrote Edna Ferber about Kipling's high opinion of her work.

How good of you to write me as you did, dear Hudson Strode. Though the letter was dated July 11th, it just reached me today. It has been bouncing all over Europe.

I'm so happy to know that Kipling likes my things. I didn't dream he'd ever heard of me. It has cheered me just when I needed cheering. You know—work is going slowly and I'm in the dumps.

My regards to you; my thanks; my best wishes—

Edna Ferber

Because of his questions about the Negro in the South, I had promised to send him a copy of Julia Peterkin's highly praised novel, *Black April,* about a noble black man. I finally did. The South Carolina Gullah dialect was all but incomprehensible to him. He wrote me from Burwash, Sussex, on December 13, 1930.

I was glad to get your letter—glad, too, to know that you are staying on on the Island instead of speculating in the thrice-infernal northern climates. Ours, just now, is beyond description for villainy.

About *Black April,* I felt it would have been more comprehensible in some tongue that was outside English. It could translate into Basuto or Swahili, and come more into key, I think, to a stranger's mind. But that's merely my own notion.

I am glad you told Miss Ferber what I thought of her if it gave her pleasure. I was not kind but merely truthful.

With every good wish for your health and fortune, Believe me,

Sincerely yours,
Rudyard Kipling

Kipling died in January, 1936, just after his seventieth birthday. Fortunately, he did not live to see World War II and the dismemberment of the British Empire which he had so glorified. He was buried in Westminster Abbey.

We were invited to dine at Admiralty House, which was about three miles from Knollwood. So we had to hire a carriage. Naturally, our place cards were far down the table from the host and hostess, who sat opposite each other at the center of the long table. But after dinner, when the men joined the ladies, I was tremendously proud of Thérèse, for Admiral Haggard sought her, sat by her on a love seat, and devoted the rest of the evening to her. Later, when we went to lunch or dinner at Admiralty House, Lady Haggard would send a hand-delivered note saying "I'll send Joey to fetch you." The first time the admiral's surrey arrived to take us to luncheon, I thought "Joey" was the name of the fat sailor-driver. I pleasantly addressed him as Joey, to his wide-eyed discomfort and my own embarrassment when I finally realized that Joey was the horse.

We really became firm friends with the Haggards at their first Christmas party, with all the young officers and their girls present. Traditional English games such as musical chairs were played. I noticed Lady Haggard, who was having some temporary difficulty with her eyes, standing alone in an arched doorway looking lost, as if she were "both there and not there." She was blond, frail, shy, even fey, and, to me, altogether lovely. I went the length of the ballroom and asked her if she would care to come and sit with my wife and me while the young folk made merry. She seemed glad to be rescued. I learned that she was born a Pisces like Thérèse, and the admiral was a Scorpio like myself. It was the beginning of a very dear friendship that was to last until both the Haggards died in 1961. Thérèse and I were sometimes weekend guests at Admiralty House. Once, when I had gone to Nova Scotia, Thérèse spent a full week with the Haggards. The loveliest photograph I have of my wife was taken by the admiral at this time. She is standing ankle deep in the Atlantic Ocean, with one hand resting lightly on a tall jagged rock and the other arm outstretched, pointing out to sea.

One winter season of six months, Inwood was leased by Owen Johnson, the author of the classic Lawrenceville boys' stories and the popular serials for *Cosmopolitan,* which brought him some $125,000 each. Owen and his fifth wife, Gertrude, called Peggy, found us companionable and took us more or less under their wing. Owen had lost three wives by death, and one by divorce. We had met him before when he came for a fortnight with Charles Hanson Towne. In fact, I was Owen's agent for his six months' rental of Inwood from Harriet Smither, for which I got three hundred dollars' commission. We dined with the Johnsons at least twice a week. Owen was a gourmet from his experiences in Paris and Rome, where his father was ambassador. He had gone to France the preceding summer and selected his vintage wines. It was not expensive to send them to Bermuda for there was one uniform import tax of ten per cent on all items, from powdered milk to Scotch whisky and Irish linens. Owen entertained like a lord of the manor about every celebrity who came to Bermuda: writers, naval officers, tennis and golf champions. All the social life we desired might be had right next door.

On Sunday afternoons the Johnsons held open house. After the strangers had left and there were only about eight intimates, Owen would cook supper on a chafing dish in the dining room. While others were drinking or otherwise enjoying themselves, Thérèse, who did not drink, would stay with Owen and watch him prepare delectable dishes, which we afterward incorporated in the Strode cuisine.

Grape Bay Beach, with its crescent coral sand, which was semiprivate, was a short walk from our house. After the first year a wealthy lady, Mrs. Helen Rogers, traveled in Europe for two years and left us the key to her spreading beach house on the sea, with roofless rooms for male and female sunbathing, a large drawing room, and wide terraces looking out to the Atlantic, where whales sometimes passed.

In the library there was a book on astrology by Evangeline Adams. My best planets were in the eleventh house. My sun was in conjunction with the radical Uranus, and Saturn was in its elevation in the planet Libra. Venus was in the mid-heaven. But Jupiter in the fourth house foretold that life would become easier after my fortieth year. I looked at all this casually and it has turned out reasonably right for me.

Numerous writers were scattered about the islands, some for vacations, some for a stay of years. Hervey Allen, who lived for three years in Somerset, at the extreme western end, wrote *Anthony Adverse* there during our stay. The only prominent American writer who had owned a house was Eugene O'Neill, but after his divorce he had given Spithead to Agnes, mother of Shane and Oona. He himself never came back.

Edna Ferber had written me about the probability of finding a house for her. By luck, I did find an ideal one at $1,500 for three months beginning in January, 1931. On December 13, 1930, she wrote again uncertainly.

Dear Hudson Strode:

It is all rather horrible here, what with one thing and another, but it now looks very much as if I couldn't get away.

The house sounds divine. When I came to "a couple of acres of green sloping to Lover's Lane" and to "an excellent tennis court in the back" I broke down and sobbed like a chei-ild. Park Avenue traffic sweeps over my knees day and night, indoors and out. I command a couple of acres sloping to the Chrysler Building. And I'm losing my mind.

It was sweet of you to write.

Various members, removed and otherwise, of my family have gone smash, financially. I am paying exactly four rents (I tell you this in confidence) and so on. Another $1,500 rent, which ordinarily wouldn't, perhaps, bother me at all, looks like madness. Still, WOULDN'T it be nice for January, February, and March, when New York is no good at all.

My thanks to you. Maybe I'll send you a wild cable before this letter reaches you.

Love to Owen Johnson.

Edna Ferber

Edna did not come.

One summer young John O'Hara took the cottage catty-cornered across the road from us. He was then married to his lovely first wife, Helen, a golden-haired English beauty. For a living John did short pieces for *The New Yorker*. He was writing his first novel, *Appointment in Samara*. In my opinion it was one that he never surpassed in his prolific career. Unlike most writers on the island, who kept regular work schedules, John wrote spasmodically. At times he needed to go on discreet binges, which often lasted days. Then he would work for long hours day after day.

Sometimes John would drop over for tea and occasionally spend an evening with us, talking on our screened veranda. John did me a very special service in reconciling me to returning to my professorship at Alabama. He could not understand why I hesitated. He declared he thought it was the ideal profession. And he claimed that he himself, if he had to make a living other than by his writing, would desire it above all others. He thought professoring was "such a gentlemanly occupation"—and with routine work for only eight months of the year it was perfect. John keenly felt the lack of a college education. He had thrown away his opportunity by his own youthful misbehavior. John had a "gentleman complex." Coming from a mining town in Pennsylvania and not having a college degree, he never felt quite a gentleman. Frequenting the Stork Club and "21" and knowing how to wear his cummerbund at country clubs did not satisfy him. Nor did marrying the second time an upper-class New York girl with a Butterfield telephone exchange. But he ended his life (with his third wife, a Virginian) on a small estate within a pleasant long walk of the ivy walls of Princeton. There he liked to think of himself as an English country squire. In his last decade he forswore alcohol, wrote with steady regularity, rarely revised, and was highly successful. I envied him his ear, that genius for catching the intonations and rhythms of speech that both he and Faulkner had.

The last letter I had from O'Hara, from Pretty Brook Road, Princeton, a couple of years before his death, was characteristic and amusing, and it seemed to breathe a certain content. It was dated August 23, 1966.

Dear Hudson:

Of course I remember that summer of '31 in Paget East. I hope I did have some influence in your decision to return to the university.

My marriage to Helen lasted only two years. My next marriage lasted sixteen years, until my wife's death, and my present marriage, now in its twelfth year and going strong, would seem to argue that we are born husbands, in view of the fact that yours has lasted forty-two years (*Who's Who* is my source). My first marriage was ill-fated from the beginning, if that is not a redundancy. After the divorce we became friends, which was what we should have been. Helen died in 1953, never having remarried.

I have been back to Bermuda several times. The war—as wars have a way of doing—spoiled the Bermuda we knew. On our last two visits we stayed at Cambridge Beach, far enough away from the honky-tonk of Hamilton to retain some of the old atmosphere, but not so remote as to keep away the motorbikes. In Princeton we live three miles from the campus on land that we cleared to make way for our house. But the bulldozers are in the neighborhood.

Although I am a member of the Loyal Legion, which means that my grandfather was an officer in the Union Army, I find that in the present circumstances I am far from unsympathetic to the Southern point of view. It was vividly expressed by a cousin of my grandfather's. He was with Sherman on the March to the Sea, and when he called on his cousins to reassure them that no harm would come to them, the young woman who received him spat in his face. Family legend is incomplete: I never learned what Captain Michael O'Hara did next, but I'll bet it was something awful. I used to tell that story to relatives of my second wife, whose parents were both born in the South. They loved the spitting part. "Good for her! Served him right!" My daughter, soon to be married, is a great-granddaughter of Confederate *and* Union army officers— and couldn't care less.

All good wishes to you!

John O'Hara

The coming of the Prince of Wales and his brother George, Duke of Kent, in April, 1931, was the event of the year. Or, rather, the garden party at Government House for their Royal Highnesses was.

Bermuda had been host to several members of the royal family who had served in the British navy. The first was a son of George III, that Prince William, Duke of Clarence and Cumberland, who ascended the British throne as King William IV, and was popularly known as "the Sailor King." He had been stationed in Bermuda as a midshipman. The Duke of Kent was already well known in Bermuda, having been stationed there as a midshipman in his naval training days.

I was eager to meet this Prince of Wales, who had captured the hearts of the world with no apparent effort. The women in our neighborhood talked much of their costumes for the occasion. Some bought complete new outfits. Thérèse, who had never made a curtsy, was instructed in the middle of the road by a plump British major friend of ours, Archie Craig, who got off his bicycle in a drizzle and gave her lessons, while she curtsied holding an umbrella over her head.

Two days before the party a bulletin was sent from Government House to the invited guests announcing that the royal princes were in mourning because of the death of a great-aunt while they were at sea. The ladies were asked to dress accordingly. Gentlemen were requested to wear black bands on their hats and black ties if convenient. I had a black band dutifully affixed to my straw hat and Owen Johnson did likewise. Peggy Johnson rechose her costume, and appeared in black velvet with a black picture hat and a corsage of lilies of the valley.

We shared a carriage with the Johnsons. All the nags had been curried and groomed almost into a new identity. Carriages and harness had been polished in relays. Flags and banners dropped from balconies interlarded with flower streamers. Barges and rowboats were draped with garlands.

Just as we reached the main part of the garden on foot an official with a megaphone announced that there would be no formal presentations. Their Highnesses would stroll about and mingle with the guests. A general murmuring of disappointment and discontent arose. As we walked about greeting persons we knew, another blast from a megaphone said that the Prince of Wales had changed his mind and that he and his brother would receive guests as presented.

I was intent on inspecting the mourning attire of the brothers. To my indignation, I saw that they were both wearing dark blue pin-striped business suits, brown suede shoes, colored shirts, and multicolored neckties, either old school or regimental. Not a black armband was in evidence.

Following Owen, Thérèse curtsied gracefully as the Prince of Wales took her hand. Then I looked him in the face. He was like his photographs, but his slightly melancholy blue eyes seemed more wistful. His thirty-seven-year-old face already had lines, as if he had some secret worry. But his smile was captivating. I paused long enough to say, "It's good of you to go through with this line of presentation." He replied in a low voice, "When I looked out on the crowd I thought I couldn't. Then I recalled how many times my father had endured such ordeals."

In my brief contact with the royal presence I had a strange desire to be helpful to this man who stood near the top of the world. He looked so vulnerable that he inspired affection. He had been destiny's darling, the most glamorous symbol of the 1920's, for too long perhaps.

At one of the dinners at Admiralty House, Thérèse's dinner partner was the personable young flag lieutenant who only three days before had attended the Prince of Wales at the exclusive club where he and the Duke of Kent had stayed. The Prince, he told my wife, was animated with "terrific nervous energy." The night before his ship docked he had stayed up until after three in the morning playing on drums in the music room. The manager of the club had spent weeks devising the perfect lunch menu to please the palate of the heir to the British throne. He was in a high state of agitation for fear something might go wrong. At last lunch was ready at the precise hour. The flag lieutenant was asked to go up to the Prince's suite to escort him down to meet the hand-picked guests. And there was His Royal Highness on his bed starko with legs pumping the air as he did bicycle exercises! Taken aback, the lieutenant hesitated. He then announced that the guests were assembled, awaiting the appearance of His Royal Highness. "Oh," said the Prince, his legs still pedaling the air, "I don't really care for lunch. Please make my excuses. And do be a good fellow and slip me up a sandwich and a bottle of beer." Dismissing his escort with a cordial wave, he continued his upside-down pedaling, while the club manager was near tears and collapse with frustration.

In memory of the garden party at Government House, when my book *The Story of Bermuda* was published in 1932, I sent the Prince of Wales an inscribed copy and received a pleasant thank you. Years later, when my publishers read that the Duke of Windsor purposed to write some book on the American War Between the States, they sent him the first volumes of my biography of Jefferson Davis. They asked me to inscribe the volumes. His prompt letter of thanks of March 11, 1961, from the Waldorf-Astoria Towers, could hardly have been more gracious. I quote verbatim:

> Thank you very much for your letter of March 5 and for sending me two inscribed copies of your biography of Jefferson Davis.
>
> As a keen student of American history, and especially the War Between the States, I much look forward to reading your books, and greatly appreciate your thought in wishing me to have these two volumes.
>
> My appetite is further whetted by the fact that ten years ago a friend of mine sent me a copy of your *Timeless Mexico,* in anticipation of a visit the Duchess of Windsor and I were about to make to that fascinating country. Not only did that book contribute in great measure to my enjoyment of the trip and some understanding of the Mexican people, it also greatly enhanced my prestige with the curator of the museum of Chapultapec, who was duly impressed by my knowledge of the fabulous characters who succeeded each other on the stage of Mexico's turbulant [sic] history!
>
> Thanking you again, and with warm regards,
>
> Sincerely yours,
Edward
Duke of Windsor

In early October, 1931, our friend Owen Johnson, whose home was in Stockbridge, Massachusetts, tactfully suggested that to effect a cure for my nerves I investigate the Austen Fox Riggs Foundation in his town. He had several times spoken of it to me and now wrote that because he had made such large contributions to the charity feature of the foundation, he could get me admitted at a greatly reduced cost. Thérèse and I decided that I should give it a try. So I turned up in Stockbridge as a houseguest of the Johnsons in that blessed month of October when the New England woods turn into flaming gold. Owen had spoken to Dr. Riggs, a friend of his, and he had a place for me in the less elegant of his two large dwellings on the main street of Stockbridge. He had a staff of some four physician psychiatrists who had their offices near the Riggses' home. The man who put me through my first examinations turned out to be a Dr. James Hiden, close friend of my student Charlie Johnson, with whom Zelda Sayre had first been in love. I felt embarrassed about being in a nerve hospital and would have liked the fact kept secret. But Dr. Hiden reassured me by saying the best people had breakdowns and that Harold Ross of *The New Yorker* had just been dismissed as cured the week before my arrival.

I was given five slim green paperback books to study about nerves and about overmobilization for flight or fight. I was to recite my lesson three times a week to a psychiatrist. Shortly I was established in a comfortable room in a frame house across the street from Ellery and Sally Sedgewick, who became friends. My meals were my only expense: I paid eight dollars a day, and very good meals they were too. Our days were organized into workshop hours, two daily walks, and sessions with the psychiatrist. Lights were out at ten. I was permitted to have tea with the Johnsons and the Sedgewicks. At night the patients played cards or talked, as they were inclined. The troubles and vagaries of the guests varied. A handsome, sturdy little boy of twelve stuttered. A man who had lost his wife so grieved that he had suicidal tendencies and had to have an attendant who walked everywhere with him. An Episcopal clergyman from Philadelphia, a manic-depressive, was great fun when he was in one of his up moods, which was generally. Newton Phelps Stokes of Greenwich, Connecticut, was there with his beautiful wife, whose portrait had been painted by Sargent. I had met them in Bermuda when they took a house near our place. They were the only husband-wife patients. I later was to stay with them in an Elizabethan manor they had had dismantled and set up in Greenwich. People came and went. There were twenty residents in our house and thirty in the more elegant stone house a couple of blocks down the street.

I enjoyed the regimen from the first day. I had thought they would put me to bed for a month. Instead they had me up at seven taking a warm shower before breakfast. I was pronounced cured at the end of four weeks. It seems that subconsciously I had been fighting against a return to my professorship at Alabama, which had thoroughly exhausted me. Mrs. Ruth Swann, a rich sister-in-law of Norman Thomas, the socialist, lent me her limousine and chauffeur and I drove to Amherst College in the incomparably beautiful weather to see if my friend Stanley King, the president, had a less taxing job for me. His professors only taught nine hours. But when I learned that it took about a thousand dollars' worth of coal a year to heat one of the frame houses, I was glad to relinquish the idea of Massachusetts winters. Besides, servants were a rare commodity. And another professor gave the course in Shakespeare. And I could not give up Shakespeare.

So I departed from the Austen Fox Riggs Foundation in a healthful state of mind and body and feeling an overwhelming gratitude that my "cure" had been so pleasant and efficacious. They had tried to teach me to work when I worked, to rest when I rested, and play when I played, all in moderation.

For Christmas someone gave me a compact little diary for the year 1932. I wrote in it—occasionally. I quote a few entries:

January 25:

Lady Haggard asked if she might bring an English lady to tea. She brought Thérèse a lovely bouquet of pale pink gladioli. The Ted Robinsons also came. He was a nephew of Theodore Roosevelt, and formerly assistant secretary of the navy. His wife Helen, a Roosevelt cousin like himself, is a darling. Ted complained that he could not understand a word anybody said except myself. Lady Haggard's accent was too English for him and Thérèse's was too Southern. Ted is a show-off. One evening at a supper party at Owen Johnson's he wallowed on the floor to get attention. A British officer said to me in amazement, "Fancy, the Second Lord of the Admiralty!"

January 30:

This morning was no good for writing, so I pleasured myself reading R. L. Stevenson's Vailima letters for an hour, and then "cultivated" my garden. He, too, poor Scorpio, took to weeding for relaxation. I do not envy his South Sea Island experiences, however exotic.

Lady Haggard arrived at teatime to stay the weekend with us. The Admiral was at sea. I moved into the empty servant room and gave her mine. She brought Thérèse a basket of delicious smelling strawberries. We took her over the wall steps into Miss Tottie Wood's garden. (An article of mine about the garden with pictures had just been printed in January *Home and Field*.) Thérèse provided a fine breakfast with thick cream for the strawberries—and broiled fresh mushrooms on toast. At eleven we went down to the beach house Mrs. Rogers had left us, but it was too rainy and windy to get into swimsuits. At night we dined at the home of Mrs. Stettinius whose late husband had been a Morgan partner. She wanted us to meet her son Carrington, whom I liked so much. Built like a coal heaver, the poor fellow had just been through a nervous breakdown, because he could not make a success on his own, while his younger brother Edward is now second to Myron Taylor, head of U.S. Steel.

March 26:

In the afternoon Katherine Meriwether, from my home of Demopolis, Alabama, brought to tea Maria-Theresa, an adopted daughter of Isadora Duncan, who had been her leading dancer. She had been crushed by Isadora's death in Nice in 1927, when she was accidentally strangled by her own long scarf caught in the rear wheel of the open automobile in which she was riding. Maria-Theresa was a charming, green-eyed woman with a beautiful body. She told stories about Isadora, to whom she had been devoted. One concerned a trip by ship from Venice to Brindisi down the Adriatic. The captain gave the star his own stateroom. After a nap in the nude she came out raging, covered with welts from bedbugs. On Italy's west coast Isadora was once lying on remote sands sunning herself. A handsome young man came up out of the sea naked. Isadora was enchanted with him. She invited him to lie with her. He did and left her pregnant. She never saw him again. Maria-Theresa regarded me speculatively and remarked with a smile, "Isadora would have eaten you for breakfast."

April 30:
Again to Admiralty House for dinner. The carriage met us at the Yacht Club landing. No other guests, just family. Over the port I asked the Admiral if he would honor me by doing a foreword to my book on Bermuda, which was almost finished. He assented somewhat boyishly. But he made me promise to chuck it, if it didn't come up to the mark.

Three days later Sir Vernon bicycled over to our place with the manuscript pages. He confessed that he had burned some midnight oil over the composition. In the garden he read it aloud to me. It was just right.

The Haggards left Bermuda in May. As a parting gift Lady Haggard gave us a handsome guest book bound in brown and henna grosgrained silk. We asked the Haggards to be the first to sign. We were sad at the parting. We felt very close to them. Thérèse and Lady Haggard corresponded until the latter's death, and I visited them in Stock, Essex, in 1938. Sir Vernon and I toured eastern England in his small car. He has remained in our affections as our favorite man in the world. His framed photograph has the place of honor in the center of my studio mantel.

In June, 1932, we gave up Knollwood and returned to the United States after an absence of three years. Clare Boothe Brokaw, later married to Henry Luce, had written to inquire if she might have the refusal on our place, which friends had told her about. In my reply I said that I remembered her as a child actress of ten in *The Dummy* and I thought her the most beautiful little girl I had ever seen. Since then Clare Luce and I have exchanged cards and occasional letters for four decades. At Christmas, 1971, she sent me from Hawaii a signed photo of herself looking incredibly young and still beautiful with a lovebird perched on her right shoulder.

Quaint, inimitable little Bermuda that strung itself out in the form of a shepherd's crook! It was a blessed chance that sent us there in 1929. But that was *then*. Now, in 1973, automobiles and motorbikes do not exactly raise the coral dust, for they are geared to travel at no more than twenty-five miles an hour, but they do disturb the peace of the land. On December 20, 1945, when I returned for a visit, I arrived by overloaded flying boat—the very last to run for Pan American. I departed for New York a fortnight hence by the first Pan Am airplane. I rode in the first licensed taxi. Already Bermuda's six physicians had discreet little cars, as well as the governor and the admiral. But otherwise not much had changed in the thirteen years I had been gone from the islands. Wages had accelerated. A few ambitious young men—all scions of top families—were seeking franchises for motorcars. I stayed at Mrs. Trimingham's guesthouse, only two blocks down the hill from Knollwood, and across the street from where Kipling stayed and where Stanley King, president of Amherst, and his wife had nearly been burned alive on New Year's Eve in 1931. Mrs. Ada Trimingham, an American, a lifelong friend of Wendell Willkie, was a widow with a beautiful home, with large high tray-ceilinged bedrooms. The house went down to the edge of the bay. Like many another, it was painted a soft coral pink.

I was taking notes for a revised edition of my *Story of Bermuda,* which had already had a sixth printing. I had for my young companion Michael Keegan, who was at home on vacation from Oxford. He went on carriage drives with me to opposite ends of the islands, to Cambridge Beach in the west and to the town of St. George in the east. Nothing seemed changed. It was too soon after the war. People had become a bit older. The horses looked the same; their harnesses were the worse for wear.

I had treasured our three years in Bermuda. Now I dined with old friends, or I went to tea and sometimes lingered on into the whisky-soda hour. I attended some evening parties. I lunched at the Yacht Club. People were still riding bikes and hiring rowboats and carriages.

I prefer to remember Bermuda as it was when we lived there from 1929 to 1932. I recall a rock-walled garden, where we went to tennis teas with a few charming old couples bearing titles, a sprinkling of *jeune filles,* British officers from the garrison, a curate or two, and half a dozen spinsters, two of them given to waving ear trumpets as gaily as tennis rackets. We would sit down to an enormous tea at a table groaning with hot scones, nut bread, seed cake, date cake, and sponge cake light as a feather, which must be rendered into portions with two forks and never desecrated with a knife.

When we returned home we would linger on our veranda and watch the strange lavender glow that suffuses the landscape at twilight. As tree frogs began their evening song, down on the road we could see people starting out to formal dinner parties on their bikes—the men with the tails of their dress suits stuffed into the trouser pockets, women with chiffon skirts inadequately tucked up about them, pedaling valiantly in high-heeled slippers, the tulle about their hair giving itself rapturously to the breeze.

If the wind was northerly we would sit before a fire of fragrant, wine-colored cedar logs, I with a Scotch and soda at my elbow, a pipe and a handy jar of the best English tobacco. At the other side of the knee-high hearth my wife would be busy with some sewing. Before we turned in at ten o'clock we would take another look at the night.

In the moonlight the silver blades of the century plant by our doorstep gleamed like hoarfrost. The white roof of the apricot-colored house across the road seemed burdened with snow. The sound of the sea came vaguely. From the cottage of a Portuguese farmer drifted the muted music of a guitar. If it was February the air would be scented with freesias growing on the lawn. We would breathe agreeably—not vigorously, not too deeply— but with a leisurely sense of utter well-being. I recall an old and pleasant myth that the mind takes color from the wine of the region. We twisted the metaphor slightly and drank peace from the atmosphere.

After some visits in the East we returned to Alabama. I was glad to get in touch with students again and give them Shakespeare and English poetry and lectures in eighteenth century literature. I again found teaching exhilarating.

In November, 1932, in the midst of the Depression, when many people were going hungry, *The Story of Bermuda* was published under the imprint of the new firm of Smith and Haas. Its format was handsome. The book was bound in white "pearl essence" with a sea horse stamped in silver, and it contained seventy-five full-page illustrations by Walter Rutherford. The price was five dollars. I feared that the high figure would be prohibitive in the increasing depression. The first reviews were uniformly favorable and bordered on the enthusiastic. The New York *Post* called it "the best book about Bermuda ever published and by far the most beautiful." In the opinion of the London *Times:* "This fascinating book could scarcely have been better done."

A second printing was ordered before Christmas. *Bermuda* eventually went into eight editions in America under three different imprints: Smith and Haas, Random House, and Harcourt, Brace. For the last publisher I wrote an added chapter after a return visit in 1945. The book remained in print for more than twenty years.

With Harrison Smith's blessing I began a narrative history of Cuba on New Year's Day, 1933. I had been delighted with an earlier fortnight's visit to the island. I spent the summer of 1933 in Cuba researching and getting the feel of the island's varied strata of civilization. On the ship *Morro Castle* from New York to Havana my deck chair happened to be placed next to that of Irene Du Pont's lawyer, Luis Machado, a future ambassador to the United States. We became friends. When Thérèse came to join me for three weeks in August, Luis and his wife repeatedly entertained us and arranged strategic appointments for me. We had been in the far easternmost city of Santiago and had come back to Camagüey when the revolution to oust the corrupt President Machado (no relation of Luis) burst out in full force. We were threatened in our hotel. Soldiers were called to protect the guests. The president's magnificent home in the Havana suburbs was looted and burned, but after that ideas of vengeance simmered down. After a week's forced immurement we were able to return to Havana.

Two days before I sailed for New York, I called on Ernest Hemingway at a modest, out-of-the-way hotel, the Ambos Mundos. Herschel Brickell, the book critic of the New York *Post,* had written me to get in touch with him and had given me his address. They had known each other well in Spain when the twenty-seven-year-old Hemingway was writing *The Sun*

Also Rises. It was published in 1926 and became an instant success. *A Farewell to Arms* followed in 1929.

Hemingway was out, or pretended to be. I left a note with the room clerk, introducing myself as a friend of Brickell and saying that I had some errands to do and would return in about an hour. I was eager to see in the flesh this man who had already written two great novels. Now he was at the height of his fame and recognized as chief spokesman of the disillusioned "lost generation," in Gertrude Stein's phrase. His lucid and succinct style had made him a powerful influence on American and British fiction.

This time I was asked to come up to his room. When I knocked, the door swung open instantly. A giant confronted me. His mass filled the whole doorway. Hemingway was not only tall, but huge of girth. His face was so sunburned from his last fishing trip that his lips were swollen and blistered. He said that he was involved in getting the manuscript of a volume of short stories packaged for mailing the next day to Scribner's. "I just have time to offer you a Scotch and soda."

The manuscript was lying unwrapped on a table. "What do you think of my title, *Winner Take Nothing?*" He handed over the title page. I read the epigraph aloud:

Unlike all other forms of *lutte* or combat the conditions are that the winner shall take nothing: neither his ease, nor his pleasure, nor any notions of glory; nor, if he win far enough, shall there be any reward within himself.

I studied it for a moment. "It's great," I said, "but I'm afraid I don't know where you got it. Is it John Donne?"

"I made it up," he said, with a hint of triumph in his swollen-lip smile.

I would follow his example a few years hence when I did a travel book on Mexico, which I called *Now in Mexico,* taken from my made-up line: "Now in Mexico you will find strange paradoxes abiding under the clearest sky."

Hemingway handed me my drink. He was forced to sip his Scotch out of the left corner of his mouth and winced even so.

I looked about the large room. On the mantel were ranged eight outsize ripe avocado pears in their burnished green coats. Doubtless they had no significance, but I somehow associated them with Hemingway's self-conscious and burly masculinity.

"I don't need much sleep," the author was saying, "so I have extra hours for writing. Four hours a night are about enough for me. If there is someone I am fond of in the room with me, I may move over to the other bed." The other bed was on the far side of the room. I knew that there was no wife in residence with him, and his three sons were in schools in the United States. I think he was between his second marriage and his third, to Martha Gelhorn.

"See my lapboard there by my bed. When I wake at dawn I reach for it and prop myself against pillows and write with pencil. In that way I disturb no one."

In that moment I knew instantly that a lapboard would be my way of writing forever. I picked it up almost as if it possessed magic. Typing gave me a pain in the back of my neck. Stark Young had already suggested using a soft number one yellow pencil, but he sat at a desk to write. When I returned to Tuscaloosa I bought a lapboard of gray stained plywood cut out with a curve to fit my middle. It cost sixty-five cents. I have written all my books except the first, *The Story of Bermuda,* on the same lapboard.

Needing nine hours sleep, I would never reach for the lapboard at dawn. I would sit in a comfortable armchair and use a number one yellow pencil on Fridays and Sundays, the days I did not teach. The only time I wrote in bed was when I was recuperating from a siege of influenza before I met Hemingway. I wrote a one-act play called *The End of the Dance* on the back of a thin atlas. It won the first prize in a national contest in New York at the Waldorf Theater in 1929 and was published by Samuel French. Gertrude Lawrence later acted in it on the radio. For this play I have received royalty checks from two continents, from Vancouver, B.C., to Dublin, Ireland.

Hemingway decided that I should have another Scotch before I left. With head tilted to the side and a corner of his blistered mouth open he now managed to get the liquid down without a grimace of pain. He stressed the importance of rewriting. He told me that he did the last two pages of *Farewell to Arms* seventy-six times. He said that it was well to read over everything you had written the previous week to see how you could better it.

He also told me where I could get the best daiquiri in Cuba—from the old barman at La Floria. I rose to go, wishing him luck on *Winner Take Nothing.* "What the artist must do," he said, "is to capture the thing on the printed page so truly that the magnification will endure. That is the difference between journalism and literature. There is really very little literature." He saw me to the door, still massive and amiable, but he had smiled only once. He had many domestic problems. I liked the man. But he lived too strenuously for my temperament.

Hemingway's stunningly terse style, which he achieved by much rewriting, was to be rewarded by a Nobel Prize for Literature in 1954. He has had many worthy imitators, but none could equal either his originality or his painstaking craftsmanship. As he said to me, "nine-tenths of genius is application of the seat of the pants to a chair," or, in his special case, the seat of his pajamas to the bed sheet. In later years I heard that he preferred to type on a bookcase while standing. Hemingway had a very special kind of genius in some of his short stories and in his three best novels. He was the all odds favorite of young men, for he glorified virility and stoic courage.

I never met a man who seemed more interested in proving his virility, shooting countless wild animals in Africa, taking boxing lessons in New York, hooking big fish, and even attempting to be a bull fighter, though he was physically made all wrong for a matador. He was too thick in the middle and too wide in the hips. At The Players in New York he had a well-publicized fight with Max Eastman, who sneeringly asked him why he didn't take the false hair off his chest.

Hemingway did seem to have something of the killer's instinct. He went from bulls and lions to marlins. He bought a finca near Havana so that he could fish to his heart's content. When he had married, for a fourth time, a woman correspondent named Mary Walsh, she proved a good wife for him. She was a plain-faced little woman, but reputed to be valiant in taking care of him. The voluptuous Martha Gelhorn, his third wife, to whom he dedicated *For Whom the Bell Tolls* (1940), had divorced him soon after its publication.

Hotel Ambos Mundos
Habana

October 8, 1934

Dear Mr. Strode:
Thank you very much for your letter and the promise of the book. I will look forward very much to reading and hope it comes soon.
Will you send it to Key West, please, and mark it *hold?*
Mail is uncertain here now. And I expect to be back there inside of a month. With best wishes and much luck with the book.

Yours always,
Ernest Hemingway

Thank you for letting me see the jacket.
This has been an interesting summer here. Please remember me to the Brickells when you see them again.

On a Caribbean cruise years later, Massaguer, the Havana artist, met me at the dock. He had done the jacket for my Cuban history and also the end papers. He was now head of tourist publicity for Cuba, and had the day free.

In the late afternoon I suggested that he take me out to Hemingway's finca. Hesitating, he said that he had offended Hemingway in a caricature portrait entitled *The Old Man of the Sea.* He had portrayed him just stepping out of the water naked and fat, with a grizzly white beard, and small, shrunken genitals. Hemingway had written him that he had debased him in the eyes of his three sons. Massaguer apologized; he had really meant it only in fun. But Hemingway had hardly spoken to him since. Accompanying me, he thought he might be forgiven.

The plantation was about twelve miles from the capital in the little town of San Francisco de Paula. It consisted of thirteen acres of flower and vegetable gardens, a cow pasture, and a swimming pool. The planting was lush about the limestone villa. A young mulatto houseboy, who spoke some English, was surprised to see us at the door. He put his finger on his lips as Massaguer explained who I was. The boy looked deeply troubled. Mr. Hemingway was asleep, he said, and his wife, too. He dared not disturb them. I left my card, and wrote that I was sorry to miss him. Then we quietly withdrew. Five-thirty in the afternoon seemed too late for a normal siesta.

Then on his ranch in Idaho, after Castro had possessed Cuba, one early morning Hemingway blew his brains out with a shotgun blast. He had felt that he was going insane, and he had wanted to spare himself that degradation. His physician father had killed himself years before. And a sister committed suicide after Ernest's death.

Today Hemingway's son Patrick at forty-five teaches wildlife conservation in Tanzania's Serengeti National Park in the shadow of glittering Kilimanjaro, where his father killed antelope, waterbuck, leopard, and any other game that moved. Neither he nor his two brothers have ever had an inclination to write anything. A heavyweight, like his father, but with twinkling eyes and hearty laugh, he trains young game wardens and national park officials.

If I had to choose among my contemporaries the foremost American writer of my generation, it would be Hemingway, above Faulkner. Both possessed genius, but Hemingway is more the artist. Faulkner let the words lie on the page as they came, in unwieldy, exhaustingly long sentences, and did not bother to better them. In their best work, however, both captured a "magnification" that will endure.

When I wrote my book, I saw Cuban history as a pageant and stressed the other-worldliness of the neighbor island. I began by quoting Christopher Columbus, writing from Baraboa, on his first voyage to Cuba's shores in 1492: "A thousand tongues would not suffice to describe the things of novelty and beauty I saw, for it was like a scene of enchantment." I ended my history with President Machado's overthrow and the assumption of dictatorial powers by a bantam-size, swart top sergeant named Fulgencio Batista, a court stenographer, who, with revolver in hand and with the same suavity he assumed when taking dictation, walked into the office of the military chief-of-staff and coolly informed him that he was relieved of duty. The amazing leap of Batista to being the most powerful man in Cuba was as sudden as the rise of Mussolini. From commander-in-chief of the army he was to win the election of the presidency. But my book ended with Batista continuing to live modestly among his soldiers at Camp Columbia, where he could keep an eye on them.

The Pageant of Cuba was released in November, 1934. The first reviews sent to me by my publishers brought me a sense of peace and satisfaction. The book was given a full-page review in the New York *Herald Tribune*

Books by Hubert Herring, the Latin-American expert. He wrote: "Mr. Strode has painted a broad canvas in the brilliant colors which the subject merits. His excellent summary of the events from the victory over Spain down to the present is by all odds the best in print." But the final encomium came from an Atlanta reviewer, who said, "It is the best one-volume history I have ever read." *The Pageant* was published in England, and then translated into German by Count Carlo von Courten, and published under the title *Kamf Um Cuba*.

Harrison Smith was so pleased with the book's critical reception that he decided I might tackle a continent, South America. I had written only about islands.

So at the beginning of June in 1935 I went to New York to confer with him. Thérèse left for a summer abroad with our friend Mrs. Robert Reese of New York and Augusta. She was the widow of a noted eye specialist and Thérèse was her guest. I saw them off on a Dutch liner with only slight misgivings. And we wrote weekly letters.

For three weeks I did intensive research in the Yale Club Library and in the New York Public Library. Then I flew to Miami and thence to the continent hitherto unknown to me. I had decided to call the book "South by Thunderbird." When the Indians of Colombia saw the first airplanes streaking across the heavens they called them "thunderbirds."

I cannot precisely remember the month in which we entertained Amelia Earhart at an impromptu supper, because the guest book given to us in Bermuda in 1932 remained packed away until November, 1937. But the year was 1934. I recall that Ted Shawn, the American dancer, came for tea with three young dancers close to the time of Miss Earhart's visit. I had met him in the Berkshires where he conducted a school of the dance at Jacob's Pillow.

A friend on *The New Republic* had suggested that I call on Miss Earhart at her hotel when she came to the university to lecture. I called in the afternoon, but I was told by the clerk that she was sleeping. I left her a note asking if I could be of service to her before her evening lecture and also if she would care to come to our apartment later for a drink. I hardly expected that I would hear from her.

But I really wanted to meet this courageous young woman who had made a solo flight across the Atlantic on May 20–21, 1932. I knew something of her history. Like Charles Lindbergh, who had made the first dramatic flight in May, 1927, when he was twenty-five, Amelia Earhart came out of the Middle West. She was born in Kansas four years before the most famous aviator of all times. During World War I she served as a military nurse in Canada. And then after some years of social work in Boston she learned to fly, against the wishes of her family. In 1928 she had acquired some small fame as the first woman to cross the Atlantic; she flew in a tri-motored Fokker monoplane with two men. She married George Palmer Putnam, the publisher, in 1931, but continued her aviation career under her maiden name. Then came her triumphant solo flight over the Atlantic in 1932.

We were having a simple dinner that evening with fried chicken as the main course. Two of my advanced students were dining with us in our apartment before the Earhart lecture. Just as the cook was putting dinner on the table, the telephone rang. It was Amelia Earhart calling. She thanked me for my note. "Would you like to come by for a drink after your talk?" I asked. She said that she never drank anything stronger than buttermilk, but she would like a bit of supper, since she never ate before her lecture. When I relayed the news to Thérèse and the two guests, she swooped up from the young men's plates the choicest pieces of chicken and sent them back to the kitchen to be held in reserve for the aviatrix's supper. We had no buttermilk, and the grocery stores were closed. But one of the students said he thought he knew of a place that stayed open, so he hurried through his meal and went in search of buttermilk. He said that if we had already left for the lecture he would leave the container at the front door.

In the early 1930's Amelia Earhart took a great interest in the development of commercial aviation in the United States and that was what she was lecturing about on this night in the university auditorium. Very few people had ever flown before 1933, and her purpose was to get them over their timidity. She made a persuasive advocate. Because she was quite tall and thin and blond, everybody thought she looked like a sister to Charles Lindbergh. When she asked the audience how many had ever flown I don't think more than six hands were raised. When she asked how many would like to fly someday she did not get as enthusiastic a response as she had hoped. But she had a nice smile, and answered all the questions put to her about the future of aviation. She was flying, she said, from city to city in her own little plane.

When I went backstage to pick her up, she was talking with a girl student who begged her to take her to her next scheduled lecture stop. She finally consented, and told the girl where to be at an early morning hour. I then introduced myself.

Johnstone Parr, my student assistant, who was driving us to our apartment, whispered that he had to go all over town, but he had finally got the buttermilk. Thérèse had already gone home and was heating up the chicken and making a delectable salad to go with it. Miss Earhart was particularly delighted with the buttermilk and drank two full goblets.

She had said all she had to say about flying, but now she was eloquent in her quiet way about birth control. Her mother held a national position in some movement to stop women from bearing children they did not want.

Planned Parenthood had not come into being by that name, but her mother and she did what they could to break down the state laws against contraceptives. The sale of diaphragms and other rubber contrivances was against the law in most states, if, indeed, not in all states. The goods were sold from under the counter. Though she never raised her voice she had firm convictions that no woman should have to bear an unwanted child. It seemed almost as passionate a cause to her as the future of aviation. While she was beautifully self-contained, yet her blue eyes blazed with indignation at the thought of man's injustice.

We next heard of Amelia Earhart when in January, 1935, she made a record solo flight across the Pacific from Hawaii to California. Then in 1937, accompanied by Lieutenant Commander Fred Noonan, she attempted a round-the-world flight in a twin-engined Lockheed. After successfully negotiating more than two-thirds of the circumference of the globe, the aircraft vanished in the vicinity of Howland Island in the South Pacific on July 2. Searches went on intermittently for years, but not a scrap of floating wreckage was ever discovered. Her husband spent a small fortune in trying to find some trace of her in nearby primitive areas, but not a clue turned up. Amelia Earhart, the foremost aviatrix of all times, was lost before she had reached her thirty-ninth birthday.

Shortly after we treated the gallant Earhart to buttermilk, a friend in Birmingham sent me tickets to hear Gertrude Stein speak in the ballroom of the Tutwiler Hotel. As a publicity gimmick she announced that if there was one more than three hundred in her audience she would refuse to speak. I had never been an admirer of Miss Stein, as either a writer or a person, but curiosity won out and I went. I had been told in the Berkshires the preceding summer by people who had met her in Paris at 27 Rue de Fleurus, a mecca for expatriate writers and painters, that she had an insatiable interest in people.

She had had an unusual bringing up. Born in Allegeny, Pennsylvania, she spent her infancy in Vienna and Paris and her girlhood in Oakland, California. She studied psychology under William James at Radcliff and attended Johns Hopkins Medical School for five years. Then she moved to Paris, where Alice B. Toklas went after the great earthquake in San Francisco and became Miss Stein's secretary and lifelong companion. Stein and her brother became astute in buying paintings by artists who were later to become famous. In Paris she perhaps knew more of the best writers of her day than anyone else, for they came to her "at homes."

I had sampled some of Miss Stein's work and thought most of it made little sense, but in her first book, *Three Lives,* published in 1908, I had been most favorably impressed by "The Gentle Lena," a sympathetic history of a serving girl. In *The Autobiography of Alice B. Toklas,* ostensibly about her secretary and companion, but really about herself, she stated that in her lifetime she had met only three geniuses: Picasso, Alfred North Whitehead, the philosopher mathematician, and Gertrude Stein. This was before there was any general recognition of the quality of genius in them. A little bell rang within her when she came into their presence.

So I went to Birmingham to hear and see the fabulous Miss Stein. When she entered the ballroom there were faint gasps of surprise in the audience. She was broad and thick through the waist and hips and had a heavy masculine face with fine dark eyes. Her iron-gray hair was cropped short like a man's and brushed forward instead of back. She wore some kind of a silk blouse with a thick short woolen skirt and heavy shoes that would have looked more appropriate behind a plow than in a ballroom.

In her rambling talk she summarized some of the great writers of British and American literature in her own Stein way. I recall nothing she said until she came to a climax after a brief discussion of Henry James, when she said, "And then I came along." She tried to explain her style and suggested that it would be the literary style of the future.

In the question-and-answer period, very few got clear-cut answers. When I rose and put some question about Faulkner to her, she told me that I knew the answer to that better than she did. At last it was over, and she moved to the small staircase winding up to the mezzanine, by which she was to escape the autographs and the signing of books. I was standing by the foot of the stairs, and when she passed I said, "Miss Stein, we have the same publisher, Random House," and I added, "I met Hemingway in Havana." She paused on the first step, turned, and looked me over, then said in a low voice, "Come up to my suite." I followed one step behind her to the mezzanine. I signaled for the elevator and we made a neat escape. Miss Toklas already had the door to the corner suite on the seventh floor open and closed it quickly after we entered.

She had collected six or seven books for Gertrude Stein to sign for persons waiting in the lobby. As she signed I regarded the other woman. Miss Toklas wore a flowered chiffon sheath and the words "flat as a board" came to my mind. The most noticeable thing about her at first glance was her black mustache, which made a heavy dark smear about her upper lip. One of the ladies called the other "Lovey" and the other used "Pussy" as a tender endearment. But I cannot remember which was named which, but that is how they addressed each other and the only way. When Miss Toklas brought up a second load of books to be autographed, she asked if the author would like to come down to the lobby to say good-by again to the parents of a marine private whom she had befriended in the war. But Miss Stein said that she had given them a half-hour in the afternoon and to let the matter rest. The newspapers had played up the friendship of the two, though I think she could hardly recall the young man from among the hundreds of American soldiers she had entertained.

We settled down to desultory talk. I can remember nothing except a discussion over the eighteenth century novelist Samuel Richardson, whom Fielding satirized. To my amazement Miss Stein admired Richardson very much and had nothing but praise for *Pamela* and *Clarissa.* I said frankly that I could not stomach his sentimentality and priggishness. In the heat of our friendly argument, our chairs, which were opposite each other and set close together, inched forward until our knees were butting each other, and I backed away.

Then I took a long shot, and said that I preferred her "Gentle Lena" in *Three Lives* above everything else she had written, and to my astonishment she confessed that it was her favorite, too. That book was her first, privately published, work before she took on the eccentricities of style which made her famous. One of the persons her later style did not fool was Amy Loveman of *The Saturday Review,* who in her criticism of Miss Stein's last book dismissed it with the crushing statement, "And not worth the paper it is written on."

In my hour with Gertrude Stein I found her a woman of such great good heart that "hearty" seemed the exact word for her. She was expansively warm. But she was also shrewd, as she proved in buying up so many paintings of Picasso and Matisse, when prices were close to rock bottom. When she saw that she did not have enough talent to be known as a great writer she began to attract attention with her weird, repetitious, and seemingly nonsensical manipulation of words; her phrase, "Rose is a rose is a rose is a rose," appeared in a circle at the top of her stationery. "Though widely ridiculed and seldom enjoyed," in Edmund Wilson's phrase, she was yet an original. Among the men who attended her salon, besides Picasso and Matisse, were Clive Bell, Wyndham Lewis, and Ford Madox Ford from England; Sherwood Anderson, Ezra Pound, Ernest Hemingway, Carl Van Vechten, and Elliot Paul from America. André Gide was a frequent Parisian guest. Without any physical attraction, she had a magnetic personality that drew people to her.

When Random House published my book on South America in 1937 I asked Bennett Cerf to send Gertrude Stein a copy, and at the same time I wrote her a note thanking her for the memorable hour with her in the Birmingham hotel room after her lecture in 1934. I said I hoped that she and Miss Toklas would find time to glance through the pages of *South by Thunderbird* and find something to please them.

Then I told her that I was preparing an anthology of English lyrics for Random House, and in my introduction, with a summary of the history of lyric poetry, I was asking a dozen notable literary persons to name two or three of their favorite lyrics from the sixteenth century to A. E. Housman.

From her new address at 5 Rue Christine I soon received an undated letter with unorthodox sentence structure, paragraphing, and punctuation. I quote verbatim:

My dear Strode

Thanks for sending us the Thunderbird we both enjoyed it a lot. You did most satisfactorily make it a continent, I don't know but you did make that earth a continent more than it has ever been done and we liked your description of the Colombian ladies, we happen to know some and you made them very real, we liked your stories, in short we liked it all we really did, both of us. And now I am sorry I cannot be equally satisfactory about lyrics of the favorite variety, but alas I cannot. It is a long time since I have read any lyrics, I like any little rhyme you have some quite nice ones in the Thunder Bird, and once in a while I see a bit of poetry in a detective story and then of course I write some, but you cannot really call any of that favorite, so I do not know quite what to say to you, but that is the way it is, what can be done about it. I wish I could be more helpful, both to please you and Bennett because certainly I would like to please you both, but I have not what you might call the favorite temperament. Something excites me when I read it and then I forget about it, but anyway I did like the Thunderbird and thank you.

Gertrude Stein

I sent Bennett Cerf a copy of her letter and I underscored the lines: "You did most satisfactorily make it a continent, I don't know but you did make that earth a continent more than it has ever been done." Coming from Gertrude Stein, I thought that it was a highly original statement of praise.

In the summer of 1937 I went to Paris for one week and thought I might call on Miss Stein, but she was in the country. During World War II and the Nazi occupation Gertrude Stein was again in the country and, despite shortages, she managed very well. Though Jewish in origin, the Nazis in no way molested her. She died in 1946 in her beloved Paris, the city that she said she found always "peaceful and exciting."

The
Air
Trip
of
My
Life

IN 1935 the largest passenger plane in existence was a DC-3, with a capacity of twenty-six passengers. I made the trip around much of the green continent in that kind of airship, including a thrilling flight over the winter Andes.

From Panama to Colombia, however, I flew in a Sikorsky S-38, called a Duck, which could land on water. It had a capacity of eight. But there was only one passenger besides myself, a North Carolinian going to sell electrical train engines to the Colombians. In the six other seats were stacked perforated green cardboard crates of baby chicks hatched only three days before in Avon Park, Florida, and consigned to a man in Medellín. The agitated chicks stuck their tender jaws out of the perforations in terrified protest and in hunger. (Chicks do not have to be fed for the first three days after hatching.) Their screeches drowned the noise of the Wasp motors and penetrated the cotton with which the pilot, the radio operator, and the two passengers had stopped their ears. We took off in a downpour of rain. The cabin began to smell as if we had been stabled with elephants.

At 9:45 A.M. the Duck alighted in Colombian territory in a yellow bay near a village called Turbo. We docked at a rude float, where I and the other passenger got out to have our passports stamped. Everywhere jungle vegetation impended. Dugouts manned by half-naked blacks slithered in and out of the green portieres of bayous, as they went about their primitive business with ageless casualness. When the refueling was accomplished the crates of chicks were shifted fore and aft, and luggage and air mail and air freight were put in the empty seats. We took off toward Medellín, the city named after the birthplace of Cortez in Estremadura, and from Medellín to Bogotá, the capital, I had to take a plane of a German company. After the Pan American Duck it seemed both spacious and elegant.

I sat by a senator from Barranquilla, who said that before the recent advent of the airplane the journey from his home to Bogotá took him two to four weeks, depending on the condition of the rivers. "You took your mule or your horse with you. You bought a ticket for the animal as well as yourself. The beast traveled upriver in a flatboat lashed to the steamer and then in the mule car on the same train with you. You had to take your own bed linen and drinking water. How different now! Breakfast with my family this morning; dinner this evening in the hotel in Bogotá. In Colombia we jumped direct from muleback to flying machine!"

Bogotá is a closed-in, narrow-streeted city of gray stone, austerely colonial-Spanish in type. It stands on a plateau 8,500 feet above the sea, only five degrees north of the equator. A blast of chill mountain air whipped about the passengers as we alighted. I looked forward gratefully to the warmth of the modern hotel. Though possessing every other comfort, the new hotel, alas, had no heating system, only one enormous fireplace in the lobby. I never felt warm in my three days in Bogotá.

At Buenaventura, which I had to reach by a miserable, creaking six-hour train from Cali because there was no air service, I met Burton Holmes taking pictures for his travelogues. He had been unable to book a room in the Hotel Estanción until a Spanish ship sailed for Panama long after midnight. I was lucky enough to get the privilege of sharing one with a Rumanian who was selling clothes out of New York.

The next morning the Panagra flying boat, named *Santa Maria* after Columbus's flagship, arrived from Cristobal at 10:30. On board was John T. McCutcheon, the cartoonist of the Chicago *Tribune*, who had plunged into fame when a youngster by sending back the first detailed report of Admiral Dewey's destruction of the Spanish fleet—he had arrived at Manila Bay on a pleasure trip just as the shooting began. With him was his attractive, much younger wife, Evelyn, and their seventeen-year-old son, Shaw. Our schedules more or less coincided until Rio, where he would take the *Graf Zeppelin* for Germany and buy wild animals for the Chicago zoo. We were booked at the same hotels. The McCutcheons made delightful traveling companions, and became lasting friends.

When I learned of their exciting trip we were five thousand miles above the earth finishing luncheon with a dessert of fresh peaches and a chocolate cake, which had been baked and iced the day before in the Canal Zone some 550 miles to the north. The pilot announced that directly below us lay the island of Gorgona where Pizarro had made his epic decision and dramatically whipped out his sword and traced a thin line in the sand. "On this side lie Panama and security," he said. "On this side lie hardship, adventure, riches, Peru. Who will join me?" He stepped across the line. Few moments have been more pregnant with destiny. At length thirteen men followed the bastard swineherd turned conquistador across the line in the direction of Peru, and finally others reluctantly moved forward.

At exactly twenty-seven minutes past three the pilot sent word by the steward that we had crossed the equator at eight thousand feet. It was as cold as Bogotá. We threw topcoats about our shoulders. But instead of some thin red line like those to be found on library globes we looked down upon the shapely black shadow of the *Santa Maria* flying in the center of a full-circled rainbow like a blackbird within a ring of varicolored flames. I thought it fantastically beautiful.

At sunset the thunderbird circled over Guayaquil, the chief port and largest city of Ecuador. It had been once regarded as a pesthole, where passengers in ships had to submit to fumigation if they merely set foot on shore. But General William Crawford Gorgas, whose elderly sisters were friends of ours in Tuscaloosa, had routed yellow fever and other contagious diseases. With the Japanese sanitation engineer Naguchi, he had transformed Guayaquil into a pleasant and healthy tropical city. A bus took the passengers into the place known before Gorgas's day as "a mouth to hell."

At a corner café on the cathedral plaza I met a group of rich young Ecuadorian expatriates swept from Paris by the "witch's broom." This is a blight that courses the evergreen cacao trees like wildfire, leaving branches as if they had been done violence with a rough broom and spoiling the seed from which chocolate is extracted. These absent landlords, out of depleted purse and impending disaster, had been forced to return and take a direct interest in their country's welfare. They were beginning to adapt themselves with grace to their enforced native environment and to give the rejuvenated port an air of sophistication. Some were learning to be overseers of their own plantations. But the bachelors of Guayaquil no longer chose to live under parental roofs; they now followed the English fashion of going into "digs."

A voluble young man arrived like a sea breeze. In the course of the evening he gave me virtually my whole chapter on Ecuador. He was not a native, but the Italian-born son of a Chilean mother and a retired New England opera singer. His name was Correll. He was small, dark, sharp-featured, with eyes piercingly astute at one flash and as naïve as those of a budding genius at the next. He spoke the cosmopolitan English of the London stage. His words poured out in cascades, spurted into geysers, babbled like a brook. He himself had appeared in one of his own tragedies in the Dallas Little Theater. He posed questions and, swift as a falcon's descent, made his own answers. He discussed the petroleum industry, the fishing, the agriculture, the minerals waiting to be exploited, even the bootleg trade in shrunken human heads. He insisted on my dining with him. His praise of life under Ecuadorian skies soared. "I have lived in Italy, France, England, New York, Ohio, and Texas," he said, "but I have never known contentment until I settled in Guayaquil. There is no place where one may have so much on small resources—where the *ambiente* is so congenial to culture and charm. I am a clerk for a local business firm. My salary is fifty dollars a month. I live like a prince. You see this excellent dinner we are eating, course after course of superior Italian cooking. For board here, luncheon and dinner, I pay $9.50 a month! Imagine!

"I share a penthouse apartment with four other young bachelors—one is a direct descendant of the Borgias. A penthouse for twenty dollars a month, divided by five! Our houseboy—butler, valet, everything—costs three dollars a month. I want you to see how comfortably we live." The walk down the sleeping, arcaded streets turned out to be about ten blocks. And the penthouse was up four flights of stairs. Correll gave me a brandy, and unfurled a sheaf of manuscript of a novel he had just written. It was a story of the Galápagos Islands entitled *Sometimes the Peace Is Broken*. He began to read. I dropped off to sleep.

At two in the morning I was lighted down the treacherous staircase by flickering matches struck one after the other, and escorted back to my hotel.

The sun was not yet shining on Bolívar's birthday when we took off into the gray morning. We would not be out of sight of land now until we reached Lima.

Suddenly, sharply, as if the curtain had dropped on one act of opera and risen on a set depicting some far remote portion of the globe, the oozing Ecuadorian jungle had vanished and now the Peruvian desert stretched southward, dry as mummy dust, unmitigated, mysterious, disenchanted.

We passed over the town of Tumbes, where Pizarro first set his mailed foot on the country known as Peru. Here the conquistador was confronted by ingenuous subjects of the Inca, who almost embarrassed him by inquiring with engaging simplicity why he had not remained at home to cultivate his own soil. Gómara wrote that they did not comprehend Spanish greed: "In those early days any Spaniard, even the poorest soldier, thought the whole of Peru was little enough for himself alone."

Since there are no continuous railway lines between the river valleys of Peru, the sea is the great transportation trunk line. Unless one flies, each journey into inland Peru must be followed by a return to the Pacific Ocean before anywhere else can be reached. As trade depends on the headlands and piers, so all life in the coastal region depends upon the rivers. If there were no rivers, there would be no irrigation, no cultivated fields of cotton, no gardens, few houses, few people. Where the last thread of irrigation ditch stops, the desert assumes its old negation and creeps up to the feet of the sharp-edged Andes, under whose mauve-and-bronze-colored walls is buried the varied mineral wealth of Peru.

No matter how high the lark soars, the saying goes, he must come down to earth for his dinner. Though this is not generally true for thunderbirds, which carry their dinner with them, the plane came down through the clouds of opalescent foam and landed near the desert town of Chiclayo. Under striped canvas awnings of orange and cream stretched on the yellow sands like Arabian pavilions, the passengers enjoyed a hot meal. To have a tasty herb soup, filet of fish, breaded veal cutlet, fresh limes, and fresh green peas set before one in a wilderness was an unexpected novelty.

We made three stops between Guayaquil and Lima, where the United States ambassador, Mr. William Dearing, was at the Lima airport to meet the McCutcheons. He also whisked Burton Holmes and me straight to the embassy for tea. Among the guests was Mrs. Forbes, wife of the British ambassador, a voluble, sparkling woman, who had been an intimate friend of D. H. Lawrence. She encouraged me by declaring that first impressions were all-important, and that if one was really perceptive he did not need to spend weeks in trying to understand the life of the people.

The essence of Lima is hard to catch. The sunbaked mud walls that bordered roads between the modern seaport of Callao and the capital called to mind Biskra and the date orchards of Algeria. The cotton fields, irrigated with Andean snow, might have been those of Alabama. The suburbs where the newly married generation of well-to-do *Limeños* live in villas of mauve, green, azure, and cream, with flowering trees and fenceless lawns, recalled Southern California and the Riviera. An ancient grove of gnarled olive trees planted in 1560 might have belonged to an Italian landscape near Sorrento. Plazas, churches, and convents breathing Spain from every stone were within sight of modernistic ferroconcrete apartment houses under construction. Bakeshops and flower shops were presided over by Japanese. Before the forty-two cinemas of Lima were placarded the faces of the current Hollywood stars. While I watched a few minutes of a chukker on the polo grounds of the most luxurious country club on the continent, a new V-8 Ford passed, with three Chunchos, savages from the trans-Andean region, in the back seat, their faces streaked tribally with blood-red paint, their heads adorned with bandeaux of parrot feathers.

Like an Oriental beauty who has granted the favor of a season by lifting her veil once, the next morning Lima was muffled in mist. But no matter how dismally the capital is choked with fog, there is escape by train or car. At an elevation of almost three thousand feet, thirty miles up the Rimac Valley, lies Chosica, in perpetual sunshine and as gay with flowers as a Swiss village in summer. "There is no question about the incalculable benefits the North American engineers have conferred on this continent," said my luncheon host from the Foreign Office, who had driven me to Chosica. "Henry Meigs, a Yankee adventurer, came to Peru to escape some trouble in California. He built a railway up into the mountains and the great repository of mineral wealth. When the staggering difficulties he would face were detailed to him by the Peruvian government, he replied with cool confidence: 'Anywhere the llama goes, I can take a train.' Rising to a height of almost sixteen thousand feet, the line passes through sixty-one mountain tunnels and over forty-one bridges."

Next day, as I drove in the Panagra bus through dim dawn-lit Lima to take the plane for Arequipa, I thought that the capital, like its climate, was half-sun, half-mist. Old Lima seemed very tired; in modern Lima the brash and the new made grating music on the seasoned and traditional. It was in the throes of economic and spiritual rebirth. The nation's four or five million people of pure Indian stock munch their wads of thought-and-hunger-drugging coca leaves and aim to keep out of white man's affairs. The wealthy darlings of the nation play polo, while the less fortunate babble of Communism and paste seditious posters on church walls.

At one o'clock we landed on the brand-new airfield at Arequipa, the city that bows before three magnificent volcanoes that bear the names of El Misti, Chachani, and Pichú-Pichú. The Quechua name "Arequipa" means "Here we rest," just as "Alabama" does in another Indian tongue. Blessed with an invigorating climate of eternal early spring, Arequipa toward the end of the Spanish viceroyalty had the largest white population in South America. An antique city of oyster white under a clear blue firmament, it is all of a piece; the composite essence seemed as nicely welded as its solid architecture, which is reared from petrified volcanic ash or lava called sillar. The fact that the citizens live in walls fashioned from the fruit of volcanoes may account for a strange mercurial vitality that agitates Arequipan breasts. For its people, more virile than the *Limeños,* are quick to flare into love, quick to hate, to forgive, to ridicule, to dance, to fight, to take holy orders.

Yet I found Arequipa a haven of rest that bore out the significance of the name's meaning, largely because of Mrs. Bates's *quinta,* where she provided comfort for a limited number of paying guests, among whom had been General Pershing, Premier Venizelos of Greece, and Noel Coward, whose three admiringly inscribed photographs hung in the whisky-soda den beside priceless Inca tapestries.

Noel Coward had been so enchanted with Quinta Bates that he composed for the guest book a three-page poem in octosyllabics extolling its virtues and the character of its presiding deity. Four lines ran:

> Her name is plainly Mrs. Bates,
> (A strange capricious whim of Fate's
> To crown with such banality
> So strong a personality).

That night I slept profoundly under fawn-colored vicuña skins. Then I went up to have breakfast on the roof garden of Quinta Bates and faced the glory of El Misti. An immaculate diadem of snow crowned the volcano's serene symmetry. Rising nineteen thousand feet against a luminous sky even bluer than Sicily's above Etna, Misti seemed as near as a morning's stroll. When I finished the last crumb of my breakfast I stretched out in a deck chair and luxuriated in an abandon of relaxation. Basking in the sun's golden elixir and gazing on the extinct volcano, I felt my breathing become more equable.

From an alleyway behind the house came the strange thin music of some passing Indian playing snatches of native melody on a reed pipe. Birds sang in the topmost branches of the mimosa and eucalyptus trees. There was nothing I had to do, no important person to see, no statistics to set down in my notebook. "This," I said, "is the quintessence of contentment."

Mrs. Bates had acquired her commonplace name from her dead English husband. She had been born Anna Montieth in the New York village of Bath-on-Hudson. Her girlhood was spent in Chile, her young married life in copper-mining towns of Bolivia. A pioneer in comfort, she had mothered two generations of mining engineers, prospectors, homesick clerks. Everybody called her *Tía,* Spanish for "aunt." Famous from Cristobal to the Straits of Magellan, she was perhaps the best-known woman in the subcontinent; legends had grown up about her in her lifetime.

"How do you achieve such contentment in your guests?" I asked Tía.

"My prescription is very simple. I feed them good American food with enough native dishes to remind them they are globe-trotters. I keep the beds soft and the water hot. And I let them be at home. Misti does the rest. They go up on my roof garden to breakfast and stretch out in deck chairs and gaze at the volcano. Misti casts its spell over them."

"I hear you've been godmother to five thousand Indian babies."

"Well, perhaps a thousand or so," she conceded. "They choose me because they say I have the *bueno mano,* or lucky hand. The Indians believe it good fortune if their children die in infancy, for then they go straight to heaven, sinless. In hard reality they reckon it a blessing to escape life. Because the proportion of my godchildren who died in infancy was great, they think I have the lucky touch. As godmother I provide a tiny shroud and a wooden coffin. Sometimes the parents also ask me to furnish a yard of white ribbon, which they fasten to the baby's shroud and let it hang out of the coffin. When I first asked the reason, they said, 'Why, Tía, it is to pull the godmother up to heaven.'

"Yes, I'm coming," Mrs. Bates called to the Chinese-Indian cook, who stuck an inquiring face through a screen of vines. "She's a perfect devil, that cook. I fire and rehire her continually. We part in rages and weep on each other's necks when I take her back. She may keep me out of heaven yet. I'll need those godchildren's ribbons."

As she started away with regal tread to interview the cook, she turned to say, "Francisco is your room boy. Look on him as your personal valet. There are no bells. He's supposed to anticipate your wishes. Join me for an appetizer before luncheon in my little get-together room."

"An amazing woman! She has imperial stuff in her." An attorney from Lima had joined me, and we watched Mrs. Bates walk away. "Half of Arequipa comes to her for advice. Her head is as full of sense as her heart is of kindness.

"Her husband deserted her," the lawyer went on, "and twenty years later asked her to take him back to die. She built a little house for him over there in the corner behind those pomegranate trees and nursed him until he died." He looked at his watch. "I must go to an office in the city. Would you care to accompany me?"

Out of Quinta's double gate we walked right into a herd of fourteen llamas, driven by their Indian owner and his boy. It was my first sight of a llama. Part sheep, part camel, with faces like pretty, inquisitive spinsters, the animals stepped shyly but precisely. Their alert pointed ears, standing perpetually erect, were pierced for the adornment of gay colored tufts of dyed yarn. On their backs they bore panniers of charcoal. They were not all dun-colored: two were smoke blue and three were dusty salmon pink. At the sight of strangers they sidled to the other side of the street and whined like newborn babies, the only sound they can make. Their master whistled to them soothingly. By various soft whistlings he directs them. The llamas are the gentlest of beasts. No one would dream of whipping one, and no one dares to overload them. At the master's whisperlike whistle the llamas turned left toward the marketplace. We watched these fascinating little brothers of the camels with their docile, virginal eyes, full of wonder. They stretched their erect heads on elongated necks five or six feet from the ground. "Like ascetic astronomers the beasts are most content when nearest to the unencumbered stars," the lawyer said. "And like the Indians of the high plateau, llamas thrive on privation, dieting on the scant grass of cold climates in rarefied air. The lushness of coastal valleys brings both of them to ruin. Between the Indian and the llama a mystic bond exists. The beast bears the Indian's burden, his wool furnishes material for the master's poncho, his dried dung provides fuel. In times of famine, his flesh saves the family from starvation. When the llama passes into the realms of ceased labor, the Indian holds communion with the beast's spirit by making music on a flute fashioned from his friend's thigh bone."

Two days later, as I left for the airport, on the veranda of Quinta Bates I bent over my hostess's hand and raised it to my lips. "It was worth journeying to South America just to meet you, Tía," I said.

"God bless you!" she responded. "I'll burn a candle for you." She put into my hands a small antique dish of hammered bronze about four inches in diameter and an inch high. "It is from the period of the Incas," she said. "There are few such artifacts left." The dish, which I was to use for the next three decades as an ashtray, was in a small chamois sack. Halfway down the stairs I turned and said, "Noel Coward expressed it too neatly in doggerel for me to try to thank you in inspired words. But that is the way we all feel.

Of every place I've been to yet
This I leave with most regret."

Shaped like a wavy two-edged sword, Chile extends nearly three thousand miles from the tropics to the glacial archipelago of Cape Horn. A fellow traveler remarked that if laid across the face of Europe the Chilean sword would reach from Portugal to Moscow. "Like ancient Gaul," he explained, "Chile is divided into three parts: the northern desert, with the nitrates, copper, and iodine; the dense southern forest with its fjords and lakes and volcanoes, where it rains thirteen months of the year; and the delightful central valley, with its fertile soil and well-ordered rainfall, where most of the people live."

A dozen persons had told me that I would like the Chileans best of all the South American people: "They have the most natural charm, they are alert, they are engaging." I heard everywhere that the women have more freedom and that no combination of blood and temperament is more attractive than the union of an Englishman with a Chilean woman.

After Rio de Janeiro, Santiago is famed for the most thrilling setting of any city in the Western Hemisphere. My eyes turned straightway to the icy heights of the Andes that glistened like a wall of fretted crystal against an azure sky. As we got into the airways bus, the purser, whose name, I learned, was Jorge Elliott, remarked to me, "Even the incomparable Rio hasn't the Andes." This bright-eyed Elliott was the well-connected offspring of an English father and a Chilean mother. He flew every other day and on his off days he devoted himself to being my guide, introduced me to his attractive young friends, and took me into their homes.

The next afternoon I was taken to the races by a handsome young man with green eyes, gold hair, and a ready smile. He was some minor official with Panagra. His name was Alberto Fox and he spoke with an English inflection learned from British masters in his private school. But he had never been out of Chile and insistently claimed to be Chilean.

Though it never goes to freezing in Santiago except on the coldest midnights in July, enormous braziers of loose woven metalwork stood breast-high on iron legs and glowed with red-hot coals before the parimutuel booths. Like the pious pausing within a cathedral's entrance before a holy-water basin, devotees of the race track stopped to warm their hands at the brazier fire.

Once inside I stopped and gazed. Before me lay the world's most beautiful racecourse, backed by the stupendous panorama of the Andes drenched in snow. Those thrilling heights might have been the grandstand of the gods, where they had set their white lacquer pavilions to watch the sport of kings and men.

My host gently nudged me out of my naïve ecstasy with the small end of his field glasses. On the marble terrace at the foot of the grandstand other basket braziers glowed with live coals. But these were only knee-high. Smartly dressed women stood in circles around the braziers like gypsies about a campfire and pulled up their tight skirts a couple of inches, holding their shapely legs to the rosy glow and twisting their Parisian shoes on their high-arched Spanish feet this way and that.

Since we could not get near the braziers, we moved among the crowd. I was introduced to race horse owners, diplomats, copper mine officials, and a number of charming ladies. I met two Philadelphians who had flown down for the salmon fishing, bringing their equipment, rubber boats and all.

One afternoon Elliott took me and Jack Buchanan, a young alpinist who was planning to ski over the Andes, to tea at the home of a widow who lived in the last villa in Santiago before one reached the real countryside.

Buchanan, who, like Fox, had never been out of Chile, was a fresh-colored, muscular young man of medium height with deep blue eyes and wavy brown hair. He radiated exuberant health and good humor. He had the well-bred assurance of the English and the spontaneous charm of the Latin. And when he smiled broadly, he revealed a more perfect set of white teeth than any native Britisher ever possessed.

Elliott volunteered the information that Jack's uncle was the head of the Buchanan clan in Scotland and worth a cool million. "The old man saw Jack's picture in a London paper about his being the champion alpinist in South America and wrote him. Jack was the first to climb Cerro Plomo just last year. The old boy sent him the latest and best mountain-climbing outfit."

Before we arrived at the villa I had some misgivings. I had pictured a grave, sallow dowager in black crepe. We were greeted by a charming birdlike woman with a laugh like the tinkle of champagne glasses touching in a toast. She wore topaz-colored velvet which prettily offset her burnished-gold hair. Here was the same piquant nose, the creamy complexion, the slightly mocking and amused eyebrows of the Chilean women I had seen at the races. Her two daughters, eighteen and seventeen years old, one fair, one dark, were dressed for a dinner dance to which their nineteen-year-old brother, an engineering student, was taking them later.

The son got out his guitar. Buchanan had brought along his mandolin. They played together and Elliott sang native songs for my benefit. During tea the atmosphere was far more lively and unrestrained than I had known in any other Spanish-blooded family. It gave the stranger a direct pleasurable kind of self-appreciation.

After tea the widow led me over to a bookcase. On either side hung a small landscape in oils. "Which do you like better?" she asked. "They are both done by one of our best artists." I indicated the vivid autumn-colored one of a boating party on a stream.

"That is Chile in autumn." She called her son to lift it off the wall. "I want you to take it home so that you will not forget Chile soon."

"But I can't possibly take your painting!" I protested.

"I can have another painted. You can't," she said gaily, touching a flaming match to the stick of gold sealing wax and affixing her calling card on the back of the picture. As the butler brought paper and string I continued to protest vigorously and called on the others to aid me in pleading the rightness of my refusal. The lady, sweetly ignoring my objections, wrapped the picture.

"I'm really overwhelmed," I said, genuinely touched. "I shall be careful not to admire this lovely eighteenth century cabinet."

I was whisked into the music room to be introduced to the *cueca,* a Chilean dance done with a pocket handkerchief. The widow sat at the piano. Her son played the mandolin. Buchanan and the fair daughter began to dance. The girl was shy at first. "Very proud. Very proud!" Buchanan coached her, as he strutted like a cock and put on the airs of a peasant who set high value on his own worth. There was much bowing and swift changing of step and tempo and fluttering of handkerchiefs. On the man's part it required great agility of leg muscles.

The young folks urged their mother to dance. The brunette daughter played the piano. The widow and Buchanan danced with spirit and finish, as if they had practiced together for weeks. The lady was properly hesitant, disdainful, coy, until at last her femininity was conquered by the male.

"Bravo!" the audience applauded. The widow laughed and held out her hand to me. "Now you must try!"

But I begged off.

"The Señora taught it to the Prince of Wales in twenty minutes," Elliott volunteered.

"Would you sign our guest book?" the lady asked.

"I am flattered," I said with a slight bow.

The dark girl left us for a moment. She brought the book, which was bound in turquoise leather. Bending over the hall table I tried out my fountain pen on an old envelope. I opened the book and found the last page that had been written on. I stared at the signature, read it again.

"Really?" I asked, glancing up questioningly.

"Yes, he was brought out to our house. That's when Mother taught him the *cueca.*"

In a large heavy black scrawl the Prince of Wales had written:

Lady—
I am at your service
    Edward P.

"Where is your picture?" the lady called, as we all started to the door.

I opened my topcoat, touched the wrapped painting, which I had put under my left arm to protect it from the rain that had begun to fall. "You see," I said with a grateful smile, "I have Chile close to my heart."

"Until the airplane we were the most isolated country on this side of the world," Buchanan was saying, as we dined that night on lobsters flown in from the island of San Juan Fernandez, 360 miles out in the Pacific. It was there that the real Robinson Crusoe, Alexander Selkirk, lived for some years after surviving shipwreck. His story, told by Daniel Defoe, was to make the author an immortal.

"When Chileans started flying it was the ambition of many to be the first
to fly over the Andes. One man after another lost his life, until the government forbade the attempt. But in 1918 a young lieutenant named Godoy made it to Mendoza in Argentina in a plane snitched from the army. The populace went wild with excitement. But the army chiefs did not know whether to court-martial him for disobedience or to proclaim him a national hero. Because the adventure was not subsidized his heroism got little publicity. Mind you, this was nine years before Lindbergh crossed the Atlantic."

I did like the Chileans enormously. I found them the most natural, the frankest, the most infectiously optimistic of all Latin Americans I had met. But beneath their charming, affable exteriors I sensed something dangerous that commanded discreet respect. As John McCutcheon surmised, "The Chilean character might be likened to the nation's commodity, nitrate. It depends on how you handle it."

The past thirty-odd days of air travel was like the prelude to a glorious love affair. The climax would be reached on this morning when I flew over the Andes.

Two planes were flying because treacherous weather in the mountains had canceled Tuesday's flight. But today the weather was propitious. I was in luck, for my young friend Elliott was the purser of our plane. He told me about Gregorio Nemsoff, a husky young Russian giant and a naturalized Argentinian, who lived in a hut built forty feet beyond the Chilean border. His was the first South American radio station that could communicate with airplanes in flight as well as with airports. He would often spend half the night clinging perilously to his ropes along edges of precipices, noting the direction and intensity of the wind, and then flashing his reports. If Nemsoff said the plane should not fly, the plane did not leave the ground.

Like two silver dragonflies just alighted on a green pool, the two Douglases were lined up one behind the other, their twin propellers twirling, their motors making harmonious thunder. The first plane filled, and was off and away.

Ten minutes later the *Santa Lucia* passengers chose their seats. Before and behind me sat young scientists with Ph.D. degrees, one from Columbia University and one from Copenhagen. They had their laps full of tubes and pumps, charts and diagrams. They had been sent by some international scientific organization to study the effect of altitude on human beings. They asked me to serve as guinea pig. Before I realized it, we were in the air, apparently headed for Aconcagua.

With celerity we climbed until we reached an altitude of fifteen thousand feet. At the scientists' request I removed my jacket and they recorded my blood pressure. A quarter of an hour after takeoff the *Santa Lucia* passed high over the foothills of the Cordilleras. Then at some invisible demarcation the plane swerved to the right as naturally as if it were turning down a hedged country lane. In another minute we had entered the stupendous gap in the high mountains known as the Pass. I demanded to be unstrapped, and walked up the aisle to the front seat on the left, the only one vacant.

The glory of Aconcagua on our left seemed as close as a New York skyscraper seen from the tip of the Battery. Everywhere was eternal whiteness—the blue tinctured whiteness of ice and diamonds, with subtle shadows of aquamarine and sapphire that shifted enchantingly before the vast crystal alcoves. Thousands of feet below the gallery's pavement was the purplish color of wet violets.

Elliott came up to me and pointed out peaks and promontories, called them by name, enumerated their respective altitudes. It was as if one were applying geography to a mystical vision of the poet Blake. The Chilean Indians say that only on the crest of the Andes can one talk with God. This corridor of carved crystal through which we tore like the west wind might have been the approach to heaven's throne. On either side of us chalky pencils of cathedral spires wrote Andean choruses on the fresh morning's azure slate. And directly in front of us the sun god, hurling gold-feathered darts of light, rose to greet the thunderbird.

Though we could not catch a glimpse of the plane that had taken off before we did, the captain knew exactly where it was. Elliott showed me on the map the spot where the other plane was at the moment. "The respective radio operators keep in constant touch with each other, giving exact positions by squares on the map of the charted territory. Most persons have the idea that the Pass is a narrow way. As you see, it's miles wide."

I looked down on land where no man had set foot, where so small a proportion of the world's people would ever set eye. It was exciting to breathe in such an age when the most ordinary of mortals was privileged to act a part that ancient seers imagined in their most extravagant dreams.

Elliott touched my arm and I went back to my seat for a better view of the famous Christ we were approaching on the right. Beneath, like a figurine in ivory, was a gigantic statue of the Lord, His right hand raised in benediction. His left grasping a cross that extended high above his head. In the shadow of the lonely Christ stood the diminutive stone hut of Nemsoff, who sent the weather reports. There, companioned only by howling pumas and mountain lions, with cyclonic winds often thundering mad symphonies, the young giant lived in Olympian isolation, controlling, with his fingertips and voice, the transcontinental movements of mail and men.

Captain Disher circled the statue and the station for the passengers' second view.

"Often magazines and bundles of newspapers are tossed from planes to brighten Nemsoff's monotonous routine," Elliott said. "And on days when no planes are scheduled to fly, he will radio that he is signing off to go down to the village 'to get a haircut.' The receiving operators in Santiago and Mendoza grin and call out into the offices: 'Nemsoff has gone for a haircut.' Everybody knows he has gone to some woman."

"What is that other house?" I asked, noticing another simple structure.

"That is the new meteorological station the Argentine government is constructing, so the Russian will no longer be entirely alone."

I strained my eyes, hoping to catch sight of this modern messenger of the gods, whose word about flying conditions airport managers and pilots heeded like the word of a deity. But the only thing stirring was the airplane's shadow, which passed like a phantom over the invisible boundary of Chile.

These hanging gardens of crystal, these blue canyons and white promontories were no different in quality from the ones we had passed. But on the map they proclaimed allegiance to Argentina. The thunderbird flew among the tempting treacheries as serenely as a dragonfly passing among clumps of white pitcher plants in a meadow brook.

Finally our plane tore away from the enchantment and we passed over a savage undulating plain with tight dry bushes and cactus growing in rocky aridity. Rusty condors flapped their huge wings above granite boulders. Below lay Uspallata, where San Martín and his liberty-seeking men began their historic climb over a way twice as perilous as that Napoleon had negotiated in the Alps.

I took one last look back at the supreme majesty of Aconcagua, now forty miles behind. It lay serene against the blue velvet of the sky, like an exhibition jewel in a showcase. Then it vanished from sight like a conjurer's trick and the plane dropped completely away from the mystery and glory.

In a state of semi-intoxication I sat back and let the two scientists put me through some quick co-ordination tests. They had me mark horizontal and vertical lines in the white checkerboard spaces on specimen paper within an allotted minute to test the effect of the altitude on my brain functioning.

When I looked out the window again we were hovering over the city of Mendoza, which reposed in the midst of irrigated vineyards 2,500 feet above sea level. The whole trip had consumed only one hour of time. As I set foot on earth I knew that never in life could any hour of travel hold so much for me.

While we were held up waiting for a fog to lift in Buenos Aires, Elliott gave some of us a brief lesson in geography. "Whereas Chile's shape resembles a long sword, Argentina's may be likened to a plowshare, the point toward the South Pole. The southern portion, Patagonia, is cold and arid, but excellent for sheep raising. The treeless, grassy pampas makes up the principal area. It is ironic that the first settlers hopefully named the land Argentina, since no silver mine has ever been discovered."

The Argentino sent to meet me at the Buenos Aires airport was sandy-haired, ruddy-skinned, and bore the name of Alberto Williams. He had been born in Argentina of British parents and thought of himself as a loyal son of his father's adopted country and not as an Englishman. "Argentina has one very concrete reason for her cordiality to England," he explained while we had a cup of tea in the Hotel Plaza, where I had booked a room. "The countries are economically complementary. For half a century now the United Kingdom has been our leading customer by a large margin. Nine-tenths of our exports are meat and agricultural products, which Britain desires. We need England's hardware and woolen goods.

"The railroad and refrigeration were the twin fairy godmothers that made poor Argentina rich. Formerly, when cattle were slaughtered for their hides, most of the meat was left to rot in the sun. Now the live cattle are sent by railway to the port of Buenos Aires, slaughtered hygienically, and preserved in ice. Only toward the end of the last century did Argentina begin her meteoric rise in world trade. British cattlemen began bringing over their blooded bulls to improve the Creole stock. Spanish and Italian immigrants arrived to work the wheat fields as sharecroppers. At the end of a few years they possessed fortunes equal to those of the richest citizen in their native villages."

Williams finished his tea and lit a cigarette.

"Argentina is almost entirely a white country," he went on. "The colonists pursued the policy of exterminating the nomadic Indians rather than eventual assimilation. Not more than a handful of the descendants of the aborigines are in the bleaker remote parts of Patagonia. We have no Negroes. Seventy-five per cent of the present population is of European descent, mostly Spanish and Italian, born in Argentina. The British community, including those of British blood, numbers about fifty thousand. By the way," he said, as he rose to leave, "I have an invitation for you to visit a great *estancia* on the day after tomorrow. Don Leonardo Periera is a delightful gentleman of the old school and an absolute autocrat. His bulls have won more blue ribbons than those of any other herder in Argentina. I would be glad to pick you up at nine. I think you will find it interesting to visit one of our cattle ranches." I accepted with enthusiasm.

In the meantime I had a good look at the city. Buenos Aires is undoubtedly a handsome capital. Resplendent boulevards are magnificent in conception. Elegantly groomed avenues of French châteaux with pretentious gateways and liveried doormen might seem to lead to the Arc de Triomphe were it not for the tropical palms, the jacarandas, and the pungent eucalyptus trees. The city superlatively evidences what man can make out of an unattractive site. Buenos Aires stands hardly thirty feet above high-water mark on a flat alluvial plain, with none of the natural beauty of Santiago, Lima, or Bogotá. Although obviously too new, too elaborate and showy, the general effect is certainly neither raw nor harsh. The city simply lacks mellow charm.

From my hotel window I again contemplated the piled stones, the lavish planting, the fountains, and the madding crowd that made Buenos Aires a great world capital. My first morning left me impressed but somewhat disconcerted at the bigness, the opulence, the smart newness, the high prices. I could not comfortably adjust to the *palazzos* in endless repetition, the streams of motorcars, the queues of businessmen with tense Chicago Loop expressions on their handsome Latin faces.

Buenos Aires, I thought, must be the most unfortunate city in the world for the not-well-to-do. To be able to sit down on a plane of equality with the millionaires in the Jockey Club, the most expensive club in the world for members, was the be-all and end-all of many an Argentino's ambition. I thought of Oscar Wilde's definition of a cynic: one who knows the price of everything and the value of nothing.

When I returned from an afternoon drive with the McCutcheons, I walked into the bathroom, drew a glass of water from the tap, and drank it, something I would not have done at that time in any West Coast hotel. No city in South America has a better or more up-to-date water supply and sewerage system. Indeed, Buenos Aires in 1935 possessed all the modern amenities and comforts: first class hotels and shops, first class opera, newspapers, race tracks, night clubs; first class physicians, prostitutes, polo ponies. I thought of the island of Tigre, a beautiful spot with its pennant-strung yachts and boating parties, its satin-smooth green lawns, and the famous Hurlingham athletic club, ultra-British in appointments and atmosphere. Perhaps no other materialistic capital offered its citizens more diversion in their diligent pursuit of wealth. Buenos Aires had just about everything except a sense of contentment.

Within forty miles of Buenos Aires lay the country seat of Don Leonardo Periera, with its 25,000 acres of park and grazing meadows. The don, with one of his sons and his Scottish overseer, was at the gate of the two-mile avenue of magnolias leading to his house, to meet me and Señor Williams. Out of a car hopped a bandy-legged little man with a white Vandyke beard. Not more than five feet tall, he wore riding breeches and a flapping Burberry raincoat that stopped at his knees. In one hand he carried a gold-headed stick and in the other a camera. With lively affability he greeted us and presented Simon, his quiet-mannered son, and then his overseer. Williams and I got into the back seat with Don Leonardo. We entered a seemingly endless pasture. The overseer at the wheel dashed in and out among the herds as if he had been a gaucho on horseback. The bulls lifted thick-necked heads, regarded the car with only mild resentment, switched their tails disdainfully. The cows looked up placid-eyed, turned their rumps to us, and went on grazing. They were all magnificent creatures, sleek and heavily padded with meat. The breed was Hereford, roan with white spots.

"They look very gentle," I commented. "Even the bulls."

"Ah, yes, they make 'quiet beef,' " Don Leonardo said. "We breed for tender quality of the meat as well as for weight. I prefer Herefords above all other cattle. Herefords have won me many championships. I have sold prize bulls for as much as $25,000 at auction. Here, Simon, you must take our picture with the herd in the background."

We left the car and posed for photographs. I asked if the surplus milk was used for buttermaking.

"Yes, now we are going into dairy farming as an alternate to beef production. In early summer our grasses are so succulent that we produce finer butter than the most delicately flavored product of Normandy."

I whirled about as the old gentleman pointed excitedly. An ostrich that had sprung up out of nowhere went tearing across the plain. "We keep one for curiosity. Ostriches eat the partridge eggs. We prefer partridges to plumes. We have some fields for the partridges fenced off so that the cattle can't disturb the grass. The birds like long grass in which"—he hesitated for the right English word—"to condense themselves. You North Americans eat Argentine partridges in your fine restaurants. The United States won't buy our beef—no, but you take our partridges."

"But we raise almost all the meat we can use," I said in courteous defense.

Back in the car we drove over hundreds of other acres. The two houses of Don Leonardo's sisters were almost a mile apart. The first house was a reproduction of a seventeenth century Touraine château. Such an elaborate and uncharacteristic structure on the pampas was like beholding a mirage. The second sister's house was a small palace lifted out of Seville. We drove through a park so lovely that it might have been in England. Don Leonardo explained that when his grandfather bought this acreage a century earlier, it possessed not a single tree. The palms, camphor trees, magnolias, mimosas, oaks, English copper beeches, and rare specimens from Madeira and South Africa had all been imported.

I saw the stables, worthy of old-time Moscovite princes. I was taken to the tiled swimming pool, where Don Leonardo's seventeen grandchildren splashed on Sundays. "The little boys at one hour," he explained, "and the little girls at another." We stopped briefly at the *estancia*'s church, where the families and servants worship regularly and a priest comes out weekly to hear confessions. Don Leonardo walked up to the altar rail and unaffectedly knelt to thank the deity for His bounty. Watching the old man say his brief prayer I thought he must be one of the happiest men in the world with such earthly possessions and with no one to question his absolute monarchy, not even his Moorish prejudice that rigorously segregated the sexes in childhood.

In the great drawing room of his own Italianate villa, where sherry and *pâté de fois gras* sandwiches were set out to refresh us, I had the uncanny sensation of being watched—perhaps the ladies of the house stealing a glance at the foreigner. Then, looking high up along the maroon walls, as if expecting secret windows such as had once made me nervous in a Muslim's house in Tunis, I realized it was the bulls' eyes. The fixed glassy orbs of a dozen regal bulls glared at me from oil paintings. On metal strips hanging from the base of their gilded frames dangled their distinguished records, with dates of blue ribbon awards and championships. The first Hereford had won the Grand Prize in 1896.

In the dining room hundreds of mementos attested to the superiority of Don Leonardo's bulls. The great room was crammed with objects in silver like the hold of a sixteenth century pirate ship returning from the sack of a city. Urns, pedestals, punch bowls, and platters lined the walls in cabinets ten feet high. The dining room windows were barred like the Bank of England and clamorous burglar alarms had been installed. Ten years before, during the family's absence in Europe, a gang of burglars had cleaned out the silver trophies. Those I now gazed on were prizes at fairs in the last decade.

When we went down the magnolia drive to our car Don Leonardo's horse, tethered to an omu tree, whinnied. We went over to speak to him. "I am in the saddle ten hours a day," the old man boasted. "Not bad for seventy, eh? Come back and we'll ride over the plain together and you can better get acquainted with our pampas."

"Would you lend me your horse?" I asked, stroking the slender neck of the handsome animal.

"I will lend you one just as good—perhaps better. Two things an Argentino won't lend: his horse and his wife." He laughed. "But"—he made a gracious Spanish gesture with his strong-fingered little hand—"the rest of my *estancia* is at your command."

After lunch at the Swift Golf Club we drove to the freezing works located on a deep-water canal. "Argentina's chilled beef is unrivaled," Williams claimed. "It is carried to the European markets at a temperature only two or three degrees below freezing and arrives with all the juice and flavor preserved."

The door of the *frigorifico* was open. A blast of chill air swept out. Attendants slipped white cover-all apron coats over our topcoats. Like medical students about to observe an operation, we walked down the corridor. A troop of señoritas dressed like nurses were separating the sweetbreads and chitterlings and tripe, potting meats, canning tongues, making sausage, and putting in glass containers the concoctions that brighten delicatessen shop windows.

A guide motioned us into the refrigeration room. The heavy insulated door closed behind us. I blinked at the uncanny monochrome in coral. A rosy glow from electric illumination was playing on the pink flanks of hundreds of vibrating beef-halves, jiggling upside down on their iron hooks two feet apart. Like dancers trooping up one by one before a ballet master for criticism they paused automatically before a solemn-faced inspector, who put an indelible stamp on flesh after appraising its quality and color. They passed over a section of cable that recorded their weights to the ounce. At last their nakedness was covered in white stockinet and finally swathed in hessian cloth made of hemp and jute. After a twenty-four-hour rest on ice the halves would be gathered up in great nets and then lowered by crane down into the cold depths of a ship's hold.

The night before I flew to Montevideo I was a guest at a dinner party at the Plaza. Fourteen sat at a round table. The lady on my right was the daughter-in-law of former President Uruburo, and very lovely. She was white-throated and delicate-featured, with soft dark hair. The host had told me she was not only beautiful but also highly intelligent.

"Oh, but you are missing the real soul of Argentina not to have stayed a night on the pampas!" she was saying in a modulated voice that was gently ecstatic. "The effect of the purple light that suffuses everything at evening is unlike anything else in the world."

"I have read about it," I said.

"But even W. H. Hudson couldn't describe it. Its essence is incomprehensible. It is uplifting and moving and yet profoundly sad." The look in her beautiful dark violet eyes seemed to bring the pampas at evening closer.

"You don't mind foreigners commenting on a strain of melancholy in the national character?"

"But why? It's so obviously there. Perhaps it's the nostalgia for the lands of our ancestors still embedded in us."

"What are you?"

"A little Spanish, more Italian, and part English."

"What do you feel you are, inside you? Italian?" There was a delicate molding of brow and a gentle harmony of feature and fragrance of disposition that matured in highborn women under Italian skies. But I guessed wrong.

She smiled, shook her head, and confessed forthrightly, "I feel as English as roast beef. My maiden name was Green."

The orchestra was playing a tango, slow, pulsing, tender, melancholy. "I had never realized that the tango is sad. It almost weeps."

"But of course. It's something like your Negro blues, with a difference.

The tango is the swan song of the gaucho, of romance and guitars, of chivalry on the purple plains."

In the tango the Mediterranean and the pampas met and fused at the turn of the century. Paris added sophistication to the primitive music and made it fashionable at *thé dansants* just before World War I. But the tango remains communal and ubiquitous. It belongs equally to the upper crust, the bourgeoisie, the slums, the brothels. It is played here, there, and everywhere.

"Listen," the lady said. "Hear how plaintive and memory-haunting the music is? One dances to relieve the heart of regret and longing."

"Where our women relieve the heart in nerve sanatoriums," I suggested, "you Argentinos dance the tango."

Smiling, she replied, "Our lives are much less complicated."

"I think security must be the most prized possession of the Latin-American woman."

"I'm afraid it is. And it isn't entirely admirable."

When Darwin paused at Montevideo in 1831 during the famous *Beagle* expedition he recognized the inhabitants as "a much finer set than at Rio de Janeiro." He commented on the men's "handsome expressive faces and their athletic figures." The people still reflect the climate's stimulation in their strong supple bodies and their sanguine countenances. In 1885, W. H. Hudson called the gallant little nation the "perfect republic." In social reform it has been its own guinea pig. Since 1877 it has had compulsory and free elementary education. It was the first Latin country to divorce church and state, the first to establish a minimum wage law, an eight-hour working day, and old-age pensions. Uruguay was the first South American republic to legalize divorce. It was also the first to give legal status to illegitimate children. And it is the only country in the hemisphere to compel adults to vote and to fine them for *not* voting. Franklin D. Roosevelt got many of his ideas for social welfare from Uruguay.

Like Argentina, Uruguay is exclusively a white man's country. Its stock is predominantly Spanish; largely, the industrious, honest Basque, with the physique and vigor that came from the Pyrenees. Even the sophisticated city people of Montevideo have the look of the out-of-doors stamped upon them.

As pleasant and homey and "progressive" as Montevideo was, there was really little of interest that could not be visited in two days. There were no ruined temples, no splendid cathedrals, no picturesque but sad coca-chewing Indians.

I went with a Mr. Morse of Armour Packing Company while he bought beef at a cattle auction on the bare terrain marked with scores of hillocks. The gauchos on their swift horses were the fences. To each herd were two or three gauchos, enveloped in windblown ponchos that fluttered like great wings behind them. On their heads they all wore Basque berets. With set expressions on their strong faces and eyes flamingly intent on the business of keeping their herds intact and separated from other herds, they looked like creatures from another planet. With their dashes and whirls and intangible circumferences they made their own corrals and shifted the cattle about over the grassless expanse for the buyer's convenience.

The color of the fringed ponchos surprised me. I expected bold, vivid colors, or sober browns. But these steel-muscled, iron-jawed men affected ethereal pastel shades. Their ponchos were primrose, champagne, soft lilac, absinthe-in-water, or palest virginal blue. And they were not of rough blanket material, but woven of expensive cashmere wool.

"I don't see any mares," I remarked.

"A gaucho would as soon be caught pushing a perambulator as riding a mare. Uruguayans have mingled scorn and respect for their female animals. Mares are treated much like harem ladies. They spend their lives plucking at clover and frolicking with their colts in green pastures and breeding in season. Their feminine flanks have never felt the goad of *nazarenos.*"

"What are *nazarenos?*"

"Those vicious spurs. The cowboys made up the name, reminiscent of Christ's crown of thorns."

After the auction was over and all the cattle sold, we went for coffee into a big barnlike café, where the atmosphere smelt heartily of leather, tobacco, ammonia, and masculinity. Gauchos were lined up on benches, sucking their yerba maté tea through silver quills out of hand-painted earthenware pots which they always carry with them. Busboys circulated with pots of boiling water. They would pour the water into the little pots, which the cowboys had stuffed with maté leaves.

I learned that yerba maté and mutton are the chief country diet. A peon's family is allowed fifty to a hundred sheep a year for his table, depending on the number of his children. Gauchos eat about four and a half pounds of mutton a day. The maté contains several vitamins, aids the digestion, and has a mucilaginous substance soothing to the throat. It is fine for the nervous system.

Strangely, my most vivid remembrance of Montevideo has nothing to do with its four hundred varieties of roses or the profusion of bougainvillaea that cascades over walls and flat roofs in a riot of magenta blossoms, but rather with the phenomenal sunset that I saw with the buyer for Armour's. The afterglow of the setting sun drenched the city's towers and the heavens with the colors of crème de menthe, absinthe, and aquamarine. In late October, 1922, from the Pincio Gardens, I had seen the dome of St. Peter's suffused in an unearthly green light, luminous as that of a firefly at first dark. And here in Montevideo in August, 1935, I beheld a second green sunset. I have never seen another.

My thoughts turned from this superb quarter-of-an-hour phenomenon to Rio de Janeiro, which, I had been told, is the ultimate in worldly beauty.

After an overnight stop in Pôrto Alegre, a city settled by Germans, our seaplane raced to reach Rio's harbor by sunset. Faintly, as if breaking through gossamer, the wavering southern silhouette of the Twin Brothers, forty miles distant, began to solidify. To the east the unstable Atlantic stretched like a continent of variegated jade. Far to the west, suffused in dusty rose color, great mountains turned their stupendous backs on Rio and stalked off toward the Brazilian jungle. Beyond the Twin Brothers the jagged peak called The Hunchback rose two thousand feet straight out of a residential district. On its summit a heroic Christ became white gold under the sun's last alchemic flare.

As the thunderbird approached its resting place, Guanabara Bay gleamed like a lake of quicksilver. Its seventy humped islands became violet-colored sea monsters, gathered for some mythological convocation. The famous Sugar Loaf Mountain reared precipitously out of the sea, like a wandering polar iceberg changed to porphyry by the tropical air.

Looking down upon the city itself spreading over seventy square miles I noted that its plan possessed little of the formal checkerboard geometry of other Latin municipalities. Its sugar-white beaches, its rocky points and spurs rushed unrestrained into various inlets and bays and made capricious outlines of new moons and butterflies. Mountains smothered in tropical luxuriance tumbled into the heart of the city, terminated shopping streets, or stepped boldly into the ocean. Orange-colored crags formed the back terraces of gardens. Rainbow-tinted villas perched on precipices like eagles' aeries. Double rows of royal palms paraded for blocks on end up avenues. The licorice-and-cream-colored sidewalks, formed of small rounded stones set in whirling patterns, were fairy-tale concoctions laid out to lure children. Such fantastic harmonies of mountain and sea, of fashionable bathing beaches and jungle wildness, of French baroque architecture and quay-ganging ships flying pennants of all nations were as unreal as a fantastic dream. Rio de Janeiro was almost beyond credibility. Like Xanadu it seemed a fabulous city created in a romantic's imagination.

I was able to get a front room at the Hotel Gloria facing the sea and the palm-bordered esplanade called the Avenida Beira Mar, often called the most beautiful drive in the world. And to crown my luck I could present a letter given me by Winthrop Scott, American chargé in Santiago, to his friend James Miller, head of the United Press in South America. The Millers were temporarily staying in the Gloria while their apartment was being redecorated. He presented me to his wife, a beautiful Brazilian, born Rosalina Lisboa, a bluestocking and an ardent patriot, who belonged to the old Portuguese aristocracy but was now a liberal in politics. Her complexion was white as milk, her eyes and hair as black as a Nuit de Noël bottle. She was that mythical *femme du monde* that one reads about, inoffensively sophisticated, completely feminine without a trace of hardness, poised and vivacious, charming and shrewd.

The Millers were to sweep my way for me: introduce me to the people I needed to meet, take me to tea at the foreign offices, to receptions. And on my last evening in Rio they gave a dinner party for twenty-four.

When I awoke at dawn, I still felt as if Rio was a place I had dreamed. I reached for my dressing gown and went to the window. The incredible harbor was there right enough—but the glamour of strangeness had not ended with the sunset and moonlight. Framed by my balcony window was the monochrome of the mercury-colored bay. The islands, now streaked with tarnished silver, were watching a boat race practice. Slashing blades of a hundred rowing sculls engraved the burnished breastplate of the bay. From afar came the barked orders of the Brazilian coxes in Portuguese.

I drew the blinds closed, went back to bed, and awoke three hours later to bird song. A fleet of birdcages had been strung across the adjoining balcony, and a chorus of canaries was greeting the ecstasy of the winter sunshine. Down on the avenue the stream of motorcars was punctuated haphazardly by bronzed men in swimming trunks crossing the street on their way to Flamenco Beach.

At luncheon, Rosalina offered a quick summation of her country's history while she peeled a dessert orange for me in the "proper Brazilian way." That the city of Rio de Janeiro should have been named River of January was due to a mistake of the explorer de Solis, who took the harbor to be a river's mouth when he dropped anchor there on a hot New Year's Day in 1516. The year 1727 might be called the real birthday of Brazil's life, for in that year diamonds were discovered and the first coffee plants set out. Then sudden glory was thrust upon Rio in 1808 by a left-handed gesture of Napoleon when he reached out to grasp Portugal. Leaving an empty shell in Lisbon for the Corsican conqueror, King John VI departed for Brazil with his valuables, his regal trappings, and "four hundred of Portugal's noble families" and their retainers. They sailed in eight battleships and forty merchant vessels, and were conveyed across the Atlantic under the protection of Great Britain. In the new colonial capital John set up an old-world court overnight. Under the title of "King of Portugal, Brazil, and Algarve," he built palaces, imported royal palms, laid out gardens, and invited the world's merchant ships to come and trade. As the opulent earth yielded quantities of coffee, sugar, timber, gold, and diamonds, foundations of great fortunes were laid. Magnificence and munificence became commonplaces in the gala doings of society.

In 1821 the king returned to the mother country at the behest of parliament. He left his popular twenty-one-year-old son as regent. When Portugal became irksomely oppressive to her prize colony, the following year the young prince uttered the cry of freedom at Ypiranga and denounced Portuguese domination. The people proclaimed him Emperor Pedro I.

At the very time the neighboring Spanish-American colonies were setting up republics, Brazil chose to be an empire. Nine years later the monarch abdicated quietly in favor of his five-year-old son, who subsequently became Emperor Pedro II and held his throne until November 15, 1889. This reign of over half a century, comparable in length to those of Louis XIV and Victoria, was one of the most benevolent, shrewd, and peaceful in history. The empire fell at last, because the abolition of Negro slavery in 1888, which Pedro favored, ruined the great planters. Brazil's behavior in both her social and her governmental upheavals was remarkable. Freeing the blacks and the exile of the royal family were accomplished without the loss of a drop of blood. "The empire fell in 1889," Rosalina said, "because it was too democratic. The republic fell in 1932 because it was too imperialistic. While the politicians in power spread corruption and crime, the boys and girls of my generation who fought for liberal ideals did not have time to be young. But we won with Vargas in 1932, and the real patriots, who do not love their own pocketbooks foremost, trust Vargas, who, incidentally, is the best friend of the United States.

"My great-grandmother, now ninety-four," Rosalina went on, "was a reigning beauty in those glamorous days of empire. When she said good-by to the emperor and empress she put on mourning and refused to go out for the next thirty-two years. In 1920 the old lady donned her bonnet and went to the harbor to receive the bodies of the emperor and empress, brought back for burial in Brazil. She hobbled behind the royal biers to the cathedral, along with other members of that fading circle, who appear like wraiths at funerals in their own exclusive set and like wraiths scatter after a brief appearance, either to musty riches or musty poverty."

Rosalina said that when she told her great-grandmother that she was going to marry a North American the old lady was horrified. "Marry a boxer!" she indignantly protested. She thought of all Americans as prize fighters. She had got the idea firmly fixed in her mind at the time of the Dempsey-Tunney fight, when her great-grandsons chattered about the championship. She refused to meet the bridegroom or go to the wedding. At last curiosity got the better of her and she asked to see this James Miller, head of the United Press in South America. She received him alone and had a long interview. At the end her eyes were atwinkle. Smiling like a shy girl, she confessed to Rosalina, "My dear, if I had to do it all over again I might marry an American myself."

On Copacabana Beach, where the local aristocrats play with the *haut monde* of Argentina, come for a winter vacation, I baked myself in the sun and cooled myself in the green surf. The sight of the golden bodies of women and bronze bodies of men tossing feathered handballs or offering themselves in voluptuous Latin languor to the sun was an eye-feast for epicures.

"What is responsible for this change in the Brazilian figure?" I asked

James. "Any book about Brazil up to 1930 says the women grow fat at twenty-five. Look, they are superb!"

Rosalina smiled thoughtfully and answered for him. "Some say *Harper's Bazaar* and *Vogue* are responsible for the change. Others say it is the introduction of sports for women. But the Prince of Wales deserves the credit."

"The Prince of Wales!" I reiterated, amazed.

Both the Millers laughed. "Yes, really. Six or seven years ago sea bathing and beach life were virtually nonexistent. We bathed at Deauville and Nice, but never in Rio. The established hours of bathing here were six to eight in the morning. Bath costumes were still hideous, like those of your nineties. Even a man whose suit was cut out too low in the back was liable to arrest. And as for a woman—" Rosalina's eyebrows elevated. "But one morning on this very Copacabana Beach Prince Edward, wanting more sun on his slender frame, unloosed his shoulder straps and dropped his top. Rio gasped. The law was thunderstruck. But the daring young men of our military school politely imitated the royal gesture and defied arrest. Fashion capitulated. If we were to show our figures something had to be done. Men rushed to gymnasiums. A troup of Swedish masseurs and masseuses was cabled for. Ladies who had never sat a horse took to riding before breakfast. Diet became the watchword. Private tennis courts were laid out in every garden. Husbands and wives engaged trainers to come for an hour each day and put them through exercises. Away went superflous flesh in chin, abdomen, and hips. Bathing kits became scanty and smart. Rio took up the cult of the body beautiful. Within four years a miraculous result was achieved. That is the simple story of our regeneration. And we owe it to the Prince of Wales."

James Miller took a day off to drive me to Petrópolis, the mountain resort where the Emperor Pedro II had held his summer court. Rosalina was writing a novel called *This Latin Blood* and begged off. The drive took us winding about peaks and precipices of sheer beauty, where nature was at its most dynamic and bountiful. Vegetation crowded every square foot of flat surface in exotic abundance. Unfamiliar flowers of mauve, orange, and scarlet packed the space of a single acre tight as squares of needlepoint in varicolored wools. From grotesque crannies crystal cascades gushed in jagged courses, spraying gigantic ferns.

Petrópolis reminded me of a Swiss village set down in the midst of palace gardens. Don Pedro created the town in 1845. He imported three thousand Swiss and German middle-class immigrants to inspire the lax and carefree Brazilians. A many-bridged canal split the shaded shopping street down the middle. Before villas stood the fragrant frangipanis with their cream-colored blossoms and "shower of gold" trees with gilded clusters drooping like wisteria. In the emperor's garden the freesias and tuberoses were in bloom. But instead of an imperial court wandering on the scented paths, schoolboys were in recess, for the summer palace had been transformed into a state school. The one-time glamour of Petrópolis was only an echo.

We lunched on a long veranda overhanging a precipice and overlooking miles of astounding beauty. All serious conversation in Rio seemed to end in gazing on the picturesque.

No fashionable dinner in Rio begins before nine-thirty. An invitation might even read "Dinner at ten," but never "Dinner at eight." The Millers took me with them to the affair they were giving at the Copacabana grill. Since I had brought along only my tuxedo, Rosalina had written the men requesting "black tie." The evening of the dinner Rosalina was demurely radiant in flame taffeta. She wore ivory-colored sandals without hose, her toenails tinted ruby. At dinner I was to meet seventeen scions of old Portuguese aristocracy. The other guests included President Vargas's daughter and his brother-in-law, and the golden-haired wife of a Danish diplomat.

"I am putting you next to a woman noted even in Paris for her elegance," Rosalina said, as she began to arrange place cards at a long table in the dining room. "She is a dear friend of mine and a political enemy. Her husband is the leading coffee king of São Paulo. He inherited a truly marvelous *fazenda*. So in politics the couple is ultra-conservative. Opposite you will be the woman a visiting maharajah pronounced the most beautiful and fascinating lady in the hemisphere."

By five minutes past ten all but one of the dinner guests had arrived. Cocktails had been served in an anteroom. I found myself with the lady the maharajah had admired so extravagantly. Tall and slender, her complexion darker than that of the other ladies present, she was quite beautiful. She was dressed in amber velvet. When she smiled, a radiance hung about her. Her voice was low, gentle, and stirring.

"Tell me, secretly," I said to her, "how do you Brazilians manage to wait so late for your dinner. Do you slip into the pantry and nibble on something before coming?"

She laughed. "Well, this evening I did have a large glass of milk about eight o'clock."

"I want to know something else. Seriously, how does a Brazilian lady of fashion spend her day?" She smiled and hesitated, as if I were making game of her. "They live much in the sun: riding, tennis, the beach." "But it rained all day. How, for instance, did you spend this particular day?" "Well, because it rained," she confessed, almost deprecatingly, "I spent most of the day in bed. I read Paris newspapers in the morning, Morgan's *The Fountain* in the afternoon. Later I told Portuguese bedtime stories to my little boy. Then I had a session with my masseuse. At eight I drank a large glass of milk, and I did eat one buttered muffin. Then I began leisurely to dress." She laughed a self-accusing little laugh, as if to say, "There is the portrait of a useless, idle woman—what do you think now?"

We turned to the others as the last guest arrived at ten-thirty. James looked at the clock and visibly scowled. The girl, a last-year's debutante of the family of the Count of Estrella, was dressed in shimmering white. She was so thin that she seemed transparent as she floated up the broad staircase. No explanation for her tardiness to the hostess, merely a wan greeting and a rather dreamy acknowledgment of introductions. Her complexion was the pallor of alabaster, her hair, palest gold. The irises of her enormous eyes were the blue of Chinese forget-me-nots. She, too, was pure Brazilian but more like the embodiment of one of Edgar Allan Poe's ethereal heroines.

At the long table in the center of the grill the twenty-four place cards rested against a bank of mauve orchids a foot thick and running the entire length of the board. The lady from São Paulo at my left looked like a Russian aristocrat and wore diamonds fit for a queen with as fresh a grace as a Devon lass wears spring flowers. Her hair was piled serenely in braided coils. Her complexion was a smooth rich cream. She told me that she and her husband spent half of each year abroad. Oh, yes, she did find Paris a bit more "sustaining" than Brazil, she said, as we got up to dance.

For all the smartness of the Brazilian women I could detect no hardness in their sophistication. They had a charm of manner to remind the world that a modern woman could be a woman and a lady at the same time.

Later, in my room my brain still danced with the champagne and the music and my good fortune in meeting the Millers and having them like me. I went to the balcony for a draft of fresh trade wind and a last look at the enchanting bay. The cathedral clock struck two. As if it had been a signal that the dream was ended, I kicked off my pumps, threw open my suitcase, and began to pack. At dawn I would begin my flight back to the routine realities on the northern side of the equator.

At the airport Brazilian blue swallows, disturbed by the transport activities, made scrawls against the night's slate, like blue neon lights loosed from their tubes. As the seaplane rose from the dark water just before the dawn, like a lover bidding farewell I looked down for a last time on Rio's voluptuous curves outlined by the incandescent night lamps. As one sometimes feels in a down-plunging elevator that he has left a physical part of himself on an upper floor, I felt I had left a vital bit of my heart in Rio.

The blackness of the night metamorphosing into day changed the landscape to purple. And as the powerful wings bore the seaplane higher above the bay's bizarre islands, the color lightened in the east to that of the orchids banked upon last night's dinner table.

The last thought I had before I drifted off to sleep was that Rio de

Janeiro held within its encircling mountains samples of everything beautiful this world could offer except stalactites and snow and volcanic flame.

I returned directly to Alabama to prepare for the fall term and to be there to meet Thérèse when she arrived from her luxurious trip to Holland, Germany, Italy, and France. She arrived two days after I did. I soon set to work to digest a continent, as it were. I had statistics to look up and report accurately. Thérèse helped me with research in the university library and she did the typing. But I wrote spontaneously according to my impressions. If I got dull or long-winded my wife did not fail to make her objections clear. I seemed to need four drafts of every chapter.

One criterion I had followed in my South American venture: I always traveled expectantly. Every place I visited was like a surprise package to be opened, and I untied strings with high expectations. Framed on a wall of our apartment was a piece of parchment with an illuminated quotation from Robert Louis Stevenson: "To travel hopefully is better than to arrive." So I traveled every hopefully, but in the arrivals I often found my high expectations exceeded the realities. And I traveled with an open mind. I left my prejudices behind. I recalled an old Spanish proverb: "He who would bring home the wealth of the Indies must carry the Indies with him."

South by Thunderbird was published in the fall of 1937 by Random House, into which the firm of Smith and Haas had merged. Bennett Cerf advertised me as "a modern Magellan." The book turned out to be my most popular seller. All over the country the reviews were excellent. Donald Adams, editor of the New York *Times Book Review,* who had recently been on some mission to South America, reviewed the book enthusiastically. The Chicago *Daily News* declared: *"South by Thunderbird* is unquestionably the best book on modern South America." Even *La Prensa* in Buenos Aires gave me a glowing review and said I had a remarkable understanding of the Argentino's character, although I had been critical of the country's compelling materialism. When the book was published in England by Hamish Hamilton, Huge Walpole wrote that it was "as alive a book as I can remember." The work was translated into Swedish under the imprint of Lars Hökerberg and handsomely reviewed in *Svenska Dagbladet* by Prince Wilhelm, the writing son of King Gustaf V and a renowned world traveler.

So Thérèse and I were highly gratified with the results. And I reflected how pleasant it was to get paid in royalties and salary for work that was my joy to do: to write of foreign travel and to teach Shakespeare and English poetry, modern drama and the modern novel.

In September, 1936, a shy girl named Harriet Hassell, born on a farm on the Watermelon Road in Northport across the Black Warrior River from Tuscaloosa, urged me to permit students in my writing class to do a novel. I said I did not think novel writing could be taught, but she was so eager that I was willing to give it a try.

The course was listed as "fiction writing," and I allowed five of my fourteen students (the enrollment limit) to work on novels as a diversion. They read aloud in class what they had written and thus they had the advantage of criticism from thirteen students of varied backgrounds, as well as my own. This procedure was anathema to Martha Foley in her course at Columbia, but I found it highly practical. The class met three morning hours a week and for a three-hour session on Monday night. Harriet Hassell won the *Story Magazine* first prize in a national contest with the first story she wrote in my class. It was called "History of the South." When she got a letter of congratulation and a check from Whit Burnett, she telephoned me promptly in exuberant excitement. Then she really plunged on with her novel. It was a family story built around her indomitable farmer grandmother, who sometimes peddled vegetables from a horse and buggy on the streets of Tuscaloosa. The old lady had named Harriet's father as heir to her eight hundred acres. And the other sons had managed to have her declared insane and incarcerated in the State Asylum in Tuscaloosa. The novel contained both passionate hatred and lyrical beauty.

Ed Aswell, editor-in-chief of Harper's, came to visit my class on a scouting trip, and took some two hundred pages of the manuscript of *Rachel's Children* off with him. Within a fortnight he offered Harriet a contract. Then he sent a first check for $250 against royalties. Harriet was inspired to push on to completion with intense concentration.

When I sailed to England in the summer of 1937 I took along Harriet Hassell's manuscript, as well as my own *South by Thunderbird*.

In London, on hunch, I sold *Rachel's Children* to the first publisher I offered it to: Peter Davies, godson of Sir James Barrie, who left him most of his fortune. Davies got the novel quickly into print, and *Rachel's Children* came out in London before it did in New York. Harper's did not release the book until April, 1938.

The reviews in the New York *Times Book Review* and *Herald Tribune Books* were close to raves. Franklin D. Roosevelt's *Public Papers* got the front page review in the *Times,* but Harriet Hassell was reviewed on page two by Katherine Woods. "Miss Hassell has had the courage to attack two of the oldest and most difficult problems in life and literature," Miss Woods wrote, "and the skill to carry through her attack with force and originality, as well as passion and sincerity and thought." Rose Feld in *Herald Tribune Books* said that it was "a work of profundity and excellence. Coming from a pen of a young woman of twenty-six it demands evaluation upon the use of the word 'genius.' " Harriet dedicated her novel to my wife and me. The book went into five printings at Harper's.

I took *South by Thunderbird* to Victor Gollancz, who, I was told, was the cleverest publisher in England. He was temporarily out of the city, but I left it with his secretary and urged her to get as quick an answer as possible. Within four days I received a letter from the publisher that surprised me very much.

July 29th 1937

Dear Mr. Hudson Strode,

It is with very great regret indeed that I find myself unable to make you an offer for SOUTH BY THUNDERBIRD.

It is, if I may say so, a brilliant book, and possesses every merit except one—but the absence of that merit is, from my point of view, I am afraid, quite fatal. Forgive me for calling it a merit—when you see what it is you won't agree with me!

I hold pretty "Left" political views, and I am one of those odd publishers who thinks it wrong to publish anything directly opposed to them. In a sense you meet possible criticism by saying: "Despite my inherent sympathy with the underdog, I shall stand accused by Marxists of not going deep enough into obvious social abuses." But I don't think you really meet it. My point is that nobody could possibly tell from reading your book that the conditions of the working classes in many parts of South America are a disgrace to civilization. . . . To me, the suggestion of advanced social legislation being the best safeguard a nation can have is anathema! I want to see the capitalist system *overthrown*.

Forgive me for having written so frankly, but the exceeding brilliance of your book, as a record of travel and as a piece of writing, makes me think that I ought to show you the courtesy of being perfectly frank, instead of making the usual evasions that a publisher does make in such cases.

And forgive me also, please, for being such an odd kind of publisher!

Yours sincerely,

V. Gollancz

P.S. The publisher in me has been sorely tempted to suppress the man of the "Left" in me—and like Jacob (was it Jacob?) I feel that as a result whatever limb it was has shrunk.

The desire to have the capitalist system overthrown astounded me. I had not known that this highly successful publisher was a Communist. I was told that he gave most elaborate and costly parties. I was flattered by his phrase "the exceeding brilliance of your book." So now I took *Thunderbird* to "Jamie" Hamilton, as all his friends called him, who had been formerly married to Jean Forbes-Robertson, the actress daughter of the great Sir Johnston and the beautiful Gertrude Elliott. He told me over lunch at his club that she had divorced him for "an actor with a beard." This was hard to understand, because Jamie was a most attractive man. He promised a quick reading.

I had brought with me to London only one letter of introduction: from Owen Johnson to Rebecca West, an old friend of his. I thought the writer might be difficult of access, so Peter Davies said to let him get the note to her by special messenger. I was at my hotel when the lady telephoned me. She invited me either to cocktails, where I would meet other people, or to lunch with her and her husband. I chose lunch.

When I was announced at 15 Orchard Court, Portman Square, Miss West was seated in the den surrounded by bookshelves on every side of the room. I was struck by the beauty of her eyes, which were very large, black, and brilliant, without benefit of mascara. She was now the wife of Henry Andrews, a successful banker in the City. She had married him when she was thirty-eight, and they had been married for seven years. Of course, I well knew the story that she had had a son by H. G. Wells when she was only twenty-one. The son preferred to be known as Anthony West and acquired a literary reputation of his own. In the 1968 edition of *Who's Who in America,* Mr. West, who became naturalized, put himself down as the son of "Herbert George Wells." Over the lunch table I was much surprised when Henry Andrews, a gentle, soft-voiced man, deliberately turned the conversation to Wells. Miss West joined in the conversation. I also talked freely about Wells, whose books I liked. When I made my adieus, they said they had taken a judge's house in Holmbury St. Mary in Surrey for August and that they would like to have me as their guest for a long weekend when I got back from Paris, where I was going immediately for a week. On my fourth day in Paris, Hamish Hamilton cabled me that he was accepting my South American book with enthusiasm. The contract was already drawn, and was awaiting my signature.

In London people were still talking about the abdication of Edward VIII in December to marry "the woman I love." I found this was also a favorite and fervid topic of conversation in Paris. On June 3, Edward, now created Duke of Windsor, and Mrs. Simpson had been married by a Protestant clergyman in France. At a dinner the Chambruns took me to, given by the diplomat brother of General de Chambrun, who was ambassador to Italy, and now married to the Princess Murat, the conversation became so heated that the eight of us were all talking at once. "It was a maneuver, just a maneuver by Stanley Baldwin to get Edward off the throne," the ambassador repeated like a refrain. "He was too social-minded for the Conservatives. He was too interested in bettering the lot of the Welsh miners, among other reforms he had in mind."

Arriving back in London I immediately signed the contract Hamilton offered me and pocketed the check.

Jamie called his former wife, Jean Forbes-Robertson, to see if she would have lunch with me while I talked about a play of mine laid in Bermuda, which might be a starring vehicle for her. The date was made for the next day. She was a charming young woman and quite pretty, but not as beautiful as her mother, Gertrude Elliott. I told her about meeting her father in

Taormina and about Blossom cutting asphodels in the ruins of the Greek theater. And I said that no man had replaced her father as my youthful idol. She told me that her father had died a few months earlier at eighty-four. She took my play manuscript home with her.

I had found a note from Rebecca West at my hotel dated August 5 reminding me of the Andrewses' invitation. So on the next Thursday afternoon I left to stay with the Andrewses. On the train going down I met fellow guests: Vera Brittain's husband, a brilliant young magazine editor, and a Yugoslavian who was helping Miss West with her book *Black Lamb and Grey Falcon,* which was laid in his country.

When Henry Andrews called his wife "Cicily," I learned she had been born Cicily Isabel Fairfield in Edinburgh. She had taken the name "Rebecca West" from the character in Ibsen's *Rosmersholm*.

We had animated conversations on politics, letters, and life, and we talked of the possibility of war that Adolf Hitler seemed to be preparing for. But a recurrent subject was the abdication of Edward VIII and the marriage with Mrs. Simpson in June. Rebecca West told me about a house party she attended in which Mrs. Simpson and the Prince of Wales were guests. "The sad thing about the whole business," Miss West said, "is that she really loved Simpson. Why, I could never understand, because to me he has the face of a pig. But she did love him. One day when she returned home from Paris earlier than expected, she found a letter in her best friend's handwriting, just delivered, on a console. Thinking it was for her, she opened it. She found that her husband and her friend were having an affair. That was when she began accepting invitations on yachting parties where the Prince was a guest. Though a year younger than he, she mothered him. She would insist that he 'take his raincoat or wear his overshoes.' On the house party Wallis Simpson was different from most of the Englishwomen, who thought she was lazy. Sparkling in conversation, she did not care for tennis or any sport that required exertion. I recall one gesture she made again and again at meals. She would reach over the Prince's plate and gently, sweetly, firmly put her hand over his wineglass. She herself did not care for alcohol. In her solicitude for the Prince's health, she spoke of him as 'the little man.' And he loved it. She was altogether a rather serene woman with a kind of mysterious charm."

Something that surprised me more than anything else in the conversations with Henry Andrews was his telling me in private that he had wanted to marry Rebecca ever since he had known of her affair with Wells and even long before he had even met her. Finally a friend had introduced them at the theater and he immediately began to court her. Now they had been married seven years, and she had made him very happy. Rebecca West told me when we were alone that she had never had any money until she married Henry, who was extremely generous. She could now live in luxury, with servants and a secretary, and devote her full time to what she *wanted* to write, instead of filling assignments.

I went down for a brief visit to Plympton St. Mary in Devonshire, whence my Strode ancestor, John, had come to Virginia in the seventeenth century. The grounds were extensive and the new manor built in the time of Queen Anne in 1699 was a large three-story structure of stone. But the house that won my heart had been built in 1400 in the time of Chaucer, and was now rented. Old Colonel George Strode had no male heir to inherit the houses. His elder daughter, who was there also to receive me, had no children, and the younger sister, Mary, was a semi-invalid who eventually produced one daughter. The elder was not pretty, but distinguished-looking and quite charming. She and her husband went skiing in San Moritz every year. She took special pleasure in showing me the eighteenth century Chinese wallpaper of the drawing room and the Chippendale furniture.

She could only stay for tea, for she lived in a manor house some miles away. Her father got out a giant-sized, handsomely bound book tracing the family tree back to King Edward I, through his youngest daughter, Elizabeth. Colonel Strode said he had paid fifty pounds for the volume. His daughter cautioned him half jestingly that it might be dangerous to let me examine the genealogy for I might lay claim to the property as the male heir. But I had no desire for anything except possibly the deer park behind the dwelling where descendants of deer that had been there since Chaucer's time roamed, and now came up to the fence to greet me. I also admired the vegetable garden, where gooseberries that we could not raise in Alabama grew to a great size. They were made into a delicious tart jam that we had for tea.

For dinner that evening we had no venison, as I might have expected, but rabbit stew. As Colonel Strode said, "to pay tribute to the Strode coat of arms," in which a black chevron lay among three black rabbits on a silver shield. On the mound above the visored helmet was an evergreen tree with pine cones. Frankly, I did not think too highly of a coat of arms that boasted only black rabbits and a pine tree, but at least it was "county."

In the course of the dinner served by a handsome butler we talked about Ralph Strode, whom Chaucer spoke of as his "philosophical friend" and who was the reputed author of *Sir Gawain and the Green Knight*. And we also talked of William Strode, the seventeenth century lyric poet, who wrote "On Chloris Walking in the Snow," and another William Strode, who had been born at Newnham Park in 1599 and was once imprisoned for his stout opposition to King Charles I. But on his death in 1645, by order of Parliament he was buried with honors in Westminster Abbey. He lay in the Abbey until after the restoration of the licentious Charles II, when the new king had his body disinterred and buried elsewhere.

Colonel Strode freely confessed to me that he had been born a Lowe. His mother was the Strode. Since the estate was to descend only to a male Strode, his name had been changed legally from George Strode Lowe to George Lowe Strode. The Strodes in England were not a prolific lot. I saw from framed escutcheons on the dining room walls that the Strode arms had been quartered sixteen times. The Colonel said that almost every time the male Strode had married an heiress. Well, I reflected, I was the last of my line in the United States and I had not married an heiress and I did not mind the name's decease with me. None of the Strodes after the seventeenth century had been particularly distinguished, though there was one general who is buried in Westminster Abbey. The Strodes had been content for the most part with the life of a country squire. And that was the life I would have enjoyed best in England. Devonshire was the county in the mild south that I found most ideal, a region I always associated with strawberries and clotted cream. On the village streets I had the strange sensation that I had come back home. The townsfolk did not look unfamiliar to me. In conversation with them, this impression was not dispelled, but augmented.

From London I went to visit our best-loved couple in the world, Admiral Sir Vernon Haggard and his lady, in the village of Stock, Essex. The Haggards lived in a charming place neighboring Lady Haggard's father's manor. The admiral had only that year retired from the British Navy. Lady Haggard was happy working in her rose garden.

The Haggards had been to the recent coronation of George VI. Because they were among the less important guests they had had to drive from Stock and be in their seats at the Abbey in full evening regalia by 7:00 A.M. "The whole thing was a terrible ordeal," the admiral said. "Edward would have hated it. He detested folderol."

The admiral said it was about time to see something of his country after so many years at sea. He would like to take me to Lady Rider Haggard's home in Norfolk. We set off in his little car on a leisurely tour and first stopped a few days at Cambridge. I was more impressed by the incredibly lovely "backs" of St. John's College on the river than anything else, and perhaps next with Pepys' Library in Magdalene. We attended Sunday church service and agreed that we had never seen so many homely women gathered together. In Cambridge, for some odd reason, every woman we saw, even the barmaids, was plain.

The big event of our trip came when the admiral drove to pay his respects to Sir Rider Haggard's widow. The lady was far advanced in her eighties and so crippled with British rheumatism that she walked with two sticks. But if her legs were halting, her mind and her conversation were as alive as her steel-gray eyes. Knowing that she had traveled with her writing husband over the face of the globe, I asked her which country remained the most vivid in memory.

For a moment she seemed to let the far-flung regions of her journeys whirl past in revolving panorama. Then she said, "Mexico. We were there in the time of Diaz. You may suffer over Mexico or laugh over it, but it stays in the memory. It is like a mural created by a collaboration of Divinity and man. In retrospect all Mexico, from the rock-studded deserts to the flowering hot lands of the coasts, is one vast mural never to be forgotten." The old lady's lips drew together in a restrained smile. "Once my husband and I came upon an absurd sight in the suburbs. Two beautiful ladies of our acquaintance had been overturned in their carriage but unhurt. They stood by a roadside ditch trailing moon flowers like some mythical creatures, half-this, half-that. Above the waist, full evening dress, jewels, and camellias for their afternoon drive on parade. Below the waist, which the world could not see in the depth of their carriage, monk-brown petticoats. On their feet they wore flapping red carpet slippers that might have belonged to their slaveys. We offered them a lift back to their home in the city—and throughout the agonizing drive the hectic flush of embarrassment showed crimson through their thick white powder. The poor creatures were prominent in society, but never during the rest of the season while we remained in Mexico did they venture out.

"Strange," she went on speculatively after a moment, "that a land so opulent and original in its natural beauty should have an upper middle class so easily beguiled by sham and show. But for all its pretensions and perversities I recall Mexico with special affection."

Now it was time to leave my dearest friends and go to Glasgow to take ship. Lucy Weir had written me to say that she would meet my train with her chauffeur and that I would recognize her because she looked faintly like her aunt, Dame Rachel Crowdy, the British woman diplomat at large, who had become my friend in Cuba.

Her husband, Jock, was pottering contentedly in his greenhouse when I first met him. He was a pleasant, large man, a Cambridge graduate, who enjoyed salmon fishing, deer stalking, and grouse shooting, as well as gardening. His father, the first Viscount Weir, owned thirty thousand acres of grouse lands to which the late King George V would come each season to shoot with him. He was president of the Weir Company, which manufactured the machinery of ocean liners and similar productions on a vast scale. Jock's father and uncle had turned out to be engineering geniuses in the late nineteenth century and got very rich. Lord Weir was to be the first air minister of Great Britain. He was also one of the founders of International Nickel of Canada and on the board of a dozen other companies, to which positions Jock would eventually succeed. The Weirs had risen to prominence out of Ayrshire peasantry and were descendants of Robert Burns through a daughter of the poet.

The house had been built by Adams in the eighteenth century and was architecturally beautiful. The surrounding gardens were handsomely kept.

We dined that night on grouse Jock Weir had shot. When my hosts saw how much I enjoyed game, we had grouse every day. Because it was late in the month of August and the evenings were cool I found a hot brick in my bed every night, placed there by a servant half an hour before I retired.

The Duke of Windsor–Wallis Simpson marriage naturally came into the conversation. And from Jock, a longtime friend of Edward, I got an intimate glimpse of the affair and a picture of the king's unpredictable behavior, much like his doing bicycle exercises starko when he was supposed to be greeting dignitaries at luncheon in Bermuda.

He told me of a gala day in Scotland, when King Edward VIII was to dedicate the ocean liner named for his mother, Queen Mary. The Weir engineering firm had made the ship's engines. Viscount Weir was giving a luncheon at his Glasgow town house in honor of the new monarch. The cream of Scotland's nobility was assembled to do him homage. After the luncheon they all were to motor down along the Firth of Clyde to the ship's dedication. The king was to speak on an international wireless hookup to the far-flung dominions of the British Empire.

When Jock went up to Edward's bedroom to escort him down to lunch he found him talking long distance on the telephone—to Mrs. Simpson in France. While the company below waited eagerly, then anxiously, and Lord Weir fumed, Edward VIII talked for one hour and thirty-five minutes to the woman he loved. Jock told me he had never seen a man so utterly in love. When he went up a third time to remind His Majesty about lunch and that they had a sixty-mile drive to the *Queen Mary,* the king waved amiably and said, "Do, please, have them go on with the lunch. I rarely care for luncheon anyhow. I'll be down shortly. I must finish this conversation." He turned back to the telephone.

Jock said his father was livid at the latest news from upstairs. He made some excuses to the assembled dukes and duchesses. The lunch proceeded, with the king's place empty until the salad course. Then Edward appeared with all his charisma, charming the most crusty Highlander, but not Viscount Weir. With police sirens fiercely screaming to clear the way, the procession went at eighty miles an hour down the estuary to where the *Queen Mary* was docked. Jock, who is a very modest man and dislikes ostentation, told me he was never so embarrassed in his life. Scotland had not beheld such a death-tempting race through its peaceful villages. King Edward, however, did not seem at all perturbed or flustered. With less than a minute's grace he arrived at the microphone, cleared his throat, and proceeded to address his millions of subjects scattered in far dominions.

After the return to the Weir home they were due at a reception given by some other nobleman. The king would have to shake a hundred hands and acknowledge a hundred curtsies. He called Jock to his bedroom, where he had had the prolonged telephone conversation. He had changed to golf togs. "Look here, Jock," he said, "I can't face it. Put on your golf clothes. You and I are playing golf."

One special factor of my visit with the Weirs has remained particularly vivid in my memory. The eldest son and heir, William, at the age of seven might well have been the boy Robert Burns himself. He looked strikingly like him. He had a radiance about him, and a devilish twinkle in his eyes, exuding an irresistible charm, as I imagine Bobby Burns did. The three children always had lunch with us. Our first Christmas greeting from the Weirs was a seven by four photograph of the three children sitting tandem but with faces turned toward the front. I have it framed in my studio.

It had been a heart-warming, as well as a foot-warming, visit. Lucy took me to my ship in Glasgow and saw me off. The Weirs had been kinder to me than I can tell and I was a profoundly appreciative guest.

I was to stay with them again the summer of 1962, when I was doing research on the final volume of my Jefferson Davis biography. This time I flew direct from New York to Prestwick, where the Weirs lived not many miles from the airport in a grand manor house called "Montgreenan," with two thousand acres of land in Kilwinning, Ayrshire. Lucy wrote hastily by air mail:

Our Chauffeur, Walker, will be at Prestwick to meet the S.A.S. 914 on May 30th. It will be great fun seeing you. We are all *so* looking forward to your visit. Jock presently fishing the Spey for salmon. He got eight today, and the thirteen-year-old son got two of 10 pounds each. All on his own. Great jubilation! See you at breakfast on the 30th. Then we will put you to bed until tea time to let you recover from the magic of jet flight. Yours ever, Lucy.

At the end of May the chill had not gone out of the Scottish winter. I was grateful to find an old-fashioned electric heater in my bedroom, which looked out on the beautiful front garden decorated with ancient tall Chinese urns. My bathroom, where the windows were kept open for "pure ventilation," was like the arctic regions even in bright sunshine. There was no heater in the bathroom, and I never got up the nerve to step into the tub. I bathed quickly standing up. But to satisfy the servants I rumpled and discarded on the tiled floor towels fit for an emperor. Except for a grate fire that was kept burning in the cozy library there was no other downstairs heat. Jock and Lucy always left the chair nearest the fire for me. Electric heat in Scotland is very expensive and when May comes it is not turned on in the enormous drawing room again until October. The only place where I found real warmth was the block-long greenhouse, where the peaches, tomatoes, and strawberries which we enjoyed at table ripened out of season.

When we dined in the late Lord Weir's Glasgow town house, where King Edward had highly displeased his host by coming late to lunch, I learned that Jock kept a staff of servants for entertaining international business guests. In time the place was to be given to William, the heir who looked like Bobby Burns, when he married. He was now in Europe.

Thoughtfully an electric heater had been set behind my dining room chair and I was given a picture window view of a perfect stretch of fresh green lawn. Suddenly, as if on cue, when we were seated a wild red fox appeared on the turf. Flambeau, the outsized golden poodle we had brought along for the ride, went almost frantic. He had never before seen a fox, but he knew it for an enemy and tried to dash through the glass. Neither of the Weirs had ever seen one on the civilized streets of Glasgow. The fox seemed as curious about Flambeau as the dog did about the strange animal. After a minute's good stare into the room, he turned and loped away.

After the little excitement we settled down to enjoying the fresh salmon and the grouse, fruits of Jock's relaxing sports.

Lucy's favorite sport was owning race horses. A Christmas card the Weirs were to send us later was a photograph of her walking at the side of What-A-Myth and his rider, when her horse had won the Cheltenham race, at which the Queen Mother presented Lady Weir with a golden bowl, and incidentally Lucy also got a purse of $20,000.

I was taken to see the Glasgow house where Jefferson Davis stayed with devoted Scottish friends who had once owned a cotton plantation in Mississippi. An especially rich dividend that came out of this happy visit with the Weirs was that Jock, one day, and Lucy, the next, would drive me to places Jefferson Davis had visited almost a century before. His traveling companion was Charles Mackay, "the poet of Perth," and the adoptive father of Marie Corelli, a best-selling romantic novelist of the 1890's. I gleaned firsthand material that I was to utilize in the third and final volume of my biography of the President of the Confederacy, which I was to title, *Jefferson Davis: Tragic Hero.*

Lady
Astor

ON the morning of January 2, 1938, I had an extraordinary "experience" in Delray Beach, Florida. I had left Tuscaloosa the day after Christmas for a fortnight's stint of special writing. In my bathing trunks I walked from my hotel the half-mile or so down Ocean Avenue to the beach. The blue-green waves of the Atlantic seemed particularly inviting and the half-past-ten morning air lifted the head higher. On this winter day I thought of Pippa's passing in spring. Suddenly a still small voice told me not to rush into the water, but to turn to the right and stroll south along the sands. I obeyed the impulse. After about a block from the lifeguard station the beach became more or less empty.

As I approached the striped canvas pavilion of Sand-O-Way East, an exclusive small hotel set in a lovely garden, I saw the figure of a woman come out of the gate and cross the road to the few square yards of private beach. She was wearing a champagne-colored bathing suit. I was struck by the distinction of her features and the wavy blond hair. I stopped in my tracks as she came nearer. Then, hardly believing it possible, I went up close to her and asked, "Aren't you Lady Astor?" She drew herself up stiffly and considered a denial. But as I regarded her steadily with such delighted expectancy, she answered with a cool monosyllable, "Yes."

"Oh!" I said, talking fast. "I met you at a party at Oxford in 1923. I was visiting Earl McGowin, a Rhodes scholar from Alabama. The Dana Gibsons were with you that night. You spoke to some club and dropped your 'g's' with gusto. A law student from Mississippi with the funny name of Jiggits introduced you, and he was so witty he almost stole a bit of your thunder." She began to relax. I went on quickly, "In your talk you told us that your old Negro mammy in Virginia said to you after your marriage with Waldorf Astor, 'Honey, you sho did out-marry yo'self.' At the informal reception afterward I spoke with you about the Langhornes of Uniontown, Alabama, distant cousins. You invited me to have tea with you at the Houses of Parliament the next week."

Then I told her my name and explained that I was a professor at the University of Alabama and was in Delray writing the introduction to an anthology of English lyric poetry which my publishers were bringing out in the fall. My credentials were accepted. "Shall we sit down?" Lady Astor invited. On the white sand we talked for two hours. She told me how Lord

Astor and she happened to be in Delray. They had come in the middle of the night from The Breakers in Palm Beach. "When I was a girl, cultivated people were guests at The Breakers. We had gone there for a much needed vacation—for both of us—to get away from the tensions of Parliament and anxiety over the waxing power of Hitler. But I was horrified at the change. The people in the lobby and the parlors were awful: hard-visaged, artificial, vulgar, dissipated. I said to Waldorf, 'Look at these people. Look at their faces! They're living in hell. We've got to get out of here. We can't stay another hour!' So we got packed, hired a car, and, with my maid and Waldorf's man, we drove down the coast. It was about eleven o'clock at night. We stopped at the Seacrest Hotel back there on the beach. They couldn't or wouldn't give us rooms. Perhaps they had no idea who we were. But they said, 'Try Sand-O-Way two blocks south.' Here we found lovely rooms. The place is run by gentlefolk. And here we are to remain for two weeks."

In the course of the conversation I mentioned that in the previous summer in England I had spent a long weekend in Surrey with Rebecca West and her husband, Henry Andrews. Other writers were fellow guests. Lady Astor confessed she knew little of the contemporary authors, though she did admire the poetry of the young Auden. Then she said an odd thing with an odd intonation. "I read virtually nothing nowadays but the Bible." I sat up straighter and looked at her speculatively. I knew that she was a teetotaler. I had learned that members of a certain faith never drank and read the Bible every day. "Are you a Christian Scientist?" I asked.

"Yes, for many years now—since 1914."

I was intensely interested as well as surprised. "Do tell me some of your experiences in Science. We have a very dear friend, Mrs. Albert Spalding, wife of the violinist, who has not had a doctor since she was healed when she was a debutante. On my birthday in late October she sent me a copy of Mrs. Eddy's *Science and Health*. I confess I can't make much out of it. My wife, though impressed that a sophisticated woman like Mary Spalding believes in it devoutly, finds it incomprehensible."

"I thought so, too," Lady Astor said, "until I was cured of ulcers on the spine by a practitioner. I suffered agonies. Physicians in London, New York, Berlin, and Vienna had failed to heal me. Whenever a soul is ready for enlightenment the answer is somewhere near at hand; the teacher comes. My beloved sister Phyllis came over to England to console me in my physical misery. She told me that there were Christian Scientists in America who believed that God never meant there to be sickness and suffering, and who could be cured by prayer. It so happened that there was in England an American Christian Science practitioner whom Phyllis knew, a friend of Alice Longworth. She was named Maud Bull. Phyllis arranged for Mrs. Bull to call on me at Cliveden. She brought with her a copy of *Science and Health* by Mary Baker Eddy. She told me to read the book and that she would pray for me, that is, know the Truth about me. When I read the first chapter on Prayer it was just like the conversion of St. Paul. Here I found the answer to all my questions and all I had been looking for. If I was a spiritual being, I would not have to suffer in the flesh, I learned. It was like a new beginning to me. My life was really made over. Fear went out of me. I was no longer frightened of anything. All this happened in March, 1914. I have never had to consult a physician since, and except for a rare head cold I have never known another sick day."

"Was this after you were the first woman elected to Parliament?"

"Before! I could never have been in Parliament without Science."

"Did Lord Astor ever take it up?"

"Fourteen years after I did. He contracted some virulent fever in India. As his ship was sailing along the coast of Africa I got a cable from the captain saying that my husband was dying. I wired him to ask if he was willing to have Christian Science work done. An affirmative answer came and I called my London practitioner. When the ship reached England Waldorf was virtually recovered. He became a student of Science and then a member of the Church. He is more devout than I. Now he occasionally writes articles for the C.S. *Journal*."

Seeing that I was mightily impressed, she told me about her intimate friend Philip Kerr, nephew of the Duke of Norfolk, later to become renowned as the Marquess of Lothian and ambassador to the United States at the beginning of World War II. "Suffering from some chronic troubles, he went to India to seek health among swamis. But he got no relief. On his return to England he came to Rest Harrow, our place in Sandwich, Kent. When he saw the change in me, he exclaimed, 'Why, Nancy, what has happened to you? You are well! What has done it?' " She told him Christian Science. He was somewhat shocked, for he was a Roman Catholic, and his uncle, the duke, looked to him to become the lay leader of the Catholic church in Britain. Lady Astor talked to him of Science until near midnight. About two in the morning he knocked at her door and said that something terrible had happened in his insides. She saw that he was acutely ill. At this time of night it was impossible to get physicians down from London.

"None of the family happened to be at Sandwich but me," Lady Astor said. "I was new in Science and I did not know quite how to work for him. I sat by his bedside and tried to know the Truth. I read to him from Mrs. Eddy's textbook. Then I read the fourteenth chapter of John to him over and over until dawn. When the surgeon arrived early the next morning he found that Philip's appendix had burst in the night and he feared peritonitis, which is often fatal. He said, 'You must have suffered excruciating pain.' Philip smiled and affirmed, 'No, really I remember only an extraordinary sense of peace.'

"Philip began to read Science. Shortly he was completely healed by a practitioner. He renounced the Catholic faith, joined the Christain Science church, and never again called for a doctor. The Duke of Norfolk and all his tribe were angry with me, though they admitted that he was cured. He became so good a Scientist that I looked upon him as my spiritual adviser."

It was nearing lunchtime and Lady Astor made a move to get up. "Waldorf has gone this morning to see an old friend at Boca Raton," she said, as I helped her rise. "But would you dine with us here tonight? And would you care to go with us to the local Christian Science church tomorrow, Sunday? We could pick you up at your hotel at ten minutes to eleven."

That evening I arrived at Sand-O-Way East and told the butler that the Astors were expecting me. Almost on the instant a tall, slender, graceful, and handsome man with enormous soft brown eyes came down the stairs. His eyes made me think of a fawn. With a welcoming smile, he announced simply, "I'm Astor," and I learned how a viscount spoke of himself. I had read that at Eton he had done wonderfully well, and then entered New College at Oxford. Here he did not bother to study hard, but pleasured himself with various sports. His university days were mostly those of hunting, fencing, and polo. He was on his college's rowing team. He just scraped through with a low degree, but he emerged with the reputation of a first class sportsman. Within three years of leaving Oxford, because of a weakness in his heart, which had caused him to give up strenuous rowing his last year, he had been forced to abandon all sports. An angina condition and a tendency to tuberculosis were diagnosed. This was a cruel blow for the young man, who had to give up winter sports in Switzerland as well as polo and hunting. It was often reported that from his youth to his last days he had a modest and quiet manner, "through which inner strength and will were visible." He possessed tact and generous consideration for others.

In 1910 Waldorf Astor was elected to Parliament from Plymouth, Devonshire. He was quick to make an outstanding impression. On his father's death he was reluctantly forced into the House of Lords, because he was now a viscount. In all his government positions he showed marked efficiency. Nancy, his wife, stood for his Plymouth seat in the House of Commons and won by a goodly majority. On December 1, 1919, she entered the House of Commons, the first woman in the British Parliament.

Lady Astor followed her husband downstairs shortly. She was wearing a simple black taffeta dinner dress and the famous Astor pearls. I wondered if I would be offered a cocktail—I noticed a few hotel guests in one of the parlors sipping drinks. But, of course, neither of the Astors drank, and we went straight into the dining room.

We talked of the increasing tensions in Europe and Hitler's menacing call for Germanic expansion. We agreed that we thought it had been a mistake to strip Germany of all of her African colonies at Versailles. After dinner in a corner of the drawing room we chatted until nine-thirty. Then, in sending me away, Lady Astor explained that she and her husband to-gether read the Christian Science Lesson-Sermon with Biblical citations before they retired.

As I bade them a grateful good night, I was frankly amazed that this famous international couple with all their knowledge of world politics really took their religion seriously.

The Astors were a few minutes late next morning, and came for me in a taxi. They had not bothered to engage a private car with a chauffeur during their Delray visit, Lady Astor said, because there was no place they wanted to go.

When we arrived at the little white wooden church the service had just begun and the congregation was absorbed in the "few moments of silent prayer." As we stood on the three steps leading up to the church stoop I realized that I might have felt embarrassed if someone I knew saw me entering a Christian Science church. Half jokingly, I said to Lady Astor, "I think I feel as strange as you must have when you first walked into the House of Commons as a member." Her expression became serious. In prophetic accent that has remained very clear after thirty-three years, she said: "Listen, my friend, listen carefully. This may mean far more in your life than my being in Parliament has ever meant to me."

The door was opened and the usher led us to the vacant front pew right. I sat between the Astors. From her handbag Lady Astor took out a small thin case of tooled Florentine leather. Within was a copy of the current *Quarterly* with the various citations for the first three months of 1938. She opened to the first lesson. The subject of the week was "God." She told me to read the responses of brief Biblical passages with her and the congrega-tion. Lord Astor took his own *Quarterly* from his pocket.

The two readers at the pulpit were both women. Christain Science, I learned, does not have ordained ministers. I was put off by the first reader's dress: white silk with tropical green palm trees running up the material.

Lady Astor sensed that I was disappointed in the service, and when we left the church she said, "I did not like the church service at first and I was critical of this and that. But you come to take in the spiritual significance."

"One thing did make a deep impression," I said. "It was the quotation from Mrs. Eddy in gold lettering on the wall facing us: 'Divine Love Always Has Met And Always Will Meet Every Human Need.' "

"If you can believe that," Lord Astor said, "you will find it very helpful."

The Astors took me back to Sand-O-Way to lunch with them. I was to lunch or dine with them every day until I returned to Tuscaloosa. This Sunday Lady Astor asked me about my special work at the university. Besides my large class in Shakespeare, I told her of my class in fiction writing, limited to fourteen, and that a novel written in my class by Harriet Hassell had just been published by Peter Davies in London and would be

225

released in the spring by Harper's in New York. In answering questions I mentioned that several talented students were extremely poor. Impulsively, Lady Astor exclaimed, "Could I help? Could I offer some scholarship money? I have a special little fund." Two checks for two girls from Alabama farming families were written out, for $300 each. Several weeks later one of the recipients, who had written Lady Astor thanking her for her generosity, came to my office holding a letter from Cliveden. She could not decipher the page and a half of hand-written postscript that followed the secretary-typed paragraph of good wishes. The holograph postscript began, "I do so admire the courage and endurance of the South." At the end, Lady Astor said she was enclosing another small check for some pretty clothes or books or any trifles the girl might desire. The amazed student held out a draft for $150 on a New York bank signed Nancy Astor. "Shall I accept it?" she asked. "Good heavens, of course," I said. My wife went with her to the best dress shop in town to help her select some things. But the girl was frugal, and preferred to save the larger part of the money.

On being questioned one evening in Delray about the anthology of English lyric poetry I was doing, I said to Lady Astor, "You could help me. I have asked a few well-known persons to tell me their favorite lyrics; among them Virginia Woolf, Havelock Ellis, Eugene O'Neill, Gertrude Stein, Stark Young, Ellen Glasgow, Robinson Jeffers, James Branch Cabell." I had in my pocket Mrs. Woolf's reply, which Thérèse had just forwarded to me. I read a part of the letter aloud:

As to your request that I should give you my opinion upon English Lyric poetry, I am greatly flattered that you should think it worth having. I began to think which are my favorite lyrics and why, and have been debating the question. The result, however, is as usual when I start reading English poetry—I am led away into hours of reading, find new lyrics as well as old ones, and in the end can no more say which I like best than I can say why I like them.

I said that O'Neill had been more direct; he had answered decisively, "First, above all others, Keats' 'Ode to a Nightingale.' " Cabell confessed "to an ancient and condoning, but inveterate friendship for Keats' 'Ode to a Grecian Urn.' " Ellen Glasgow chose A. E. Housman's "Be Still, My Soul, Be Still; The Arms You Bear Are Brittle."

When I asked Lady Astor if she would tell me her favorite English lyric and permit me to quote her in my introduction, she said to let her think. She had a copy of *The Oxford Book of Verse* with her and would glance through it. The next evening at dinner she had three choices: Shakespeare's "Poor Soul, the Centre of My Sinful Earth," Donne's "Death, Be Not Proud," and Blake's "Never Seek to Tell Thy Love." I was delighted, for those poems were among my favorites.

When not talking Christian Science, Lady Astor was the most amusing conversationalist I have ever known. Her quick wit came forth like a flash.

One evening when Mrs. Ross Smith of Birmingham, a longtime friend of my wife and me, made a fourth at dinner, Lord Astor knocked over his iced-tea glass and the tea spilled across the table. In mock lament, Lady Astor exclaimed, "Men are never properly housebroken. Mrs. Smith, would you please take Waldorf outside and walk him around the bushes?"

Though her wit was often barbed, Lady Astor had the kindest of hearts. But she might blurt out something she would not have said if she had stopped to think. One evening while she was knitting some baby garment for the infant of a young man who had thought himself in love with her and whom she had steered into a good marriage, she made a remark that made me wince. I do not recall what Lord Astor was expounding in his gentle way, but his wife stopped her needles, looked at him, and said without emphasis: "You know perfectly well, Waldorf, that every really good idea you ever had you got from me."

Except for a flicker in his eyes, Lord Astor did not react. He neither denied nor corroborated. He changed the subject, and his wife went on quietly with her knitting. I thought to myself, "It is well she married an angel." In London in 1962, as we were looking at a framed photograph of her dead husband, Lady Astor said with feeling, "You know, I married an angel." I had known that in Delray in 1938 and thought then that this scintillating, extroverted, witty, politically minded, deeply religious, and irrepressible woman had had a special need of an angelic husband.

Lady Astor had the reputation of never being nonplused, no matter what the circumstance. But on one occasion a twelve-year-old girl innocently accomplished the trick. As a member of Parliament from Plymouth, in campaigning, the viscountess would often call on her constituents in depressed districts and take along with her a "man of the people." One afternoon in Plymouth her companion was a well-scrubbed, strapping young sailor in uniform. They chose cottages at random. When the sailor knocked at one door a timid girl answered and let them in. "Is your mummy at home, my dear?" Lady Astor inquired sweetly. The child looked the couple over appraisingly and went and opened wide a front bedroom door. "No, she's out. But she told me to say that you could use the front room, and, when you're done, would you please leave five bob on the mantelpiece?"

Lady Astor had an easy winning way with all sorts of people, from the highest to the lowest. She had no trouble being elected to Parliament again and again for twenty-five years. Then her mild husband said, "It is enough."

Knowing that Lady Astor was an intimate friend of Bernard Shaw I had ventured to hope that if I came to England I might get to meet the famous man. "I'll gladly take you!" she promised impulsively. "For years," I said, "I have taught his plays in a modern drama course; but I might be a little afraid of his tongue." "Have no worry. Shaw is a gentleman. He'll behave well. He is really extremely genial. His wife, Charlotte, incidentally, is a Christian Scientist. We go to the same Ninth Church in London." But I was never to meet Shaw, for he died on November 1, 1950, at ninety-four, and I did not get back to England again until 1962.

Lady Astor took a real joy in being helpful. When I told her that Thérèse and I would be going to Scandinavia for a year in January, 1939, she quickly said, "Would you like to meet the Crown Prince of Sweden? He is a very dear friend of mine. Just let me know when you want it, and I'll send you a letter for him. He'll be king someday if his aged father ever decides to die." I have a note from her dated November 29, 1938, from 4 St. James's Square.

The Crown Prince of Sweden dined with me last night, and I spoke to him about your forthcoming visit. However, I am also enclosing a note of introduction.

I was to present the note to His Royal Highness in March of 1939, and he was most helpful.

Lady Astor invited Thérèse and me to stay with her at Cliveden late in September of 1939. But the declaration of war came earlier in the month and cut short our Scandinavian sojourn. We never got to Cliveden.

When I went to Sand-O-Way East to thank the Astors for their hospitality and for explaining their religion to me, Lord Astor put in a word of caution. "Don't get the idea," he said, "that Christian Science is just an alternative to medical treatment. But it does reveal health to be spiritually natural and shows us how to demonstrate it here and now." Lady Astor loaded me with gifts—mostly books from England that had been sent to her at Christmas—and a set of twelve exquisitely produced illuminations from some medieval holy book for Thérèse.

One of the books was *Great Contemporaries,* "By the Rt. Hon. Winston S. Churchill." In the chapter on George Bernard Shaw, while discussing the playwright's and the Astors' visit to Stalin, Churchill etched Viscountess Astor in two incandescent paragraphs:

For his co-delegate or comrade in the trip to Russia Shaw selected Lady Astor. The choice was happy and appropriate. Lady Astor, like Mr. Bernard Shaw, enjoys the best of all worlds. She reigns on both sides of the Atlantic in the Old World and the New, at once as a leader of fashionable society, and of advanced feminist democracy. She combines a kindly heart with a sharp and wagging tongue. She embodies the historical portent of the first woman Member of the House of Commons. She accepts Communist hospitality and flattery, and remains the Conservative Member for Plymouth. She does all these opposite things so well and so naturally that the public, tired of criticizing, can only gape.

'It is now some sixteen or seventeen years ago,' to parody Burke's famous passage, 'that I first saw the present Viscountess Astor in London society, and surely never lighted on these shores, which she scarcely seemed to touch, a more delightful vision.' She had stepped out of a bandbox from the United States to animate and charm the merry and still decorous circles through which she had then begun to move. Every door opened to her approach. Insular and masculine prejudices were swept aside, and forthwith the portals of the House of Commons, barred by immemorial tradition to women, also difficult of access to those of foreign birth, were thrown wide to receive her. In a trice she was escorted to her seat by Mr. Balfour and Mr. Lloyd George, was soon delivering her maiden speech, and offering a picture of the memorable scene to be preserved in the Palace of Westminster. These are indeed startling achievements.

I had told Lady Astor that my Virginian Strode ancestor had come from Plympton St. Mary in Devonshire about 1640 and settled around Amherst near Lynchburg. When I had visited the Strode estate in 1937 I found in the park deer descended from those of 1400 in the time of Chaucer, who spoke of Ralph Strode as "my friend, the philosophical Strode."

Lady Astor asked for my pen and inscribed the flyleaf of the Churchill book: "To Hudson Strode of Devonshire from Nancy Astor, M.P. from Plymouth. 1938." Then she thought for a moment and in her almost illegible hand wrote of Churchill: "He was a great writer and just as bad a politician as ————. His description of Lawrence of Arabia is brilliant."

On the trip home to Tuscaloosa I reflected on the enriching memories that impulse to turn to the right and stroll down the beach had brought me. It still seemed miraculous that Lady Astor had suddenly appeared at that special moment. I did not know that she was in the States and I had not seen her in sixteen years. I knew nothing of her interest in Christian Science. In our conversation on the sands that morning she said that we were destined to meet in this way. "If you keep yourself in a receptive frame of mind I think that you will meet in your travels precisely the persons who will be helpful." "Of course," she added, "it is sometimes well to take 'human footsteps' to bring about the meeting." In the ensuing years I was to believe what she said was largely true. Her simple remark encouraged me to follow leads and to get to know certain kings and princes, foreign Nobel Prize winners, and Olympic champions.

When I related to Thérèse the story of the Astors' metaphysial healings, I said, "You know Lady Astor to be a worldly, sophisticated woman. Let's clean out our medicine chest, and try again to read Mrs. Eddy."

We had never heard of a C.S. in Tuscaloosa and I knew there was no church edifice. Then, two nights after my return, David Clay, a representative of the publishing firm of Harcourt, Brace, came to call. He was a practicing Scientist in New York. He told us that there were about twenty church members in Tuscaloosa and that Sunday morning services were held in the Druid Motion Picture Theater. David took us the next Sunday and we found several friends there, intelligent people whom I would no more have suspected of being interested than I would the Astors.

Lady Astor and I exchanged occasional letters during 1939. From

Stockholm I wrote her to tell her that a practitioner had cured me of bronchitis. On May 11 she replied from her home on St. James's Square.

At this moment my hair is being permanently waved. Your wife will know what that means, but it is my only chance of sending you a line.

First, let me say how delighted I am that Christian Science is helping you. It gives me more joy than anything you could tell me.

I am so glad that your visit is a success and am happy that you saw the Crown Prince and that he helped you.

We are very busy, but still hopeful that we may avoid a war.

Please do not fail to let me know what you decide to do.

I wrote Lady Astor again after the war had begun and we were about to sail for New York. From Cliveden she replied on October 7.

I am so happy to receive your letter and to know that you have had a successful time in the Scandinavian countries. What a blessed thing it must be to have money to spend on your own people's conditions, instead of having to spend every penny on armaments to try to save Democracy for the world!

I cannot write you about the war. It is too terrible to contemplate, and when one has five sons of serving age, it is all too near home. C.S. is the only thing which makes life possible for me just now.

Late in 1940 I sent Lady Astor a copy of the published novel of twenty-two-year-old Helen Norris, one of the girls to whom she had given scholarship money. I had entered the manuscript of *Something More Than Earth* in the Atlantic Monthly–Little, Brown $10,000 prize contest for the best novel from any part of the world. Edward Weeks, editor of *Atlantic Monthly,* wrote me that it had been chosen one of the three finalists. Helen's novel did not win, but it got a good critical reception. The book had been forwarded from Cliveden to Plymouth, where Lady Astor spent months living in her extremely vulnerable house at 3 Elliot Terrace on the Hoe to give courage and succor to her constituents during the German raids. She wrote me that she read the book during a dreadful night of waves of bombers and became so absorbed in it that it distracted her mind from the awful devastation going on around her.

By March 30, 1941, Plymouth had suffered thirty-nine bombing raids and hundreds of alerts. On the morning of the twentieth, King George VI and Queen Elizabeth arrived by royal train for a brief official visit. They were met at the station by the Lord Mayor, who was Lord Astor, and the Lady Mayoress, who was Lady Astor. The king and the queen went on a tour of the city, remarking the terrible damage caused by the bombing raids, and inspected the defenses and shelters. The visit ended with tea at 3 Elliot Terrace with a few chosen guests.

After tea, escorted by the mayor and mayoress, the royal couple drove to the station through the streets filled with cheering subjects. Just as the king and queen were saying good-by to the Astors, an alert sounded, and the train got under way. Two hours later Plymouth suffered an air raid which was perhaps the most devastating on any English town during the course of the war. The city's center was almost obliterated.

All the tubs in the Astors' mansion were filled with water, and spades were ready for the incendiaries. As a stick of bombs came nearer and nearer everybody fell flat on their faces by the hall door. A bomb exploded close enough to the house to shatter the glass of the windows on the Hoe side of Elliot Terrace. An air warden appeared and ordered the inhabitants down to the basements. The Astors and their few guests obeyed. In the shelter, Rose Harrison, Lady Astor's devoted maid, spent the time picking bits of glass out of her ladyship's hair, while Nancy chattered about her Virginia childhood and the tobacco fields. When the group emerged from the basement Lady Astor stopped by a blasted window to gaze at Plymouth, which for miles was a blazing fire. Tears filled her eyes. "There goes thirty years of our lives," she ruminated, "but we'll build it again." She never lost her courage or her hope.

In another letter, dated May 11, 1941, from Plymouth, thanking me for a family-size box of pecans, she wrote:

Poor Plymouth! It is impossible to describe to you what it is like here. The people are simply magnificent. I find that when the test comes you are given strength to carry on and it takes away all fear.

I have been given such strength and courage. I was (word illegible) Lord Mayor of Plymouth for 5 weeks. I had no idea I could do it. Now I feel I should be on a War Cabinet!

Please stick to C.S. Love to you all. And oh, the pecans! I do feel you are too generous.

On April 30, 1944, the sirens wailed at three o'clock in the morning for the last time in Plymouth. Twenty-seven persons were killed. This day marked the end of fifty-nine German bombing raids.

In November, Lord Astor told Nancy of his and the entire family's wish that she should retire. She had served twenty-five years in the House of Commons. The Labour Party had become very strong all over the country, and Waldorf felt that she, who had never known defeat, would be certain to lose. The chairman and other members of the Conservative Party urged Bill to dissuade his mother from standing again. Lord Astor explained calmly, gently, and firmly that if she refused the family's advice and stood for Parliament again, he could give her no support.

A letter of early 1944 is the only one of that year I can find in my files. But at the end of the year she wrote to tell me, with deep hurt and indignation, that Waldorf refused to campaign with her in the next election and she could not make it without his help.

The blow to Lady Astor was shattering. It was one from which she never completely recovered. On December 1, 1944, together Lord and Lady

Astor announced in the press that she would not contest her seat again. The announcement said that since Lord Astor's health did not permit him to undergo the exertions of an election, she was giving up out of consideration for him.

At a large dinner for women in celebration of her twenty-five years as an M.P., in her unsentimental speech, she declared, "I will not fight the next election, because my husband does not want me to. It is a terrible thing for me."

She had endeavored to enlist the support of Bernard Shaw, who was sympathetic to her cause, but he dared not write to Lord Astor to ask him to reconsider. The truth is her husband may have saved her from humiliation. When the election returns were counted, the Labor members numbered 396 against a Conservative opposition of 189. Winston Churchill himself failed to win re-election. Clement Attlee was the new Prime Minister.

But Nancy persisted in thinking that her husband had injured and betrayed her. They were mildly estranged for the next five years, and she never entirely forgave him.

On her first return to Virginia after the war, because my mother and mother-in-law were then pressing obligations, we could not invite Lady Astor to stay with us in Tuscaloosa until too late. She wrote from the Langhorne family place, "Mirador," in Greenwood, Virginia, on May 23, 1946.

It's not fair for you to wait until I am northern bound and ask me to 'Paradise.' I long to come, but it's too late. Give me a 'Rain Check.' (That's an Americanism which the English should borrow—A and Gt. B are as one.) I do appreciate you both wanting us. However, Waldorf sailed last week, and now I go to Boston after settling many family problems here in Virginia.

Besides seeing you I should relish the *peace of a house that's not convenient to visitors.*

Thank you both many, many times. It's nice to feel we have 2 firm friends in Alabama.

Ever yours,
Nancy Astor

In 1952 Lord Astor's heart condition made it dangerous for him to walk more than a few steps. He had to use a wheelchair. He never complained, though his suffering was acute. As death approached, his calm demeanor was troubled by one thought: how would Nancy face life alone? His last words to Bill, repeated many times, were "Look after your mother." He died on September 30, 1952, and was buried at Cliveden.

Lady Astor wrote me, "Waldorf suffered terribly, but remained true to his religion." She wrote to a mutual friend, "We had forty happy years together. No people ever worked happier than we did. These last seven

232

years have been heartbreaking, but thank God he was like his old self the last ten days, and, oh, how it makes me grieve for the years wasted."

The next time Lady Astor returned to the United States she planned to stay a week with us in the early spring of 1955. But Mrs. Dana Gibson became critically ill and she had to cancel the visit. She wrote on March 31, 1955:

I must sail for home tomorrow. I really did love to hear from you. I will certainly try to get to you when I come back.

I have had great protection, and my sister Irene Gibson, a wonderful healing. C.S. is my only hope in this reeling, rushing world. I wish I could write more, and above all *see* you both.

Occasionally I would ask if she would let some talented student of mine in Britain call on her at 4 St. James's Square. She would write back, "Send him to me, I'll look after your young friend for you." When David Clay Jenkins, on a Fulbright at a Welsh university, was asked to lunch and arrived with a box of chocolates from me, Lady Astor immediately challenged him: "Are you wearing your woolies? They're absolutely necessary in this damp winter climate. British houses are never properly heated. Buy long drawers as soon as you leave after lunch. And the next time you come to see me be sure you have them on!"

When I purposed to go to England in 1962 to do research on Jefferson Davis in the British Museum, Lady Astor asked my wife and me to stay with her at Sandwich in Kent in August. I replied that I was coming over at the end of May and that Thérèse was staying home. She wrote back that, alas, she had no proper guest room at her Eaton Square apartment, but added, "You can have *all* your meals with me: and very good meals they are too." She kindly offered to invite to dinner any persons in London I might want to meet. From 100 Eaton Square on May 16, 1962, Lady Astor wrote:

I have just received your letter. I am really delighted that you are coming over.

You can certainly see my son David, who is nicer than the people you mention. I will get David here, when you let me know the day of your arriving from Scotland. I will write Lord Stansgate [Anthony Wedgwood Benn] and tell him you are coming over and invite him to dinner. I believe Lord Attlee is still in the hospital. I can't understand why he wanted to become a Lord. I would far rather be in the House of Commons! and *oh,* how I miss it!

As I read your letter over you seem to know more people than I do.

I find being alone very strange, being one of 8 children and having 6 of my own.

Best wishes, and Great Expectations, but not by Dickens.

My second night in London I dined with her and her favorite son, David, the second of her Astor children, and publisher and editor of the liberal

Observer. Lady Astor received me in her library, where a fire blazed in the grate. The first thing she said to me, as she took both my hands, was, "You know, I made a dreadful mistake in giving up Cliveden to Bill. Waldorf left me a fund to keep the place in style the rest of my life. But I let Bill have it. And now it makes me miserable that I can't ask my friends to stay with me there."

I admired a silver framed profile photograph of Lady Astor wearing a tiara and taken years before. "You know," she said, "Waldorf's father, the first viscount, gave us Cliveden as a wedding gift and millions to maintain it. And as a personal gift he gave me the famous Sanci diamond, which had been worn by Louis XIV at his coronation and has a history that goes back to Constantinople. But I had no tiara. Going to so many regal parties with all those duchesses wearing glittering coronets, I felt a bit drab. So, after his father's death, I said to Waldorf, 'Look here, didn't your father leave any diamonds?' Waldorf said he didn't know, but that he would go down to the bank and see. He came back with two great leather bags crammed with diamonds. They looked like the goatskin bags Lawrence drank from in the Arabian desert. We poured out the gems on a tabletop. I called a jeweler down to Cliveden to select stones, match them for size, and design me a tiara. He did a superb job, I think. I never saw one that delighted me more."

Lady Astor would quickly change a subject. "I've recently had visitors from Texas here. I rejoice that Texas is so rich! When I was young I remember people saying, 'Where *do* you come from?' 'Texas, dammit, don't laugh!' Nobody laughs at Texans now!" She gave a little triumphant chuckle as David arrived from a cocktail party. He was blond and blue-eyed like his mother, but his temperament and personality came from his gentle father. He was warm, shy, and charming. I was drawn to him immediately.

I hardly expected to be offered a drink, but the butler entered with Dubonnet and glasses on a tray. He asked me if I would care for some Du*bon*ny, pronouncing the word heavily on the second syllable, as in a "bonny lass." David said that he was full of martinis, but he took a glass. Lady Astor, the teetotaler, hesitated for a moment and then she, too, took a glass and sipped.

In the large dining room a small table had been attractively set before one of the great windows that gave on the green treetops of Eaton Square park. (The handsome Sheraton table gracing the center of the room was used in the days to come when there were ten or more guests.) The intimacy of the small table for three was reminiscent of my being with the Astors in Delray. Lady Astor remarked the fact before our conservation began to range the globe.

The devotion of mother and son did not prevent differences of opinion. She took no stock in David's ultra-liberal views and his "idealization" of

African blacks, whose pictures he sprinkled generously through *The Observer*'s pages. "You know," she reminisced, "my family was ruined by the Yankees in the war, like almost every other Southerner. My father lost his tobacco plantation, his home, his money, his labor. When virtually penniless, his knowledge of black psychology saved us. A new railroad was to be built, and my father applied for the job of construction manager. He told the railroad officials that he had one talent: he knew how to handle Negroes. He got the job and made a spectacular success. When I was thirteen, in 1892, he bought 'Mirador,' an estate with a spreading 1820 house in the peach country near Charlottesville. I was the seventh child. Irene, the second daughter, was the beauty of the family, and, as you know, married Charles Dana Gibson, who immortalized her as the Gibson girl. My blessed mother, who was a Virginian of Irish extraction, bore eleven children. And she hated having to birth every single one. She never cared for children. I wasn't born until fourteen years after the war, when Reconstruction had run its hideous course. But I felt its aftereffects. And I have never ceased to admire the Confederates passionately and to love the South. The very thought of Yankees may keep me out of the Kingdom of Heaven."

She ate a bit of the lobster mousse and then said, "Because we were poor when I was a child, I have this enormous sympathy for persons living in poverty and for the overburdened British mothers. I tried my best to help women through legislation."

The gentle David took decided exception when Lady Astor casually remarked to me: "You know, I married beneath me." He sat up straight, glanced my way, and murmured out of the side of his mouth, "I've heard *this* before." He reproved his mother with a touch of indignation. "I don't see how you continue to say that. I like my Astor relatives quite as well as my Virginia kin, and they certainly have better manners than some of the Langhornes I know."

Lady Astor seemed to let the matter drop. Then she decided to prove her point.

"David, you know that the Astors stem from the son of a poor butcher in the German village of Waldorf. John Jacob emigrated to New York at the age of twenty, and promptly went into the fur business and laid the basis of the family fortune by skinnin' skunks in Canada." Turning to me, she went on, "Then he shrewdly began to buy up Manhattan real estate. By 1835 he was reckoned the richest man in the Western Hemisphere. But he was never really received in what was called 'society.' " To David, she said, "Your great-great-grandfather's manners would not do. They say he ate ice cream and peas with his knife."

David winced. His plain-speaking mother had got under his skin. Lady Astor added a softener: "He married a wonderful, level-headed woman, the daughter of his boardinghouse keeper, who brought him three hundred dollars. All the reports say that Sarah Todd was an odd combination of shyness and ambition, reserve and pride. Her characteristics have come down to the Astor descendants. Your father was like that. And aren't those traits yours, too, my darling?"

David did not deign to reply, but changed the subject.

I ate at 100 Eaton Square several times again. Lady Astor never had more than a dozen at table. At the last luncheon, on my right sat Lady Helen Nutting, the charming Scottish aunt of Angus Ogilvy, who had recently married Princess Alexandra, daughter of the Greek beauty Marina, Duchess of Kent. I amused her by remarking that if I lived in London I would prefer to live in Eaton Square above any other location. "I imagine you would!" she said, with a mischievous twinkle in her eye and a soupçon of mockery. "Who wouldn't?" So I gathered that the rent of large apartments facing the small park was astronomical.

After all the other guests had gone, I remained to have a last brief chat with Lady Astor on the long gallery outside the drawing room. It was one of those perfect June days that can be so marvelous in London. I felt that I would never see her again. Though she seemed in excellent health and even still played golf occasionally, she had reached her eighty-third birthday in May. Her beauty was by no means all faded. Though her hair was gray there were still streaks of gold through it. And that exquisite facial bone structure she would carry to the grave with her. She had been a wonderful friend to me and I was extremely fond of her.

Again deploring the fact that Thérèse and I had never stayed with her at Cliveden, a sudden thought struck her as I rose to leave. "Have you ever *seen* Cliveden? Could you go right now? My amiable young chauffeur, who doubled as footman at luncheon, is here. The car is here. It's not a long drive. I do so want you to see Cliveden. We could have tea there."

The idea was more than tempting. But I had an afternoon appointment, and I had to be at Covent Garden at seven-thirty for a gala performance of *La Traviata*—the two hundredth. The beautiful young Mary Costa was making her London debut. Six years earlier, in Tuscaloosa, I had been excited by her voice, her acting, her face, and her figure in a performance of *Candide*. I had predicted her success in grand opera. The porter at my hotel had miraculously secured a stall in the middle of the first row despite the sellout. I could not be late. So with painful regret I was constrained to give up Cliveden.

I may have missed an adventure. I might have met Christine Keeler nude in the swimming pool. For just at this time Lord William Astor was renting one of the estate houses to the "society" osteopath, Stephen Ward, who exhibited Christine's naked charms to the British Minister of War, John Profumo, in the Cliveden pool. The unfortunate man was to retire in disgrace when the scandal broke that he was sharing the favors of the luscious call girl with a high Soviet agent. The osteopath, who had treated

Winston Churchill and a string of other notables, was often at the poolside in late afternoon that June with two or three high-priced beauties he employed for voyeur parties in London. While he was on trial for "immoral conduct" he committed suicide.

I was later told that when the sensational story broke, Lady Astor's secretary and her butler did everything possible to keep it from her. Papers would be destroyed or declared undelivered or the scandalous news clipped out and thrown away. The butler arranged that at a minute to one o'clock and six o'clock every day a friend should telephone and keep her in conversation until the Profumo case had passed on the BBC news. When Lady Astor went to stay with David at Sutton Courtenay the routine was followed. Then one morning his mother got up early before anyone else was stirring and brought in the papers herself. To her horror, she learned everything. Her reaction was instant and typical. At breakfast she told David they must drive to Cliveden that morning to rally around Bill so that the world might see that she was by her son's side. On the way she turned to David and said, bemused, "Why are we going to Cliveden?" Her mind was slipping and she had forgotten.

Thinking it over a few months after the lurid tale filled the papers, I reflected that Christine in the pool might have been a piquant memory for me. Certainly the performance of Mary Costa in *La Traviata* that evening was triumphant, with more fervid enthusiasm from a British audience than I had ever witnessed. She sang divinely and her body was still as perfect as I have seen on any operatic stage. I went backstage to congratulate her. I told her that a few years earlier, when she was virtually unknown, I had been thrilled by her in Tuscaloosa, Alabama. Sweetly, in a genuine Southern accent, she said, "Why, Ah come from Knoxville, Tennessee. That makes us something like kissin' kin, doesn't it?" So I kissed both her hands.

When I had kissed Lady Astor's still graceful octogenarian hand in farewell, I told her that I was to be received by her friend King Gustaf VI Adolf of Sweden at "Sofiero," the summer palace, on June 19. I reminded her that she had given me a letter to him in 1939 when he was the crown prince. She sent His Majesty affectionate messages.

Waiting for the private lift in the foyer I recalled to her the incident in Delray in January, 1938, when the "still small voice" had sent me down the sands to meet her face to face. "Always heed that voice!" she admonished. Then as the lift arrived, she said, "In Isaiah 30, we read this glorious promise: 'Thine ears shall hear a word behind thee, saying, this is the way, walk ye in it, when ye turn to the right, and when ye turn to the left.' " Though her secretary had told me that Lady Astor was "forgetting," she could certainly quote passages from the Bible.

It was my last sight of this fascinating, amusing, generous-hearted woman, beloved by her friends, and darling of the world's pressmen, who "buzzed about her," as *Time* declared, "like bees around a honeypot." I doubted if one of them ever had an inkling of her Bible reading.

Before her death I received three letters from her, all signed "Nancy Astor, Rebel from Virginia." After 1963 she wrote few letters to any of her friends. On April 18, 1964, the day she arrived at Grimsthorpe, the home of her daughter, Lady Ancaster, she had a stroke and was carried up to her bedroom. After two days she was able to sit in a chair for an hour. She had not lost her spirit of jest. She told the doctor who had been called in that, "considering I am dying, I am very well indeed." She tried to read *Science and Health*. When her son Michael read some of it aloud to her, she dozed. Then suddenly she opened her eyes and cried out, "Waldorf, Waldorf, wake me up. *Please!*" On April 30 Michael read her the twenty-third Psalm, over and over again, as she had read the fourteenth chapter of John to Philip Kerr the night his appendix burst. Michael thought that she had moved on, as it were, into the spirit world. When her end was very near, Jakie, another son, was sitting beside her. "Am I dying?" she asked. "Or is it my birthday?" "A bit of both," he answered tenderly.

In the afternoon of May 1, when Rose Harrison sat by her bedside, she raised her hands, looked straight before her, and cried out, "Waldorf!" Then slowly, painlessly, she lapsed into a coma. Early in the morning of May 2, 1964, she made the transference, just a few days before her eighty-fifth birthday.

Phyllis, according to her dying request, covered her casket with a Confederate battle flag, which had been carried in the War Between the States. Her ashes were laid in the same grave with those of her husband.

Scandinavian Summer

IN 1938 Norman Foerster, one of our foremost authorities on American literature, invited me to come to the University of Iowa for a summer school session. The offer tempted me because I planned on spending a year in Scandinavia and I thought I should see something of the Middle West to which so many Swedes and Norwegians had emigrated. I was so ignorant of the section that I imagined that, excepting the cities, the land was one vast cornfield. I wrote Dr. Foerster that I would come if I were allowed to teach a course in Shakespeare's tragedies, as well as his requested course in fiction writing. He accepted my conditions. Then I learned that the other visiting English professor was to be Dr. George Parrot, a Shakespearean specialist from Princeton, now retired. But Parrot amiably offered a course in Elizabethan Literature.

A furnished house was to be secured for two summer months, since a professor from New England with his wife, born a Sedgewick, would be abroad. A maid who "lived in" went with the place. We found the house was furnished with antiques. The best china, silver, and fine linens had been left for our use. Instead of facing a cornfield, trees met in a graceful archway over our street, as in Montgomery and Tuscaloosa.

In Iowa City one of our neighbors was the artist Grant Wood, who often dropped in for tea or a drink. In the chapter on my childhood in Demopolis I have recounted my remembrance of his wife's singing voice in the operetta *Robin Hood*. Baldwin Maxwell, second in command to Norman Foerster, had been born in Montgomery, and his fascinating Iowa wife, named Georgia, reminded us of Scarlett O'Hara.

The Norman Foersters lived in a charming house surrounded by woods on the brink of a hill. We thought that when we did build our own home, we would like it to be a retreat something like theirs. In 1939, the next year, when we saw Isak Dinesen's "Rungstedlund" in Denmark, we got many more ideas from her estate, for it had a meadow and a large garden, as well as acres of surrounding woods.

The summer turned out to be the coolest Iowa City had known in decades. In those days before air conditioning we were told that people carried their mattresses out onto porches to try to endure the sweltering nights of July.

I was asked to be the commencement speaker for summer graduation at the University of Iowa and received a substantial extra check for the performance. Iowa was the only summer school I was ever to teach in. We really enjoyed our six weeks in the Midwest. The greatest boon that came out of it was that I persuaded Dr. Parrot to come and lecture on Shakespeare for me at Alabama for the second semester beginning at the end of January, 1939. When I returned to Tuscaloosa I felt a stronger compulsion to go to Scandinavia at midyear than ever, though I doubt if E.S.P. told me that World War II would break out in September. The university authorities wanted me to remain until June. But with an eminent name like Professor Parrot of Princeton to take my place, they finally relented.

It was icy February when we sailed from New York on the old *Drottningholm* for Göteborg, Sweden. Somewhere south of Greenland Captain Ericsson turned north sharply into the teeth of a terriffic storm to attempt to rescue twenty Norwegian seal hunters bound for Newfoundland. For two days and nights, like a good Samaritan, the Swedish American liner searched the tempestuous seas for the lost men. Finally, when hope was almost extinguished on both sides, we saw the dim lights of the disabled little tub. In a blinding hailstorm, with waves forty feet high, ships officers and men volunteered, at the risk of their lives, to effect the rescue. The lowered boats were held away from the ship by sturdy oars, which split like matchsticks at the impact when dashed against the *Drottningholm*'s side. After a night of suspenseful hours, all twenty Norwegians were able to climb up the ladder to the deck in a state of semiexhaustion, the captain of the crew coming last with his little satchel of documents. Each man was cheered as he was helped over the rail.

After the grim, tempest-tossed voyage, in which I had to tie Thérèse in her bed for two days (we had been given Greta Garbo's suite) we arrived in Göteborg on March 1, three days late. The prosperous city was bathed in brilliant sunshine. Little round flowers called "golden balls" peeped through the snow and made bright pools of yellow under trees. Everything was extraordinarily clean. The sailors' district looked new with neat, comfortable cottages. It was exciting to find no slums and no squalor in a seaport of more than 300,000 inhabitants, where the harbor bristled with international shipping and the foremost shipbuilding activity in Scandinavia was going full blast. In a hilly park pink-cheeked old gentlemen, wearing Persian lamb caps and carrying canes, took their brisk morning constitutionals, while young children, watched by nursemaids, played in the snow or on the green grass.

A letter from a friend to the handsome young Baron Göran von Essen had brought him to the ship to meet us after breakfast. He was pleased to drive us about and to point out manifestations of the state of general welfare. The focal point of the city is the modern Civic Center, completed in 1935, with a modernistic Concert Hall, the new Municipal Theater, and the Art Museum with Carl Milles' Poseidon Fountain before it. We were told that Göteborg's shipbuilders and merchant princes delighted in continued munificence to make their city ever more beautiful. On the way to the baron's home for luncheon we stopped to see a great conservatory filled with rare specimens of orchids like those I had admired in Colombia and Brazil in 1935.

At luncheon, where his pretty wife presided, cocktails were served in fox-hunt-scene glasses, exactly like those that had been given us at Christmas in Bermuda in 1929. They, too, had been purchased at Goode's in London. I have never seen like ones in any other house. The sun poured in through the high windows of the dining room over vases of narcissuses and pots of bright pink azaleas.

When Baron von Essen put us on our afternoon express train for Stockholm he slipped letters of introduction to friends in the capital into my hand, along with our seat reservations and an airmail edition of the London *Times*. So our introduction to these far-northern latitudes could hardly have been more warm or auspicious.

On our arrival in Stockholm that night, though in a flurry of snow, it was almost as cheering as our day in Göteborg. For at the Stockholm Hotel we found a corner sitting room and bedroom waiting for us, with a vase of tulips, daffodils, and anemones, with sprigs of budding elm sent to my wife by the young Countess Madeleine Hamilton, who had crossed on the *Drottningholm* with us, and who had taken a morning train to Stockholm. We went to bed with high expectations of the Scandinavian year to follow.

By the time war came in September, we had traveled in almost every part of the four northern countries and I had eight books packed with notes and interviews. We had been to the northern tip of Norway by ship, to Finland's Arctic Ocean coast by bus from Rovaniemi, to the Russian border of southeast Finland, and to the German border in Denmark, where I stood with one foot on Danish earth and the other foot on German soil. I was tempted to borrow Laurence Sterne's first sentence from *A Sentimental Journey* and write: "They order this matter better"—in Sweden or Denmark or Norway or Finland, as the case might be.

"If you will pardon me," said Dr. Gunnar Heckscher, a Swedish professor of political science at Uppsala University who consistently voted Conservative, "Sweden is twenty years ahead of the United States." He had lectured at Princeton and traveled the U.S.A. from California to Florida. On the whole he was right—in 1939. I came to look upon the four northern countries as something like models which other nations might observe with profit.

We were to find that the three Nordic peoples differ as much in temperament and personality as the New Englander, the Midwesterner, and the Southerner. And the geography of differences is even more marked.

243

Norway towers over Sweden in the magnificence and splendor of its breath-taking mountains and fjords. And Sweden has little of that idyllic charm of Denmark's smiling countryside. Yet Sweden in 1939 was a nation so well-ordered, so reassuring and admirable, that it gave a sense of peace in its harmonious and even-keeled commonwealth that was exciting. A country without slums or degrading poverty, with no illiteracy, no unemployment, with medical care provided for all, and assurance of old-age support, Sweden's standard of general culture for low-income groups exceeded that of the United States in every particular except the possession of motor-cars.

In talking with the head of the youth movement of the Social Demo-cratic Party, whose father had been an effective labor agitator thirty years before, I was agreeably surprised when the young man said, "After all, education's chief goal is to give men the power of distinguishing what is first rate." An urbane Czech author, who had preceded me to Sweden, wrote his consummate opinion: "The wanderer in this strange land feels more of a man and a gentleman than anywhere else in the world."

The next morning Börje H. Brilioth, editor of the Stockholm *Tidningen*, called to present me with a check for my wireless story of the rescue of the Norwegian fishermen, which he had requested. He had known that I was a passenger, because he had had me interviewed by his paper's representative in New York the day before we sailed. Now he brought me a copy of the morning paper with our photographs prominently displayed on the first page, and pictures I had taken of the rescue in the storm, which a man from his paper had asked for when our ship docked. He had had them developed quickly, and my wireless report and the pictures were what was called a scoop. Brilioth also presented me with a silver medal for special services, which he said was rarely given by his paper, and then he invited us to luncheon. I learned that both of his brothers had achieved promi-nence. One was a bishop of the Lutheran church and the other had been private secretary to Ivar Kreuger, called the Swedish match king, who committed suicide when his stock manipulations got hopelessly fouled. But Brilioth's brother, who had been kept in the dark about the tricky trans-actions, was completely exonerated.

The emphasis Swedes put on flowers and house plants as amenities of daily living the stranger notes quickly. And he is also immediately aware of the part water in fountains plays in enhancing the beauty of Stockholm's handsome buildings. The square called Haymarket (Hötorget), just off King Street, one of the busiest commercial thoroughfares in the city, has a fluidity all its own and abounds in color. In the very shadow of Ivar Tengbom's porticoed Concert House, where the Nobel Prize ceremonies are held, as well as symphony concerts, stands Carl Milles' fountain with his sculptured Orpheus. On tiptoe the god of music plucks an unheard melody on his magic lyre that draws up four dead youths and four dead maidens in wonderment from the nether world. The broad steps of the Concert House were crowded with sun worshipers, who threw back their faces and drank in the sunshine of early March, after four months of dreary winter.

The flower market spreads out between the Concert House and the co-operative department store called P.U.B., where Greta Garbo was once a shop assistant. Thérèse bought while tulips and yellow Dutch iris and first sprays of pear blossoms from the south from among this half-acre of potted plants and cut flowers.

Within three days of our arrival I was asked to speak on the Swedish radio and to be received by the Crown Prince on the second day following. I had contracted bronchitis in the Scandinavian snows and was hardly able to talk. In the Stockholm Hotel, coming up in the elevator, Thérèse had noticed a door with the lettering: Christian Science Reading Room. I asked her to go back down there and get someone to recommend a practitioner. She returned with a copy of the C.S. *Journal* containing the names of the eight Stockholm practitioners. She said the librarians were extremely nice, but I should choose my own practitioner. I selected a man and the only teacher of C.S. in Scandinavia. "Please go back and ask them about this Count Sigge Cronstedt."

Thérèse returned with remarkable news. "Count Cronstedt, who drops by the reading room about twice a month, happened to walk in just as I was inquiring about him! He is charming and distinguished. He says that if you decide you want his help, he will be glad to drive back to the hotel after dinner. Here is his telephone number—just as in the *Journal*." With my chest paining me and my voice a croak I debated back and forth. I was afraid a medical doctor would send me to a hospital. Finally I said, "Let's give C.S. a try. Ask him, please, to come."

When Count Cronstedt arrived, I got out of bed, put a robe on over my pajamas, and came out to greet him in our little sitting room. He had been a well-known architect until he had a healing in Science. Then eventually he had become a full-time practitioner. He had a fine-featured face and wore a white imperial. He looked about sixty-five. He seemed in no sense concerned about my condition. With smiling assurance, he told me that God never made sickness, that all that He made was good. So physical discomfort, though it might seem very real, was an illusion, often based on fear. "If Jesus the Christ had believed in the reality of a man's sickness he could not have healed."

As he and Thérèse chatted about various things, I could feel the congestion in my chest breaking up. Thérèse saw the color return to my cheeks. On leaving, Count Cronstedt reassured me, "I will work again tonight and tomorrow. You will rest well, and tomorrow night you will speak on the radio."

I had a good night's sleep. By midafternoon I knew how much better I was. The radio station manager had been told of my indisposition and called on us. He said that they could manage by rigging an elevator device outside to our six-story window. That evening men brought along the necessary complex equipment. I got dressed and read over my prepared speech aloud. My voice was improving minute by minute. Half an hour before I was to go on at eight, I said to the radio men, "I believe I am well. Let's do it at the station." Bundled up in a heavy overcoat and a thick scarf, I was driven off through the snow. All trace of nervousness and anxiety left me as I was being introduced, first in Swedish and then in English. When I spoke my voice was clear and strong. I received compliments and was handed a check. People began calling the station to ask where I was staying in Stockholm.

Back at the hotel I found that Thérèse was very pleased with my voice and my performance. "I am well," I announced triumphantly. "Christian Science *worked.*"

So our real "conversion" or "leaning to" that metaphysical religion, which Lady Astor had led me into, came about in Sweden in 1939. But we were never to become active members of the church. Thérèse was wary of any kind of organization, particularly that of a church. I was too worldly to give up smoking and "social" drinking, and I would never have considered renouncing all forms of medical aid. I was to remain, as I had been christened and confirmed, an Episcopalian, although of "the going-to-church-on-Easter" kind. But we both were to read Mrs. Eddy's books with profit and later to know healings from resident practitioners in various parts of the globe—from Mexico City to Athens and New Delhi and Madrid.

In any case, I feel that I can attest to positive virtues in Christian Science which have helped me in my effort to overcome anxiety neuroses, impatience, and a rather intense self-will.

Two days after my radio appearance I was received by Sweden's Crown Prince, to whom Lady Astor had commended me. The American ambassador, Mr. Frederick Sterling, wanted me to wear his frock coat and striped trousers to the interview, but I declined and went in my own dark blue business suit. The Prince was wearing a dark blue suit with chalky white stripes.

I had been glad to accept the offer of our ambassador's chauffeured limousine, for it was snowing when I arrived at the Royal Palace. The Crown Prince was then acting as regent for his aged father, King Gustav V, who was playing tennis on the Riviera for a month.

In the course of conversation, His Royal Highness, called Gustaf Adolf, told me that the head of the Swedish Labor Federation and his wife had dined with the king at the palace the night before he left for the Riviera. He said, "I don't see how we could be more democratic." He told me that I should meet this August Lindberg, a "most admirable and reasonable" man. "Would it be convenient for you to call on him tomorrow?" On my assent, he rang for his equerry, who telephoned and straightway made the appointment. "There has been no 'class-interest' fanaticism in Labor's leadership," the Prince said. "By their prudence and moderation the trade unions have been a wonderfully stabilizing agency in the labor market." The Crown Prince also gave me a letter to Thorsten Laurin, the publisher, his closest friend among commoners (although, of course, he did not use the term "commoner").

We talked of Lady Astor, whom the Prince had known for decades and thought beautiful. "Her photographs never quite do her justice," he said. "There is an incandescence about her no photographer can catch."

I told the Crown Prince that his brother Prince Wilhelm had reviewed my *South by Thunderbird* in the *Svenska Dagbladet* when the book appeared in Swedish in October and that the review delighted me. He said he remembered it, and that his brother had traveled extensively in South America.

He thought that my wife and I would enjoy performances at the Opera and also at the Royal Dramatic Theater. He said that Swedes took considerable pride in their productions. I told him that our hotel porter had already booked seats for us to hear the young Jussi Björling in *La Bohème*.

The Crown Prince kept me in audience for one hour, and minute by minute I had come to admire him more. I had read of his archeological interest and his personal digging. On parting, he said to me, "If you should ever write about the Swedes, please don't merely praise us. Do point out our faults, as a foreign observer like yourself may see them. We know we still have plenty wrong with us. And we don't want to become smug."

At labor headquarters the next morning August Lindberg received me. He was a tall, handsome, reddish-blond man in his middle fifties. His splendid lumberjack physique and his sympathetic way of speaking both inspired confidence. When I asked him about his education, Lindberg smiled and said, "Like a character in a Jack London novel, I hardly knew what the inside of a schoolhouse looked like. But, seriously, I did attend a short-term backwoods school until I was ten. Then I began to work twelve hours a day at a sawmill. My job was to fetch timber and pile. For that kind of work you must be strong." He had inherited his good constitution, he said, from his father and his grandfather, who had both been employed in an ironworks.

"Now, for my health's sake, because of the present sedentary life, I walk the four miles from my home to my office instead of taking a bus." He could not afford an automobile since his salary was only two thousand dollars a year. In 1939, that was the standard annual salary for a shop foreman; and he did not think he should have more.

"Certainly," he said, "an improved economic condition of the working classes increases the cultural standard too, and with that the spiritual, if I may say so. The Swedish people are much better off spiritually than they were forty years ago. For instance, when I was a youth, the working classes spent their money mostly for alcohol. Now, they buy books—and enroll in adult education classes."

As the Crown Prince had arranged for me to meet the Labor Federation head, so now Mr. Lindberg telephoned and made an appointment for me to interview Gustav Söderlund, head of the Swedish Employers' Association. In Sweden, back in 1902, only four years after the founding of the Labor Federation, the Employers' Association came into existence to offset the workers' waxing power. In the United States the bulk of employers had never yet organized to treat effectively with labor.

Mr. Söderlund was an affable man, who might have doubled for Spencer Tracy, the cinema actor. Though his salary was exactly six times that of Lindberg's, he had much the same background as his opposite number in labor. He grew up as a small boy in Dalarna, where his father worked in the same sawmill with the young August Lindberg. But he had received considerably more formal education.

"In Sweden," Söderlund said, "labor has far more potential power than in America. It is not split into jealous camps like the A. F. of L. and the C.I.O. It is all under one federation. It possesses its own press, with thirty-four daily papers that have a circulation of more than half a million. Swedish labor has its own political party: the Social Democratic. It does not divide its votes between Democrats and Republicans. The Social Democratic Party is today almost as large as all the other parties—Conservative, Liberal, Farmers, and Communist—combined. So you can see employers have a mighty opponent, and we must be wary in our procedures." He paused, and then went on, with the knowing smile of one born in a workman's family, "You have to treat workers very carefully. 'Give, give,' they keep saying. We might give them the whole factory and some of them still wouldn't be satisfied. So we have to make them feel they have *earned* what we give.

"In December, 1938, the leaders of both sides got together and talked tough problems over for several weeks at Saltsjöbaden, a seaside resort near Stockholm. You see, we knew each other well enough to call one another by first names, and that makes argument easier. At night we dined together and played cards or billiards. Five days before Christmas we signed a basic agreement, guaranteeing the public against interruption of essential services and delaying strikes and lockouts. Factory owners in Sweden stick together. If some individual labor union makes utterly unfair and unreasonable demands, the whole bunch could be fired.

"Because Swedish labor is virtually one hundred per cent organized there is no picketing and no indulging in sit-down strikes. The American practice called 'feather-bedding,' which forces employers to hire more workers than are needed, is unknown and would be looked upon as unprincipled. Since the beginning of 1938, except for one ill-advised strike in the metal workers' union, which was engineered by the Communists and ended in defeat for the workers, Sweden has enjoyed a remarkable industrial peace."

As practiced in Sweden, I learned that socialism means little more than social security: co-operatives, where men may buy commodities at near wholesale prices; an opportunity for the clever of humble background to rise; medical care for all, and a social structure where ability and achievement supersede financial rating as criteria.

Yet I was also to find that a good address is tremendously important to the Swede. The aristocrats are still the aristocrats. Swedes want to know by whom you have been entertained. Danes seem to know instinctively who and what you are, while Norwegians don't give a tinker's damn, any more than Texans do, if they happen to like you. But the Swede moves cautiously and may entertain you in the degree that your connections or attainments merit, after he has perhaps made inquiries in what households you have already been received.

I soon discovered that Sweden is a man's country, where the women have equal rights, but the men most of the fun. It is more of a man's country even than England. The Swedes are men's men, but never in the vaunted cinematic version of the two-fisted, hairy-chested American. A Swede merely prefers the company of men, where he can talk alone with men and drink as much as he pleases. If they took their wives or sweethearts with them they would feel under obligation to make conversation with the women, and they do not want to be bothered. Though the well-brought-up Swede knows how to kiss a lady's hand correctly and even with masculine grace, he is the least romantic of men. The word "flirt" has no counterpart in the Swedish language, and the average Swede would be ashamed to belittle himself by flirting. If a foreign girl attempts to charm him, she is often politely squelched. I heard a glamorous, vivacious Polish girl cry out with despair at a party. "Oh, you Swedes! I am frozen here twenty times a day!"

But Thérèse had no such misgivings. When Thorsten Laurin, the Crown Prince's friend, took us to lunch at his home, he could not have made himself more attentive or agreeable. Yet it was Mrs. Laurin, his wife, whom we both came to regard as the most admirable and charming among all the women we knew. She was an ideal of the lady, sympathetic and wise and delightful. I recall that towards the end of luncheon she said to my wife, "Mrs. Strode, I have been watching you and I must say that you skoal perfectly, with unstudied grace. It is sometimes difficult for a foreigner to get the hang of what we call 'skoaling.' " I said that Thérèse had been taught on the *Drottningholm* by Captain Ericsson himself.

After six weeks in Sweden I came to agree with Marcus Wallenberg, the banker, that the Swedish woman is really a finer human being than the Swedish man. Yet in 1939, the offbeat, unspoiled Swedish male, one who possessed the dependable Nordic virtues and a sense of humor, without a trace of stuffiness, was about as pleasing and finished a specimen of humanity as contemporary civilization has produced.

The Swede is more concerned with "making a good appearance" than any race I have known. The Swedish proletariat on a Sunday is better dressed than any laboring class in the world. I recall running into a crowd of workers coming from a Sunday football match in the factory suburb of Jönköping and my surprise at the uniform good cut and quality of the men's topcoats and the smartness with which they wore their fedoras. The young clerk who went about in what is called "society" had his clothes made by a first class tailor, just like the banker or industrialist. This correctness of dress, I think, derives from a strong motive force in a Swede's life: fear of criticism. From birth a Swede is trained in "doing the right thing," obeying the code, making that proper appearance.

In Sweden politeness is a science or an art, as you choose. After meals little boys bow and little girls curtsy and thank their parents for the food. At the end of a formal dinner the hostess stands by the grand piano or the mantel and each lady guest in turn comes up to thank her for the dinner and to kiss her on the cheek if they are old friends. The gentlemen line up to kiss her hand.

The Swedish housewife and the Danish, too, is well trained for her work. There is no better housewife in the world than the Swede or the Dane, though neither are the hausfrau type of women known in Switzerland and Germany. Nobody can get his degree at an agricultural college until he has completed two years of active work on a farm, besides passing his examinations. Count Bonde, who inherited one of the finest castles and estates in Skäne, had to labor for two years on someone else's farm before attaining his degree. The young Countess Wachtmeister served two years as a dairymaid before she got her diploma in agriculture. Twenty-year-old Count Jack Hamilton, who had dinner with us our first night in Stockholm, was working on such a farm, and his mother had to make a long-distance call to the farmer to ask permission for him to stay over another twenty-four hours to meet us.

Though the virile Swedes have courage aplenty—I had personally witnessed their risking their own lives to save the lives of the Norwegian seal-hunters—they have a special horror and hatred of war, as something unworthy of civilized man. Since 1814 Sweden has been at peace. She has managed to stave off invasion and retain her official neutrality when world conflagrations raged about her.

The Swede has a devotion to nature: he feels especially close to the forest. Here he comes into harmony with himself: hiking, camping, shooting, or collecting specimens for his herbarium. Lumberjacks spend most of their lives in the forest, and these steadfast men, tall, strong, and silent, contribute a special quota of stamina to the national health and character. On holidays city laborers hike or bike to the woods. Business and professional men maintain lodges or shacks in the forests, and retire there for refreshment of soul as well as body.

The Swede also has a natural affinity with the sea. To know the real Swede behind the conventional mask, go sailing with him in summer, if you can't go with him on skis through a wintry wood.

Mrs. Bertil-Arpi, the handsome gray-haired director of the Hotel Stockholm, who looked like Queen Marie of Rumania, thought that we should go north to Dalarna while the snows were still thick on the grounds and the slopes were ideal for skiing. Her unmarried daughter Britt managed the resort hotel up there and would be glad to reserve a comfortable room for us. So we took the train for Darlana and the Siljansborg Hotel.

Swedes of all latitudes have their pet epithets for the province of Dalarna, or Dalecarlia, as the English call it. It is the most beloved, because it is the most "typically Swedish" as well as the most colorful. Its sturdy blue-eyed people have accepted what they need of mechanical devices, without disturbing the familiar contenting rhythms. One still finds the same cheerful red farmhouses, with hand-carved gables and gaily decorated porches and cupboards and standing hall clocks painted with tulips and roses. One sees timbered haylofts dating from 1500 and carved fifteenth century reredoses in old blue and white churches. High in the hills, at the *säters,* from midsummer to Michaelmas the cowgirls still yodel on birchbark horns for their cows.

The Maypole dances surpass those of any other part of the land, and the men take pride in their dancing in knee breeches. Nowhere else in Sweden are found such gala beribboned Maypoles, such lilting music, such brilliant native costumes.

On March 21, 1939, the day spring officially arrives, Thérèse and I got out at the station of Rättvik in a flurry of snow. Everything was white and red like a Santa Claus costume as we drove two miles through a frosty Christmas card to Siljansborg. Snow blanketed the rolling hills. The roofs of red barns and red cottages glistened with white. Between the farms birch trees stood naked and graceful with their ankles deep in snow, their milk-white trunks striped with black like a zebra's flank.

In our hotel room on a table between two large windows were narcissus and pink tulips for Thérèse. The windows opened on a balcony overlooking a white garden with an ice-sheeted lake beyond and distant blue-white hills. As Thérèse said, the world looked purified.

On winter evenings a kind of congenial house-party atmosphere exists in Siljansborg. Coffee is taken in one of the several drawing rooms, where one gathers with his own circle of friends, old or new, around open birch log fires or in cozy corners. The handsome black-haired young ski instructor, a

Count Jens Trompi, introduced himself to us our first evening at coffee. We became friends at once. He brought over to our table a beautiful, statuesque blonde, with the name of Ambra. She had a Polish mother and was the wife of a Swedish army colonel. The four of us were to be almost continually together except when Trompi was giving skiing lessons.

Our second afternoon we went with a sleighing party to a place high in the hills. Our new Swedish friend Ambra sent Thérèse a covering for her head, a white woolen cap and a peaked white goatskin cap to go over that. We had misread the markings of temperature on the thermometer outside our window; it said zero, but that was in Centigrade, not Fahrenheit, and we had wondered why we weren't colder at zero.

A few minutes before the appointed hour of the sleigh ride we looked out a window at the head of the stairs and saw a storybook picture. Grouped like figures on a clock dial around the snow-covered circular drive were twelve gaily painted double sleds, piled with red and yellow cushions. The sorrel horses blew their frosty breaths into the air. The stalwart drivers stood with the collars of their fleece-lined coats turned up over the ears to meet the edges of their pulled-down sheepskin caps.

One tall rubicund driver helped Thérèse into the back of a sleigh and then motioned her to snuggle down and lean on the pillows. He wrapped her feet and legs in a soft green blanket and pulled two fleece-lined covers about her, tucking her in like a baby. He went through the same routine with me when I took my place beside her. And then he did as much for Ambra, who was resplendent in a white fox coat and ermine toque, and for the ski master at the opposite end of our sleigh, facing us and traveling backward. In the posture one assumes in a Venetian gondola, we half reclined, as excited as if we were to view for the first time the palaces along the Grand Canal.

Off we went at what is called a merry clip, the honey-colored manes of the horses flying in the wind and the strings of bells jingling like a Christmas chorus from twelve sets of harnesses. The motion of a holiday sleigh behind a fast horse on a frosty afternoon is something to induce little thrills of pleasure all the way. When we took the curves, our sleigh slipped and skidded with just enough uncertainty to add a fillip of danger. Sometimes we came so close to whitened branches of fir trees that they brushed our horses' flanks and flicked snow against our cheeks.

We reached high country, where stood the gray log huts of the *säters,* where the cowgirls live in summer tending their animals and making cheese. The twelve sleighs drew up before the cottage owned by the Swedish Tourist Association. It was like hundreds of others erected about the land for the convenience of hiking vacationists. A bright fire burned in a corner fireplace, the short split birch logs up-ended in the customary Swedish manner. The aroma of good strong coffee mingled pleasantly with the aromatic odor of burning birch and pine cones. At a long table covered with blue-and-white oilcloth we sat down forty strong to eat cake and drink coffee. Having lost their natural reserve and restraint on the invigorating ride, the Swedes chattered like Danes and addressed other Swedes to whom they had not been formally introduced. Musicians appeared and made music with old-fashioned country instruments, the harp and buckhorn, the bagpipe and fiddle. In the late afternoon, after the place had been cleaned and the woodbox filled for the next visitors, we drove back to the hotel under the stars to the tintinnabulation of the twelve sets of sleigh bells.

On Sunday we went to a church service in nearby Leksand. We went early to see the congregation gather. The women wore short white lamb-skin jackets and black skirts with aprons embroidered in narrow vertical stripes of different colors. The married ladies wore white caps with many ribbons; the unmarried, red or flowered caps. Widows were to be recognized by bright yellow aprons and white veils, very fetching indeed on young widows, and quite a contrast to the crepy black of Stockholm widows. The church was comfortably full. Since earliest times the "Dale folk" have had an excellent record for church attendance. The singing was mighty, true, and impressive. For generations men of Dalarna have been renowned for their fine voices and their choral singing. Jussi Björling came from this region and as a youth sang good old Lutheran hymns before he did operatic arias at La Scala and the Metropolitan.

For his text the minister chose a verse from Proverbs: "And he that is of a cool spirit is a man of understanding." This struck me as being emphatically Swedish, and especially significant in the war-imminent year of 1939.

After the service we lingered awhile in the serenely ordered cemetery. For us, one inscription on a headstone stood out above all others:

> How sweet to have lived,
> How beautiful that one can die.

Adjoining the churchyard cemetery is the handsome house, built in the old manor style of white stucco with black metal trimmings, of Dr. Axel Munthe, psychiatrist and physician-in-ordinary to King Gustav V, and author of the international best seller *The Story of San Michele*. The slate roof of the house was now snow-covered. An avenue of white birches led up to the portal. I was told that the author-physician found the Leksand church cemetery the most satisfying in all the world and expected to rest eternally there in this very heart of Sweden. On February 11, 1949, at the age of ninety-one, Dr. Munthe died at the Royal Palace in Stockholm, where he had been the houseguest of the king since 1943.

I delight in recalling that stay in the snows of 1939. I think of what Hans Christian Andersen had written as a tourist in Sweden: "Painter and poet shake hands and go up to Dalarna. That country is rich in beauty and poetry and richest at Lake Siljan." Whatever one's experiences in winter or in summer, if there is response or affection in him, he leaves a bit of his heart in this heart of Sweden.

"The Swedes, more than any other Nordic people," Sigrid Undset remarked when she was our houseguest in Alabama in 1942, "know the desire to create an imaginary world above the real one. See how the lyricist Carl Michael Bellman with his songs lifted the Stockholm underworld into a realm of golden clouds of beauty and music and melancholy." And as the songs of wastrel Bellman turned the traffic of sailors' dives into a roseate region of enchantment, so, in her stories, Selma Lagerlöf cast such glamour over the province of Värmland that today travelers often see the region with the author's imagination. Since the publication of *Gösta Berling's Saga* in 1891, the novel has held the key to the spell of Värmland.

It was largely because of Selma Lagerlöf that we visited Värmland. "Mårbacka," Selma Lagerlöf's home, is the best-known private residence in Sweden. The author has written several books about her childhood home. But in 1939 the stucco house was much grander than when she was born there on November 20, 1858, in a two-story frame house painted the country red, and which had been possessed by the Lagerlöf family for almost three centuries. With the $40,000 that came with the Nobel Prize she won in 1909, the school teacher was able to redo the house. With its creamy stucco walls and gabled black metal roof Mårbacka was rebuilt in the traditional Swedish manor style. Across the front veranda rose six sets of double Doric columns. Here Selma Lagerlöf resided with a secretary and two servants. She received visitors only rarely, and shied away from interviews as assiduously as Greta Garbo, who starred in the silent motion picture version of *Gösta Berling's Saga* before she came to Hollywood.

Dr. Lagerlöf sat on her sun-splashed veranda dictating to her Austrian secretary, a pretty, slender, dark-haired girl who looked like the young Duchess of Windsor in Tyrolean peasant dress. Though the day was quite warm, the author wore a white knitted sweater that reached almost to her knees. Across the back of her chair was folded a fringed blanket of white cashmere. Wrapped about her throat several times was a blue chiffon scarf. Her feet, encased in high-top country walking shoes, rested on a low footstool beside a white Eskimo dog named Kerr. The Austrian girl's fingers paused above the typewriter keys, and Selma Lagerlöf rose slowly to greet us.

The moment she spoke and held out her small hand we were under her spell. We were unprepared for her genuine sweetness. We might have expected the only woman elected to the Swedish Academy to be somewhat austere. Her inherent shyness and reserve she covered up in graciousness. As she showed us about the ground floor of her home, an aura of humility emanated from her, as if she had never become accustomed to the blessings Providence had showered upon her: security and world fame.

The walls of her drawing room were hung with family portraits—generations of clergymen, who sometimes were also dirt farmers and who married daughters of other farmer-clergymen.

"We were not from a noble family," she commented. "Good, but not ennobled."

As I glanced at the foreign editions of her books in the study, testimonials to her widespread success, she seemed to read my thoughts. "It all came from here," she said, pressing her heart. "I was just a school teacher, and a poor little school teacher, too."

I knew that no living Swedish man approached her in literary fame in 1939. That bitter, cynical genius, August Strindberg, who was only nine years older than she, had died in 1912. Now in her eighty-first year, she had enjoyed decades of fame as a living classic, like Rudyard Kipling.

I stopped before a great stuffed wild goose that stood on the hall mantel. "This, of course, is the magical gander that carried Nils Holgerson about Sweden," I said. "The very same," she answered whimsically. "A schoolboy who liked my fanciful tales about Nils shot it, had it stuffed, and sent to me."

Out on the veranda again she let me take half a dozen pictures of her with my Leica, the last pictures of Selma Lagerlöf ever taken.

"They say I am not as well as I should be," she said, "so they are giving me injections of vitamins. But I think sunshine is the best medicine."

When she came to the edge of the veranda to say good-by, we spoke of the beauty of her pastures decked with field flowers and cows. Thérèse said, "I think the flowers must be the reason for the extra sweetness of Värmland butter."

Selma Lagerlöf's eyes twinkled and she gave a little laugh. "It is a pretty thought. But if you notice the meadows closely, you will see that the cows nibble all around the flowers and leave blossoms untouched. Cows just don't like the taste of flowers."

We all laughed at my sentimental wife, as a farmer's boy arrived with the morning newspaper and handed it up to the secretary. I had seen the paper at breakfast and noted possible intimations of war on the first page. It seemed as if a shadow passed over the frail figure of Selma Lagerlöf, who was standing in a shaft of sunlight. "I do hope whatever happens in the world, the peace of Sweden will not be broken."

Selma Lagerlöf lived just long enough after World War II began to donate her gold Nobel medal to be melted down to contribute aid to the innocent sufferers of devastation. A few weeks before the Nazi invasion of Norway, Selma Lagerlöf died, on March 16, 1940. Sweden managed to remain neutral and the peace of Mårbacka was not broken.

When we returned to Stockholm we stayed in a front room of the Grand Hotel. The large windows proved magic casements. In the very center of the city, the long thrusting arm of the Baltic Sea and the capricious Lake Mälaren meet and divide and subdivide the site of Stockholm into chunks of many shapes and sizes, making beauty out of diversity and offering reasons for quantities of picturesque bridges, great and small, high and low.

Some of the islands rise in sharp escarpments and others heave themselves barely above the water's edge. But the webs of electrical illumination linked them all together in slender chains of flame-gold. The city's shimmering incandescence reflected in myriad waterways gave the scene redoubled loveliness. Numerous cities have exciting waterfronts, but no other I know, except Venice, has water before, behind, around, between, beneath, flowing here in natural curves and confined there in long, slender, man-made diagonals. With the possible exception of Rio de Janeiro, where the mountains tumble dramatically into bays, Stockholm has more variety in contour than any other capital. Though Rio is fantastically beautiful, Stockholm has a more harmonious beauty, for the multiplicity of its lights and waterways keeps a certain decorum, offering peace in the same breath with excitement.

I would arise in the night, pull back the dark velvet curtains, and feast my eyes on Stockholm's glories. My window looked directly to the granite bridge called Norrbro, which joins the island of the Old Town with the richest segment of the mainland. Under the bridge the sweet waters of Lake Mälaren meet and commingle with the salty Baltic in perpetual foam-flecked delight. The slender arm of the sea lay between the hotel and that magnificent pile, the Royal Palace, built early in the eighteenth century and designed by Sweden's great architect Nicodemus Tessin the Younger.

High to the left and beyond the island known as "the City Between the Bridges" rose the cliffs of Söder, with villas along the ridge and, at sea level, docks marked for London, Hamburg, Antwerp, Riga. To the near right side of the swirling confluence of waters lay the square honoring Gustavus Adolphus, Sweden's greatest king-hero. There, looking out upon his bronze replica on horseback, stood the Foreign Office and the Royal Opera House. The small island between Gustavus Adolphus Square and the Royal Palace held the House of Parliament on its high embankment and down on the water's edge was an out-of-doors co-operative café embowered in willows. Here on the terrace Carl Milles' famous statue "the Sun Singer" faced the east and a harbor where merchant ships and visiting foreign men-of-war docked. Directly beneath the hotel's front windows were moored three small white passenger steamers that plied the waters of the archipelago. Farther along, beneath the quay, reposed the fishing boats of Stockholm's old timers, who still caught Baltic smelts in great round basket nets right under the walls of the king's palace.

The unearthly quality of the light fell upon this most rational capital city like a gossamer of white-blue transparency. The façades of stone and marble, the quay and the cobbled street glimmered dimly, as if possessing the properties of glowworms. With the seagulls and most of the citizens settled in sleep, Stockholm lay wrapped in countrylike stillness.

At my third-story casement I was enjoying a gentle delirium. Rodin's last words to Carl Milles came to my mind and I felt justified. "Carl," Rodin had said, "whenever you see beauty, look a long time."

In 1851 Bayard Taylor wrote of Copenhagen: "Its streets are gay, brilliant, and bustling and have an air of life and joyousness which contrasts strikingly with the gravity of Stockholm." If the American author-traveler were reminiscing in this age of bicycles and motorcars he would not need to change this description written more than a century ago. The tone of the Danish capital and the whole nation seems to have been set around 1600 by King Christian IV, that irrepressibly buoyant monarch, "plump as a wine barrel and a heavenly fencer." Christian believed that all his subjects should take some joy in their brief passage between the limbos of unknown worlds. He reigned for sixty years (1588–1648), displaying a mighty gusto for life, whether he feasted, made love, directed naval battles, or built lasting monuments to his and Denmark's glory.

Of all Europe's people, none has a more innate garden sense than the Dane. It is both a talent and a hunger with them and runs through the entire population from royalty to the humblest tenant. This flair for making things grow and bloom gives grace to scenery and citizen alike, just as the surrounding seas give savor and vigor to the whole commonwealth. Beyond the city limits, the island of Zeeland is one vast garden with occasional towns of great antiquity. A radiance lies lightly on the quietly composed landscape. Behind farms forests rise like cathedrals. Cottages belonging to folk sagas dot lime-shaded highways. Meadows stretch beyond vision over the gently rolling hills. As the national anthem proclaims, "Denmark is a lovely land."

But if Christian IV had never been born, Copenhagen would be a far less beguiling city today. At least two score of the finest palaces and churches are owed to this king, who was contemporary with Shakespeare and who died only one year before his nephew by marriage, Charles I of England, was beheaded. It was Christian who first embellished roofs and steeples with glittering copper that changes, chameleonlike, with shifting lights of the hours and seasons. His penchant for towers and spires was expressed in opulent variety. Of his numerous copper-covered towers the climax is that of the Stock Exchange, completed in 1640. The long many-gabled building is topped by a fantastic spire fashioned of the entwined tails of four dragons standing on their heads. It is a creation one might expect to find in ancient China rather than in a brisk modern capital. The energetic monarch is reputed to have worked with his own hands on the construction of the dragon-tail spire. A stout advocate of commerce, Christian believed that business might as well be transacted in gay and graceful surroundings.

The burly Round Tower, which rises 117 feet just off a business street, was erected by Christian to serve a double purpose as an astronomical observatory and as a steeple to the adjoining Church of the Trinity. Built stoutly of brick and stucco and ornamented with deep-set double windows in perpendicular rows nine stories high, the cylindrical, phallic Round Tower is as different in style as could be from the fanciful Stock Exchange. To reach the high summit there is no staircase and, of course, no elevator, only a spiraling causeway broad enough to drive up in a carriage and pair, though the only person ever to do so was Russia's Peter the Great.

For his own summer residence Christian erected Rosenborg, a palace in rose-colored brick that rises from a moat in the King's Garden like something conjured up by incantation. Its graceful towers are adorned with copper turrets and pillared belvederes, ending in spears of flying pennants. Originally outside the city, the last king to live there was the mad Christian VII, who died in 1808. Now it has been turned into an authentic and somewhat fabulous memorial museum of the Royal House. In the center of a room in Christian IV's private apartments stands a tall octagonal case holding the crown jewels. One room contains a fantastic throne of narwhal tusks taken from those rare arctic sea unicorns that are endowed with a single tusk of twisted ivory. Another throne is of solid silver guarded by three kittenish lions carved out of the same precious metal.

Anyone may roam at will in the lovely Rosenborg park and when he comes upon the serene seated statue of Hans Christian Andersen he will note the cryptic smile on the homely face, hinting that no tale-spinner need conjure up a castle more fanciful than this one beyond the rose trees. His parents did not even possess a regular bed in Odense in April, 1805, and Hans was born on a bunk fashioned from discarded boards, which had recently served as a frame for a nobleman's bier. The son of a frail cobbler and a buxom, illiterate washerwoman who went on periodic sprees, the child tasted the bitter dregs of penury and humiliation. He grew up physically unattractive, with a long bony face, a large nose, small squinty eyes, and a loose-jointed, lank frame that made him awkward in every movement. He heard the hoots and jeers of his schoolmates continually ringing in his ears. Perhaps his boyish wretchedness was the essential soil for the incubation of his genius. When he was fourteen, with just that number of Danish crowns in his pocket, he set out to seek fame in Copenhagen.

The rawboned, grotesquely ugly boy imagined himself before audiences applauding nightly, as actor, singer, or ballet dancer, he did not care which. So appealing and winning was his manner that shortly several persons of note to whom he had offered his talents were giving him small financial handouts and occasional meals.

At last, he hit upon the genre that was to bring him to the pinnacle of fame. His first volume of fairy tales was published in 1835 when he was thirty. It was a success. His special genius gave him an extraordinary perception of the soul of inanimate things—a tin soldier, a spinning top, a darning needle. He made the world of make-believe seem so real that grownups as well as tiny tots could accept his stories with delight. Hans Christian Andersen soon became a household name with the children of the world.

In background, temperament, and the subject matter of their stories no contrast could be greater than between Hans Andersen and Denmark's foremost contemporary writer of tales, Baroness Karen Blixen, who wrote under her father's name of Isak Dinesen.

When Irita van Doren, editor of the New York *Herald Tribune Books,* asked me to review *Out of Africa* in 1938, I was so moved by its strange beauty that I gave it an ecstatic review which won the front page. When *Seven Gothic Tales* had been published previously the identity of the author was a mystery even to her publisher. When it was chosen as a Book-of-the-Month selection and became a distinguished success, such a clamor of curiosity arose that Isak Dinesen removed the mask sufficiently to reveal that she was a woman and listed correctly in the Danish census as the Baroness Karen Blixen of Rungstedlund, Rungsted. I felt a compulsion to meet the author. So when we left for Scandinavia, Dorothy Canfield gave us a letter to her old friend Frøken Westenholtz and hoped that she would arrange a meeting "if her niece was well enough to see us." Since her return to Denmark after her coffee plantation failed, the Baroness Blixen was virtually a recluse. Her husband was a Swedish nobleman, an adventurous sportsman and hunter who attempted to raise coffee on the side. She had divorced him in 1921 and tried to manage the coffee plantation alone. After seventeen years in Africa, she returned to Denmark and now lived alone in the house where she was born and bred, with only family servants.

The lady had liked my review so well that, after we had been personally recommended by a man from the Danish foreign office with whom she had attended dancing school when a little girl, she consented to have luncheon with us on a Sunday.

There, sitting on a small sofa in the D'Angleterre lobby with a half-finished cigarette still smoking between her fingers, a woman was regarding me with a quizzical smile. She had the most extraordinary eyes I had ever seen; they were deep set, and reminded me of black diamonds. Their brilliance was intensified by long black lashes, black penciled lids, and a white powdered complexion. Her mouth was painted dark crimson. She wore a chic black hat with a nose-length veil and a fox fur stole. When she rose she was not tall, but her slimness, like that of a spear the proud Masai nomads use for killing lions, made her seem so.

When Thérèse came down, Baroness Blixen suggested that we lunch at the Yacht Club Pavilion on the Langelinie, where she had booked a table by a window. Far down the shrub-lined walk Hans Christian Andersen's Little Mermaid, sculptured in bronze by Edvard Eriksen, sat demurely on her sun-warmed rock, gazing wistfully toward the sea.

"You will see here in Denmark," Isak Dinesen was saying as sherry was set before us, "the plus and minus of true democracy. With democracy we seem to give up all ideals other than those which can be reached. It's a mediocre happiness that is purchased at the price of no great art, no great music. With utter democracy the quality of culture is bound to come down. I don't think it's well for a nation to give up its elite completely." She smiled with a hint of wryness and then said, "There should be a few versed in the classics.

"I don't mean to imply," she added quickly, "that the Danish aristocrat was a highly educated man. He wasn't—although a few men did go to Oxford or to one of our universities, some of them were hardly educated at all. Besides agriculture, the males were generally interested only in shooting. But our girls were sent to boarding schools in Paris or Switzerland, taught languages and continental culture."

She would talk fast, then stop suddenly, puff rapidly on a strong Egyptian cigarette with lips pursed and eyes looking into the beyond. Then as suddenly she would begin speaking again.

As she went on talking I saw before me like changing screens the contrasts between her sheltered existence in sophisticated Copenhagen and the primitive life on a Kenya coffee plantation, where for years she was the only white woman among thousands of black people and where she often saw zebras and wildebeasts fleeing before hungry lions.

Along with the stimulations and the satisfactions of living in a mysterious, alien earth, she had known the heavy burden of "carrying a farm on her," as she said—a 6,000-acre tract of land where fruition or dearth affected the well-being of her horde of native workers and numerous squatters to whom she had become attached. She had played physician and nurse, assisted at births and funerals. She had acted as tribal justiciar. She had helped shoot preying lions by the light of a pocket torch. In a book of memoirs, her divorced husband, Baron Blixen, pays high tribute to her courage and audacity in driving a menacing lion away from a bullock cart with only a long whip for a weapon. Because of her frailness, she looked as if she might subsist on a rarefied diet of tea, biscuit, and Malaga grapes. It was gratifying to see this slight woman, bright as a flame, eating with obvious appetite substantial filet of beef with Bordelaise sauce.

I remarked carefully the high-bred face, the nose with nostrils keen as a deerhound's, the lips with a perpetual little twist to the left. The bony structure lay close to the surface of her skin as if proud to reveal its fine, distinctive modeling.

When a very ragged man, such as one almost never sees in Denmark, passed beneath our window, Baroness Blixen looked pained and said, "There are still things for democracy to accomplish in its way. Yet, even so, I don't think poverty and illness are fit subjects for art—nor the rights and wrongs of society, for that matter."

"But what of Dostoevsky?" Thérèse said.

"Ah, that was between man and God!" she said quickly. "His work is like a cry to God. That is, I think, the basis of his art. Perhaps it should be in all art—just as a touch of religion should be in all great art." After a bite, she added with an oblique smile, "It doesn't matter at all whether the Capulets or the Montagues were right or wrong. . . ." She paused, and then said feelingly, "But I could not have lived my life without Shakespeare."

When Baroness Blixen invited us for tea the next Wednesday we drove the fifteen miles along the coast road to Kronborg, the setting of Shakespeare's *Hamlet*. The ivy-clad white house, more than two centuries old, is in the shape of an L—one part, two-story, one part, one-story. The easternmost room of the one-story looks across a narrow white beach over three miles of blue water to Sweden. Here, more than two centuries ago, the lyric poet Johannes Evald composed his songs. In the very same room at a desk before the eastern window Isak Dinesen wrote.

When we rang the bell at Rungstedlund, a woman wearing two black sweaters and a black woolen fascinator wound about her throat came to the door. Her hair was drawn skull-tight into a plait at the nape of her neck and tucked under and tied with a black grosgrain hair ribbon. At first we both thought it was some elder relative, until the characteristic deep voice came—this time from unrouged lips in a face powdered dead white. It was a startling change from her town smartness on Sunday, when she wore her fox fur with elegance.

The tea table was set in a Victorian drawing room cluttered with bric-a-brac, whatnots, antimacassars, and hassocks, just as her mother had left it on her recent death. Here and there a profusion of greenhouse flowers were beautifully arranged. Baroness Blixen talked rapidly while she cut cake with an enormous knife, as if she were hacking into a suckling pig. I thought of lion hunters pausing on the plain for a feed, and yet this was all happening in a white willow drawing room with thick lace curtains and embroidered cushions.

After tea we went into the study that had been Evald's and later her father's, where he wrote Danish outdoor sketches. Before she was born he had sailed to America and for three years lived among the Pawnee Indians in the wilds of Minnesota. They had called him "Boganis" and that was the nom de plume under which he had published. Dinesen had got on quite as well with the redskins as his daughter had with blacks. In the study there was no scent of Victorianism, but old screens from China and chests from

Africa containing treasures and memorials. In one corner were some tall lethal spears and in another a spear-long tusk of spiral ivory from a male narwhal of the Arctic Ocean.

The chief brightness in Karen Blixen's African life had been an Eton-schooled Englishman named Denys Finch-Hatton, who had come adventuring as a white hunter. He would take her up in his Moth plane and fly her about, and then he would sit through long evenings reading aloud to her from the English poets. I had read about this paragon among men in *Out of Africa*. I spied what I thought must be Finch-Hatton's photograph on her desk. I was right. We had never seen a handsomer man in profile. He recalled the early nineteenth century beauty of both Lord Byron and Shelley, but at the same time it was a strong and modern face. It was to this young Englishman, who had conducted lion hunts for Edward, Prince of Wales, and Prince Wilhelm of Sweden, that Isak Dinesen owed some of the felicity of her prose style, for she read him her first attempts at story writing, sitting on the floor before her African fire beside her two Irish deerhounds and Lulu, the pet gazelle. It was Denys who nurtured her love of the English poets, especially Shakespeare and Keats. And like the Polish Conrad, who wrote his books in English, she wrote in English and later translated them into Danish.

Baroness Blixen brought out another photograph of Denys in a frame of worn gray-green silk, a full-face view. We studied the two photographs for some time. She must have loved him very much. We recalled that he was buried in the Ngong hills after he had crashed in his plane the only time he ever refused to take her up with him while he scouted for lions. In *Out of Africa* she had said how lions would sometimes come and sit on his grave at sunrise and sunset. "It was fit and decorous," she had written, "that the lions should come to Denys' grave and make him an African monument. Lord Nelson, himself, I reflected, in Trafalgar Square has his lions made only of bronze."

The lady of Rungstedlund disappeared, but in a second she was back wearing a shaggy brown fur coat. Out on a side veranda she kicked off her shoes and stepped into wooden peasant clogs. We were going to have a look at the garden, several acres of mellowed beauty—ancient beeches, smooth velvety turf, a century-old boxwood hedge. The gravel paths were bordered by blue hyacinths and violets. A white bridge made a graceful arc over a pale amber stream. The wilder ground was still carpeted with white anemones, for the beech trees had not yet unfolded. Beyond the thatched fairy-tale cottages of the gardener and the cook, half hidden by lilac bushes, came the kitchen garden. Suddenly the baroness stopped short. An odd expression of caution and indecision came over her face. I followed her glance. A gray gander, accompanied by his favorite goose, stretched out his neck and hissed. She stepped over to the foot of a gnarled tree and picked up a stout stick. "That gander is a vicious beast," she said, "I don't trust him."

I laughed. "You who have fought lions, afraid of a gander?"

"That's all very well," she said. "But yesterday as I was sitting there on the ground writing, he suddenly rushed at me without warning and gave me a nasty pinch on my thigh. The blood came."

A skylark shot straight up from nowhere and began a song as he ascended. "Let's see if the nightingales are beginning to stir in the thickets. Last night they sang divinely." In the meadows three red cows were grazing contentedly near the outcropping of rock resembling a Viking's monument. We sat down on the rock and turned our faces to the sun as Scandinavians do in early spring.

Baroness Blixen told us that she had renewed her girlhood passion for bicycling in Skagen, that tipmost northern town on the peninsula of Jutland, where she had gone in the dead of winter to work on *Out of Africa*. There she had spent the worst of the winter months in an inn without a heated bathroom. "Life was somewhat hard in Skagen," she admitted, "but it was by no means dismal. I went to fish auctions, chatted with pilots, made friends with commercial travelers, whom I found to be intensely human, full of zest and vigor. I feel sure the same type of men must have been the mercenary soldiers of past centuries. But my boon companions were three little boys around eight or nine. I taught them to play casino in my bedroom, and we went bicycling together. Now whenever I get out of touch with humanity," she said with a merry look in her eyes, "I get on my bike and ride in the throng. There is something very humanizing about a bicycle. It makes all men brothers. You ride along on roads and soon you are conversing pleasantly with someone. There is a kind of snobbish class distinction among motorcars, but with bicycles the model counts for nothing, nor the age, nor even the sex."

We did not hear nightingales on this afternoon, but as she enchanted us with her stories, I thought how inexorably Fate had ripened her for the art of writing. It had plunged her into a stirring primitive activity, which tore at her heart and brain and nerves and muscles with both ecstasy and despair, then it lifted her back into the seclusion of a more or less sheltered life in a sophisticated culture. Her African solitude had given her opportunities to ponder, to judge, to value, to extract subtle emanations of beauty, and to see in the casual incident the significance of the cosmic.

Back at the house we were joined by the baroness's tall, hulking, soft-spoken brother, Thomas Dinesen, who had won a British V.C. in World War I for killing seven Germans single-handed. He had come to take his sister to a family dinner at Frøken Westenholtz's. The baroness kicked off her wooden clogs, put her other shoes back on, and then fetched a tight-knitted white cap and stuck it firmly on her skull. It made her look strange, as if she had just been scalped and thought it quite jolly. Twenty years were wiped away at a stroke. The youthful Nijinsky in some bizarre conception came to my mind. It was fantastic how the woman's aspect and manner could change.

The last thing she said to us was that she would write her relations in Fyn and they would ask us to stay with them. One lived in a castle with a moat and the other in a white palace by the sea. One was the Countess Bernstorff-Gyldensteen and the other, her elder sister, the Countess Wedell, first lady-in-waiting to Queen Alexandrine of Denmark.

More or less in the heart of the island called Fyn lies the provincial capital Odense, named after Odin, chief deity in the hierarchy of Valhalla, god of war, god of wisdom, and god of poetry. In the very core of the old city was born Denmark's favorite son, Hans Christian Andersen. Until the cobbler's boy began to write his fairy tales, St. Canute, great-nephew of Canute the Great, who ruled over England as part of the Danish Empire, was ranked as the foremost personage. In the crypt of the Cathedral lie the bones of this Canute II, who was not saintly at all.

From Odense it was only a short train journey to Wedellsborg, one of the most beautiful castles in Fyn. The estate, with vast farmlands, was owned by Count Julius Wedell. Countess Wedell had reached us by telephone to ask if we could postpone our arrival by three days, because something had gone wrong with the drains. But it was really because she wanted us to be there for the leafing of the beech trees.

The day we arrived happened to be gray, which is rare in the first week of May. An old man was waiting at the station for us in a Studebaker. As we drew near Wedellsborg, the sun appeared and turned the cloudy day into blue and gold. Two white cottages with thatched roofs stood just within the great gate, like a double welcome to the beech forest that rose nobly all about. The trunks of the beeches were like columns of pale olive green marble, supporting an azure roof. The tender buds of the branches were swollen to the very verge of unfolding, while the floor of the forest was inlaid with millions of white anemones. The old man, pointing upward, indicated the approaching climax of leafing and said "tomorrow." On the left side of the drive the park eventually ended and the meadows began, but on our right the beeches extended all the way to the body of water called the Little Belt. Directly ahead the castle loomed up somewhat in the shape of the letter Z with its middle line straight instead of on the bias. Like the royal residence of Fredensborg, it was all white and not the usual pink or red brick of the other Danish castles.

Without embellishments of towers or a lilied moat, it sat solidly on the earth that gave it *raison d'être* and sustenance. When the car stopped in the pebbled courtyard before the main entrance two menservants welcomed us with dignified smiles. They led us to our rooms, first up the broad main staircase, and then through the block-long Knights' Hall with magnificent oak beams, armor, carved chests, tapestries, and all the appurtenances of a noble seat.

Down three steps we turned left into the corridor of the east wing. Doors of the bedrooms had typed cards inserted into copper frames bearing the names of the weekend guests who were to occupy them. Our suite with two bedrooms and a shared bath lay at the extreme end. Mine was masculine enough, done in yellow chintz, with a portrait over the fireplace of the Danish Alexandra, queen to Britain's Edward VII. Our bags were already in our rooms, brought up a circular stairway. One of the men helped me unpack. Shortly a manservant came to fetch us for tea, and said the Greve would now receive us. Downstairs again, we were ushered into a bright drawing room furnished in green and gold Louis Quatorze.

Count Wedell greeted us with even more than Danish affability. He was a typical Dane, fair and pink with sandy hair, and dressed in English country clothes. He presented a young diplomat just returned from some Balkan state. The count busied himself at a high side table, preparing tea. Then the four of us gathered about a round table set with a pink cloth and much toast and fresh orange cake. At the first sniff of the aroma and a sip of tea Thérèse recognized it as Earl Grey, and remarked that it was her favorite tea and that we drank it at home in Alabama. Count Wedell raised his eyebrows in surprise and relief. From that moment the American strangers were "accepted."

In the midst of our second cup an American lady, Mrs. James Hazen Hyde, who lived in Paris, arrived. Frightened by talk of Hitler's probable imminent move on France, she had closed her house and fled to Copenhagen with four trunks of clothes and her more precious bric-a-brac. Through her sister's husband, who was Danish minister to France, she had been invited to Wedellsborg.

"How do you like your tea?" the count asked.

"My dear, like poison." From then on, for two days, the conversation was chiefly hers. Petite, smart, with shrewd and witty eyes, she was like a character created by Noel Coward. Born rich in Pittsburgh, twice married and twice divorced, she was a rootless cosmopolite. When she was a girl her father had been American ambassador to numerous European countries. "My dear, when father was in diplomacy we left bathrooms in half the capitals in Europe. That's where our fortune went—in plumbing."

While Marte Hyde was enjoying her third cup of poison, Countess Wedell came in with two bounding springer spaniels. She had been shopping in a nearby town. Dressed in a green sweater suit and a green felt hat, she was an attractive, slender woman with pale red hair, a narrow face, keen intelligent eyes, and a distinguished nose. She never took tea, she said, for she was generally too busy at teatime.

I proposed a walk through the park to the sea. The count said he would be happy to accompany me. Countess Wedell decided to come with us and brought the spaniels along for a run.

From the seaside view the castle was more impressive. A double balustraded staircase of white marble curved up to a rounded balcony and a formal entrance into the Knights' Hall. A stretch of green turf lined with enormous old boxwoods clipped in pineapple shape reached to the edge of the park. Three diverging avenues through the beechwoods pointed their arrowheaded formation at the castle, so that one could stand on the lawn and get three different glimpses of the Little Belt.

"In that upper room at the end nearest the forest," the countess said, "Karen Blixen wrote several of her *Gothic Tales*. She was absolutely secluded, but sometimes she would read her stories to us in manuscript about a winter fire."

In our walk down the central avenue I paused for an admiring backward glance at the gleaming white house. "The castle was first heard of in the fourteenth century," Count Wedell explained. "But only the main hall existed then. The present restoration with the added wings dates from 1672. That was the year the feudal entail was established by a Wedell ancestor of mine."

The Little Belt was churning restlessly when we reached its shore, and the seagulls were circling low. We climbed stairs to the top level of a pavilion set near the water's edge, fine in summer for watching ships sail between the Baltic Sea and the Kattegat.

The Wedells were very easy to talk with, the count as naturally loquacious as any Dane; the countess more reserved, but an excellent listener. Both lived busy lives. The count attended to all the bookkeeping of the farm and the tenants and the students working toward their degrees in agriculture. The countess directed the domestic affairs herself without a housekeeper. Besides being mistress of Wedellsborg, the countess owned Frijsenborg, the largest castle in Jutland, where she had been born and where she spent every June discussing farming and dairying with the overseer and going over business accounts. Beyond these responsibilities, Countess Wedell had to be at Queen Alexandrine's side as her first lady-in-waiting during the court season.

During our absence the Dutch ambassador and Mme. Scavenius, divorced wife of a former foreign minister of Denmark, had arrived. To join us for dinner that evening Baroness Rosencrantz, Count Wedell's sister, drove over from a neighboring estate where she was visiting. Mrs. Hyde told me *sotto voce* that when Theodore Roosevelt met the baroness as a debutante, he pronounced her the most beautiful blonde in Europe. Though her hair was a lustrous gray now, she was still an extremely handsome woman and her gray-blue eyes seemed strangely clairvoyant. Her deceased husband had been head of the Rosencrantz clan and owned Rosenholm Castle, an estate in Jutland.

Despite *Hamlet,* the name of Rosencrantz is uncommonly well spoken of in Danish annals. The Guildensterns had long since died out in Denmark even before Shakespeare's day.

At dinner Baroness Rosencrantz instructed me in the etiquette of eating hard-boiled seagull eggs, which was the first course. In Denmark they are considered a rare delicacy, like plover's eggs in England. These were the first of the season and had been gathered fresh on the estate. You put the peeled egg end-up in your left palm and then smash it gently with your right palm until the white falls open. You discard the white, which is never eaten, touch the yellow ball with salt, and eat it in two bites.

When we returned to the drawing room for coffee, one of the footmen was perceptibly agitated as he spoke to Count Wedell in an undertone. The count went to one of the long windows and drew back the draperies. The Little Belt blazed with illumination, as if a city had suddenly been raised upon the water. Thirteen Nazi warships were anchored at the foot of the garden. They had come quietly while we were dining. One of the gardeners had been strolling along the shore and had seen them arrive. He had run to inform the household just as we were finishing dessert.

"There has not been a fleet of German warships in the Little Belt since the last war," Countess Wedell said.

"This must be *it,*" Mrs. Hyde said with dramatic underemphasis. "I have fled Paris only to run into invasion here."

"We might as well have a good look," I said, stepping out on the terrace.

Through the screens of the beech branches the luminosity was impressive. But everything was intensely still. There were no shouts, no music, no sounds of any kind. The gardener's word was to be depended upon, the count said, for he had once been a sailor and was knowledgeable in foreign vessels.

Presently Baroness Rosencrantz, who had thrown a cape about her shoulders, joined me at the balustrade. "If another war comes," she ruminated after a silence, "it may well mean the end of all this." She touched the marble balustrade lightly, then looked up at the walls of the castle where she had been born, and gazed out into the park. She was indicating a way of life. "For some years now I have wondered if this will last out our time."

When we returned, the Dutch ambassador was complimenting Mrs. Hyde on her dress of purplish-blue velvet with gold embroidery made by Schiaparelli. "It's really nothing," she said, "just a house dress. It's got a zipper—it zips all the way down the front. That makes it for the house. Schiaparelli would have a conniption fit if she saw this dress *out.* Black is the thing in Paris these days. Of course, white is lovely—if you only knew where you would end up in the evening. But there is no telling nowadays—

and in black you can slip in and out of almost any kind of place." We all laughed and the tension was further eased.

Out of the west windows lights from the warships blazed steadily. We all went to bed that night with varying degrees of disquiet. But the next morning when the servants set out breakfast in Thérèse's room the sun was shining brightly. We were told that the German ships had departed at dawn as quietly and strangely as they had come at dusk.

As we passed Mrs. Hyde's suite on our way downstairs to meet Count Wedell, who was taking us over his farmlands, she was at the door to greet us. The two-centuries-old clock in the outside wall above her sitting room was just striking ten. "Did you hear that clock make that dreadful noise just before it struck? My dear, it gave me the fright of my life at midnight. You know how jumpy we all were with the German navy staring at us within a long rifle shot. Well, I had just come up and put aside the Schiaparelli diaphanous nightie my maid had laid out in case Countess Wedell came in for a second goodnight. Then I reached down into my bag and dug out the good old cotton flannel nightgown I always carry when I visit in castles. You never know what shivering drafts you may run into in these ancient houses. I had just put it on and got into bed when I thought I heard a crunching on the gravel below, and then came the terrible grating and grinding in the clock before it struck with a crash bang. 'My god,' I said to myself, 'the doors are broken. The admiral is here!' My dear, like lightning I hopped out of bed, slipped out of the cotton flannel and reached for the Schiaparelli. Then I jumped back into bed and began running through my German verbs. If I was to be taken, I wanted to be taken elegantly."

Downstairs, when we looked out on the back terrace, the beech forest shimmered with ethereal green. A glory lay upon the crowns of the beeches and made the shadowy atmosphere of the woods luminous like the Aurora Borealis. Songbirds flocking to their restored choirs voiced rapture. We walked down the stairs into the near wood. To move under the trees through the anemones was like walking along the bottom of the sea among myriads of small white starfish. If we looked up it was like sauntering through a cathedral of pale green glass. As an esthetic impact I can rank nothing higher.

Count Wedell came to join us and I requested to see his pigs being readied for the English market. Nowadays one rarely saw a Danish pig except in a model pighouse with a well-scrubbed cement floor. Mechanized farming and social legislation had brought revolutionary changes in the commonwealth, so the home life of Denmark's pigs had undergone a change as radical as their breeding, which was planned for bacon-leanness in the British market. I said I wondered if the pigs did not enjoy their existence more under the old order, when their pens were less sanitary and they were not hedged about with quotas, scientific feeding, and other forms of twentieth century materialism, but left free to wander in woods or wallow in puddles.

But the farmer said, no, pigs were instinctively clean animals. They only wallowed in mud to get the lice off. These contemporary pigs had no lice. They lay on beds of clean, fresh straw. They never dirtied it, the farmer said. There was a runway at the back of their stalls where they could go to an outdoor toilet. The pigs had very pink skins and white hair. The farmer picked up a piglet and offered it to Thèrése. She cuddled it like a puppy. "Pigs in Denmark," she said, "do not even smell like pigs."

The way of the manor might be singing its swan song, as the Baroness Rosencrantz had suggested. The probable future of the entailed estates was forecast in a political crisis of 1919 when a law was passed by which they were lifted from entail at the death of the owner. Once more powerful than most kings, the Danish nobility had virtually no political power in 1939. But the estates do contribute financially to the national economy. Farming them is big business that requires managerial ability and constant vigilance. The owners know each farm activity from the apple crop to sugar beets and wood cutting and pasture lands to processing the milk of a thousand cows. Just as royalty in Scandinavia is considered a symbol of national unity, so the aristocrats add tone to Denmark's socialized society.

We took the train trip from Oslo to Bergen because it was said to be particularly beautiful in late May with snow still on the mountaintops and with the apple trees bursting into bloom along the Norwegian railway tracks. We had never seen such a profusion of huge blossoms. Interspersed among the apple trees were blooming lilacs which drenched the air with their fragrance at the little stations when we alighted for a stretch. We were bound for Bergen to take the *Stella Polaris* on a cruise up to the North Cape in the time of the midnight sun. The scenery of the fjords with the jagged snow-covered mountains and fertile green valleys is as varied as it is magnificent. We made four stops along the way. With the glory of the midnight sun almost at the full, it was hard to take ourselves to bed.

At Hammerfest, the most northern town in Europe, I was immediately impressed by the ruddy cheeks of the little boys, which looked as if they had been heavily rouged. All in all they were the healthiest-looking kids I had seen in any part of the world. Next, I was also attracted to the display of fur skins for sale, particularly the Spitzbergen blue fox and the ermine. Thérèse was tempted by the elegant skins, which she held up to her face. But she could not make up her mind to close the deal before the *Stella Polaris*'s whistle politely summoned us to return to the ship.

We hardly got to our stateroom when the rosy-cheeked woman who had offered the skins knocked on our door. She had brought them with her. She thought that my wife might have had time to consider further. "You will never again see such rich quality in fur," I encouraged her. So Thérèse quickly signed the proper number of American Express checks, and the Hammerfest lady departed happily, to be rowed across the bay back to her place of business.

In Bergen, a furrier, among whose patrons was Juliana of Holland, took great interest in fashioning a short ermine cape with a high Elizabethan collar for Thérèse, and he made a blue fox stole that pleased us immeasurably. He charged a fraction of what such expert workmanship would have cost in New York and which we could never have afforded.

Gösta af Geijerstam, whose idyll called *Northern Summer* had inspired my Scandinavian visit while reading the book in mid-Atlantic in 1937, telephoned me when we were visiting in the guesthouse of an electrical manufacturing concern. Because he did not speak English, our hostess had to translate the conversation. Several persons, he said, had sent him cuttings from various Scandinavian papers in which I told reporters about his influence on my trip. He was very pleased with all this praise from an unknown American, and he was now inviting us to stay at his home in Dale in Sunnfjord. He said he would fetch us in a motorboat. Impulsively I accepted his invitation.

Geijerstam's father was an ennobled Swede and an author of distinction. Gösta had married a Norwegian and become a Catholic convert, as had his godmother Sigrid Undset, the person I desired to meet above all others in Norway. He came and spent the night with our new friends in the company guesthouse. At dinner much translation ensued, amid exchanged smiles. We left in the morning. Somehow Gösta and I managed to communicate by gestures. No matter what remark I made he would smile. A carefree rapport was established between us.

Gösta was a sweet-natured fellow, who apparently had never had a regular job in his life. Before *Northern Summer,* his first book, published with success by Dutton in the United States, he had written only short pieces and spent a lot of time with his sketchbook. In the meantime he had begat four sons and a daughter in rapid succession, who were reared in a two-story house his wife had inherited in the village of Dale on Sunnfjord. All the children were grown-up now; only two remained at home.

Thérèse and I spent two nights at the home in Dale, where a few polished antique pieces gave evidence of Gösta's background. Astri, his energetic wife, was a capable woman with wind-blown blond hair, who managed entirely without maid. Fortunately Astri spoke some English and understood it well. There was no bathroom in the house, only an outdoor privy. But we had a really heartwarming visit climaxed by a trip to the island they owned, Storevik, where the nineteen-year-old third son, Peter-Lorenz, lived alone, trying to raise vegetables for the family table and hay for the cow. This young man was an ideal son, tall and handsome, and as industrious as his father was seemingly lazy.

"Sigrid Undset often spent her holidays with us," Astri said, "and stayed in the hut vacated by the death of our octogenarian milkmaid, Marthe. She would come at haymaking and always she helped rake hay. Her children offered childish help and ran about the fields like ours, naked under the sun.

"Sometimes, before the potatoes and peas were mature, we had little to eat but clabber, and maybe fish, but Sigrid can live on clabber as content as anybody. She can milk and make butter and cheese. And she is so good, so good! She gives all her money away—to her church, to charities, to needy friends. People borrow and borrow and never pay back. Her purse is hardly full before it is empty again. She gave every øre of her Nobel Prize money, forty thousand dollars, to a home for crippled children. Her only daughter was born a partial cripple, and retarded as well."

Gösta, with Astri interpreting, told us of the drowning in the bay of the second son, Svante, in a squall, when he was returning from the island in an old boat to the mainland. "We heard him crying, crying," meaning "calling for help." "But we had no way of reaching him. And then the crying stopped and we knew he had gone under. His body was washed ashore two days later."

Thérèse and I had admired the admirable qualities of Peter-Lorenz and we had seen his inferior old rowboat tied up on the island. I casually asked him what a new boat and new oars would cost. Peter-Lorenz said it would be about twenty-five dollars in American money. So after we returned to Dale, when we were saying good-by to the Geijerstams, I put into his mother's hand thirty dollars in American Express checks and said, "Let Peter-Lorenz select his own boat when he next goes to the city." Her face lighted with gratitude. "We shall name the boat the *Alabama!*" she exlaimed.

I had been told that in Europe it was easier to gain an audience with all the crowned heads than to meet Sigrid Undset. I had called on the Norwegian ambassador, Wilhelm Morgenstierne, in Washington, to make this special request. It was the one thing he could not do for me, alas, he said regretfully.

We were scheduled to go to the charming, idyllic town of Lillehammer, where Sigrid Undset lived, to spend Midsummer Eve. I knew that she resided there in a sixteenth century house brought down from somewhere farther north and set up in her garden. Astri had told me that she was not well. And because she was extremely reticent, she protected her shyness with forbidding frigidity. But behind a seemingly impenetrable façade, Astri declared, there beat a mighty heart, full of kindness. Gösta gave me a brief note to her the morning we left for Oslo.

Except for its splendid situation on the water, I could not say much for the beauty of Oslo itself. The new architecture seemed heavy and without grace. However, the blooming lilac trees that marched from the Grand

Hotel up the avenue to the very gates of the king's palace were superb, and I was fascinated by the Viking ship museum with three magnificent vessels of Viking days.

We were guests for the weekend of the American minister, Florence Jaffray Harriman, a good-looking, stylish, lively widow of seventy, who had caught herself a handsome admirer ten years younger than herself. While we were staying with her, she gave a farewell white-tie dinner to the Danish minister, who was being transferred to Washington. After dinner we danced, and Mrs. Harriman did all the latest dance steps with her beau as partner. She had learned to ski at sixty-nine. She may have been an indifferent ambassador, but she was immensely popular with the Norwegians.

Confidentially, Mrs. Harriman told me she was certain war was coming and that the United States would become involved, because we had told England she must stop the appeasement of Hitler or we would not help her. But the Norwegians seemed little concerned, and could not quite take in the iikelihood of armed conflict.

After our weekend at the embassy we moved to the Grand Hotel for my convenience in seeing the prime minister, Foreign Minister Halvdan Koht, and Carl G. Hambro, President of the Norwegian Parliament. The latter took up much time with me. He was interested in the theater and had married the widowed mother of Lilibel Ibsen. It was at the Grand after his triumphant return from years in Italy, Hambro told me, that the dramatist Henrik Ibsen would take his afternoon coffee by a window in the ground-floor dining room to be seen by the world at large if it cared to look. But he was not to be spoken to or ever interrupted in his reading of the hotel's newspapers. He had known such great success that at one time his *Pillars of Society* was playing simultaneously in five different theaters in Munich, in February, 1878.

We had a letter from Irene Ibsen Bille in Copenhagen to her brother Tancred Ibsen, who lived in the fashionable suburbs. We went to tea with him and his wife, Lilibel, a noted dancer and an actress. Tancred was the grandson of both Ibsen and Björnstjerne Björnson, playwright, novelist, social reformer, and patriot, who had received the Nobel Prize in Literature in 1903. Tancred had had his youthful adventures, and once shipped out to Antarctica on a whaling vessel. Then he had become a motion picture director. When he was a boy, his father was prime minister of Norway. Lilibel remained a favorite in the theater, but she had virtually retired from dancing. We found them the most attractive couple we had known in Norway, and Thérèse said that Tancred was the handsomest man she had set eyes on. Neither of them had ever seen Sigrid Undset, but Tancred told me she lived across a Lillehammer street from his Björnson relatives at the edge of the town.

Lillehammer is one of those towns one is apt to fall in love with at once, even when it is crowded with tourists at midsummer. But my objective was to meet the woman who had written *Kristin Lavransdatter*. Ever since we had read the book in Bermuda in 1931 I had had this desire, though I had foreseen no possibility of fulfilling it. I was convinced that she had no equal among women novelists of this century, and who among male novelists was her superior?

"But it is impossible to see her! Impossible!" the hotel manager told me. "She receives no one. If strangers approach her and speak to her, she breaks out in red splotches."

"But I have a letter from her godson, Gösta af Geijerstam, the writer," I said with confidence.

"It will make no difference. Her German publisher came all the way from Germany just to meet her. But he didn't."

The highly intelligent editor of Lillehammer's newspaper was hardly more reassuring. "Sigrid Undset is really extremely shy," he said. "A few years ago the booksellers of the four northern countries held a convention here. I know Sigrid moderately well, and I told her 'You must entertain them. Let them come to see your garden and give them tea. It is not for your literary reputation or the increased sale of your books that you must do this, but for Norway's sake.' Although her mother was a Dane, she is an intensely patriotic Norwegian. Finally she consented to give them tea in her garden. After all the booksellers had arrived on the appointed hour, I went into the house to bring her forth. As she stepped out on her porch to greet her guests, two Danes rushed forward and snapped her picture. She fainted dead away at their feet. You may know that Sigrid is a rather large woman and heavy, so we had a struggle to carry her back in the house. When her housekeeper and I had revived her she asked me what she was to do now. I told her she should walk among her guests with her teacup in her hand and say 'skoal!' I escorted her down into the garden to sit at my reserved table. Then I tucked her arm into mine and she went from group to group with her teacup raised saying 'skoal.' "

The editor told us this when we were having lunch with him at his home. He had invited Anders Villier, headmaster of a boy's boarding school in Lillehammer, whom I came to regard as a most admirable man. Casually, the editor remarked that the wife of Villier, who spoke hardly a word, was the youngest daughter of the "Swedish poet, Strindberg." I was considerably surprised, for she was so painfully shy. She was a tall, slender, blond young woman, who had two boys of twelve and ten. Her mother was the actress Harriet Bosse, the third and last wife of August Strindberg, who still played at the Stockholm Dramatic Theater. We were to meet her later in her dressing room after a performance, and find her very sweet.

On one of those incomparable Northern afternoons in June, just before St. John's Day, the twenty-fourth, scorning the dismal auguries, with a reluctant Thérèse I walked the flowery mile from our hotel to the home of Sigrid Undset, which was called "Bjerksback." My expectations were a bit dampened by the eight-foot stockade of split logs that surrounded the house and extensive garden. When I rang the bell at the stout forbidding gate, we were greeted by the ferocious barking of dogs. There was a delayed fumbling of heavy bolts. The gate was cracked six inches, and instantly the fangs of three dogs were through, thigh-high, knee-high, and ankle-high. Above the snarling muzzles of the dogs shone the hostile eyes of a maidservant. "The Fru is sick," came in quick Norwegian.

I held out my letter. The woman regarded the white envelope coldly. I explained in the few Norwegian words I knew who it was from and stuck it through the narrow opening. The maid took it grudgingly, shut the gate, fastened the bolts. Thérèse said, "I shall not be a party to this," and wended her way back to the hotel. I stood in the road and waited and waited—the dogs ceaselessly barking. Finally I decided the incident was closed and was turning away just as the bolts grated again. The woman hailed me and stuck a correspondence card through the crack. It was a note in pencil from the lady herself.

> Thursday
> June 23
>
> Dear Mr. Strode
>   I am so sorry to be unable to see you, but I am ill and must stay in bed some days.
>   Hope you have enjoyed your stay in Norway.
>   Please excuse this writing but I am not allowed to sit up.
>
> Yours truly,
> Sigrid Undset

"We said you would not see her," the hotel manager remarked on my return. But the note in Sigrid Undset's own handwriting impressed him. And it gave me courage to send Fru Undset a note expressing sympathy for her indisposition and saying that we had hoped to give direct news of the Geijerstams. I said we were so charmed by Lillehammer that my wife and I were staying over until the next Tuesday, and that if she were mended before then I still hoped to have the honor of meeting her.

On Monday, when I returned from a morning climb, the manager and his staff looked at me with new eyes. Fru Undset had herself telephoned while I was out. She had recovered. Would I be so good as to call on her at five that afternoon?

At five I presented myself at the gate of the stockade. The maidservant, all dimpling smiles and ducking curtsies now, led me over a stretch of lawn to the largest of three gray weathered houses. The dogs had been banished to the cellar. Two of the structures had been reconstructed from log houses brought down from the Gulbrandsdalen mountains. One, I learned later, dated from 1700, the other, in which Sigrid Undset lived, had been built in 1590. I was left alone in the spacious high-ceilinged living room of the latter. Its walls were of paneled pine. The enormous stone fireplace gleamed with bronze and copper utensils and racks of pewter platters. Peasant antiques of simple beauty, with shaggy goatskins thrown over chairs, comprised the furniture. The colors were primitive and cool— ivory, weathered gray, the bronze of pine cones, the pale silver of birch bark, the white of goat hair. Not only did Sigrid Undset re-create bygone centuries in her novels as no other person could do so well, but she had made her drawing room a breathing evocation of the past.

Her love of the past, I reflected, might stem back to her birthplace in the medieval town of Kalundborg in Denmark, for she was born at the old home of her Danish mother, but went to her father's country, Norway, when a small child. More likely its source was in her Norwegian father, a distinguished archeologist, who let her render him youthful assistance in his work of delving into past epochs.

The windows—curtainless to let in the full golden flood of Norwegian sunlight—looked out over lilac bushes to the blue-green mountains beyond the river. As I was examining a picture on the wall, the atmosphere suddenly became suffused with the scent of lavender, as if a wind had blown over a whole bank of the pungent plants. I turned. Sigrid Undset was standing in the center of the room. She was very light on her feet and had come in silently. She gave me a searching look, then held out her hand stiffly and said, "How do you do," with a get-it-over-as-quick-as-you-can handshake. Then she glanced sidelong at the floor. We stood silent for a moment in the middle of the room.

Dressed in a black-and-white silk print, Sigrid Undset stood there uncomfortable in her own drawing room, radiating—as if against her will—an aura of greatness. She was broad-browed, with great brooding blue-gray eyes, and in stature she suggested a Brünnhilde. She was a paradox: a shy woman of commanding presence who made a man feel strangely protective toward her.

"I was just admiring that sketch of Gösta Geijerstam's," I said, after the pause. "Gösta and Astri send you devoted love."

Fru Undset glanced at me again in shrewd appraisal, as if she saw not with her eyes but something behind her eyes. Then she said, "In my study I have two earlier drawings of Gösta's, which I like better."

We moved into the narrow study that opened off from the drawing room. It was lit by one long narrow window high in the wall above her desk. A half-finished page of manuscript in Norwegian curled in the old portable typewriter. "You do your own typing?" I asked.

"Yes, and my letters, too. Sometimes I have so many letters to write that there is little time left for fiction."

"Why no secretary?" I asked.

A faint line of smile curved her mouth. "I can't bear to have one around."

"But you waste so much priceless energy doing your own typing," I protested.

"I would use up more energy resisting the personality of a secretary in the house," she said crisply. "I had one once, but I could not dictate. So all the secretary could do was to address envelopes. When she had finished the envelopes she would say, 'What shall I do now?' Then I would have to stop and think up a task for her. Oh no! With a secretary in my house—all my strength goes."

Back in the drawing room Sigrid Undset looked about uncertainly. "Where shall we sit?" she asked. "I almost never use this room."

Glancing about, I said, "Why not over here?" indicating a corner where rich white goatskins had been thrown over chairs. It was evident that I had to make my hostess at ease in her own house.

"But where is your wife?" she asked, sitting down. "Is she coming later?"

I told her that Thérèse wasn't coming—that the hotel clerk did not make it clear she had been invited.

"But, of course! We must telephone for her."

"I doubt if she will come—she is very shy."

Fru Undset gave me a skeptical glance, and said with subtle emphasis, "An *American* lady—*shy?*"

I laughed and she smiled. "Some are," I said. "But, please, you telephone her and tell her I say she must come immediately—not to change, but come as she is."

"I shall ask her *politely,*" Fru Undset said, putting me in my place as a husband.

The ice was broken. Thérèse arrived sooner than we expected. She told me later that the hotel manager had rushed up to her room, wildly excited, and said that Fru Undset herself had telephoned and that she was to come at once. "We have already ordered a taxi," he said.

When Sigrid Undset saw that my wife really was shy, she at once began putting her at her ease. For the rest of the long afternoon, over tea or wandering about the garden, where delphiniums grew ten feet high, Fru Undset talked easily.

She came quite naturally by her rooted attachment with the past, she said. She was nursed in museums, more than in a nursery. For her mother helped the father, too. The little girl became a pet of the scientists and curators, who would rifle cases of their treasures to find temporary playthings for her and deck her out with arm rings, neck chains, and diadems from the Stone Age.

When she was eleven her father died in Oslo. The widowed mother was hard put to bring up her three girls on the small annual pension from the government and the little she could make taking in sewing. But scholarships were immediately offered for the girls' education. Sigrid Undset did not choose to go to a university, however. At seventeen she entered a commercial school. Her first job was as a clerk in a hardware store in a rough part of the town frequented by seafaring folk. She enjoyed selling rope and hammers and iron pots, and chatting with the hardy and simple customers, she said. But after the first few weeks a scandalized friend of her father's rescued the daughter and got her a job as secretary in a highly respected engineering concern. This position she held for ten years.

It was at the business conferences that the future novelist learned about men. "You can't know the truth about men when they are in love," Fru Undset said, "for then you see only their best side—or their worst. But in business dealings you see men as they really are. I would sit demurely, poker-faced, taking down shorthand, but secretly making mental notes of masculine traits and reactions, of men's bluff and fallibility.

"When I went to my tiny room after a fatiguing day I would try to write stories. For years I did not get more than four hours' sleep a night. As a working girl I gained firsthand knowledge of what we Norwegians call 'the Poor Fates.' I found little time for frivolous pleasure. The first luxury I felt I could afford from my earnings was a bottle of English lavender toilet water. I have never swerved in my allegiance to the cool, clean scent that sweetened my imagination in my restricted young-ladyhood."

At twenty-five Sigrid Undset's fame in Scandinavia was established with a novel called *Jenny*. The heroine was a twenty-eight-year-old girl who had never known love and who deluded herself into believing she loved a weak man who adored her. The marriage was disastrous and Jenny ended by running away.

Shortly after *Jenny*'s success Sigrid Undset married a well-known artist, A. C. Svärstad, who already had three children by a former wife. She bore him two sons and then a daughter. The girl was an invalid from birth. Living in a city apartment among Bohemian friends, with an artist husband and with three small children, it was impossible for her to write. So she bought the place in Lillehammer and in seclusion again pursued literature, writing in the night after her noisy household had quieted down.

This marriage proved unharmonious, and after ten years of it, she divorced her husband. In 1920–22 she wrote her masterpiece, the trilogy *Kristin Lavransdatter*. Shortly afterward she was converted to Catholicism. In 1928 she was awarded the Nobel Prize for literature.

"I have always wanted to see America," Sigrid Undset was saying, as she poured me a second cup of tea. "But while my daughter was alive I couldn't leave her. She died early this year. Now, if this war does not come to Europe perhaps I may go to America very soon. My publisher in New York has often invited me. But I greatly fear war will come." Her large eyes stared at the white cloth for a moment and then looked directly at me. "Hitler means war," she said, with hardly a change of expression, like a sybil that had foreknowledge. "When he cannot get what he wants without fighting, he will fight." Then she added grimly, "I do not like the German traits—they are cringing when down; insufferably arrogant when up."

As far back as 1932 Fru Undset was urging as strong defensive measures as Norway could provide. She was apprehensive for Norway's undefended position, but she was no pacifist. "War is not always madness," she said, as she pressed us to take more seed cake. "Not when you are defending yourself against a foreign atmosphere in which you know you cannot breathe happily. Then war is the lesser of two evils."

"But Sweden and Norway have been untouched by war for more than a century," I said. "Will the mothers want their sons to fight?"

"There are women," she replied steadfastly, "who would rather lose their sons than see them grow up in conditions they regard as loathsome. After all, children are not mere house pets for women to play with."

We touched on politics. Sigrid Undset distrusted constant reforms, and thought true progress must be a growth of unity. She didn't concern herself much with political parties. "The Conservatives are housewives with paring knives," she said. "The Socialists are often mere kitchen slatterns." She admired the stable, the permanent. Her outlook was that of a natural conservative attuned to the peasant traditions of Norway.

"In olden times," she said, "men made what was needed and took joy in their work. Today industrial workers know that they are occupied in making a heap of things which the world could just as well do without. There is both spiritual and material danger in overindustrialized nations."

She paused for a sip of tea, and then said, "If the South had won the Civil War I think it would have rendered impossible such a hectic wave of prosperity in the North, which I regard as unsound."

"Do you know anything about the South, our part of the world?" Thérèse asked.

Fru Undset's smile was warming. "I know a great deal, I think. You see, my elder son's hero of all times is Robert E. Lee. In his room he has whole shelves of books on the Civil War. I have read many of them, including Douglas Southall Freeman's four-volume biography of Lee. I like the voices from the Southern states in *I'll Take My Stand*. I applaud their strong cry against hustling for hustling's sake." She again passed the little cakes with ground nuts sprinkled on top. "To achieve a just distribution, people should abandon their hysterical rush, as well as their rampant greediness."

The cakes were delicious and I complimented them heartily. "The basis of one of my ardent friendships," Sigrid Undset confessed, "is cookery. I have a woman novelist friend in Oslo, and when we get together we immediately begin swapping recipes or recommending new cookbooks.

"Occasionally I go to Oslo on a shopping expedition and to look after a boardinghouse run by nuns for young working girls from the provinces. Here my husband's daughter of a former marriage lives, and I am devoted to the girl. In Oslo I always stay at a certain old run-down hotel, because I stayed there years ago when I was poor and unknown. As long as the head porter lives I can't go anywhere else—it would hurt his feelings too much to hear I had been the guest of another hostelry."

As we were about to make our adieus I said, "May I take your picture?"

"Of course." She acquiesced without a moment's hesitation, and smiled as if it was going to be a lark. She came out into the garden, picked up the smallest dog and stood by some lily plants. The little dog that had been let loose in the garden was too young "to bite seriously yet." The two older dogs, who had been shut up in the cellar, began a terrific barking. "The big dogs are really bitish." Fru Undset smiled maliciously. "So we have to imprison them if guests come."

"I never heard such hostile dogs," I said. The barking became so frenzied that the maidservant went to quiet them. Their mistress smiled with satisfaction. "That's why I keep 'em. And they would rather go for a reporter than a rabbit." A reporter had flagrantly misquoted her years ago, and she had been morbidly suspicious of them ever since.

The little dog became very friendly during the picture-taking. When he kept trying to get to Thérèse, who has a way with dogs, Fru Undset put him in her arms, and he kissed her on the nose. The maidservant, who had bolted the gate in my face on Thursday, curtsied and smiled and smiled as she let us out on Monday. Sigrid Undset came out into the road to say good-by to us. In an atmosphere of warm graciousness and promise of future welcome, we departed. The great lady slipped back into the sanctuary of the rose garden behind the stout stockade.

The situation was to become worse for Sigrid Undset. The Nazis treacherously occupied Oslo on April 9, 1940. She was in the capital on the night of April 8 denouncing the Germans over the radio. At 12:30 A.M. an alert sounded. The guests in the old hotel huddled in the cold cellar. Some said they had seen airplanes over the Oslofjord. But no one suspected that the Germans were actually landing in Norway.

In the morning when she went to church the black bombers circled over the houses so low that the national insigne, the iron cross, could be clearly seen. As she and her younger son, Hans, were boarding the train for Lillehammer, a couple of bombs dropped just outside the railway station. But she could not believe that the Germans would ever get up to Lillehammer, until the afternoon when a German transport plane dropped down just outside her garden fence.

She was persuaded to flee to escape Nazi wrath. She went north, then over the mountains into Sweden. Both her sons had joined up immediately in the futile defense of Norway. The elder, who so loved Robert E. Lee and who was so able and admirable that several citizens prophesied that he would be a future prime minister, was killed by the Germans on the seventh day after the occupation. His mother learned that he had been shot in the temple only when she reached Stockholm. Since there was no possible passage over the Atlantic, she was forced to go across Siberia and the Pacific to get to San Francisco.

I was in the Berkshires staying with the Albert Spaldings when I read in the paper that the escaped Sigrid Undset had arrived in San Francisco. I telegraphed her to ask if I might see her in New York. I received a wire with two "verys." She would "be very very glad to see me." Her second night in New York I took her and her younger son, who had also managed to escape, to dinner in the Finnish Pavilion at New York's 1939 World's Fair.

And that was how she came in February of 1942 to stay with Thérèse and me for a fortnight in Alabama in the new home we had built in twenty acres of woods.

When in conversation with Sigrid Undset I had mentioned that we were going to Finland for August and September, she had said spontaneously, "The Finns are the most gifted of all modern people." I knew little enough about them except of Paavo Nurmi, the runner, and Sibelius, the composer. The only Finn I had actually ever met was named George Paloheimo, a tall, good-looking fellow, now a naturalized American and the New York head of the Finnish Tourist Association. He owned property in Finland next to the country estate of the great composer. His elder brother, Arvi, was married to the oldest daughter of Sibelius. He gave me a letter to this brother, who was ostensibly a manufacturer of glassware, but mostly a country gentleman.

He also wrote to a young poet friend and cousin named Lorenz von Numers, who turned out to be possessed of uncommon charm, as well as a golden and robust handsomeness. In our first meeting Von Numers was to say something that more or less gave me a key to his people. "In our Finnish world, where everything must be paid for, we have our solitude in exchange for our endless space, and the darkness of our winters, rich with snow, against our marvelous summers, brimful of light. The melancholy you find in our music and in our poetry is the black flower of the silent wilderness. You cannot find the same thing among orange blossoms. You might say that the key words to the Finnish character are space, solitude, struggle."

Later I was to learn another key word, even more significant. It is the Finns' favorite word, *sisu,* pronounced see-su, with the accent on the first syllable. Like so much of Finland the word eludes precise definition. It is a thing felt, like religion or love. It surpasses fearlessness and extraordinary endurance, and acts as a kind of inner fire or superhuman nerve force. It makes an athlete scorn fatigue and pain to risk his life to win. Sibelius was to define *sisu* to me as "a metaphysical shot in the arm, which inspires men to do the impossible."

It was almost noon when we reached Helsinki. My admiration for the Finns rose high the instant the smallish porter began to strap our seven bags about him, before, behind, on both sides. All but his feet and head disappeared. I protested, and vainly insisted that he summon an extra porter or two. He scorned my suggestion, and he would not let me lend him a hand. Smiling reassuringly, he said what I imagined was: "This is nothing," and walked off stout as a load-bearing ant. Though I was not yet familiar with the word *sisu* I witnessed the thing personified on our arrival in Helsinki.

In front of Eliel Saarinen's railway station, the neighboring buildings are not the usual bobtail conglomerations to be found surrounding many American stations. The National Theater, the Atheneum Museum, the yellow Post Office, and two of the best hotels open directly upon the square. And across an elevated street to the west stands the most imposing Parliament House in the north, designed by the architect Sirén and built of pinkish-gray granite with fourteen towering columns across the noble façade.

We stood and marveled at the urban space under the blue of a high noon sky. But where was the vaunted silence? The Finnish capital was noted for its noiseless streets. We knew that by law no motor horns honked, no bicycle bells tinkled, no street vender cried his wares, no factory whistle sounded the work hours. A great hubbub of excavation, of blasting and drilling, was going on. "Building all over the city!" we were told by the young woman secretary, whom Paloheimo's brother had thoughtfully sent to meet us. "Dozens of new apartments going up, hundreds of villas in the suburbs. We have so little time!"

The Olympic Games were scheduled for the next summer of 1940. Through the streets, in shopwindows, like a herald Mercury bearing the glad tidings, the green-bronze nude of Paavo Nurmi was running on posters announcing the next Olympiad to be held in Helsinki. The posters were printed from Väinö Aaltonen's statue of Nurmi in the Atheneum. They had been printed in twenty languages. Nurmi was running like that all over the globe. As if no rumors of possible war had reached Finland, the city was building furiously to be ready to accommodate athletes and spectators.

Much of Helsinki is new. Although the city had occupied its present sight since 1640, it is difficult to find a structure built before the nineteenth century. A new crop of gifted architects matured, led by Eliel Saarinen, Sirén, and Lars Sonck, whose Michael Agricola Church is the handsomest ecclesiastical building in Scandinavia. A younger generation, led by Alvar

Aalto, in employing the modern style, which dominates contemporary architecture, has made spectacular architectural history. Finnish architects have sought to capture the light, making abundant use of glass.

I wanted to know how Finland, a nation of less than four million population had within a score of years accomplished such an exemplary state that foreign countries sent commissions to study details. The foreign minister, Eljas Erkko, gave me a simple answer with a smile: "Because they are an intelligent and gifted people." He pronounced the pronoun "they" as if leaders of recent years had merely carried out the general will. "And"—he paused significantly—"because the Russian domination under the last czar sharpened every virtue they possessed. But mark you"—his friendly eyes shone frank and keen behind his glasses—"they have not been timid about innovations and experiments. As you know, we were the first European nation to give the vote to women. The Finns *planned* their future to accord with their natural resources and their native mentality. In Helsinki a man must paint his house every seven years. If he refuses the city paints it and sends him the bill. A property owner here is not permitted the indulgence of maintaining an eyesore for speculation."

"In Helsinki," I said, "then it is all a restricted area."

"Just about," he said with a grin. "And no one is permitted to cut a beautiful tree in his own front yard, unless a committee approves."

With Olaf Gummerus, a young official on the Olympic Games Committee who had been brought up largely in Rome when his father was minister to Italy, I drove out to Olympic Village. Here three hundred men and two hundred young women were working to prepare to house three thousand foreign athletes. The thirty modern apartment houses, with a shopping center and rock gardens, were set on a hilly slope among spruce trees some four miles from the city's center. With the usual Finnish astuteness the Village had been planned for permanent use. The up-to-the-minute apartments were already being bought on the co-operative plan.

Within pleasant walking distance from the center of Helsinki the Olympic Stadium had been built. The stadium tower that shoots straight as a javelin twenty-two stories tall and lustrous white against the deep blue Finnish sky is spectacular and exciting. "The stadium belongs to the people," Gummerus said. "By means of tag days they have been collecting the money since 1927. Now it is just completed, to hold sixty-three thousand spectators. The tickets for the Olympics have almost all been sold, a year in advance."

We climbed aloft and sat down in the empty stadium. "Despite the universality of skiing," Gummerus told me, "long-distance running still holds first place in the ambitions of athletes seeking the fame of a Paavo Nurmi."

Gummerus opened a fresh box of cigarettes, "Club No. 7," long and thin with an inch of hard paper holder attached in the Russian manner. I regarded the slender young man who wore a blue beret and who looked as much like an English Pre-Raphaelite as a Finn. He wore three rings on one finger, but he rose at six every summer morning to keep fit by rowing a shell in the bay. I imagined his rearing in Rome in diplomatic circles had something to do with his sophisticated grace.

"We have no professional athletes," Gummerus said. "Our sportsmen run, leap, wrestle, and ski for fun and national glory."

"By the way," he added, "on June 16 a world record was made in this new stadium. Taisto Mäki ran the 5,000 meters in 14 minutes 8¾ seconds. That's beyond anything anyone had believed humanly possible. In 1924 the champion Paavo Nurmi brought it down to 14 minutes 28⅕ seconds."

We drove back into the heart of the city to meet the phenomenal Taisto Mäki, who also held the world's record for the 10,000-meter, the two-mile, the three-mile, and the six-mile. "Remember," Gummerus emphasized, "Finland does not pamper her champions. Mäki works for his living as a baler and wrapper in the Alcohol Monopoly. He lives in the village of Rekola and commutes. He gets up before six and runs up and down the road. Then he takes a train to Helsinki. He works from nine to four, handling bundles and receipts. Then he runs in the stadium and afterward takes a train for Rekola. His salary is about fifty dollars a month—hardly a widow's mite to an American world-record breaker."

Although I had heard that Taisto Mäki had suddenly become the most popular athlete in the north since Nurmi, I was not prepared for the Mäki personality. We found the contemporary idol of the Finns in a below-the-pavement office. As he came forward, he was smiling, the most engaging smile I ever saw. He looked as much like a handsome Irish-American as a Finn. He was middle-sized, with wavy brown hair and dancing eyes. In the midst of the city he carried an atmosphere of new-mown hay about him, and his twenty-nine years had not robbed him of his eager, little-boy charm. Superlatively likable, he was a bit shy, and he flushed easily. There was no hint of heroics or pose about him.

I regarded him almost incredulously and looked down at the famous fleet feet in their rusty cheap shoes. Here before me stood a man the gods loved, for they had blessed him from toe to crown; they had given him legs to outrun the world and a smile to outface any victory or defeat.

Mäki was the son of a small farmer, he told me, and in his youth he had been a shepherd boy. He said he first did running after lost sheep. Later, while hired out as a farm laborer, he ran in local rural competitions. Then in 1934 at Tampere he ran the 5,000-meter race as a dark horse and won. Nurmi coached him a few times, and in 1937 he began smashing world records.

"The Finnish athletes live normal lives," Mäki said, "with no great palaver about training." He himself ate just as he pleased, ice cream whenever he wanted it, though not just before a race. He did not smoke and he drank no alcoholic beverages.

On invitation I promised to drive out to his place in the country some Sunday to meet his wife and his little daughter, Marie Anita, and to see his vegetable patch. "It's only a half acre," he said with a deprecating smile.

Because Lapland is at its best in mid-August, between the end of the mosquito season and the first frosts, we were advised to go to the Arctic while the weather was salubrious. Two days before we were to leave we were invited by Otto Schreck, the head of Suomi Films, to a private showing of documentary motion pictures revealing varied aspects of Lapland. Then we were taken by the Schrecks to dine at the Hotel Kämp on the tree-lined Esplanade. The Arvi Paloheimos were the other guests for dinner. We had not yet met Eva Paloheimo, the daughter of Sibelius, though her husband, George's brother, had been most attentive. She could not interrupt her three weeks' fruit-preserving period.

Great platters of cold scarlet crayfish decorated with dill were already spread on the table. We knew that a crayfish dinner was something rare and special, but we were unprepared for the ritual. Mrs. Paloheimo took off her rings and bracelets and laid them beside her plate. The hostess, wife of the cinema head, whose name was Aino, took off her rings and a necklace of aquamarines. Paloheimo stowed his wrist watch in a pocket. We wondered if we were being kidded. But, doing as in Rome, Thérèse removed her one ring and laid her pearls beside it by her plate. Mrs. Paloheimo tucked her napkin over the bosom of her flowered chiffon dress. The party was ready to begin.

A glass of icy schnapps was tossed off or sipped to skoals and then we set to work enjoying the delicacies that are perhaps God's greatest culinary gift to man. The technique of properly eating crayfish must be learned. The first move is to break the crustacean in two and then suck the cool, dill-flavored juice. We tossed back our heads and partly poured the juice, partly sucked it into our mouths, before we bit into the succulent flesh. I had eaten crayfish before as hors d'ouvres at a men's luncheon in Stockholm, but Thérèse had not. Paloheimo at her left instructed her and pointed out how to get the most delicious morsels tucked away in crevices, and how to suck to the best advantage. The fashionable Swedes had decreed it *de rigueur* to eat crayfish noisily. In Sweden sophisticates are rather formal fifty weeks out of the year. Then for one fortnight (in crayfish season) they relax, abandon proprieties, drink a glass of akvavit with every crayfish, and make a hilarious, rip-roaring, very un-Swedish holiday.

When finger bowls bearing lemon slices were set before us, we enjoyed a bathing of hands and mouths and chins. Then rings and necklaces were put back on, watches replaced on wrists, and ladies' lipsticks repaired damages.

Fresh napery was now laid, wine glasses were set, and the dinner proceeded to the second course: stuffed squab and green asparagus.

When the dinner was over, Thérèse and I both tried to get the conversation on Russia during the domination. Thérèse said that she had not met a single Finn who had ever been to a Russian's house or a Russian party, or even had a speaking acquaintance with one.

"Certainly not," the Finns shouted as one voice. "We had nothing to do with them."

"I've never seen people so united in detestation as you Finns are for the Russians," Thérèse said, "except oldtime Southern Confederate hatred for Yankees during Reconstruction." They had all read *Gone With the Wind* and readily understood and nodded in agreement.

"But didn't any Finnish girl ever go to a Russian ball?" I persisted.

"Of course not!" they cried.

"But, Mr. Paloheimo, you and your wife lived for a few years in St. Petersburg. You told me that you enjoyed the city and had charming Russian friends."

"Oh, yes," he admitted. "But that was different—that was *in* Russia."

"I once knew a Russian scientist in Arequipa, Peru, a Baron Korff," I said. "His father was governor-general of Finland when the Bolshevik revolution came. Korff seemed a very nice chap. Did you know the Korffs?"

Paloheimo slanted an eye at me and grinned sardonically. "No name that ends in two f's is any good in Finland."

We all laughed, and I did not pursue the question further.

It was almost midnight, so we thought we should get a good rest before we took the two o'clock afternoon train for Rovaniemi, the capital of Lapland, which was as far as the railway went. Then we were to take the *posti bussi* for two more days with a night stopover. At the thought of my delicate Thérèse jolting in the post bus, the Finns were aghast. "The bus will shake your teeth loose," one declared. "The roads are not paved." "You will be smothered by Lapps and chickens and maybe pigs," said another.

When our train reached Rovaniemi, with its gay, gypsy-sounding name, we were surprised to see the Pahjanhovi Hotel standing modern white beside sparkling blue rapids and a yellow hayfield. It was far more attractive than any hotel in Helsinki. The lobby soared three stories high and had enormous round columns of lustrous white enamel supporting an electric blue ceiling. The east wall, built of glass blocks, opened on terraces where guests sat under sky blue umbrellas taking tea. The furniture was of chromium, glass, and blue leather. We had not expected to find such a gala hostelry at the edge of what was hardly more than a trackless wilderness not many years ago.

A glass elevator took us to the lounge of an upper floor, where mirrors reflected daisies and blue cornflowers in vases on tables of glass. Our room and bath was all that one could desire in comfort, smartness, and equipment. A great corner window gave on a swirling river, where men fished from little boats. In hayfields girls in red blouses and young men naked to the waist raked fresh-scythed hay and stacked it in cocks. The Arctic Circle lay less than five miles to the north.

A lithe young man who spoke some English knocked politely at our door, and introduced himself as Eero Eho. He was carrying a red pocket dictionary in his left hand. He said one of my Helsinki friends had telephoned and asked the governor to look after us. He was on the governor's staff temporarily and adjudged cases of social welfare. He bore an invitation from the governor and his lady to lunch with them next day. Eho was a lawyer by profession, and his wife was a dentist in Helsinki, where their two children were in school.

Just now, he said, Rovaniemi was in the throes of growing pains. One block gave the impression of a mining town in the gold rush days of forty-nine, and the next belonged to an architectural dream of the future. In the middle of the town co-operative shops displayed German cameras, fancy fruits from California, topcoats from London. At the end of the town reindeer grazed in primeval peace. Through the main street ran the blue fish truck carrying fresh fish from the Arctic Ocean down to Helsinki.

The governor of Lapland lived in a recently completed mansion of tasteful ultramodern architecture. He was youngish, unbound by tradition, and physically stout as an oak stump. He had a powerful chest, a determined jaw, and a grip of iron. He radiated good nature, purpose, and limitless energy. His lady was a tiny thing, pretty, blond, and bubbling. Neither the governor nor his wife spoke English. So Eho, the only other luncheon guest, turned his tongue to English or to Finnish as rapidly as possible, while his fingers flipped pages in the pocket dictionary.

With our luncheon we drank lemonade. The governor was a teetotaler, and so was Eho. For dessert we had bowls of golden berries, a Lapland specialty, called "cloudberries." The last three Russian czars, the governor told us, were especially fond of cloudberries and the regal court got their supply from the very district whence these came.

As the halting conversation progressed, I gathered that Governor Hillilä was the busiest man in Lapland. By car, by boat, by ski and afoot, he traveled over twenty thousand kilometers a year. He commanded one-third of the territory of Finland and ruled over more land than the King of Denmark. He had his fingers on the pulse of every section of his commonwealth. As a sportsman, he said, he always took his rods or his gun along. "The poor in Finland," he commented with pride, "have all the blessings of shooting and fishing that only the privileged rich do in England."

"Don't expect to see Lapps everywhere, just because this northern province is called Lapland," he said as we were leaving. "There are no more than two thousand Lapps in all Finland. Sweden has three times as many, and Norway has twenty thousand."

Eho drove us back to our hotel, and later came again to initiate me in the rites of the Finnish sauna. The sauna is a place not only for family bathing, but for entertaining one's guests. It has something of the special value of the Japanese tea ceremony. The offer of a sauna bath is the height of Finnish hospitality.

The superintendent of the new hospital had invited Eho and me to have a steam bath down at the river's edge. Eho and I arrived at the hospital just before eight. The evening air was so cool, we were glad we had worn our topcoats. We were joined by two young physicians not long out of medical college. The shorter one had grown a crisp black mustache to make him look older and more professional. The other was taller, clean-shaven, and auburn-haired. They both spoke English.

The sauna was built in modern style. It had a small veranda with benches, a dressing room, and a steam room. In the dressing room were a couch and chairs spread with bathrobes and towels. On a table were bottles of mineral water and Valencia, a Finnish orange drink.

We stripped to our skins and went into the breath-taking hot air of the steam room. The inside walls were paneled with small split logs to soften the atmosphere and absorb moisture. On scrubbed wooden benches lay bars of soap and gourd sponges. On the floor stood wooden buckets and basins for washing and throwing water over the body. Utensils of metal would be too hot to the touch, just as stone benches would be impossible to sit on. In a corner was a nest of rocks, about breast-high. The rocks were fist-sized, from boys' fists to lumber-jacks' fists. They were rounded black cobbles that had lain in the wash of the shore. Now they were grayish-white with heat. In these fancy new saunas a turned spigot would send water from a pipe flowing onto the hot rocks and creating steam—dry steam, not wet like a Turkish bath.

Reached by eight broad steps—something like bleachers at a ball park— was the slightly sloping platform where the bathers lay with heads toward the back wall and where they could just sit up straight and miss bumping their heads on the ceiling by inches.

I waited to follow the moves of the initiated. One of the doctors turned the spigot and hot vapor rose from the sizzling stones and swirled about the room. The vapor became hotter and denser. Eho wondered how I liked it. I liked it just fine.

They had forgotten the birch twigs, so the auburn-haired doctor went out, naked as Adam, into the garden, and tore off two fistfuls of leafy birch twigs about a foot and a half long. He brought them in and seared them by switching them briefly against the gray-hot stones. Then he dipped them in a bucket of warm water. A pungent, tonic scent, faintly medicinal, filled the

287

air. The black-haired physician took his place on the platform by the wall where he could manipulate the spigot and the intensity of heat.

I went up the steps into the hotter air and lay on the warm planks. The hot vapor bulged out. My skin began to tingle. I had to open my mouth to breathe. Sweat drenched me from head to foot. As I lay in a puddle, I felt the wooden boards beneath me getting hotter. The heat crept into every pore and routed out every impurity.

"Are you ready for the whipping now?" the red-headed doctor said, climbing down from his high perch and handing me a birch whisk. I began to slap my back as I saw the others doing. With the crash of aromatic birch leaves on my skin I began to sting and tingle pleasurably. We all sweated in quiet gusto for another ten minutes. When the draft of the oven was opened the heat became too intense even for the seasoned Finns.

Then came the washing with soap and warm water, the scrubbing with gourd sponges, followed by the relentless pouring of buckets of cold water over glowing bodies. The mustached doctor, who finished first, went out to sit on the veranda to cool. It was a gesture of bravado an uninitiated American might think the shortest route to pneumonia. But if physicians did it perhaps there was no great harm in it.

"And now for a quick plunge in the river," Eho called, leading the way. I paused on the veranda steps, as the hospital clock chimed nine. The river at night on the Arctic Circle? I had an hour ago arrived in a topcoat and now, stark naked, I was supposed to run along the grassy path to the river. Mentally I shivered at the thought, and then boldly tossing to the winds the cowardly thought of catching cold, I ran leaping after the leader. As I struck the river I let out a yelp of horror and delight. The water was shockingly icy and quite wonderful.

"In the winter," Eho called out, "we roll in snowdrifts."

Back in the dressing room we sat about in bathrobes to complete the cooling-off process. We drank mineral water or orange juice and settled back for quiet talk and surrender to a preternatural sense of well-being. I began to have an inkling of why Finns are champion runners, why they don't seem to get flustered, and why sometimes in crises their strength is said to be as the strength of ten.

The indispensable Judge Eho had reserved seats for us on the yellow *posti bussi*. It was well that he had, for three young men from Oxford had taken up the last three seats. We crowded into our places while the passengers scrooged together to make room for us. But being packed tight as tinned kippers prevented us from jouncing about. Besides the three Oxford boys, a librarian from Dartmouth College, and ourselves, the twenty-odd passengers were Finns. A mother with two obedient tow-headed children and a baby at her breast sat in the row behind us, with two shaggy axbearing woodsmen and a toothless old woman with a head rag tied under her chin.

In the right-hand forward corner of the bus the sharp-eyed postboy sat wearing his official yellow-billed cap, his eyes alert to warn the driver when to make a stop. The passengers' accommodation was a by-product of the desultory mail service. We collected and delivered not only mail but empty milk cans, flowering plants, sacks of grain, squawking hens. The clangor of the milk cans atop the vibrating bus and the constantly changing passengers added to the confusion and the sociability.

The white dust flew when we passed another car. And sometimes the bus vibrated so on the rough stretches that if we did not hold our teeth clamped together, they began to chatter. I began to wonder if I had not done a dastardly thing in bringing my wife on such a journey. But she was amused and seemed to be surviving well.

At intervals we stopped for coffee at farmhouses which carried on a refreshment business in the front rooms, invariably painted white with muslin curtains and pots of flowers on the window ledges.

At a place called Vuotso, where rude log buildings gathered about a yard to serve as post office and restaurant for the community, we stopped for evening coffee. Because it was Sunday, several Lapps from a nearby Lapp village had come dressed in Lapp costume. They were sitting about the stoop in thick blue woolen suits embroidered in colored wools of red, yellow, and purple. The long, shirtlike jackets, which flared at the bottom, were belted low on the hips and made them look incredibly long-waisted. Lapps have short legs at best, because for generations they have squatted on the floors of tents around a central fire and nature has shortened their legs to make squatting more convenient.

The men were all wearing "four winds" caps, with the points sticking out in four directions like the pricked-up ears of a dog listening to the wind. The women wore billowy woolen skirts and gay cotton print blouses and head kerchiefs tied under their chins.

One of the older men, who had a sweeping sandy mustache that drooped like the pictures of old Viking chieftains, wore a knife with a carved bone handle hanging in a leather holster. It looked ready to spring into action. I had not yet learned that the Lapp people are exceedingly gentle and peaceable and that where much strong drink may make a Finn run amok and clean out a whole tavern, alcohol makes a Lapp increasingly affectionate and dovelike.

While we drank weak, bitter coffee and munched on delicious fresh baked bread several Lapps came in to inspect us and sat on board benches around the walls and stared at us frankly and silently. One fair, slightly built youth with an elfin expression leaned forward with elbows on his knees, cocked his head to the side and regarded us with the eager curiosity of a slightly daft wood creature. But his childish, soft lips smiled at us and his blue eyes were wistful, as if he were eager to learn about the outside world. With his "four winds" cap and sidelong whimsical glances, he seemed like a court jester come to life after centuries of sleep. It was a strange meeting of two worlds at this crossroads where the yard was littered with reindeer antlers.

The bus crossed the watershed, which sent all the rivers flowing north to the Arctic Ocean instead of to the lakes or the Bothnian Gulf. When we crossed the timber line again, the pine and spruce and birch came to meet us—little fellows at first, then came whole virgin forests with tall, straight trees standing among fallen ancestors. The dead ones, lying prostrate on the ground, had stood for centuries without having been seen by mankind, and then had dropped onto their shadows from old age. Now they lay, bleached pale as skeletons, their whitened roots and limbs spreading out like mammoth antlers from gigantic, prehistoric elk and reindeer.

When the bus turned into the drive of the Ivalo Inn, a building of squared logs stained red, university student waitresses stood on the steps to receive us in native costume. Within, a cheerful fire blazed on the hearth and brought out the bright colors of the handwoven rugs and curtains. In our upstairs room I touched the radiator. The steam heat was on. Our window gave on a silver river with a sandy beach on the opposite shore, which the northern sunlight turned to grains of gold. A canoe glided swiftly by leaving in its wake a chain of glinting ripples. When it had passed a young stag came over the green fields down to the beach for a drink. The sun at nine-thirty was still above the horizon.

"Don't look," I said over my shoulder to Thérèse, "unless you want to catch Lapland fever. I've got it already."

But she looked—and tired as she was from the day's hard journey, she succumbed too.

The next morning we took the seven o'clock bus for Petsamo, the most northern province, which in 1920 Russia was forced to cede to Finland, with its valuable ice-free harbor on the Arctic Ocean.

At first glance, Liinahamari was like Rovaniemi, obviously teeming with the future. Seventy lorries were lined up on the harbor road. Supplies for constructing the new hydroelectric plant came through the port. Trawlers from Italy, Spain, and Africa, having discharged their cargoes of olive oil, fruits, and vegetables, were loading up with salted cod. Though already prepared to handle seventy tons of herring daily, the fish-packing plant was extending its warehouses.

Captain Haikola, the harbormaster, spread blueprints and architectural drawings over his office table to indicate the future town that the new prosperity would bring into being. It was a beautiful layout with the residential streets as winding as in an English village. Before the public buildings was plenty of space for planting. And in this protected spot, warmed by the Gulf Stream, shrubs and flowers and birch trees did fairly well. Each citizen had to submit his plans and color schemes to a committee before proceeding to build.

Captain Haikola took us out in his private boat to visit nearby coves of industry on the ocean front. The sun was golden and the water seemed bluer than in the Gulf of Mexico. But a cold wind was blowing, so we sat huddled together on the bow deck, with Thérèse in the middle on robes made of reindeer faces. The cheek of the reindeer is the softest, silkiest part of the hide and by far the most costly.

"The wind is always cold on the Arctic Ocean both winter and summer!" The captain sounded slightly bitter. He was tall and thin, with strange hazel eyes, an attractive fellow, like a character in a Conrad novel.

"The long dark days—" Thérèse suggested.

"No," the captain said quickly. "The dark isn't really bad." He looked off—his seaman's eyes peering into the distant horizon. Then, coming back to reality, he turned to her and repeated gently, "The dark isn't bad. We work as on ordinary days and we read much more. Once you know the spell of the winter dark it isn't easy to be happy anywhere else. Two years ago I thought I could not stand it any longer. I asked to be transferred south. They gave me a good post and life was much easier. But I wasn't happy. I asked to be sent back there. My wife felt the same. We were impelled to return."

Before us lay the whole expanse of the Arctic Ocean. Directly north there was no more land between us and the North Pole. The waves dashed spray on our faces and we licked arctic salt off our lips. We had been at sea for some two exhilarating hours.

Sibelius had asked his son-in-law to bring me out to his country place, "Järvenpää," when we returned from Lapland. His wife unfortunately was ill and confined to her room. On the drive we talked mostly of music. "Finland is very much what you in America might call 'musically minded,'" Paloheimo said. "The concert season in Helsinki is heartily well attended. Sometimes we have two or three concerts scheduled for one evening. And it isn't just the city folk who like good music. In peasant cottages far out in the wilds you can hear Sibelius' tone poems on gramophone records."

Sibelius was born in an atmosphere of culture, Paloheimo explained, in a family moderately comfortable but not rich enough to sap his ambition. He was born in 1865, the year in which Lee surrendered at Appomattox. His father was an army physician in a fortress town in the pastoral province of Häme. As a stripling he entered law school and dutifully took his degree. But he studied the violin more assiduously than the law, for he hoped to become a violin virtuoso. Impelled to follow his genius, when he was twenty-three he went to study music in Berlin. Then he moved to Vienna,

291

the glittering capital that he said "lived entirely for music." "At last I have found a place made for me," he wrote to his grandmother in an exuberant outburst. But in his compositions, he was inspired by the Kalevala legends, rooted in soil of his fatherland. When he returned to Finland in 1892 his music created something of a sensation. To make a living for his increasing family of girls he taught theory at the Academy.

The Finnish government voted him a life pension in recognition of his genius. The world at large first heard of Sibelius at the 1900 Paris Exposition, when a Finnish orchestra played his First Symphony. Soon his fame penetrated the rest of the continent and England.

Off to the right just before we reached Sibelius' place was George Paloheimo's estate, with three rented houses which he planned someday to turn into a psychiatric estate for the poor. The broad acres along the road were richly laden with profitable sugar beets.

The Sibelius house sat on a rise of ground in a pine grove. It was built of logs, stone, and vertical white clapboards. Its roof was painted a deep rich red. "Ah, the peace of this place," Paloheimo murmured luxuriously. And then as the chauffeur stopped, he looked suspiciously at a large car parked under a tree. "Who *are* those people?" he asked, puzzled and resentful.

The front door was wide open. The son-in-law rang the bell perfunctorily, and we immediately went inside without waiting for a servant to answer. At the entrance to the drawing room, balls of silver light burst before our eyes. Tripods like wigwam skeletons were set up about the room. Three men and a woman stood by them like soldiers at machine guns. They were London photographers come to get pictures of Sibelius for British periodicals as advance publicity for the 1940 Olympics.

In a double-breasted white linen suit, with the coat casually unbuttoned and displaying a square-cut white waistcoat over an ample stomach, the composer rose and came through the barricade of tripods to greet us. In his trembling fingers he held a smoking cigar.

Because I was a friend of his neighbor George, now in New York, I was thrice, thrice welcome. He had not expected to be photographed this afternoon, but here they all were, and they seemed insatiable. Would we sit down? Would we have cigars? What could he offer us to drink?

The first impression I got of the great man was his warm humaneness. He had a magnificent head, bald as a birchwood bowling ball, and his neck was as thick as that of a wrestler.

We walked softly about the edges of the large drawing room, a mixture of town and country in its furnishings, sophisticated and peasant, but bright and spacious. We moved into the newly added library, paneled in butter-colored wood. Sprawling armchairs were upholstered in beige homespun. Draperies were in shades of copper, brown, and parchment. It had a relaxing atmosphere as if made for masculine conversation. "Sometimes my father-in-law will sit up until dawn talking to a congenial companion,"

Arvi Paloheimo said. "My brother George compared his conversation to 'an arc of flame.' Let's take a walk in the garden."

By no means did the photographers seem ready to release the composer, who called out through the cordon of tripods: "Show him my peonies."

Sibelius made a specialty of peonies, which were late bloomers in these northern latitudes. We strolled among the beds of stiff-stemmed blossoms that burst into pompoms of crimson and white. Where a group of alders stopped and before the vegetable garden began, we came upon a large doll house that resembled a miniature crofter's cottage. Sibelius himself had built it for his little girls, his "five best symphonies," as he called them. "He built it not only for their pleasure," Paloheimo said, laughing, "but to get them out of the house while he was composing. But he claims he has never really done his best composing indoors. He does it wandering about in the woods, or sitting on a remote log, or staring at a smiling lake. Most of his work is done, he says, before he touches the piano."

We sat on the steps of the doll house to smoke a cigarette. "I am distressed that Mme. Sibelius is not well enough to see you," Paloheimo apologized. "When you have met her you have met a woman! She is superb, and beautiful, too, with the finest face you've ever seen."

With that profound tribute to his mother-in-law, we returned to see if the Britishers had gone. They were just packing up. But another car drove up and out of it stepped Väinö Aaltonen, Finland's most famous sculptor, and Mme. Toivala, wife of the foreign office's press chief, who had been most helpful to me, and a noted woman photographer from Paris. The latter was equipped with camera, tripod, and two cases of flashbulbs. Paloheimo swore, and not inaudibly.

The seventy-three-year-old composer was visibly surprised. Tired and nervous, he groaned faintly, excused himself to both groups and led me into the wood-paneled library. "I must have a break," he said. He proceeded to mix me a Scotch and soda. He regretted he could not join me until the French photographer had gone.

He took my arm that held the whisky glass and led me over to the long window. "Do you know who lived over there in the woods only a few miles away?" he asked. "Alexis Kivi, our greatest writer. I fancy I can see his rooftop. Often I sit here by the window and look towards Kivi's roof. Poor fellow, he went mad and died poverty-stricken at thirty-eight. *Kivi* in Finnish means 'stone.' We have a pun and apply the biblical saying to him. 'The stone that the builders rejected has become the head of the corner.' The writer neglected in his young days is truly appreciated now as an immortal." I had read Kivi's *Seven Brothers* and was delighted with the novel, particularly with its unorthodox humor.

As I was half through a sentence, asking the composer if as a child he could recall ever seeing Kivi, Mme. Toivala came in with Aaltonen to say the French photographer was waiting. "We must be careful not to tire Mr.

Sibelius," she warned me with a frowning glance. Though irritated, I remembered my manners and did not say that I had thought that *this* was *my* afternoon. I gave her only a cold stare as she led Sibelius into the drawing room to begin the routine of posing again.

Paloheimo had slipped away to pay his respects to Mme. Sibelius in her sickroom upstairs. Aaltonen sat down in one of the big chairs, a powerfully built man with jutting jaw and heavy-lidded eyes. He had done the green bronze life-sized statue of Nurmi and also the massive head of Sibelius emerging from a huge block of marble. I mixed him a whisky and soda.

As we finished our drinks, Paloheimo came in to say that coffee was served in the drawing room. Sibelius was again posing at his piano for the Frenchwoman, looking like an amiable little boy being brave about an unjust punishment, while flash bulbs burst with sudden light. We gathered about the coffee table, with Mme. Toivala pouring and continuing her refrain: "We mustn't tire Mr. Sibelius. We must all leave as soon as this is over."

Paloheimo now in turn gave the lady a cold stare. Then to me he said, under his breath, "We'll come back another day."

When the last picture had been taken Sibelius passed cigars from an inscribed silver box, a gift from the Yale Glee Club. He came out into the yard and shook hands with everybody. Then he stood white against a pine tree looking like a monumental statue of himself. As we drove off he waved a white-sleeved arm, at the end of which was a glowing cigar in his right hand.

"I feel as if I had taken you on a lion hunt," Paloheimo said, "and we had been devoured by swarms of mosquitoes."

The next day in Helsinki the Minister of Defense, Juho Niukkanen, received me in his office. He was wearing a suit of cream-colored wool. In answering some questions about defense, he told me that Finland had several factories, state and private, for making guns and explosives and gas masks. "During 1938," he said, "we spent $32,000,000 on defense. That is a lot of money for a small country." He led me to a map that covered half a wall. It was merely an enlarged sector of that part of southeast Finland tracing fortifications and lines of tank traps and barriers that curved like sickles.

The minister had a cold, and when I asked a question he did not want to answer, he sneezed into a silk handkerchief.

"By every means possible," he said, "we shall certainly try to avoid being drawn into war. Our army officers and all those serving in defense work agree not to mix up in the struggle that may come. But Finland will not give up easily, like Czechoslovakia. Quite independent of any pact that may be made, Finland will fight the minute a foreign army crosses our border."

A secretary came in and announced that General Mannerheim was waiting. The minister of defense rose and said that he would arrange for the colonel in charge of constructing the antitank barricades on the Karelian Isthmus to meet us at Viipuri Sunday morning and take us to the frontier. Foreign Minister Erkko had already offered us an interpreter for the trip into Karelia, where only Finnish was spoken. I asked for one of his own men, Heikki Brotherus, a Finn in his late twenties, who looked like portraits of Napoleon and whose father was chancellor of Helsinki University.

In the anteroom a tall, distinguished-looking man in a smartly tailored gray suit arose as we entered. I refrained from asking to be presented. Baron Mannerheim's athletic figure, his hair and eyes, belied his seventy-one years. He was the product of aristocratic breeding and military training. The epithet used to explain his reputation to Americans was "the George Washington of Finland." In the Soviet press he was still called "the White Butcher." It was in World War I that he became a great hero when the small Finnish army held back the might of the Russians under his inspired leadership. After the successful formation of the Finnish republic he had retired to private life, but in 1931 he had been recalled to help organize the nation's defenses. As the inner door closed on his soldierly back I knew I had seen another Finnish "immortal." Soon his name would be publicized in world headlines in the defense of the Mannerheim Line.

When I made my exit from the building that housed the defense ministry I ran into a dramatic critic I had met. "Ah, yes, *defense,*" he said with an odd inflection. "But remember, Russia can put fifty men in place of one dead one. When a Finnish soldier is killed there is none to take his place."

Accompanied by the genial and interesting conversationalist Brotherus, Thérèse and I left by train for Viipuri, Finland's second city. It is on the Helsinki-Leningrad railway, and only seventy miles from Leningrad. The cobbled streets led down to the separate quays where the harbor was crowded with foreign ships. Viipuri was doing a big export business of wood products from eastern Finland.

Within a seven minutes' walk stood the warlike thirteenth century castle built by the Swedes, its masonry sides nine feet thick, and Alvar Aalto's new municipal library with walls of glass. This gem of modernity was like a crystal palace held together with white stone and chromium.

Although less than fifty miles from the Russian frontier and under Russian domination for 108 years, Viipuri, Brotherus told us, was Finnish to the core. "It would be easier to get borsch," he said, "in Peoria, Illinois, than in Viipuri. Such is the tenacity of Finns for the mores of Western civilization."

The colonel called for us in his car. He was a tall, slender, slightly stooped man in his middle forties with sandy hair and a sensitive, English-type face. His winning smile radiated good will, but his dark gray eyes hinted at sadness for the follies of mankind that made defensive fortifications necessary.

As we drove in a chauffeured official car, the colonel explained the work of the civic guard. It was a volunteer organization and evolved out of the White Guard of 1918. Because the government had no money for wages, men and youths offered their services in constructing fortifications. For two years now Finns had spent their vacations at hard labor, digging, blasting, and transporting rocks for the country's protection. Sons of rich men, landlords, lumbermen, musicians, actors, students, and country boys worked side by side for the defense of Suomi, as the Finns call their native land. Volunteers came for a week or a fortnight. Since the first of June, the colonel said, thirty-five thousand civilians had worked under his direction in setting up antitank barricades.

In the midst of a spruce forest the car came to a halt. We had come upon a line of antitank defense, jagged pinkish boulders chest-high. The blocks were set in holes two meters deep in nests of concrete and pebbles. The stones could not be moved except by blasting. Blasting, the colonel explained, would leave such holes that enemy tanks could not pass until they had been filled. During the delay, Finnish soldiers would be at work sniping and blowing up the tanks. The soundness of the colonel's ingenuity was to be proved a few months later when hundreds of enemy tanks were stopped at the barricades and blown to smithereens. But now in late August the atmosphere of this sector of volunteers was like that of a summer camp. There was no feeling of imminent war. A group sang for us. The man who led the singing with a resounding baritone came from Oulu in the west. He was going to be a Lutheran priest and would finish his theological course in six months.

We drove on to Terijoki. In imperial days before the revolution it had been a favorite summer resort for Russian society. Villas were still standing on either side of the road, many of them with their windows boarded up, just as the Russians had left them twenty-three years before. The well-to-do owners had never returned to rehabilitate them. We presumed that they had been executed by the Soviets. An air of decadence and dismay pervaded the ghost-thronged properties. High grass choked the struggling annuals that still volunteered gallantly in neglected gardens.

Farther on, at Rajajoki, a narrow river separated Finland from Russia and formed the common frontier. On the Soviet side vicious tangles of barbed wire stretched along the river bank. In the center of the railway bridge white Finnish paint met the broad streak of red Russian paint. On the Soviet side the train passed under an iron arch decorated with a great red star.

A youthful Finnish guard with a bayoneted rifle stood in the doorway of a sentry house by the bridge. The colonel borrowed field glasses from him for me. The powerful lens brought the Red guard within seeming touching

296

distance. The Russian also had a pair of field glasses to his eyes. He stared back at me. He lowered his glasses and hid behind a screen of bushes. He was young, slim, and pale, with reddish hair. He would peep over the bushes and then duck back out of sight, as if hating my curiosity.

The foreign office in Helsinki was calling Brotherus to tell him that Germany and Russia had suddenly signed a pact. He was to return at once. Naturally we went with him. He was puzzled and troubled. "The Nazis and Communists are the most bitter enemies," he reiterated. "They probably want to split Poland between them."

Back in Helsinki at lunch we met Urho Toivala, chief of the foreign office's press department. He was calm and cheering. "Britain," he said, "issued an ultimatum to Germany to withdraw her invading troops from Danzig, Poland. But she sets no definite time limit. War is, of course, probable, but not inevitable. In any case, it is quite safe for you to stay in Finland—the little countries will hardly be drawn into war." But the six-foot-five nephew of Neville Chamberlain, who was in the Coldstream Guards, was not so optimistic. We had run into him several times. With a Finnish friend he had sailed his small yacht to Helsinki. While he claimed no inside knowledge, he said prophetically war would be declared on September 3. He himself was sailing home to England immediately.

On Sunday, September 3, we lunched out-of-doors at the Royal Café at the head of the Esplanade. The terraces were not as crowded as usual. Most of the tourists had cleared out. The Finns had gone to the beaches for their last Sunday swim of the summer. Helsinki stood at the threshold of autumn. Because of the tang in the air Thérèse wore the blue fox scarf. Occasional leaves from the horse chestnuts detached themselves and drifted leisurely to rest among the pigeons on the grass. On its dais a string quartet played muted music.

While waiting for coffee, Miss Brent, an English teacher we had met, passed. We asked her to join us. Yesterday she told us she had put her luggage on the boat that was to take her back to England and had gone away to do some last-minute shopping. When she returned, she was informed that there would be no more passenger boats from Finland to England. The agents had routed her by train through Sweden and Norway and hoped she could get a ship from Bergen. "I think it definitely means war," she said.

Even while she spoke I noticed a newsboy passing in and out among the tables selling half-sheets of newsprint. I bought two. It was a Swedish language sheet. I read the large-print headline: EUROPA I BRAND (EUROPE ON FIRE). A brief paragraph below the headline announced that England had declared war on Germany at eleven o'clock, September 3—one o'clock by Finland time. Now it was almost two. I returned to our table with the news. Thérèse turned slightly pale. Miss Brent, who was a

Socialist opposed to war, said in anguish, "Oh, I wish they hadn't done it. Why didn't they wait a little longer and try to compromise?"

No loud speakers blared the devastating news. The newsboy walked about until all his papers were sold, never once having raised his voice. There was no outward interruption in the Finnish Sunday peace.

The next morning at the Swedish American Line office I booked the last cabin on the *Gripsholm* sailing on the nineteenth. I had accepted an invitation to a P.E.N. dinner in honor of Thomas Mann and H. G. Wells for the next Saturday in Stockholm and had intended to fly over for the week-end. But now we broke a fortnight of engagements in Finland and booked reservations on a Stockholm boat from Turku.

When I got back to the hotel, Ralph Enckell, who was to become the first Finnish ambassador to the United Nations, telephoned that he had arranged for me to meet Paavo Nurmi that afternoon at three. He said that the champion would show me his collection of modern paintings. I told him that we were suddenly leaving on the boat train at five and could not make it. Could he possibly persuade Nurmi to come to the hotel at four? Enckell said he would try to bring him, but that he was difficult and extremely shy.

At three he telephoned that Nurmi had agreed to come. And at five minutes to four Enckell arrived at the hotel with the athlete who had caught my imagination beyond all others.

In features Paavo Nurmi was obviously a typical Finn. He was blond, with a broad face, high cheekbones, and pale gray eyes. He was dressed in a gray suit that seemed too small for his five-feet-nine form. Outwardly, my hero looked superlatively average.

I had learned in these last weeks something of the private life of the Finnish idol, who by 1930 held thirty-seven world records for distance running. The son of a working man, the "Phanton Finn" began his career as a twelve-year-old errand boy for a foundry. After his first success in Antwerp some people interested in his future paid his expenses at an industrial school. He finished second in his class and became a skilled mechanic. His wife had divorced him and taken his son, who was now eleven. Like an ascetic, Nurmi now lived in a one-room apartment and invested money in modern art, for which, Enckell had told me, he had an astute appreciation. Enckell said his walls were covered with paintings and crated pictures leaned against the walls, while others were stored in a warehouse.

These odd facts ran through my mind as we sat in the parlor of the hotel, my eyes periodically on the clock, just as Paavo Nurmi used to consult the watch he always clutched in his fist when he ran a race.

"It is somewhat idiotic," Nurmi said, "a man chasing after a record." Enckell skillfully interpreted. "God did not intend a man to train himself into a perfect machine."

But this was no case of a forgotten champion sour because his medals were tarnished.

"Success in sport, as in almost everything," Nurmi was saying philosophically, "comes from devotion. Devotion is the essential. It cannot be forced on anyone. You simply have it or you don't. I happened to be born with it, and so I do not boast about it. I never desired to be taken for an exceptional being. I made a champion's career, but still I have no happy memories. Perhaps it is regrettable, but that's the way it is."

He spoke in a low, monotonous tone, as impassive as his mask. Then Nurmi raised his voice, as if he wanted to drive home a point. "The fault with sport nowadays is that it tends to overreach itself. It has been driven to a higher level than it should be. If one desires gold medals in the Olympics, one must sacrifice too much."

I countered by quoting a favorite line from Joseph Conrad: "What matter the price if the trick be well done?"

"I'm not sure the Pole was right," Nurmi said with a half grin. He turned directly to me and looked at me with quiet challenge. "At the present time sports hardly interest me."

"But," I protested, "you encourage youth in sports—you sometimes help train them."

"Ah, because I have acquired experience, I think it is my duty to give the younger generation the profit of it—if they want it."

I asked Nurmi what he did for exercise now, and drew an amused smile. "I walk," he said. "Now that the government has stopped the sale of gasoline for private cars, I walk all over the place to look after my construction business. But soon there won't be any more building—for lack of materials. Work on the Olympic Village has been halted—temporarily, I hope."

Our luggage was brought down. Thérèse came and Enckell presented Nurmi to her. He said they would both go to the station with us and see us off. At the station we could find only one free porter. Enckell and I picked up some of the stuff from the sidewalk. So did Nurmi. Thérèse in horror said, "But you can't let Mr. Nurmi carry luggage!" The old champion understood and grinned, and we all went through the gates, Paavo Nurmi carrying one of Thérèse's suitcases.

After the luggage was stowed in the reserved compartment, and we stood outside the train again, I asked Nurmi for his definition of *sisu*.

"Every Finn has his own pet definition," he said slowly. "To me, *sisu* means patience without passion. It is something in the soul. It comes from within oneself. For instance, it makes a soldier do brave things because he himself must, not because he was ordered to by a superior officer."

I told Nurmi that I had profited from something he had said to a reporter early in his career: "I always finish a race a little taller than when I began." That dictum, I told him, had inspired me through the years to overcome a tendency to stoop, and whenever I thought of Nurmi I straightened my shoulders and lifted my head higher. Nurmi smiled to think that a remark of his to some reporter had helped someone in another hemisphere to hold his spine erect.

At that moment Lorenz von Numers, the young Swedo-Finnish poet and scion of a noble family, came down the platform with a bunch of red roses for Thérèse. He was a close friend of Ralph Enckell. One evening we three had sat in his one-room apartment in Töölö, in highbacked leather chairs that belonged in palaces, talking Finland and poetry and drinking wine. He laughingly confessed to being perhaps the only Finn who longed for a monarchy. But he loved the root and soul of Finland with a poet's passion.

Von Numers was going to join his regiment tomorrow, he told us, with the air of one invited to a wedding feast. He stood with his hat off, the sun gleaming on his gold hair. Thérèse looked tenderly at the smiling, handsome face. "I pray that Finland will be able to keep out of this war," she said fervently, meaning that it was too dreadful to contemplate having this young man with a bullet through his head.

Nurmi smiled gently at Thérèse when he shook her hand in good-by. We said the quickly forgotten things one says in farewell. From the glass vestibule I raised a hand. The three waved back. Against the other parallel train the sun shone in afternoon splendor and illuminated the three Finns: the athlete, the diplomat, and the soldier-poet. Behind them like a stretched banner the embossed white letters SUOMI stood out boldly on the red railway carriage. As our train moved away the symbolic letters drew together and became one vertical white line.

I came into the compartment and sat beside Thérèse. Both our hearts were full.

"The papers used to say that Nurmi always finished a race a little taller than when he began," I said, settling down beside her, after laying the roses gently on top of the piled luggage. "I think that's the way I feel in leaving Finland—a little taller than when I came."

I met H. G. Wells in Stockholm under tense circumstances four days after Britain had formally declared war on Germany. He and Thomas Mann were to be the guests of honor at a dinner for about thirty given by the Swedish members of the P.E.N. Plans for the full International P.E.N. Congress had been canceled by the threat of war, but three writers from Balkan countries had already arrived. A whole cargo from Britain, including E. M. Forster and Stefan Zweig, had been stopped just before they left England. The official delegate from the United States had left New York on a Polish liner, which dodged German submarines in the North Sea for five days and finally reached harbor in a British port. H. G. Wells, who had been touring Sweden with his last longtime companion, the Baroness

Budberg, was the only Englishman present. Thomas Mann had fled Stockholm that afternoon on advice of Swedish police, for Nazi agents were threatening to kill him because of his derogatory remarks about Hitler.

Since a youth I had read Wells and found his fiction and histories and polemics stimulating. He was a sickly, skinny, undernourished boy, the only son of a servant mother in an aristocratic house with a fine library, where he developed a love of literature when visiting his mother. His father preferred playing cricket to running a little crockery shop in Kent. Wells escaped the dreary life of a draper's assistant by winning a scholarship to London University, where he came under the strong influence of T. E. Huxley. He turned out to have a rare gift for journalism, as well as science, and in 1895 he was producing highly readable popular novels. As his health improved and he was more robust, he became a Don Juan. After his first marriage with a cousin, he seduced her best friend. He said that he used sex chiefly as a relief from tension and boredom.

Wells's looks were not impressive. He was short, plump, and red-faced. His voice was high-pitched and thin. Despite his sophistication and expensive tailoring, his "lower middle class origin" was on his face like a map. But his pale blue eyes glowed with his supersharp intelligence.

My wife and I were the only Americans at the dinner. We were now awaiting the sailing of the *Gripsholm* on September 19. During the cocktail hour the hospitable Swedes put forth their best efforts to disguise the general anxiety and make the party gay. I spent most of my time talking about travel with Prince Wilhelm, the author-brother of the Crown Prince, who had reviewed my book *South by Thunderbird* for the *Svenska Dagbladet*. The prince had given the book a flattering review, and I told him how honored and immensely pleased I was.

At dinner, because Thomas Mann was absent, my place card had been set where his would have been, at the head table with Mr. Wells and Prince Wilhelm. With the superb food, vintage wines, and champagne, the dinner went off so pleasantly that at one point I thought of the Duchess of Richmond's ball before the cannonading began at Waterloo.

After three brief welcoming speeches from prominent Swedes, the seventy-three-year-old Mr. Wells was introduced. It had been rumored that he had prepared a "highly provocative" address. He had disapproved of Britain's war declaration and of her original guarantee to Poland. With all the new devices for killing and maiming he envisioned the deaths of millions. His speech was intensely pacific. He urged the Swedes to use all the means in their power to keep their well-regulated country from any kind of involvement. Turning directly to me, he said he hoped for the sake of the world that the United States would not mix in destructive squabbles across an ocean. Wells's thin voice remained calm throughout his reading of a written text.

As Wells sat down a kind of awed silence held the company for some moments. Then came a flurry of applause, and the master of ceremonies thanked the author for his frank and deeply felt opinions.

As the guests began to move about, I saw that Thérèse was fascinated by the towering greyhound, Prince Wilhelm, who had a devilishly attractive left eye. He told her that he had gone out to Africa on the same boat with Isak Dinesen. He had stood witness at her wedding in Kenya to the Swedish Baron Blixen, an adventurous young coffee planter and lion hunter.

When I told Mr. Wells I hoped to talk with him again, he invited me to have breakfast with him at the Grand Hotel the next morning. We sat at a table for two before one of those long picture windows of the dining room that give on a view of the Royal Palace across the sparkling Lake Mälaren. It was a glorious blue-and-gold September morning. We gazed on the movements of sailing craft and motorboats and the fishermen dipping their great round nets in and out of the fish-rich waters. With its curving bridges and the beautiful eighteenth century Parliament House in the right background, this is one of the views I favor above all others in the world. Wells seemed affable, even cheerful, as he looked upon so much beauty, but when he turned to take up his coffee cup he gave a kind of shiver that told me his mind was back on the unholy trouble the world was getting itself into.

To steer his talk away from Armageddon, I brought up the subject of publishing. I expressed surprise that most of his later books had each been released in the United States under different imprints. Wells professed to be cynical about publishers. Where he himself was personally concerned, he was a pragmatist, and he felt no loyalty whatever to any one American publishing house. He said that he now sold each new book to the firm that offered him the largest advance and advertising allowance. "I want my ideas dispersed," he said, "and, incidentally, I like to make money. As a youth I endured the humiliations of poverty, which, as you may know, brought tuberculosis on me. If a publisher has a big initial investment in my book, he will do his damnedest to sell it."

Despite the gloom that now hovered about Wells, a warm humanity exuded from this man. And every now and then he revealed a bubbling sense of humor. He was in midsentence of an amusing anecdote when a bellboy approached with a message from the Baroness Budberg: journalists had already arrived at his sitting room to interview him. "Such is life when you get a bit of fame," he murmured. At the elevator he took my hand, wished us a safe voyage home through the now perilous waters. Then he gave me the strangest look, which seemed a combination of disappointment, disgust, hopelessness, and sly mischief. "Strode," he said in his squeaky voice, "I may never see you again, but I want you to remember carefully the words I want incised on my tombstone: 'You damn fools, I told you so!' And with an exclamation mark, please." He grinned almost boyishly and I grinned back. "Will you help see that my wish is carried out?" he called as he walked into the elevator. As the door was closing he gave me a conspiratorial wave and winked. I never expected to see him again.

But I did, within less than five months. Wells came to Birmingham to deliver the first of twelve speeches across the continent and I was asked to come up and introduce him.

Two days after the fractured P.E.N. dinner, my Social Democrat friend Nils Horney, foreign editor of the Labor Paper *Morgontidningen,* secured for me a coveted seat in the press gallery at the opening of Parliament in extraordinary session on Saturday, September 7. Horney and I arrived at the west entrance of the Royal Palace courtyard. Inside the palace we climbed a broad curving sweep of marble stairs between lines of royal guardsmen, the cream of Swedish youth, dressed in Charles XII uniforms, with chamois-colored jackets, silver breastplates, and black tricorn hats trimmed with gold braid. Behind the guards, the stairwell was hung with tapestries of deep blue and faded yellow. The proud young men stood as motionless as the woven figures behind them, with their rifle butts resting on the stair treads and bayonets at a sharp angle.

In the reception room ladies-in-waiting stood by windows in black taffeta evening dresses with puffed sleeves, regulation court costume of ladies of rank below princesses—a Swedish innovation of bygone days to prevent extravagances and feminine rivalry.

We were ushered through a series of rooms made into corridors by gold tooled-leather screens and then down a short flight of blue carpeted steps into the Hall of the Realm, where on the right rose a broad stage ornamented with a silver throne. The 380 members of the Riksdag were already seated. The thirty of us with press invitations sat in a two-rowed gallery against a side wall raised a few feet above the floor. My reserved seat was in the upper row of the narrow gallery, second nearest the throne stage, between Horney and the Swedish correspondent of the *Christian Science Monitor.* As notable persons entered, my two companions identified them for me.

Over the back of the empty silver throne was draped an elaborate robe of ermine with a long train of ruby-colored velvet, richly embroidered with small golden crowns. To the right of the throne stood a small square table covered with blue velvet embossed with more golden crowns, which, Horney told me, King Gustav had never worn at any ceremony. On this table lay other symbols of vanished regal power—an orb, a scepter, and a horn of anointing oil. At a signal, two high officers entered and took their places at right and left of the throne. Eight other dignitaries came and ranged themselves across the back of the stage. Then the ladies of the court entered, carrying their black trains over white-gloved arms. They sat according to protocol in the gallery opposite that for the press. In a corner of the stage itself was a lower box where three ladies now entered. The first two were top ladies-in-waiting with titles centuries old. The third was the wife of socialist Prime Minister Per Albin Hansson. She had been in her youth a lady's maid and a milliner. With her husband's consent I had called on her in the simple Hansson cottage in the suburbs and found her most amiable and intelligent.

After the last of the foreign diplomats came the Bishop of Stockholm, adorned with the pale blue silk of the Order of the Seraphim. The last to enter was the commander of the Swedish armed forces, his breast agleam with medals, though he had never had to lead soldiers to war, Sweden having been at peace for 125 years.

In the upper box above Mrs. Hansson, wife of the Prime Minister, and her companions, appeared three royal princesses: first, Sibylla, wife of the Crown Prince's eldest son; then Ingeborg, Danish-born sister-in-law of King Gustav and mother of the Crown Princess Martha of Norway and the late Queen Astrid of the Belgians. Last, to the front seat of honor, came Crown Princess Louise, sister of England's Lord Louis Mountbatten and aunt of Philip, later Duke of Edinburgh and consort of Queen Elizabeth II. All three ladies wore their court jewels and evening gowns of pastel colors. As a hush fell upon the assembly, the princesses came to the front of their box, one by one. Each made three sweeping bows, two to the members of Parliament and the spectators and one toward the empty throne.

Then entered the hereditary princes of the royal house, the aged king's two brothers, Prince Carl and Prince Eugen, two of his grandsons, Prince Gustaf Adolf and Prince Bertil. They were followed by his two sons, Prince Wilhelm and the fifty-seven-year-old Crown Prince. Finally the octogenarian monarch himself entered, spruce in military attire. He seated himself on the throne draped with the ermine and velvet robes. He rose to address his Labor-dominated Parliament, whom he saluted as "Swedish men and women." He began with the time-honored statement, "Sweden's relations with other powers are good."

The gravity of Europe's situation, the sadness for the inevitable suffering of war to come, and the alerting to the potential danger to Sweden were all in the king's prepared speech, and, most important, the nation's determination to hold to a course of armed neutrality in keeping with national honor and dignity.

The pomp and ceremony seemed as archaic in these democratic days as the occasion was solemn and ominous.

Though we had misguidedly felt that Norway and Denmark, as well as Sweden, would be safe from invasion, no one encouraged us to remain. They thought we would be lucky to get home safely. Even when we dined with Axel Jonsson, the widowed president of the Swedish American Line, at the home of his son-in-law, Baron von Essen, the night before we sailed from Göteborg, we had a ray of hope that he might urge us to stay. But he shook his head, and doubted how long his ships would be able to carry passengers. As it turned out, ours was to be the last westward crossing of the *Gripsholm*.

The handsome Baron von Essen came to see us off, and I snapped smiling pictures of Thérèse and him on the deck. It was Von Essen who had entertained us at our first lunch in Scandinavia in February and at our last dinner in September. Between those months we had stored up hundreds of happy memories of the four northern countries. And in my briefcase were scores of pages of notes that Thérèse and I had taken. When we went to our cabin I set the briefcase on the floor by my bunk and kept it there through the first half of the homeward voyage so that I might smuggle it into a lifeboat under my overcoat if we struck a floating German mine.

Just after the *Gripsholm* had sailed, a steward knocked politely on our open door and delivered two steamer letters. One was from the Crown Prince of Sweden, regretting deeply the cause that was cutting short our stay. He asked me to introduce myself on shipboard to his second son, Sigvard, the scenic designer and worker in silver. He was going to New York to work on designs at Jensen's on Fifth Avenue.

The other letter was from Sigrid Undset.

I am so glad I received your letter today, so I can send you some words before you leave Europe and wish you safe passage over the sea and a happy homecoming—If I had had your message in the afternoon it would have been too late, as I am going for Oslo by the midday train to assist at the funeral of Olav Duun, our great novelist. It seems to me, since the burial of my daughter last winter I have done nothing but attend funerals and send wreaths—Oscar Brache, the author, the authoress Rozine Nooman (who was also my special friend and my daughter's godmother), last month my mother and her sister, now Olav Duun. And in a way I think they are lucky to be out of this present awful world.

I stretched on my bunk for a while and closed my eyes, thinking of Sigrid Undset's letter. I could not help but be moved, for I had really appreciated and loved the four northern countries and their people, just as I had acquired an everlasting love for Italy in 1922. The startling three-word headline that broke the Sunday peace of Helsinki loomed up now in dire significance: EUROPE ON FIRE. I began to think of the homeward voyage as an escape.

Index